Ibn Katheer

Early Days

(Stories of the beginning of Creation and the early Prophet from Adam to Yoonus)

Taken from
Al-Bidayah wan-Nihayah

1st Edition: October 2010
Supervised by:
Abdul Malik Mujahid

HEAD OFFICE

P.O. Box: 22743, Riyadh 11416 K.S.A.Tel: 00966-1-4033962/4043432 Fax: 4021659
E-mail: darussalam@awalnet.net.sa, riyadh@dar-us-salam.com Website:www.darussalamksa.com

K.S.A. Darussalam Showrooms:

Riyadh
Olaya branch: Tel 00966-1-4614483 Fax: 4644945
Malaz branch: Tel 00966-1-4735220 Fax: 4735221
Suwaydi branch: Tel: 00966 1 4286641
Suwailam branch: Tel & Fax-1-2860422

- Jeddah
  Tel: 00966-2-6879254 Fax: 6336270
- Madinah
  Tel: 00966-04-8234446, 8230038
  Fax: 04-8151121
- Al-Khobar
  Tel: 00966-3-8692900 Fax: 8691551
- Khamis Mushayt
  Tel & Fax: 00966-072207055
- Yanbu Al-Bahr Tel: 0500887341 Fax: 04-3908027
- Al-Buraida Tel: 0503417156 Fax: 06-3696124

U.A.E
- Darussalam, Sharjah U.A.E
  Tel: 00971-6-5632623 Fax: 5632624
  Sharjah@dar-us-salam.com.

PAKISTAN
- Darussalam, 36 B Lower Mall, Lahore
  Tel: 0092-42-724 0024 Fax: 7354072
- Rahman Market, Ghazni Street,Urdu Bazar Lahore
  Tel: 0092-42-7120054 Fax: 7320703
- Karachi, Tel: 0092-21-4393936 Fax: 4393937
- Islamabad, Tel: 0092-51-2500237 Fax: 512281513

U.S.A
- Darussalam, Houston
  P.O Box: 79194 Tx 77279
  Tel: 001-713-722 0419 Fax: 001-713-722 0431
  E-mail: houston @dar-us-salam.com
- Darussalam, New York 486 Atlantic Ave, Brooklyn
  New York-11217, Tel: 001-718-625 5925
  Fax: 718-625 1511
  E-mail: darussalamny@hotmail.com

U.K
- Darussalam International Publications Ltd.
  Leyton Business Centre
  Unit-17, Etloe Road, Leyton, London, E10 7BT
  Tel: 0044 20 8539 4885 Fax:0044 20 8539 4889
  Website: www.darussalam.com
  Email: info@darussalam.com
- Darussalam International Publications Limited
  Regents Park Mosque, 146 Park Road

AUSTRALIA
- Darussalam: 153, Haldon St, Lakemba (Sydney)
  NSW 2195, Australia
  Tel: 0061-2-97407188 Fax: 0061-2-97407199
  Mobile: 0061-414580813 Res: 0061-2-97580190
  Email: abumuaaz@hotamail.com

- The Islamic Bookstore
  Ground Floor-165 Haldon Street
  Lakemba, NSW 2195, Australia
  Tel: 0061-2-97584040 Fax: 0061-2-97584030
  Email: info@islamicbookstore.com.au
  Web Site: www.islamicbookstore.com.au

CANADA
- Nasiruddin Al-Khattab
  2-3415 Dixie Rd, Unit # 505
  Mississauga
  Ontario L4Y 4J6, Canada
  Tel: 001-416-418 6619

FRANCE
- Editions & Librairie Essalam
  135, Bd de Ménilmontant- 75011 Paris
  Tél: 0033-01- 43 38 19 56/ 44 83
  Fax: 0033-01-43 57 44 31
  E-mail: essalam@essalam com·

MALAYSIA
- Darussalam
  Int'l Publishing & Distribution SDN BHD
  D-2-12, Setiawangsa 11, Taman Setiawangsa
  54200 Kuala Lumpur
  Tel: 03-42528200 Fax: 03-42529200
  Email: darussalam@streamyx.com
  Website: www.darussalam.com.my

SRI LANKA
- Darul Kitab 6, Nimal Road, Colombo-4
  Tel: 0094 115 358712 Fax: 115-358713

INDIA
- Islamic Books International
  54, Tandel Street (North)
  Dongri, Mumbai 4000 09, INDIA
  Tel: 0091-22-2373 4180
  E-mail: ibi@irf.net

SOUTH AFRICA
- Islamic Da'wah Movement (IDM)
  48009 Qualbert 4078 Durban,South Africa

Ibn Katheer

Early Days

*(Stories of the beginning of Creation and the early
Prophet from Adam to Yoonus)*

Taken from

Al-Bidayah wan-Nihayah

Translation and Researched by

Research Department of Darussalam

© **Maktaba Dar-us-Salam, 2010**
King Fahd National Library Cataloging-in-Publication Data
Ibn Kathir
  Early days. / Ibn Kathir - Riyadh, 2010
  pages: 408 Size: 14x21 cm
  ISBN: 978-603-500-044-4
1- Prophets stories 2-Prophets - Biography 1- Title
229.5 dc   1431/8751
L.D. no. 1431/8751
ISBN: 978-603-500-044-4

Contents

In the Name of Allah, the Most Beneficent, the Most Merciful

Preface to the Revision

All praise and thanks be to Allah, Who revived knowledge of His religion and caused it to blossom forth after it had all but disappeared, and Who demolished the false conjectures of the apostates. I praise Him and I seek refuge with Him from the sins which weigh upon the backs of mankind. I worship Him and seek His aid in removing hindrances and difficulties in the practice of my religion. I bear witness that none has the right to be worshipped except Allah, Alone, without partners and I bear witness that Muhammad – who, by Allah's leave, brought about the dawn of faith to the darkness and misguidance which existed in the hearts of mankind – is the slave and Messenger of Allah. May the

Blessings and Peace of Allah be upon him in perpetuity.

O, Allah! We seek Your favor and through You we seek to ward off affliction. We ask You to protect us and to grant us mercy. Our Lord! Make not our hearts deviate after You have already guided us. Make it easy for us to perform our deeds in the way that You have taught us. Make us grateful for what You have given us and make plain a path for us which leads to You. Open up the doors between us and You by which we may arrive before You. To You belong the keys to the heavens and the Earth and You are Most Able to do all things. To proceed:

Among the blessings which Allah has bestowed upon us, the community of Muslims is that He has made it easy for us to follow the path of guidance, and He has opened the doors of knowledge by making available to us these new publications, which present to us the writings of the early scholars and reveal to us what they said regarding legal verdicts, history, events, information and lessons. These scholars opened a clear beacon of light for all those Muslims seeking guidance and they set up for us a signpost in which there is neither deviation nor crookedness. Whoever follows it will arrive safely at his desired destination and whoever diverts from it will be lost forever. They have written these books and treatises and made clear to us therein events, information and virtues. Among such books is this unique work, *Al-Bidayah Wan-Nihayah*, by the Imam, the *Hafiz*, the master scholar of *hadeeth*, 'Imaduddeen Isma'eel Ibn Katheer Al-Qurashi – may Allah have mercy on him. This book was greeted with approval by the vast majority of Muslims. No Islamic library would be complete without it. In it, the author has recorded what Allah, Most High has made easy for him about the history of mankind, from the beginning of creation, starting with the creation of the Throne and the

Kursi (Footstool), the heavens and the Earth and all that they contain and all that lies between them, such as the angels, the jinn and the devils. He also described how Adam ﷺ was created, and told the stories of the prophets up to the days of the Children of Isra'eel and the Days of Ignorance (*Jahiliyyah*), until the advent of Prophet Muhammad ﷺ, which heralded the end of Prophethood. He then recorded his *Seerah*.[1] Then he recorded the events which took place up to his own time. He also spoke of the trials and battles, the signs of the approach of the Hour, then the sending forth of mankind and the terrors of the Resurrection, which he described in detail. He then described the Hell-fire, with all its horrors, and Paradise and all the good things contained therein. He called this particular volume of his book: *An-Nihayah Fil-Fitan Wal-Malahim* (*The Ending in Trials and Battles*). As for the book which is in our hands today, it is *Al-Bidayah*.

By Allah's Grace, I came to know brother Abdul Malik Mujahid, the general manager of Darussalam Publishing in Riyadh. He visited me in my humble office in Damascus and suggested to me the idea of creating a summarised version of this wonderful book. I prayed for Allah's Guidance in the matter and sought help from Him in completing the project. Allah enabled me to make the acquaintance of a number of people of knowledge and experience in this field and a plan of action for the work was written. It consisted of ten principal points and we then started the task, seeking help from the Lord of the heavens and the Earth. All of us exerted our utmost efforts in this task, making repeated revisions and corrections, until we reached the point where, by Allah's Permission, we completed it and it was published in the form which is in your hands today.

---

(1)   *Seerah*: Biography, life story, in particular, of Prophet Muhammad ﷺ.

The Plan of Action for This Book:

1. Summarization of the text. This was achieved by concentrating on the most important events narrated in the book. In doing so, we took care not to leave out any important details which would cause loss of meaning or import.

2. We relied on a number of printed and handwritten copies of the book and in cases where any contradiction or omission was found, we succeeded in establishing the most accurate and authentic text.

3. We left out the *ahadeeth* which proved to be baseless or weak and confined ourselves to the *ahadeeth* which are authentic or *hasan* [1] and those which are acceptable due to the existence of other supporting narrations. On rare occasions, when it was found that there were no other *ahadeeth* in the chapter, we included some weak *ahadeeth* whose weakness was not of an extreme nature.

4. We performed *takhreej* [2] of the *ahadeeth* with ascription of the number of the section and the page, the number of the *hadeeth* and in many cases, the precise location of the *hadeeth* in the original source, then the ruling on its authenticity, if it was not from the *Saheehain,* [3] because the *ahadeeth* therein do not require any ruling on their authenticity and they have been widely accepted by the

---

(1) *Hasan*: Good, sound. An acceptable *hadeeth*, although it does not reach the level of *saheeh* (authentic).

(2) *Takhreej*: Referencing the sources of a *hadeeth* and evaluating them.

(3) *Saheehain*: Saheeh Al-Bukhari and Saheeh Muslim.

Muslim *Ummah*. [1] As for the *ahadeeth* in this book, we have relied on the opinions of the Imams and scholars of *hadeeth* – including the earlier scholars, the later scholars and those of the present day. On some occasions, we have recorded the weak *ahadeeth*, while making it plain that they are not authentic. We have not omitted them because the author has included them in order to warn the people against them due to their widespread popularity amongst the Muslims in general. In such cases, we desired not to oppose the author in this effort and so we left them, at the same time making the scholars' ruling on them clear, so as to warn the people against them.

5. We summarised the *asaneed* [2] present in the book, in most cases mentioning only the Companion who narrated the *hadeeth*, or the person who reported it from him.

6. We omitted many of the *Isra'eeliyyat* [3] found in this book which the author referred to in the preface, where he said: "We do not record the *Isra'eeliyyat* except those which the Lawgiver has permitted, i.e., those which do not contradict the Book of Allah and the Sunnah of His Messenger ﷺ. These are stories which are neither believed nor belied and they have been recorded because they provide details of unclarified narratives that we have, or they provide names for people and places that have only been mentioned in passing in our Revelation, due to there being no benefit in specifying them for us. Thus we have reported them in order to provide extra detail and not with the intention of citing them as evidence or placing any reliance on them. Only the

---

(1) *Ummah*: Nation or people; in this case, what is referred to is the scholars of the *Ummah*.

(2) *Asaneed* (sing. = *isnad*): Chains of narrators of the *ahadeeth*.

(3) *Isra'eeliyyat*: Narrations of Jewish origin.

Book of Allah and the authentic Sunnah of His Messenger 鐵 may be relied and depended upon. It is from Allah that we seek help and it is He in Whom we place our trust; there is no help and no power except in Allah, the All-Powerful, the Most Wise, the Most High, the Almighty.

7. In some instances, we have referred back to the original manuscript in order to verify the wording of a *hadeeth* from its source. In some cases, the author has combined two narrations of the same *hadeeth* together and so where this has occurred, we have noted it and separated the two narrations, placing our own words between brackets, i.e., (and in another narration…) and we have also identified the source of the addition in the footnotes.

8. We have written the Qur'anic Verses in the Uthmani script, in conformity with the copy of the Qur'an published by Al-Madinah Al-Munawwarah Printing Complex.

9. We vowelised the words of many of the *ahadeeth* in the book and, in addition, the poetic verses, wherever possible.

10. We mentioned the meters of the poetic verses between parentheses.

11. We explained the meanings of some difficult or obscure words, relying on dictionaries, books containing *ghareeb* [1] *ahadeeth* and narrations and other sources.

12. We furnished a brief biography of the author, Hafiz Ibn Katheer though in reality, he requires no introduction and no description.

Finally, I ask Allah, Most High, to accept this humble work from us and to acknowledge it as having been done purely and sincerely with the aim of pleasing Him and to grant us and our

---

(1) *Ghareeb:* A *hadeeth* which is reported at one or more stages in its chain of narrators by a single narrator.

brothers, who assisted us in the production of this book, pardon and forgiveness in religious and secular matters. In addition, we ask Him that He include this work in the weight of our good deeds on the Day of Resurrection – a Day on which neither wealth nor sons will benefit anyone – except for those whom Allah has blessed with pure hearts.

And our final declaration is that all praise and thanks are due to Allah, and we invoke blessings and peace upon Prophet Muhammad and upon all his righteous family and Companions until the Day of Reckoning.

Yoosuf Al-Hajj Ahmad,
The humble slave of Allah.
Damascus, Ash-Sham (Syria).
2nd of Dhul-Hijjah, 1428 A.H.

Publisher's Preface

Verily, all praise and thanks are due to Allah. We seek His aid and we ask forgiveness of Him. We seek refuge with Allah from the wickedness in ourselves. Whomsoever Allah guides, there is none who can misguide him and whomsoever He sends astray, there is none who can guide him. I bear witness that none is worthy of worship except Allah and that Muhammad is His slave and His Messenger. He sent him with guidance and the true Religion and with the light (of truth), the admonition and wisdom, at a time when no Messengers were sent for a long period, when there was little religious knowledge and the people had gone astray, when the Hour was drawing nearer. Whoever obeys Allah and His Messenger has followed the right course, while whoever disobeys Allah and His Messenger erred from it and gone far astray. To proceed:

The book *Al-Bidayah* (*The Beginning*) by the *Hafiz*, the *Imam*, the scholarly critic, Ibn Katheer is an incomparable work regarding the study of the events and their chronological order, the knowledge of which he strove hard to acquire. He began by describing the start of creation – from the creation of the Throne and the *Kursi* and the heavens and the Earth and all that is in them and all that lies between them, such as the angels, the jinn and the devils and he described the manner of Adam's creation ﷺ. He recounted the stories of the Prophets and the events that took place therein, up to the times of the Children of Isra'eel and the Days of Ignorance, which ended with the advent of the final Prophet, Muhammad ﷺ. Then he gave a detailed description of his life and what happened after that, up to the time in which he, lived. He then wrote a separate volume called *An-Nihayah Fil – Fitan Wal-Malahim* (The Ending With Trials and Great Battles).

Furthermore, Allah inspired us to undertake the noble task of making this book easily accessible to both the students and the scholars and then to translate it into several languages, by Allah's Permission.

I suggested to my brother, Yoosuf Al-Hajj, the necessity of summarizing this book in a suitable manner, through the omission of unbeneficial repetition, weak *ahadeeth*, lengthy poems, etc. I am thankful to brother Yoosuf for assembling a team that consisted of Abdul Malik Wadih, Abu Muslim Al-Jaza'iri, Muwaffeq Khaleel Hammad, and himself. Darussalam funded the entire project, paying each team member for his contribution and work. After they completed their portion of the project, the work then went through numerous people in the Research Division of Darussalam, who meticulously went through the work, adding and subtracting materials. After this, the project went through another round of editing of the Arabic material before it was sent to the translation department. The translation was then checked for accuracy and then sent for editing, resulting in the final project that you see before you. All praise and thanks be to Allah for allowing us to produce such a classical work for the first time in the English language.

O Allah! We ask that You bless us with sincerity and success and that You spread goodness through our hands.

'Abdul Malik Mujahid.
Jumadal-Oola 1431 A.H.

In the Name of Allah, the Most Beneficent, the Most Merciful

Biography of Al-Hafiz Ibn Katheer

He is the *Shaikh*, the *Imam*, the *Hafiz*, 'Imaduddeen Abul Fida' Isma'eel Ibn 'Umar Ibn Katheer Ibn Daw' Ibn Katheer Ibn Dir', originally Al-Busrawi, then Ad-Dimashqi Ash-Shafi'i.

He was born in Mijdal, a village on the outskirts of Busra, in the year 701 A.H., where his father was a *khateeb*. [1]

In the year 706 A.H., he moved to Damascus where he studied Islamic Jurisprudence (*fiqh*) under Shaikh Burhanuddeen Al-Fazari and others. He married the daughter Al-Hafiz Al-Mizzi and reported many traditions from him. He delivered formal legal verdicts, was a teacher and debated with other scholars. He was a leading scholar of Islamic Jurisprudence, *tafseer* and Arabic grammar, in addition to which he applied himself assiduously to the study of *rijal* [2] and weaknesses or

---

(1) *Khateeb*: The one who delivers the Friday sermon (*khutbah*) in the mosque.

(2) *Rijal*: Literally man; here it is used to refer to the narrators of *ahadeeth*.

discrepancies in *ahadeeth*.

He was appointed as head of Umm As-Salih School and At-Tankaziyyah School, after Adh-Dhahabi.

Adh-Dhahabi referred to him in the explanatory notes of *Tabaqat Al-Huffaz,* and in *Al-Mu'jam Al-Mukhtass* he said: "He is a sound scholar of Islamic Jurisprudence, a verifier of *hadeeth*, a scholar of *tafseer* and a critic. He has written many beneficial works."

Among his written works are

1. *At-Takmeel Fee Ma'rifatith-Thiqat Wal-Majaheel* (The Complete Book of Criticism and Praise and Knowledge of the Trustworthy Reporters and the Unknown Reporters). It combines *Kitab ut-Tahdheeb* and *Al-Meezan* and consists of five volumes.

2. *Jami' Al-Masaneed Was-Sunan Al-Hadi Li-Aqwam Sunan* (The Combined *Musnads* and the *Sunan* Which Guide to the Most Precious *Sunan*); this is said to be one of Ibn Katheer's finest works in the field of *hadeeth* and it is one of the last books that he wrote, though not the very last one. He died before completing it – may Allah have mercy on him. In it, he combined the *musnads* of Imam Ahmad, Al-Bazzar, Abu Ya'la and Ibn Abi Shaibah with the Six Books.

Shaikh Muhammad Abdur-Razzaq Hamzah said in the introduction to the book *Al-Ba'ith Al-Hatheeth*:

His lineage, his birth, his teachers and his upbringing [1] *:*

---

(1) Quoted from *Al-Manhal As-Safi Wal-Mustawa Ba'd Al-Wafi* by the fa-

'Imaduddeen Abul Fida' Isma'eel Ibn Ash-Shaikh Abu Hafs Shihabuddeen 'Umar – the *khateeb* of his village – Ibn Katheer Ibn Daw' Ibn Katheer Ibn Dir' Al-Qurashi, originally from Al-Busrawi, then Ad-Dimashqi.

His birth, his upbringing and his education:

He was born in Mijdal, a village on the outskirts of the city of Busra, to the east of Damascus, in the year 701 A.H. His father was a *khateeb*; he died in the year 705 A.H., when Ibn Katheer was just four years old. He was then brought up by his brother, Shaikh Abdul Wahhab, from whom he learned the fundamentals of Islamic Jurisprudence.

Then he moved to Damascus in the year 706 A.H., when he was six years old. There he studied Islamic Jurisprudence under the tutelage of Shaikh Burhanuddeen Ibraheem Ibn Abdur-Rahman Al-Fazari, better known as Ibn Al-Firkaah (d. 729 A.H.). In Damascus he learned from 'Eesa Ibn Al-Mut'im and from Ahmad Ibn Abi Talib, better known as Ibn Ash-Shihnah and Al-Hajjar, who lived for more than a hundred years (d. 730 A.H.). He also learned from Al-Qasim Ibn 'Asakir, [1] from Ibn Ash-Sheerazi, Ishaq Ibn Al-Amidi [2] and Muhammad Ibn Zarad. He also attended the lectures of Shaikh Jamaluddeen Yoosuf Ibn Az-Zaki Al-Mizzi, the author of *Tahdheeb Al-Kamal* and *Atraf Al-Kutub As-Sittah*, who died

---

mous historian, Abul Mahasin Jamaluddeen Yoosuf Ibn Saifuddeen, better known as Ibn Taghri Bardi Al-Atabki Az-Zahiri, the author of *An-Nujoom Az-Zahirah Fee Akhbari Misr Wal-Qahirah* (812-874 A.H.)

(1) He is Baha'uddeen Al-Qasim Ibn Muzaffar Ibn 'Asakir. He died in the year 723 A.H.

(2) He is Ishaq Ibn Yahya Al-Amidi, the Shaikh of the Zahiri movement. He died in the year 725 A.H.

in the year 724 A.H. He benefited greatly from his association with him and married his daughter. He also learnt and benefited greatly from *Shaikh Al-Islam* Taqiyuddeen Ibn Taimiyyah (d. 728 A. H.) with whom he kept company and whom he loved dearly. In addition, he studied under the *Shaikh*, the *Hafiz* and historian, Shamsuddeen Adh-Dhahabi Muhammad Ibn Ahmad Ibn Qayimaz (d. 748 A. H.). In Egypt, he was endorsed by Abu Moosa Al-Qarafi, Al-Husaini, Abul-Fath Ad-Dabboosi, 'Ali Ibn 'Umar Al-Wani, Yoosuf Al Khatani and others.

Al-Hafiz Shamsuddeen Adh-Dhahabi said in *Al-Mu'jam Al-Mukhtass*: "(He was) the *Imam*, the *muhaddith*, the *mufti* (deliverer of legal verdicts), the outstanding scholar of Islamic Jurisprudence and *tafseer*; he wrote many valuable works."

Al-Hafiz Ibn Hajar said in *Ad-Durar Al-Kaminah*: "He worked on *ahadeeth*, studying their texts and their chains of narrators and he had a phenomenal memory and was a good-humored man." During his lifetime, his written works spread throughout the lands and the people benefited from them after his death." [1]

As-Suyooti commented on this, saying, "(He was) a reliable source of *ahadeeth* knowledge, of their authenticity or weakness, of the various sources from which they were reported and of their *rijal* and their strength or weakness…"

The renowned historian, Abul-Mahasin Jamaluddeen Yoosuf Ibn Saifuddeen, better known as Ibn Taghri Bardi Al-Hanafi said in his book *Al-Manhal As-Safi Wal-Mustawfa Ba'd Al-Wafi*; "(He was) the *Shaikh*, the *Imam*, the most erudite, 'Imaduddeen Abul-Fida'… he was constantly occupied and tireless in writing, compiling, categorizing, studying, narrating *ahadeeth* and authoring. He possessed huge knowledge of

---

(1)   See: *Ad-Durar Al-Kaminah Fee A'yan Al-Mi'ah Ath-Thaminah* (1/218).

hadeeth, *tafseer*, Islamic Jurisprudence, Arabic language and other subjects. He delivered legal verdicts and he continued to study until he died."

He was renowned for his ability to correct and revise and he was acknowledged as a leading historian, scholar of *hadeeth* and *tafseer* and it was he who said,
"The days pass us by, one after another,
Only driving onto the appointed times, while the eye watches,
And that youth which has gone will never return,
While this irritating old age remains."

His Students:

The number of students who heard from Ibn Katheer and reported from him is great; they include Al-Hafiz 'Alauddeen Ibn Hijji Ash-Shafi'i – may Allah have mercy on him – who said of him: "He had memorized more *hadeeth* texts than any other scholar of our acquaintance and he was the most knowledgeable of them regarding the authentication and disparagement of narrations and their *rijal*. His contemporaries and his teachers all acknowledged this. Every time I met him I gained some benefit from him."

Ibn Al-'Imad Al-Hanbali said in his book, '*Shadharat Adh-Dahab Fee Akhbari Man Dhahab*: "(He was) the great *Hafiz*, 'Imaduddeen; he memorized *At-Tanbeeh* and presented it in the year 718 A.H. and he memorized *Mukhtasar Ibn Al-Hajib*. He had a phenomenal memory and seldom forgot anything. He had good understanding and was a scholar of Arabic language who wrote average poetry." Ibn Habeeb said of him: "He heard (from the scholars), he collected and authored and he delighted the ears of his listeners with his words. He taught and he benefited (his listeners) and the pages of his legal verdicts spread throughout the lands and he became famous for his accuracy and his writing and editing skills."

His Writings, Including Detailed Works and Brief Treatises

1. *Tafseer Al-Qur'an Al-'Azeem* (Explanation of the Noble Qur'an), [1] which is one of his most important works. It is considered to be one of the best books of *tafseer* whose author depended primarily for the interpretation of the Verses of the Noble Book on the *ahadeeth* of the Messenger of Allah (*sall Allahu 'alaihi wa alihi wa sallam*). It was ordained by Allah that this great volume should become accepted and spread throughout the Muslim lands.

2. *Al-Bidayah Wan-Nihayah* (The Beginning and the End): This is a highly estimable book and scholars through the times have benefited from it and it has passed through the hands of researchers in every corner of the large Islamic world. In it he spoke of Earthly affairs, beginning with the start of creation, touching on the lives of the Prophets (*alaihimuss-salatu was-salam*) and speaking in depth and at great length about the life story of the Messenger of Allah (*sall Allahu 'alaihi wa alihi wa sallam*) and recording in beneficial depth the period that followed the Prophet's life, from the era of the rightly-guided Caliphs and ending in the year 767 A.H., with a description of the trials that would appear before the Hour.

---

(1)   Popularly known as *Tafseer Ibn Katheer.*

3. *At-Takmeel Ma'rifati Ath-Thiqat Wal-Majaheel* (The Complete Book of Criticism and Praise, and Knowledge of the Trustworthy Reporters and the Unknown Reporters). There is a version of it in Dar Al-Kutub Al-Misriyyah, No. 24227, which is in two volumes, but it is incomplete. (It combines *Kitab At-Tahdheeb* and *Al-Meezan*, which consists of five volumes).

4. *Jami' Al-Masaneed Was-Sunan Al-Hadi Li-Aqwam Sunan* (The Combined *Musnads* and the *Sunan* Which Guide to the Most Precious *Sunan*); this is said to be one of Ibn Katheer's finest works in the field of *hadeeth* and it is one of the last books that he wrote, though not the very last one. He died before completing it – may Allah have mercy on him. In it, he combined the *musnads* of Imam Ahmad, Al-Bazzar, Abu Ya'la and Ibn Abi Shaibah with the Six Books. [1]

5. *Tabaqat Ash-Shafi'iyyah* (The Levels of the Shafi'i Scholars). An evenhanded estimation of the Shafi'i scholars, including a description of the virtues of Imam Ash-Shafi'i.

6. *Takhreej Ahadeeth Adillah At-Tanbeeh Fee Fiqh Ash-Shafi'iyyah* (*Takhreej* of the *Ahadeeth* of "*Adillah At-Tanbeeh*" in Shafi'i Jurisprudence).

7. *Takhreej Ahadeeth Mukhtasar Ibn Al-Hajib* (*Takhreej* of the *Ahadeeth* in the original version of *Mukhtasar Ibn Al-Hajib*); this was published recently with an authentication by Al-Kubaisi and published in Makkah.

8. *Sharh Saheeh Al-Bukhari* (Explanation of *Saheeh Al-Bukhari*); unfortunately, it is incomplete.

---

(1) The Six Books: *Saheeh Al-Bukhari, Saheeh Muslim, Sunan Abi Dawood, Sunan At-Tirmidhi, Sunan Ibn Majah* and *Sunan An-Nasa'i.*

9. *Al-Ahkam Al-Kubra* (The Major Rulings); sadly, he did not complete it, reaching as far as the topic of *Hajj*.

10. *Ikhtisar 'Uloom Al-Hadeeth* (An Abbreviated Book on the Science of *Hadeeth*); it was published in Makkah in the year 1358 A.H., with an authentication by Shaikh Muhammad 'Abdur-Razzaq Hamzah and an explanation by Shaikh Ahmad Shakir and it was printed in Cairo in the year 1355 A.H. Al-Hafiz Ibn Hajar Al-'Asqalani said of it, "It contains many benefits."

11. *Musnad Ash-Shaikhain* (*Musnad* of the Two *Shaikhs* – i.e. Abu Bakr and 'Umar – may Allah be pleased with them both).

12 & 13. *As-Seerah An-Nabawiyyah* (Biography of the Prophet ﷺ) – a full version and a summarised one. He mentioned it in his *Tafseer*, in the explanation of *Soorah Al-Ahzab*, in the story of the Battle of the Trench. The summarised version was printed in Egypt in the year 1358 A.H. and was entitled *Al-Fusool Fikhtisar Seerah Ar-Rasool* (Summarised Chapters of the Biography of the Messenger ﷺ).

14. *Al-Muqaddimat Fee Usool Al-Fiqh* (Introductions to the Science of *Usool Al-Fiqh* [the Principles of Islamic Jurisprudence]). It was referred to in the summary of *Muqaddimah Ibn As-Salah*.

15. *Mukhtasar Kitab Al-Madkhal Ila Kitab As-Sunan Lil-Baihaqi* (Abbreviation of The Introduction to the Book of the *Sunan* by Al-Baihaqi).

16. *Risalah Fil-Jihad* (A Treatise on *Jihad*), which is available in print.

His Death

The author of *Al-Munhal As Safi* said· "He died on Thursday, the 26th of Sha'ban, in the year 747 A.H., aged seventy-four years."

Al-Hafiz Ibn Hajar said: "He had become blind in the latter years of his life, may Allah have mercy on him and be pleased with him."

Author's Preface

The *Shaikh*, the Imam, the scholar, the most erudite, Abul Fida' 'Imaduddeen Isma'eel – may Allah have mercy on him – said: "All praise and thanks be to Allah, the First and the Last, *Az-Zahir*, *Al-Batin*, Who has complete knowledge of all things. He is the First, because there was nothing before Him and He is the Last, because there will be nothing after Him. He is *Az-Zahir*, because there is nothing above Him and He is *Al-Batin*, because there is nothing below Him. He is the Eternal, Who is continuously and permanently present with all of His perfect and complete Attributes, forever, without end and without interruption. He is Aware of even the crawling of a black ant on a solid rock on a dark night, and He knows the exact number of the grains of sand. He is the Sublime, the Greatest, Who created everything and ordered them in due proportions. He erected the heavens without any supports and adorned them with the shining heavenly bodies and He placed therein a lamp (the sun) and a luminous moon. Above them He created an elevated seat, which is wide, domed and circular and that is the Mighty Throne, which has legs borne by noble angels known as the *Karoobiyyoon* [1] - may the Blessings and Peace of Allah be upon them all. They sing Allah's praises and glorify Him. Likewise, all corners of the heavens are filled with angels and every day seventy thousand of them arrive in *Al-Bait Al-Ma'moor* [2] in the Seventh Heaven. When they leave it after completing their saying *la ilaha illallah,* praise, glorification, prayers and greetings etc., they never return to it (but always a fresh batch comes). He placed in the Earth rivers and streams for the animals and He placed therein tall mountains and blessed them, and provided nourishment of every kind for mankind and their livestock both in summer and in winter.

He began the creation of man from clay and He made his offspring from his semen, composed of worthless water, in a safe lodging (womb). Then He fashioned him in due proportion, and breathed into him the soul (created by Allah for that person), and He gave him hearing (ears), sight (eyes) and hearts, after he had been nothing to be mentioned and He honored him with knowledge and teachings. He created Adam صلى الله عليه وسلم, the father of the mankind, fashioned his body and breathed into it His Spirit. He made the angels prostrate before him and created from him his spouse, Eve, the mother of the mankind for his company. He placed them in His Paradise and showered His Blessings upon them. Then, in His Wisdom, He sent them down to the Earth and He produced from them numerous men and women and in His infinite Wisdom, He made some of them kings and others subjects, some of them poor and some of them wealthy, some of them free and some of them slaves. He made them reside in all corners of the Earth, throughout the length and breadth of it. He made them in generations, succeeding one another

---

(1) *Karoobiyyoon*: The most exalted among the angels.

(2) *Al-Bait Al-Ma'moor*: The house in the Seventh Heaven where the angels congregate daily to offer prayers.

until the Day of Reckoning, when they will be presented to their Lord, the All-knowing, Most Wise. He blessed them with rivers in all the lands. These rivers varied from large to small, according to the needs of the people. He caused springs and wells to flow for them. He sent them rainclouds and brought forth for them all manner of plants and fruits and gave them all that they requested: ❴ And if you count the blessings of Allah, never will be able to count them. Verily, man is indeed an extreme wrongdoer, a disbeliever (an extra ingrate who denies Allah's Blessings by disbelief, and by worshipping others besides Allah, and by disobeying Allah and His Prophet Muhammad. He gave you of all that you asked for. ❵ (*Soorah Ibraheem* 14:34). Glorified be He, the Most Generous, the Self-Sufficient, Most Forbearing. One of the greatest blessings which He bestowed upon them – after He created them, gave them provision, made the path easy for them and gave them speech – was that He sent Messengers to them and revealed to them Scriptures which made clear what He had made lawful and what He had made unlawful, His communications, His Rulings and details of everything from the beginning until the return to Allah on the Day of Resurrection. The happy man is the one who believes in these communications and submits to them and complies with His Commands and extols His Prohibitions. Such a person succeeds in attaining eternal bliss and will avoid the abode of the rejecters in Hell, where *Az-Zaqqoom* [1] is located, along with *hameem* [2] and a painful punishment.

I praise Him abundantly with pure and blessed praises, filling the expanses of the Earth and the heavens for all time until the

---

(1) *Az-Zaqqoom*: A bitter tree in Hell, which has a bad smell and whose fruit is the food of the inhabitants of the Fire.

(2) *Hameem*: A boiling hot drink given to the inhabitants of the Fire.

Day of Resurrection, as befits His Great Majesty, His Eternal Dominion and His Beneficent Countenance. I bear witness that none is worthy of worship except Allah, Alone, without partners, without offspring, without any female companion, without peer, without minister, without adviser, without equal, without rival and without sharer. I bear witness that Muhammad is His slave and His Messenger, His beloved, His *Khaleel*, [(1)] *Al-Mustafa*, [(2)] of Arab origin, the Seal of the Prophets, who has been given the great *Hawd* [(3)] of sweet water and who will be permitted by Allah to intercede on behalf of the Muslims on the Day of Resurrection. He will hold the banner which Allah will send to *Al-Maqam Al-Mahmood*, [(4)] a banner under which all of mankind will desire to gather, even Allah's *Khaleel*, Ibraheem – may Allah's Blessings and Peace be upon him and all of his brothers among the Prophets and Messengers and may He be well pleased with all of his esteemed, noble and excellent Companions, who are the best of all people after the Prophets.

In this book, I will record – with Allah's Help and Guidance – what Allah, by His Strength and Power, makes easy for me of the beginning of all created things, such as the creation of the Throne and the *Kursi*, [(5)] the heavens and the Earth and all that is in them and what lies between them, such as the angels, the jinn and the devils, how Adam ﷺ was created, the stories of the Prophets and the events that surrounded them, up to the

---

(1) *Khaleel*: Friend, loved one.

(2) *Al-Mustafa*: The Chosen One.

(3) *Al-Hawd*: A vast pool or lake given to the Prophet ﷺ by Allah. The Believers will drink from it on the Day of Resurrection, after which they will never feel thirsty.

(4) *Al-Maqam Al-Mahmood*: The Exalted Station.

(5) *Kursi*: Foot-stool.

times of the Children of Isra'eel and the *Jahiliyyah*, [1] which ended with the coming of our Prophet, Muhammad ﷺ. We will give details of his life story, as appropriate, thereby healing hearts, quenching thirsts and banishing the ills of the sick. Then we will report the events which followed that, up to the present time. We will speak of the trials, the battles and the Signs of the Hour. Then we will describe the Sending Forth and the Gathering, the terrors of the Resurrection and its description, including what will occur on that Day. Then we will describe the Fire and after that, the Gardens (of Paradise), the good things therein and other matters relating to this. We will also mention what has been said regarding this in the Qur'an, the *Sunnah,* and the traditions accepted by the scholars.

We shall not mention the *Isra'eeliyyat* [2] except what is permissible according to Islamic Law, i.e., which does not contradict the Book of Allah or the *Sunnah* of His Messenger ﷺ. Such narrations are neither believed in nor rejected and we will only mention those which contain details where all we have is summary or names where our narrations do not supply them, due to there being no benefit for us in providing them. And we only mention them for the purpose of embellishment, not with the intention of citing them as evidence or relying upon them. We only depend upon and have confidence in the Book of Allah and the authentic and sound narrations from the *Sunnah* of His Messenger ﷺ. As for those narrations in which there are some weaknesses, we have identified them. Allah is the One from Whom we seek aid and upon Whom we depend and there is no strength and no power except with Allah, the Almighty, the Most Wise, the Most High, the Great. Allah says

---

(1) *Jahiliyyah*: Days of Ignorance.

(2) *Isra'eeliyyat*: Early literature of various types attributed by Muslim scholars to Jewish and Christian sources.

25

in His Book, ❲ Thus We relate to you (O Muhammad) some
information of what happened before. And indeed We have
given you from Us a Reminder (this Qur'an) ❳ (*Soorah Ta Ha*
20:99). And Allah has recounted to His Prophet ﷺ information
from the past concerning the creation of all things and He has
mentioned the previous nations and what He did to His *Awliya'*
and what He caused to befall His enemies. The Messenger
of Allah ﷺ conveyed all of this clearly to his people and in
each chapter, we shall narrate what has come to us from him
ﷺ following the relevant Qur'anic Verses. He informed us of
what we need to know in this regard and ignored matters of no
benefit. We will only mention a few of such things in brief and
we shall point out what is true in them and accords with our
information and whatever contradicts that, we shall hold to be
rejected.

As for the *hadeeth* narrated by Al-Bukhari in his *Saheeh*, on
the authority of 'Abdullah Ibn 'Amr Ibn Al-'As ﷺ, in which it
is stated that he said: The Messenger of Allah ﷺ said, "Convey
from me even a single Verse. You may relate from the Children
of Isra'eel without objection. (Relate from me and do not tell
lies about me). If anyone deliberately tells a lie against me
let him prepare his seat in the Hellfire." [1] This refers to the
Isra'eeliyyat on whose authenticity we offer no opinion, for
we have nothing with which to confirm or refute them. So it
is permissible to relate them for the purpose of reflection and
contemplation and that is what we have done in this book. As
for those narrations whose authenticity is confirmed by our
sources, there is no need to relate them, since we may suffice
ourselves with what we have (in the Qur'an and *Sunnah*). As for
those narrations whose falsehood is established by our sources,
they are rejected and it is not permissible to relate them, unless

---

(1)   Narrated by Al-Bukhari (3461). See also *Al-Musnad* (3/46).

it is with the intention of pointing out that they are false and rejected. And since Allah – all praise and thanks be to Him – has sufficed us with His Messenger, Muhammad, against the need to avail ourselves of all other sources and with His Book against the necessity of referring to all other Scriptures, we will not resort to what is in their hands for information, when we know that it contains confusion, mixed-up facts, lies, fabrications, distortions and substitutions and in addition to all that, deletions and alterations.

That which we require has been made clear to us by our Messenger, and he has explained it and elucidated it – some know it, while others are ignorant of it – as 'Ali Ibn Abi Talib said: "The Book of Allah contains information about what occurred before you and tidings about what will occur after you and rulings on what takes place among you; and it is true, not a thing to be taken lightly. If any tyrant or oppressor who abandons it, Allah will destroy him and if anyone seeks guidance from any other source, Allah will cause him to go astray." [1] And Abu Dharr said: "When the Messenger of Allah died, no bird flapped its wings in flight except that he had taught us some knowledge about it." [2]

Al-Bukhari said in the Book of the Beginning of Creation: It was reported on the authority of Tariq Ibn Shihab that he said: I heard 'Umar Ibn Al-Khattab saying, "The Messenger of Allah stood up among us for a long period and informed us about the beginning of creation (and talked about everything in detail) till he mentioned how the people of Paradise will enter their places and the people of Hell will enter their places. Some

---

(1) This is a weak *hadeeth* narrated by *At-Tirmidhi* (2906) and by Ahmad (706).

(2) This is an authentic *hadeeth* narrated by Ahmad (20854).

remembered what he had said, and some forgot it." [1]

Imam Ahmad Ibn Hanbal reported in his *Musnad*, on the authority of Abu Zaid Al-Ansari ﷺ that he said: "The Messenger of Allah ﷺ led us in the *Fajr* prayer, then he ascended the pulpit and he delivered a sermon to us until midday, then he descended and offered the *Zuhr* prayer. Then he ascended the pulpit once again and delivered a sermon to us until it was time for the *'Asr* prayer. Then he descended and offered the *'Asr* prayer. After that, he ascended the pulpit once more and delivered a sermon to us which lasted until the sun set. In these sermons, he spoke to us about what had been, what was (at that time) and what would be (in the future) and the most knowledgeable of us (regarding these things) was the one with the best memory." [2] Muslim also recorded it in his *Saheeh*, with a different chain, narrating on the authority of Ya'qoob Ibn Ibraheem Ad-Dawraqi and Hajjaj Ibn Ash-Sha'ir, who both reported on the authority of Abu 'Asim Ad-Dahhak Ibn Makhlad An-Nabeel, who reported on the authority of 'Azrah, who in turn reported on the authority of 'Ilba', who in turn reported on the authority of 'Amr Ibn Akhtab Ibn Rfa'ah Al-Ansari ﷺ, who reported it from the Prophet ﷺ. [3]

Imam Ahmad reported on the authority of Abu Sa'eed Al-Khudri that he said: "The Messenger of Allah ﷺ delivered a sermon to us after the *'Asr* prayer which lasted until sunset. Some of us remembered it and others forgot it." 'Affan said: "Hammad said: To the best of my recollection, he said: (it was about) the events that would take place up until the Day of Resurrection." Then he praised and thanked Allah and said,

---

(1)   Narrated by Al-Bukhari (3192).

(2)   This is an authentic *hadeeth* narrated by Ahmad (22381).

(3)   Narrated by Muslim (2892).

"Verily, the life of this world is green and beautiful, and Allah made you dwell in it generation after generation so that He sees what you will do. Therefore, beware of the life of this world and beware of women." Then he reported the rest of the sermon and he said: Then when it was sunset, he said, "Verily, the likeness of what remains of the life of this world, compared to what has passed of it, is as the likeness of what remains of this day, compared to what has passed of it." [1]

Then Imam Ahmad narrated on the authority of Abu Sa'eed Al-Khudri ﴿ that the Messenger of Allah ﷺ led us in the *'Asr* prayer one day and then he stood up and delivered a sermon to us which lasted until sunset; during this sermon, he did not neglect to mention anything of the events which will occur up until the Day of Resurrection. Some of us memorized it and others forgot it. One of the things that he said was, "O people! Verily, the life of this world is green and beautiful and verily, Allah has made you dwell in it generation after generation so that He sees what you will do. Therefore, beware of the life of this world and beware of women." Then he reported the rest of the sermon and he said, "Then as the sun was about to set, he said, "Verily, what remains of the life of this world, in comparison with what has already passed of it is like what remains of this day, in comparison with what has already passed of it."[2] This is what has been recorded and Allah knows better.

---

(1) This is a weak *hadeeth* narrated by Ahmad (10759).

(2) This is a weak *hadeeth* narrated by Ahmad (11193); in its chain of narrators is one 'Ali Ibn Zaid Ibn Jud'an, of whom Ahmad and Ibn Ma'een said, "He is not strong (i.e., he is weak)."

A Description of the Creation of the Throne, the Kursi, Al-Lawh, the Heavens and the Earth

Chapter On The Words of Allah, Most High: ❨Allah is the Creator of all things...❩

Allah, the Most High, says in His Noble Book: ❨Allah is the Creator of all things and He is the *Wakeel* (Trustee, Disposer of affairs, Guardian, etc.) over all things ❩ (*Soorah Az-Zumar* 39:62). So everything besides Allah was created by Him, is under His Dominion and His Disposal, and was brought into being, having previously not existed.

The Throne, which is the ceiling of all created things, including everything that lies beneath the Earth and all that exists between it and the Throne – whether animate or inanimate – all of it is His Creation, His Kingdom, His slaves and all are under

His Subjugation and His Power and they are subject to His Disposal and His Will. ﴾ **He it is Who created the heavens and the Earth in six days and then rose (*istawa*) over the Throne. He knows what goes into the Earth and what comes forth from it, and what descends from the heaven and what ascends thereto. And He is with you wheresoever you may be. And Allah is the All-Seeing of what you do.** ﴿ (*Soorah Al-Hadeed* 57:4).

The scholars of Islam, without exception, are in complete agreement – and no Muslim has the slightest doubt of this – that Allah created the heavens and the Earth and all that lies between them in six days, as proven by the Noble Qur'an. But they differed as to whether these days are like Earthly days, or whether each day is equivalent to a thousand years of what you reckon. [1] In this matter, the scholars are divided into two camps, as we have made clear in the *tafseer* of this Verse and we shall explain this in the relevant place.

They also differed regarding the question of whether or not there existed any creation before the formation of the heavens and the Earth. Some groups among the rationalist theologians supported the idea that nothing existed before them and that they were created from absolute nothingness. Others said that no, before the creation of the heavens and the Earth there were other creations; and they based this claim on the Words of Allah, Most High, ﴾ **And He it is Who has created the heavens and the Earth in six days and His Throne was over the water.** ﴿ (*Soorah Hood* 11:7). In the *hadeeth* narrated by 'Imran Ibn Husain it was stated that "Nothing existed before Allah and His Throne was over the water. He wrote everything in the Tablet,

---

(1)   See *Soorah Al-Hajj* 22:47.

then He created the heavens and the Earth." [1]

These people disagreed regarding which of them was created first:

Some said that the Pen was created before all of these things and this was the preferred view of Ibn Jareer At-Tabari, Ibn Al-Jawzi and others. Ibn Jareer said: "After the Pen, the fine clouds, and after it, the Throne." They cited as proof for this the *hadeeth* narrated by Imam Ahmad, Abu Dawood and At-Tirmidhi, on the authority of 'Ubadah Ibn As-Samit ﷺ, who said: The Messenger of Allah ﷺ said, "The first thing that Allah created was the Pen, then He said to it, 'Write.' In that very hour all that was to occur (was written) up to the Day of Resurrection." [2] This is the wording of Ahmad's narration and At-Tirmidhi said of the *hadeeth*, "(It is) *hasan-saheeh-ghareeb*."

The opinion of the majority of scholars, according to what has been transmitted by Al-Hafiz Abul-'Ala' Al-Hamdani and others, is that the Throne was created before that and this is what was narrated by Ibn Jareer [3] via Ad-Dahhak, on the authority of Ibn 'Abbas ﷺ, as proven by the *hadeeth* narrated by Muslim in his *Saheeh*, in which it was reported on the authority of 'Abdullah Ibn 'Amr Ibn Al-'As ﷺ that he said: I heard the Messenger of Allah ﷺ say, "Allah ordained the measures of the creation fifty thousand years before He created the heavens and the Earth – while His Throne was over the water." [4] They

---

(1)   The *takhreej* has already been given.

(2)   This *hadeeth* has been narrated authentically due to other supporting narrations (*saheeh lighairihi*); it was narrated by Ahmad in his *Musnad* (22705).

(3)   Narrated by Ibn Jareer in his *Tareekh* (1/39).

(4)   Narrated by Muslim in the *Book of Al-Qadar*, in the Chapter: The Ex-

said that this *taqdeer* was His writing of the measures with the Pen. This *hadeeth* proves that this took place after the creation of the Throne, so it is confirmed that the creation of the Throne preceded that of the Pen, with which the measures were written – and this is the opinion of the majority of scholars. The *hadeeth* of the Pen must therefore be understood to mean that it was the first of the created things in this world and this is supported by the narration of Al-Bukhari, on the authority of 'Imran Ibn Husain 🙵 that he said: The people of Yemen said to the Messenger of Allah 🙽, "We have come to you to learn the Religion and to ask you about the beginning of this universe." The Prophet 🙽 said: "There was Allah and nothing else before Him…" [1] In another narration, he said, "There was nothing else with Him…" [2] In a narration transmitted elsewhere, it was reported that he said, "His Throne was over the water and He wrote everything in the Record; and He created the heavens and the Earth." [3] In another version, it was reported that he said, "Then He created the heavens and the Earth." [4] They asked him about the beginning of the creation of the heavens and the Earth and that is why they said: "We have come to you… to ask you about the beginning of this universe." So he answered only what they had asked, which is why he did not inform them about the creation of the Throne.

Section Regarding What Has Been Said Concerning the Description of the Creation of

---

change of Arguments Between Adam and Moosa (Peace Be Upon Them).

(1)   Narrated by Al-Bukhari, in the *Book of the Oneness, Uniqueness of Allah* (7418).

(2)   I have not found this wording in Al-Bukhari's *Saheeh* or anywhere else.

(3)   The *takhreej* for this *hadeeth* has already been given.

(4)   The *takhreej* for this *hadeeth* has already been given.

the Throne and the Kursi

Allah, Most High, says,

❨Owner of high ranks and degrees, the Owner of the Throne❩ (*Soorah Ghafir* 40:15)

He, Most High, says,

❨ So Exalted be Allah, the True King, *La ilaha illa Huwa* (none has the right to be worshipped but He), the Lord of the Supreme Throne! ❩ (*Soorah Al-Mu'minoon* 23:116)

He, Most High, says,

❨Allah, *La ilaha illa Huwa* (none has the right to be worshipped but He), the Lord of the Supreme Throne! ❩ (*Soorah An-Naml* 27:26)

He, Most High, says,

❨ And He is Oft-Forgiving, full of love (toward the pious who are real true believers in Islamic Monotheism). Owner of the Throne, the Glorious ❩ (*Soorah Al-Burooj* 85:14,15)

He, Most High, says,

❨ The Most Beneficent (Allah) *Istawa* (rose over) the (Mighty) Throne (in a manner that suits His Majesty) ❩ (*Soorah Ta Ha* 20:5)

He, Most High, says in a number of Verses of the Qur'an,

❨ And then He *Istawa* (rose over) the Throne (really in a manner that suits His Majesty) ❩ (*Soorah Al-A'raf* 7:54)

❨ Those (angels) who bear the Throne (of Allah) and those around it glorify the praises of their Lord, and believe in Him, and ask forgiveness for those who believe (in the Oneness of Allah) (saying), "Our Lord! You comprehend all things in mercy and knowledge..." 》 (*Soorah Ghafir* 40:7)

He, Most High, says,

《And eight angels will, that day, bear the Throne of your Lord above them 》 (*Soorah Al-Haqqah* 69:17)

He, Most High, says,

《 And you will see the angels surrounding the Throne (of Allah) from all round, glorifying the praises of their Lord (Allah). And they (all the creatures) will be judged with truth, and it will be said, "All praises and thanks be to Allah, the Lord of the *'Alameen* (mankind, jinn and all that exists)." 》 (*Soorah Az-Zumar* 39:75)

In the supplication against distress narrated in an authentic *hadeeth*, it was said: "None has the right to be worshipped except Allah, the Great, the Most Forbearing. None has the right to be worshipped except Allah, the Lord of the Noble Throne. None has the right to be worshipped except Allah, the Lord of the heavens and the Lord of the Earth, the Lord of the Noble Throne." [1]

It has been established in an authentic *hadeeth* in *Saheeh Al-Bukhari* from the Messenger of Allah ﷺ that he said: "When you ask Allah for Paradise, ask for *Al-Firdaus*, because it is the highest and best place in Paradise and above it is the Throne of the Most Beneficent." [2]

---

(1) Narrated by Al-Bukhari in the *Book of Invocations* (6346) and by Muslim (2730).

(2) This is an excerpt from a *hadeeth* narrated by Al-Bukhari, on the authority of Abu Hurairah ☙, in *the Book of Jihad and Military Expeditions* (2790).

It has also been reported in one tradition that "The inhabitants of Al-Firdaws listen to the groaning of the Throne and it is its glorification and extolling of Allah." [1] And that can only mean that they are near to it.

It has also been authentically reported that the Messenger of Allah ﷺ said: "The Throne of the Most Beneficent shook due to the death of Sa'd Ibn Mu'adh." [2]

Al-Hafiz Ibn Al-Hafiz Muhammad Ibn 'Uthman Ibn Abi Shaibah wrote in his book "*The Description of the Throne*' on the authority of one of the *Salaf*: [3] "The Throne was created from a red ruby and the distance between its two sides would take fifty thousand years to traverse." We mentioned when citing the Words of Allah, Most High, ❴ The angels and the *Rooh* (Jibrael/Gabriel) ascend to Him in a day the measure whereof is fifty thousand years ❵ (*Soorah Al-Ma'arij* 70:4) that the distance between the Throne and the seventh Earth would take fifty thousand years to traverse and its breadth is also fifty thousand years.

Some of the rationalists have contended that the Throne is a circular heaven that encompasses the world on all sides and that is why they referred to it as the Ninth Heaven, the Starless Heaven and *Al-Atheer* (the Ether). But this is not good, because it has been established that it has legs which are borne by the angels and the heaven does not have legs, nor is it held and in

---

(1) This was narrated on the authority of Jubair Ibn Mut'im, on the authority of his father, who reported it on the authority of his grandfather.

(2) Narrated by Al-Bukhari in the *Book of Virtues* (3803) and by Muslim in the *Book of the Virtues of the Companions* (2466).

(3) *Salaf*: The first three praised generations from the Companions ﷺ and those that followed them (the Tabi'oon) and those that followed them (*Atba' At-Tabi'een*).

addition, it is above Paradise and Paradise is above the heavens and there are a hundred levels between each of its seven levels,* the distance between each of which is equivalent to the distance between the heavens and the Earth. And the distance between the Throne and the *Kursi* is not the same as that between one heaven and another. In addition, the word *'Arsh* (Throne) in Arabic refers to the throne of a king, as Allah says, ❨ And she (i.e. the Queen of Sheba) has a great throne... ❩ (*Soorah An-Naml* 27:23). It does not mean a heaven and none of the Arabs understands it to mean that; and the Qur'an was sent down in the language of the Arabs and so it is a seat, which has legs that are borne by the angels and it is like a dome over the world and the ceiling of creation. Allah, Most High, says, ❨ Those (angels) who bear the Throne (of Allah) and those around it glorify the praises of their Lord, and believe in Him, and ask for forgiveness for those who believe (in the Oneness of Allah) (saying), "Our Lord! You comprehend all things in mercy and knowledge..." ❩ (*Soorah Ghafir* 40:7)

And He, Most High, says, ❨ and eight angels will, that day, bear the Throne of your Lord above them ❩ (*Soorah Al-Haqqah* 69:17)

In the poetry of 'Abdullah Ibn Rawahah ﷺ which he recited to his wife, when she accused him of impropriety with his slave-girl ('*Al-Bahr Al-Wafir*'), he says:

"I bore witness that Allah's Promise is true

And that the Fire is the abode of the disbelievers,

And that the Throne is above the water, floating,

And above the Throne is the Lord of the worlds,

And it is borne by noble angels,

The angels of the (one true) Deity (who are) commanded."

This was recorded by Ibn 'Abdul-Barr and other scholars.

Abu Dawood narrated on the authority of Jabir Ibn 'Abdullah that the Prophet ﷺ said: "I was permitted to speak about one of the angels of Allah, the Almighty, the All-Powerful, who is one of the bearers of the Throne and (to tell you) that the distance between his earlobe and his shoulder is a journey of seven hundred years." [1] It was also narrated by Ibn Abi 'Asim with this wording, "(The distance is) like that of a bird flying for seven hundred years." [2]

And it is reported on the authority of Ibn 'Abbas ؓ and Sa'eed Ibn Jubair that they said regarding the Words of Allah, Most High, ﴾ His *Kursi* extends over the heavens and the Earth, and He feels no fatigue in guarding and preserving them. And He is the Most High, the Most Great ﴿ (*Soorah Al-Baqarah* 2:255), "It means, His Knowledge." But what is known from Ibn 'Abbas ؓ is that he said, as reported by Al-Hakim in *Al-Mustadrak* – who said that it is authentic according to the criteria for acceptance cited by Al-Bukhari and Muslim – "The *Kursi* is the Footstool and no one is able to properly estimate the Throne except Allah, the Almighty, the All-Powerful." [3]

Ibn Jareer At-Tabari said: Yoonus told me: I was told by Ibn Wahb that he said: Ibn Zaid said: My father told me that

---

(1)   This is an authentic *hadeeth* narrated by Abu Dawood, in *The Book of the Sunnah* (4727).

(2)   In his explanation of *Soorah Al-Haqqah* (4/415), Ibn Katheer attributed this narration to Ibn Abi Hatim and he said, "And this chain of narrators is good."

(3)   This narration is authentic, though *mawqoof* (i.e. it can only be traced back to Ibn 'Abbas ؓ, not to the Prophet ﷺ). It was narrated by Al-Hakim in Al-Mustadrak (2/310, No. 3116).

the Messenger of Allah ﷺ said, "In respect to the *Kursi*, the heavens and the Earth are no more than seven *dirhams* thrown into a shield." [1]

Abu Dharr ⌖ said: I heard the Messenger of Allah ﷺ saying, "The *Kursiyy* in relation to the Throne is no more than a ring of iron thrown into an open desert on Earth." [2]

Section: Regarding What Has Been Said Concerning Al-Lawh Al-Mahfooz

It is reported on the authority of 'Abdullah Ibn 'Abbas ⌖ that the Prophet ﷺ said, "Verily, Allah created a Preserved Tablet from a white pearl; its pages are made from a red ruby and its Pen is light and its record is light. In each day, Allah has three hundred and sixty moments in which He creates, sustains, causes death and gives life, honors and humbles and does as He wills." [3]

Ishaq Ibn Bishr reported on the authority of Ibn 'Abbas ⌖ that he said: Verily, at the beginning of *Al-Lawh Al-Mahfooz*, it is written: 'None has the right to be worshipped except Allah, Alone. His Religion is Islam and Muhammad is His slave and His Messenger. and so whoever has faith in Allah, believes in

---

(1) This is an authentic *hadeeth* narrated by Ibn Jareer At-Tabari in his *Tafseer* (3/10).

(2) This *hadeeth* is raised to the level of *saheeh* (authentic) by all of the sources from which it was reported; it was narrated by Ibn Jareer At-Tabari in his *Tafseer* (3/10). See also *Silsilah Al-Ahadeeth As-Saheehah* by Shaikh Muhammad Nasiruddeen Al-Albani – may Allah have mercy on him – (109).

(3) This is a weak *hadeeth* narrated by At-Tabarani in *Al-Kabeer* (10/260, no. 10605).

His Promise and obeys His Messengers, He will admit him to Paradise." He (Ibn 'Abbas ⚬) said, "And *Al-Lawh Al-Mahfooz* is a tablet made from white pearl; its length is equivalent to the distance between the heaven and the Earth, its breadth is equivalent to the distance between the East and the West and its edges are pearl and ruby, its two sides are red ruby, its Pen is light, its words are hung upon the Throne and its base is in the lap of an angel." [1]

Anas Ibn Malik ⚬ and others from among the *Salaf* said, "*Al-Lawh Al-Mahfooz* is on the forehead of Israfeel." [2]

---

(1) This is a *mawqoof* narration and it is a baseless fabrication. In its chain of narrators is one Ishaq Ibn Bishr, who was known to be a liar and a fabricator of *hadeeth*.

(2) This is a weak *hadeeth* narrated by Ibn Jareer in his *Tafseer* (30/140).

Chapter: What Has Been Said Regarding the Creation of the Heavens and the Earth and All That Lies Between Them

Allah, Most High, says, ❨ All praise be to Allah, Who created the heavens and the Earth, and originated the darkness and the light, yet those who disbelieve hold others as equal with their Lord ❩ (*Soorah Al-An'am* 6:1)

He, the Most High, says, ❨ Indeed, your Lord is Allah, Who created the heavens and the Earth in six days ❩ (*Soorah Al-A'raf* 7:54). This is repeated in a number of verses in the Qur'an.

Scholars of *tafseer* hold two different opinions regarding the measure of these six days: The majority holds that they are like our (Earthly) days. It is reported on the authority of Ibn 'Abbas ؓ, Mujahid, Ad-Dahhak and Ka'b Al-Ahbar that: "Every day of them is equivalent to a thousand years of your reckoning."

This was narrated by Ibn Jareer and Ibn Abi Hatim and it was the preferred view of Ahmad Ibn Hanbal in the book in which he refuted the arguments of the *Jahmiyyah*. It was also the preferred view of Ibn Jareer and a number of the later scholars – and Allah knows better. Later, we shall present evidence to support this opinion. Ibn Jareer narrated, on the authority of Ad-Dahhak Ibn Muzahim and others, that the names of the six days are: "*Abjad, Hawwaz, Hutti, Kalemun, Sa'fas* and *Qarasht*." Ibn Jareer also reported three sayings relating to the first days. He narrated, on the authority of Muhammad Ibn Ishaq, that he said, "The followers of the Torah say that Allah began the creation on Sunday, while the followers of the *Injeel* say that Allah began the creation on Saturday, while we Muslims, according to what has come to us from the Messenger of Allah ﷺ, hold that Allah began the creation on Saturday." And this saying which is reported by Ibn Ishaq from the Muslims was favored by a number of *Shafi'i* scholars of Islamic Jurisprudence and others. It was reported in a *hadeeth* on the authority of Abu Hurairah ؓ that the Messenger of Allah ﷺ said: "Allah created the soil (or clay) on Saturday." [1]

Allah, Most High, says, ﴾ He it is Who created for you all that is on Earth. Then He *istawa* (rose over) toward the heaven and made them seven heavens and He is the All-Knowing ﴿ (*Soorah Al-Baqarah* 2:29)

He, Most High, says, ﴾ Say (O Muhammad): "Do you verily disbelieve in Him Who created the Earth in two days and you set up rivals (in worship) with Him?" That is the Lord of the *'Alameen* (mankind, jinn and all that exists). He placed therein (i.e. the Earth) firm mountains from above it, and He blessed

---

(1) Narrated by Abu Dawood in the Description of The Day of Judgment, Paradise And Hell (2789), by Ahmad (8141) with similar wording.

it, and measured therein its sustenance (for its dwellers) in four days equal (i.e. all these four days were equal in the length of time), for all those who ask (about its creation). Then He **istawa** (rose over) toward the heaven when it was smoke, and said to it and to the Earth: "Come both of you willingly or unwillingly." They both said: "We come willingly." Then He completed and finished from their creation (as) seven heavens in two days and He made in each heaven its affair. "And We adorned the nearest (lowest) heaven with lamps (stars) to be an adornment as well as to guard (from the devils by using them as missiles against the devils). Such is the Decree of Him the All-Mighty, the All-Knowing". (*Soorah Fussilat* 41:9-12) This proves that the Earth was created before the heavens, because it is like a foundation for the structure, as Allah, Most High, says, ⟨ Allah, it is He Who has made for you the Earth as a dwelling place and the sky as a canopy, and has given you shape and made your shapes good (looking) and has provided you with good things. That is Allah, your Lord, then blessed be Allah, the Lord of the *'Alameen* (mankind, jinn and all that exists) ⟩ (*Soorah Ghafir* 40:64)

He, Most High, says, ⟨ Have We not made the Earth as a bed? And the mountains as pegs? ⟩ (*Soorah An-Naba'* 78:6,7) – up to His Words, ⟨ And We have built above you seven strong (heavens). And have made (therein) a shining lamp (sun) ⟩ (*Soorah An-Naba'* 78:12,13)

He, Most High, says, ⟨ Have not those who disbelieve known that the heavens and the Earth were joined together as one united piece, then We parted them and We have made from water every living thing. Will they not then believe? ⟩ (*Soorah Al-Anbiya`* 21:30) – That is, "We parted the heaven and the Earth so that the winds blew, the rains fell and springs and rivers flowed and the animals were refreshed." Then He says, ❨ And We have made the heaven a roof, safe and well-guarded. Yet they turn away from its signs ❩ (*Soorah Al-Anbiya'* 21:32) – That is, from what He has created in the heavens, such as the fixed and the moving celestial bodies, the shining stars and the illuminated heavenly bodies and the proofs of the Divine Wisdom of the Creator of the heavens and the Earth, as Allah says, ❨ And how many a sign in the heavens and the Earth they pass by, while they are averse therefrom. And most of them believe not in Allah except that they attribute partners unto Him ❩ (*Soorah Yoosuf* 12:105,106)

As for His Words: ❨ Are you more difficult to create or is the heaven that He constructed? He raised its height, and has perfected it. Its night He covers and He brings out its forenoon. And after that He spread the Earth. And brought forth therefrom its water and its pasture. And the mountains He has fixed firmly, as provision and benefit for you and your cattle ❩ (*Soorah An-Nazi'at* 79:27-33) – some people have taken these Verses as proof that the heavens were created before the Earth, thus contradicting the clear evidence provided by the abovementioned two verses. They have not understood this Verse, because it must be understood from this Verse that the flattening out of the Earth and the bringing forth of water and pastures from it was in fact after the creation of the heaven. This was the measuring of sustenance, as He says, ❨ And measured therein its sustenance ❩ (*Soorah Fussilat* 41:10) – That is, He prepared the places of cultivation and the locations of springs and rivers.

Then when He had completed the creation of the form of the higher and the lower world, He spread out the Earth and brought forth from it that which had been deposited therein, so that the springs gushed forth and the rivers flowed and the crops and fruits grew. This is why the flattening or spreading was explained as meaning the bringing forth of water and pasture from it and the fixing of the mountains. He says, ❨ And after that He spread the Earth. And brought forth therefrom its water and its pasture ❩ *(Soorah An-Nazi'at* 79:30,31) and He says, ❨ And the mountains He has fixed firmly ❩ *(Soorah An-Nazi'at* 79:32) – That is, He settled them, made them firm and established them in their places.

And He says, ❨ With Hands We constructed the heaven. Verily, We are able to expand the vastness of space thereof. And We have made the Earth a *firash*; how excellent the Spreader (thereof) are We! And of everything We have created pairs, that you may remember ❩ *(Soorah Adh-Dhariyat* 51:47-49). His saying, ❨ With Hands ❩ means "With Strength."

❨ Verily, We are able to expand the vastness of space thereof❩ - That is because all that is above is wider and so each heaven is wider than the one below it – and since the *Kursi* is higher than all of them, it follows that it is wider than all of them. And the Throne is much greater than all of these. After that, He says, ❨ And We have made the Earth a *firash* ❩ *(Soorah Adh-Dharyat* 51:48) – That is, "We spread it out and made it a bed, i.e, fixed, calm, undisturbed and unshaken, which is why He says, ❨ How excellent the Spreader (thereof) are We! ❩ *(Soorah Ad-Dhariyat* 51:48) The word "And" in Allah's saying, ❨ And We have made the Earth a *firash* ❩ does not indicate the order of the sequence of events; it only indicates general information – and Allah knows better.

Al-Bukhari narrated on the authority of 'Imran Ibn Husain ﷺ that he said: I went to the Prophet ﷺ and tied my she-camel at the gate. The people of Banu Tameem came to the Prophet

who said, "O, Banu Tameem! Accept the good tidings."
They said twice, "You have given us the good tidings, now
give us something." Then some Yemenis came to him and he
said: "Accept the good tidings, O, people of Yemen, for Banu
Tameem refused them." They said, "We accept it, O Messenger
of Allah! We have come to ask you about this matter (i.e. the
start of creation)." He said, "First of all, there was nothing but
Allah, and (then He created His Throne). His Throne was over
the water, and He wrote everything in the Book (in the heaven)
and created the heavens and the Earth." [1]And Imam Ahmad
Ibn Hanbal narrated on the authority of Abu Hurairah ﷺ that
he said: The Messenger of Allah ﷺ took me by the hand and
said: "Allah created the dust on Saturday and He created the
mountains on Sunday, and He created the trees on Monday, and
He created the unpleasant things on Tuesday and He created
the light on Wednesday and He spread the creatures throughout
it on Thursday and He created Adam ﷺ after *'Asr* on Friday.
He was the last creation during the last hour of Friday, between
'Asr and the night." [2]

And An-Nasa'i reported in the *Tafseer* on the authority of Abu
Hurairah ﷺ, who said: The Messenger of Allah ﷺ took me by
the hand and said: "O Abu Hurairah! Verily, Allah created the
heavens and the Earth and what lies between them in six days,
then He *istawa* over the Throne on the seventh day and He
created the dust on Saturday." [3]

'Ali Ibn Al-Madeeni, Al-Bukhari, Al-Baihaqi and other
hadeeth masters discussed this *hadeeth*; Al-Bukhari said in

---

(1) Narrated by Al-Bukhari in the *Book of the Beginning of Creation* (3191).

(2) The *takhreej* for this *hadeeth* has already been given.

(3) An-Nasa'i narrated something similar to this in *Al-Kubra* (6/427, No.
11392), but the author disputed that it was *marfoo'* (i.e. attributed to the
Prophet ﷺ) and attributed it to Ka'b Al-Ahbar.

his *Tareekh*: "Some have said that it was on the authority of Ka'b and that is more correct." That is to say, this *hadeeth* was heard from Ka'b Al-Ahbar by Abu Hurairah, because they were Companions and used to sit together to study *hadeeth* One of them would recite from his papers and the other would recite from what he believed to be from the Prophet ﷺ. So this *hadeeth* was obtained by Abu Hurairah ﷺ from Ka'b, who read it in his papers and so some of the narrators assumed that it was narrated from the Prophet ﷺ. He confirmed that it was *marfoo'* by his saying, "The Messenger of Allah ﷺ took me by the hand…" After that, there is something extremely singular in its text, such as the fact that there is no mention of the creation of the heavens in it, but the creation of the Earth and all that is in it in seven days is mentioned. This conflicts with what the Qur'an says, because the Earth was created in four days, then the heavens were created in two days from smoke. This is the steam from water which rises when the great water – which Allah created by His churning of the Earth, through His All-Encompassing Omnipotence – is agitated, as narrated by Isma'eel Ibn 'Abdur-Rahman As-Suddi in a tradition which he reported on the authority of Abu Malik and on the authorities of Abu Salih, Ibn 'Abbas ﷺ, Murrah Al-Hamdani (who reported on the authority of Ibn Mas'ood) and on the authority of people from among the Companions of the Messenger of Allah ﷺ that he said regarding the Words of Allah, Most High, ﴾ He it is Who created for you all that is on Earth. Then, He *istawa* towards the heaven and made them seven heavens and He is the All-Knowing ﴿ (*Soorah Al-Baqarah* 2:29) They said that Allah's Throne was over the water and He had not created any part of His creation before the water. Then when He wanted to create the creation, He extracted smoke (i.e. steam) from the water and it rose above the water and He called it the heaven. Then

He dried the water and made it into a single Earth and then He rent it apart and made seven Earths in two days - Sunday and Monday – and He created the Earth on a whale, that being the whale (Noon) mentioned by Allah in the Qur'an: ❨ Noon. By the Pen and what they (the angels) write ❩ (*Soorah Al-Qalam* 68:1) The whale was in the water. The water was upon the back of a (small) rock. The rock was upon the back of an angel. The angel was upon a rock. The rock - the one mentioned by Luqman - was in the wind, neither in heaven nor on the Earth. The fish moved and became agitated. As a result, the Earth quaked, whereupon He firmly anchored the mountains on it, and it was stable. Allah created the mountains and the beneficial and useful things that are in them on Tuesday and on Wednesday, He created the trees, the water, the cities and the cultivated and barren land. He rent apart the heaven, which had been one single unit, and made it into seven heavens in two days – Thursday and Friday – and He only called Friday *Al-Jumu'ah* because on that day He combined in it the creation of the heavens and the Earth and inspired His Command in every heaven. He created in each heaven the angels, the seas, the mountains of hail and all of the other things which none knows but He. Then He beautified the heaven with the stars and made them as adornments and as a guardian against the devils. Then, when He had finished creating what He loved, He *istawa* (ascended) over the Throne." In this narration As-Suddi mentions a great number of strange things, and many of them are derived from *Isra'eeliyyat*. This is because when Ka'b Al-Ahbar embraced Islam during the Caliphate of 'Umar ﷺ, he used to speak in front of 'Umar Ibn Al-Khattab ﷺ about things from the knowledge of the People of the Scripture and 'Umar ﷺ would listen to him out of friendliness toward him and from surprise at the things he said that concurred with much of the truth that is contained in the Qur'an and the authentic sayings of the Prophet ﷺ. As a result, many people deemed it permissible to transmit what Ka'b Al-Ahbar said. But much of what he conveyed was incorrect and far from the truth.

Al-Bukhari narrated in his *Saheeh*, on the authority of Mu'awiyah ﷺ, that he used to say regarding Ka'b Al-Ahbar, "Even though he was the most truthful of those who transmitted things from the People of the Scripture, we found that some of what he said was lies." [1] This means that he regarded the transmissions as untrue, not that he held Ka'b to be a deliberate conveyor of lies – and Allah knows better.

We relate them and then follow them with *ahadeeth* which either prove them to be true or disprove them, while the rest remain neither proven nor disproved. Allah is the One Whose Help is sought and upon Whom we depend.

Al-Bukhari narrated on the authority of Abu Hurairah ﷺ that he said: The Messenger of Allah ﷺ said: "When Allah ordained the creation, He wrote in His Book which is with Him above the Throne: Verily, My Mercy has overcome My Anger." [2]

Then Al-Bukhari said: Chapter: What Has Been Said Regarding Seven Earths and the Words of Allah, Most High: ﴾ It is Allah Who has created seven heavens and of the Earth the like thereof (i.e. seven). His Command descends between them (heavens and Earth), that you may know that Allah has power over all things, and that Allah surrounds (comprehends) all things in (His) Knowledge ﴿ (*Soorah At-Talaq* 65:12) – and

---

(1)   Narrated by Al-Bukhari in the *Book of Holding Fast to the Qur'an and Sunnah* (736).

(2)   Narrated by Al-Bukhari in the *Book of the Beginning of Creation* (3194), by Muslim in the *Book of Repentance* (3751) and by An-Nasa'i in *Al-Kubra* (4/417, No. 7750).

then he said: It is reported on the authority of Abu Salamah Ibn 'Abdur-Rahman that there was a dispute between him and some people and so he visited 'A'ishah (may Allah be pleased with her) and acquainted her with the details of the dispute and she said, "O Abu Salamah! Avoid the land, for the Messenger of Allah ﷺ said, 'Whoever takes even a span of land unjustly, his neck shall be encircled with it down seven Earths.'" [1]

Then Al-Bukhari narrated on the authority of Salim, on the authority of his father ؓ that he said: The Prophet ﷺ said, "Whoever took some land without right will sink down the seven Earths on the Day of Resurrection." [2]

Here Al-Bukhari mentioned the *hadeeth* of Muhammad Ibn Seereen, on the authority of 'Abdur-Rahman Ibn Abi Bakrah, on the authority of his father ؓ, that he said, "The Messenger of Allah ﷺ said, '(The division of) time has turned to its original form which was current when Allah created the heavens and the Earth. The year is twelve months.'" [3] What he meant by it – and Allah knows better – was to determine the meaning of the Words of Allah, Most High: ﴿ It is Allah Who has created seven heavens and of the Earth the like thereof (i.e. seven) ﴾ (*Soorah At-Talaq* 65:12) – That is, the like thereof in numbers. That is to say, just as the number of months, which is now twelve, corresponds with the number of months with Allah in His first Book, so these correspond in time, just as they correspond in place.

Imam Ahmad narrated on the authority of Ibn Mas'ood that he said, "I said: O, Messenger of Allah! Which injustice is

(1) Narrated by Al-Bukhari in the *Book of the Beginning of Creation* (3195).

(2) Narrated by Al-Bukhari in the *Book of The Beginning of Creation* (3196 and 2454).

(3) Narrated by Al-Bukhari in the *Book of the Beginning of Creation* (3197).

greatest?" He said, "That a Muslim should decrease a single cubit from the land of his brother, for there is not a pebble from the land that a person takes which does not encircle his neck on the Day of Resurrection down to the bottom of the Earth and none knows the bottom of it except Allah." Ahmad was alone in narrating this, but its chain of narrators is acceptable.

These *ahadeeth* are similar to *mutawatir* [1] narrations in their affirmation of the existence of seven Earths. What is meant by that is that each of them is above the other. The scholars have disagreed regarding whether or not they are piled up, with nothing separating them or whether there are spaces between each of them. There are two opinions in the matter and there is a similar disagreement regarding the celestial bodies. It would appear that between each of them there is a distance, based on what is apparent from the Words of Allah, Most High: ❴ It is Allah Who has created seven heavens and of the Earth the like thereof (i.e. seven). His Command descends between them ❵ (*Soorah At-Talaq* 65:12)

As for what one of the rationalists said regarding the *hadeeth*: "…his neck shall be encircled with it down seven Earths." [2] - that it means seven regions, this opinion contradicts the clear meaning of the Verse and the authentic *hadeeth* which we have narrated via *Al-Hasan*, on the authority of Abu Hurairah ﷺ. [3]

Then he interpreted the *hadeeth* and the Verse in a way that

---

(1)　*Mutawatir*: A *hadeeth* which is reported by so many reliable narrators at each level in its chain of narrators that it negates the possibility that they could have conspired together to concoct a fabrication.

(2)　The *takhreej* for this *hadeeth* has already been given.

(3)　It is weak, which is why we have omitted it. See *Sunan At-Tirmidhi* (3398) and Ahmad's *Musnad* (2/370) and in it is: "…if all of you lowered one of you by a rope down to the seventh and lowest Earth, it would reach Allah."

contradicts their clear meaning, without any support and without any proof – and Allah knows better. It is the same with much of what is said by many of the People of the Scripture and which has been accepted by a group of our scholars, which states that this Earth is made from dust and what is below it consists of iron, and the other is from sulphur stone and the other from such-and-such. But all of this, if it has not been authentically reported with a chain of narrators reaching to the Prophet ﷺ is rejected. Likewise, regarding the tradition narrated on the authority of Ibn 'Abbas ﷺ which states that he said, "In every Earth of the creation there is something similar to what is in this one, even an Adam, like your Adam and an Ibraheem, like your Ibraheem," it was reported in a summarised form by Ibn Jareer and it was examined by Al-Baihaqi in *Kitab Al-Asma'i Was-Sifat*. If it is authentic, it must be understood that Ibn 'Abbas ﷺ took it from the *Isra'eeliyyat* – and Allah knows better.

Geographers have mentioned the number of mountains in the Earth in all of their locations, east and west and they mentioned their length, how far they stretch and their height and they have spoken at great length on these matters, and it would not be fitting to explain all that they have said on the subject here. Allah, Most High, says, ﴿ And among the mountains are *judad,* white and red, of varying colors and (others) *gharabeeb,* black ﴾ (*Soorah Fatir* 35:27)

Ibn 'Abbas and others said that the Arabic word *judad* means pathways and 'Ikrimah and others said that *gharabeeb* means tall, black mountains. This is the case of the mountains all over the Earth. They differ in their locations and their colors.

Allah has mentioned Al-Joodi by name in His Book; it is a great mountain which lies to the east of Jazeerah Ibn 'Umar, by the side of the River Tigris, near Al-Mawsil. It stretches from the south to the north, for a distance of three days' journey. Its summit is half a day's journey and it is green in color, because it is covered in oak trees. To the side of it is a town known as Ath-Thamaneen, which was the home of those who survived the flood in the ship with Nooh ﷺ, according to what has been related by more than one scholar of *tafseer* – and Allah knows better.

Allah also mentions Mount Sinai and Al-Hafiz Ibn 'Asakir narrated on the authority of Ka'b Al-Ahbar that he said: "On the Day of Resurrection, four mountains – and they are Al-Khaleel Mountain, Lebanon, At-Toor (Mount Sinai) and Al-Joodi – each of them will become a white pearl that shine between the heaven and the Earth and they will return to Bait Al-Maqdis (Jerusalem), so that its corners will be illuminated and His *Kursi* will be placed on it and there He will judge between the people of Paradise and the people of the Fire. ﴾And you will see the angels surrounding the Throne from all around, glorifying the praises of their Lord. And they will be judged with truth. And it will be said, "All praise and thanks be to Allah, the Lord of the worlds." ﴿ (*Soorah Az-Zumar* 39:75)

Section Regarding the Seas and the Rivers

Allah, Most High, says, ﴾ And He it is Who subjected the sea (to you), that you may eat from the fresh tender meat, and that you bring forth out of it ornaments to wear. And you see the ships plowing through it, that you may seek from His bounty and that you may perhaps be grateful. And He has driven firm standing mountains into the Earth, lest it should shake with you; and rivers and roads, that you may guide yourselves. And (by the) landmarks; and by the stars, they guide themselves. Is then He Who creates the same as one who creates, not Will you not then reflect. And if you would try to count the favors of Allah, you would never be able to count them. Truly, Allah is Forgiving, Most Merciful⟩ (*Soorah An-Nahl* 16:14-18)

He, Most High, says, ⟨ And the two seas (kinds of water) are not alike: this is palatable, sweet and pleasant to drink, and that is salty and bitter. And from them both you eat fresh tender meat (fish), and derive the ornaments that you wear. And you see the ships cleaving, that you may seek of His bounty, and that you may give thanks.⟩ (*Soorah Fatir* 35:12)

He, Most High, says, ⟨ See you not that the ships sail through the sea by Allah's Grace that He may show you of His Signs? Verily, in this are signs for every patient, grateful (person). And when waves cover them like shades, they invoke Allah, making their invocations for Him only. But when He brings them safe to land, there are among them those that stop in between. And Our *Ayat* are not denied except by every perfidious ingrate. ⟩ (*Soorah Luqman* 31:31,32)

He, Most High, says, ⟨ Verily, in the creation of the heavens and the Earth, and in the alternation of night and day, and the ships which sail through the sea with that which is of use to mankind, and the water (rain) which Allah sends down from the sky and makes the Earth alive therewith after its death, and the moving (living) creatures of all kinds that He has scattered therein, and in the veering of winds and clouds which are held between the sky and the Earth, are indeed *Ayat* (proofs, evidences, signs, etc.) for people of understanding. ⟩ (*Soorah Al-Baqarah*)

So Allah, Most High, has blessed His slaves with the things

that He created for them, such as the seas and rivers. The vast seas which stretch across the Earth and that which they produce in all corners of it is salty and bitter and in this there is great wisdom for the health of the atmosphere, for if it were sweet, the atmosphere would become malodorous and the air bad, because of the large creatures that die in them and that would lead to the extinction of mankind and the spoiling of their environment. But (Allah's) far-reaching Wisdom necessitated that it should be the way it is in order for this advantage to be attained. This is why, when the Messenger of Allah ﷺ was asked about the sea, he said, "Its water is pure and its dead things are lawful (to eat)." [1]

As for the rivers, their waters are sweet and permissible to drink, for those who wish to do so. The fact that Allah has caused them to flow freely, making them spring forth in one land and sending them to other lands as sustenance for His slaves. Some of them are large, while others are small, according to the need and the benefit.

Scholars of geography have spoken about the number of seas and about the major rivers, their sources, and where they end in words containing wisdoms and proofs of the Omnipotence of the Creator, Most High. It also shows that He acts by Choice and with Wisdom. Allah, Most High, says, ﴿ And the sea kindled by fire (or kept filled ﴾ (*Soorah At-Toor* 52:6). There are two opinions regarding this; one states that it is the sea which is under the Throne, mentioned in the *hadeeth* of the goats [2] and that it is above the seven heavens. The distance

---

(1)   This is an authentic *hadeeth*, narrated on the authority of Abu Hurairah ﷺ by Abu Dawood in the *Book of Purification* (83), *At-Tirmidhi* (69), *An-Nasa'i* (332), *Ibn Majah* (386), *Ahmad* (7192), *Malik* (43) and *Ad-Darimi* (729).

(2)   This *hadeeth* has been declared as weak by scholars of *hadeeth*. See *Silsi-*

between the lowest part of it and the highest part of it is like the distance between each heaven. It is from this that the rain will fall before the Sending Forth and from it the bodies will be restored to life from their graves. This is the preferred opinion of Ar-Rabee' Ibn Anas. The second opinion states that the word *bahr* is a generic collective noun, meaning all the seas on Earth – and that is the opinion of the majority.

Scholars disagreed regarding the meaning of *Al-Bahr Al-Masjoor* in the abovementioned Verse. It was said that it means "filled" and it was also said that it means "that which will become a kindled fire on the Day of Resurrection and that it will surround *Ahl Al-Mawqif*," [1] as we mentioned in the *Tafseer*, on the authority of 'Ali Ibn Abi Talib ﷺ, Ibn 'Abbas ﷺ, Sa'eed Ibn Jubair, Mujahid and others. It was also said that what is intended by *masjoor* is prevented, restrained and preserved from overflowing and inundating the land, and drowning those upon it. This was narrated by Al-Walibi, on the authority of Ibn 'Abbas ﷺ and it was the opinion of As-Suddi and others. It was reported on the authority of 'Umar Ibn Al-Khattab ﷺ from the Messenger of Allah ﷺ that he said: "There is not a single night when the sea does not rise three times and ask permission from Allah, the Almighty, the All-Powerful to unfold and flow over them (mankind), but Allah prevents it." [2]

This is one of the blessings which Allah bestows on His slaves, that He prevents the evil of the sea from inundating

---

lah Al-Ahadeeth Ad-Da'eefah Wal-Mawdoo'ah (1247).

(1) *Ahl Al-Mawqif*: Those on the Day of Reckoning who will be facing what they deserve because of what they did in the life of this world. Those people will seek intercession from Adam ﷺ, Nuh ﷺ and other Prophets and Messengers, but none of them will be permitted to intercede except Muhammad ﷺ.

(2) This is a weak *hadeeth* narrated by Ahmad in his *Musnad* (1/44, No. 305).

them and makes it subservient to them, so that it carries their ships so that they may reach distant lands with their trading goods and other things. And He guides them on it, with what He has created in the heaven and on Earth, such as the stars and the mountains, which He has made as landmarks by which they are guided on their journeys. He has also blessed them with the precious, rare, and beautiful pearls and gems that He has created therein, which are not found anywhere else and with the strange creatures that He has created in it and which He has made lawful for them to eat, even when they are dead, as He, Most High, says, ﴾ To hunt and eat the creatures of the sea is made lawful to you ﴿ (*Soorah Al-Ma'idah* 5:96) and the Prophet ﷺ said, "Its water is pure and its dead things are lawful (to eat)." [1] In another *hadeeth*, he said, "Two dead things and two types of blood have been made lawful to us: Fish and locusts and the liver and the spleen." [2]

Al-Hafiz Abu Bakr Al-Bazzar reported in his *Musnad* on the authority of Abu Hurairah ﷺ – in a *marfoo'* form – that he said: "Allah spoke to this western sea and He spoke to the eastern sea. He said to the western sea, 'I transport some of my slaves upon you, so what do you do with them?' It said, 'I drown them.' Allah said, 'May wretchedness be in (all of) your regions.' And so He deprived it of jewels and game (i.e. fish etc.). Then He spoke to this eastern sea and said, 'I transport some of my slaves on, so what do you do with them?' It said,

---

(1) This is an authentic *hadeeth*, narrated on the authority of Abu Hurairah ﷺ by Abu Dawood in the *Book of Purification* (83), At-Tirmidhi (69), An-Nasa'i (332), *Ibn Majah* (386), *Ahmad* (7192), *Malik* (43) and *Ad-Darimi* (729).

(2) This is an authentic *hadeeth* narrated by Ahmad in his *Musnad* (2/97, No. 5690) and Ibn Majah (3314), on the authority of 'Abdullah Ibn 'Umar ﷺ.

'I carry them in my hand and I am to them like a mother to her child.' And so Allah rewarded it with jewels and game." [1] Then he (Al-Bazzar) said, "We do not know of anyone who narrated it on the authority of Suhail except 'Abdur-Rahman Ibn 'Abdullah Ibn 'Umar and he narrates *hadeeth* which are *munkar*." [2] He added, "And Suhail narrated it on the authority of An-Nu'man Ibn Abi 'Ayyash, on the authority of 'Abdullah Ibn 'Amr in a *mawqoof* [3] form.

I say: To say that it is *mawqoof* at 'Abdullah Ibn 'Amr Ibn Al-'As is more correct, because on the day of the Battle of Yarmook, he had found two pack-animals, loaded with books which contained knowledge of the People of the Scripture; and he used to relate things from the *Isra'eeliyyat* from them, some of them well-known and accepted and some of them unknown and rejected. As for the *marfoo'* narration, it was narrated only by 'Abdur-Rahman Ibn 'Abdullah Ibn 'Amr Ibn Hafs Ibn 'Asim Ibn 'Umar Ibn Al-Khattab Abul Qasim Al-Madani, the chief justice of Al-Madinah. Imam Ahmad Ibn Hanbal said of him, "He is nothing. I heard it from him, then I tore up his *hadeeth*. He was a liar and his *ahadeeth* were *munkar*." He was also declared weak by Ibn Ma'een, Abu Zur'ah, Abu Hatim, Al-Juzjani, Al-Bukhari and Abu Dawood. Ibn 'Adiyy said, "In

---

(1) Recorded by Al-Haithami in '*Al-Majma*'" (5/281) and he said, "It was narrated by Al-Bazzar; but in its chain of narrators there is one 'Abdur-Rahman Ibn 'Abdullah Ibn 'Umar Al-'Amri, who is abandoned (by scholars of *hadeeth*). The author also denied its being *marfoo'* and said that it is from the *Isra'eeliyyat*.

(2) *Munkar*: A weak narration which contradicts something that has been authentically reported.

(3) *Mawqoof*: With a chain of narrators that does not reach to the Prophet ﷺ, but only as far as the Companions.

general, his *ahadeeth* are *munkar* and the worst of them is the *hadeeth* of the sea."

The geographers – who deal with latitude, longitude, seas, rivers, mountains, terrains and the cities, ruins, buildings, the seven true regions, according to their terminology, and the numerous commonly known regions, what is contained in the cites and the countryside – including private property and plants and trade that exists in every area – say that the land is flooded by the great water (i.e. the seas), except for about a quarter of it and that is ninety degrees. And Divine Providence necessitates that the water be held back from this area, in order that animals might live on it and that crops and fruits might grow on it, as Allah, Most High, says, ❴ And the Earth He has put for the creatures. Therein are fruits, date-palms producing sheathed fruit-stalks (enclosing dates). And also corn, with (its) leaves and stalk for fodder, and sweet-scented plants. Then which of the Blessings of your Lord will you both (jinn and men) deny? ❵ (*Soorah Ar-Rahman* 55:10-13)

They said that the inhabited portion of this land is about two-thirds of it, or a little more than that; and that is ninety-five degrees. With regard to the Western ocean – which is known as Oceanus (Okeanos) and which borders the lands of the West, including the Canary Islands – between them and its coast is ten degrees, which is approximately one month's journey. It is not possible to travel or sail across it, due to its waves and the varying winds and waves that exist therein. It contains no fish or other edible life and has nothing that can be extracted from it. It cannot be traveled on for the purpose of trade or anything else and it stretches in the south to the Mountains of

Darkness, or the Mountains of the Moon, wherein is the source of the Egyptian Nile. It traverses the equator and then stretches eastward and reaches the south of the land. In it there are the islands of the black people and on its coast there are many ruins. Then it stretches to the east and to the north, until it connects with the Sea of China and India. Then it stretches eastward until it borders the end of the exposed eastern land – and there are the lands of China. Then in the east of China, it turns northward, so that it crosses the lands of China and faces the Dam of Ya`jooj and Ma jooj. Then it turns and encircles lands whose circumstances are unknown. Then it stretches westward and borders the lands of the Russians and passes them, then turns westward and southward and encircles the land. Then it returns toward the west and the strait pours out from the west to the body of the land, the furthermost point of which ends at the western borders of Ash-Sham (Syria). Then it crosses the lands of the Christians, until it reaches Constantinople and other lands of their.

They say that between the Indian Sea and the China Sea there are mountains which separate them and between them there are lanes on which ships travel and they are caused to do so by their Creator. He has also made paths similar to them on the land. Allah, Most High, says, ❴ And We have placed on the Earth firm mountains, lest it should shake with them, and We placed therein broad highways for them to pass through, that they may be guided. ❵ (*Soorah Al-Anbiya'* 21:31). And Ptolemy, one of the kings of India, [1] mentioned in his book,

---

(1) Claudius Ptolemaeus (Greek: Klaudios Ptolemaîos; after 83 – C.168 C.E.), known in English as Ptolemy, was an ancient mathematician, astronomer, geographer and astrologer in the Greek tradition. He lived in Roman Egypt and was probably born there in a town in the Thebaid called

Al-Mijisti, which was translated into Arabic during the reign of Al-Ma'moon – which is the source of this information – that the seas which flow from the western, eastern, southern and northern oceans are very numerous. Some of them are in fact, one sea, but bear different names, according to the lands which they border; these include *Bahr Al-Qulzum* (the Red Sea) and Al-Qulzum is a village on the coast, near Aylah. There is also the Sea of Persia, the Khazar Sea (Caspian Sea), the Sea of Warnak, the Roman Sea (the Mediterranean Sea), the Bantash Sea and the Blue Sea – a city on its coast – and it is also known as Al-Qarm Sea. It becomes narrow until it pours into the Roman Sea, to the south of Constantinople, i.e., the Gulf of Constantinople. This is why the ships move quickly on its current from Al-Qarm to the Roman Sea, while they move slowly when they come from Alexandria to Al-Qarm. This is because they encounter a current of water; and this is one of the wonders of the world, because every flowing water is sweet, except this. And every non-flowing sea is salty, except for the Khazar Sea, which is also known as the Georgian Sea and the Sea of Tabaristan and has a large portion of sweet water in it, according to what has been reported by travelers to the area.

They (the geographers) have mentioned the limits of these seas, their origins and their end-points. And they have also mentioned the lakes on Earth into which the rivers empty and other flow – and they are the wide beds. They have also mentioned the well-known great rivers that exist on Earth,

---

Ptolemais Hermiou; he died in Alexandria around 168 C.E. Ptolemy was the author of several scientific treatises, three of which would be of continuing importance to later Islamic and European science. One of them was the astronomical treatise now known as *Al-Magest*, or *Al-Mijisti* (The Great Treatise). He was not a king of India.

along with their sources and where they end.

But we are not concerned with lengthy explanations of such things here; we only wish to speak of what relates to the rivers which are mentioned in the *hadeeth*. Allah, Most High, says, ❴ Allah is He Who has created the heavens and the Earth and sends down water (rain) from the sky, and thereby brings forth fruits as provision for you; and He has made the ships to be of service to you, that they may sail through the sea by His Command; and He has made rivers (also) to be of service to you. And He has made the sun and the moon, both constantly pursuing their courses, to be of service to you; and He has made the night and the day to be of service to you. And He gave you of all that you asked for, and if you (try to) count the blessings of Allah, never will you be able to count them. Verily, man is indeed an extreme wrongdoer, ungrateful ❵ *(Soorah Ibraheem* 14:32-34)

In the *Saheehain*, it is reported on the authority of Malik Ibn Sa'sa'ah ﷺ that when the Messenger of Allah ﷺ spoke of *Sidrah Al-Muntaha*, he said: "Two hidden rivers and two visible rivers ran from its roots. As for the two hidden rivers, they are in Paradise, and the two visible rivers, they are the Nile and the Euphrates." [1]

In *Saheeh Muslim*, it is reported on the authority of Abu Hurairah ﷺ that the Messenger of Allah ﷺ said, "Saihan, Jaihan, the Euphrates and the Nile are all among the rivers of Paradise." [2]

---

(1) Narrated by Al-Bukhari (3207) and Muslim (164)

(2) Narrated by Muslim (2839).

What is meant – and Allah knows better – by this is that these rivers resemble the rivers of Paradise in their clarity, their sweetness, their courses and other such attributes, as he ﷺ said in another *hadeeth*, narrated and declared authentic by At-Tirmidhi, on the authority of Abu Salamah, who reported on the authority of Abu Hurairah ﷺ that the Messenger of Allah ﷺ said, "The *'ajwah* dates are from Paradise and contain a cure for poison." [1] That is, they resemble the fruits of Paradise, not that they are harvested from Paradise, because practical experience proves otherwise; so it is clear that it refers to something else. Likewise, the Prophet ﷺ said, "Fever is from the breath of the Hellfire; so cool it with water." [2] And he ﷺ said, "The severity of the heat is from the breath of the Hellfire." [3] In the same way, the sources of these rivers have been witnessed on Earth. As for the Nile, it is the river which is without equal on Earth in its lightness and its fineness and the distance for which it flows from its beginning to its end. It starts in the mountains of Al-Qumr, i.e. of white. Some said that they are the mountains of Al-Qamar, i.e. the moon and they are in the west of the land, beyond the equator, lying in a southerly direction. It is said that ten streams of water – all of them distant from one another – combine to form it and that each five of them combine to form a lake, then six rivers flow from it, then all of them combine to form another lake and then one river flows from it and that is the Nile. It then passes through the lands of Sudan and Abyssinia

---

(1)　Narrated by At-Tirmidhi (2066), who declared it *hasan saheeh*.

(2)　Narrated by Al-Bukhari on the authority of 'Abdullah Ibn 'Umar (3264) and Muslim (2209), Ibn Majah (3472), Ahmad (4705) and Malik (1761).

(3)　Narrated on the authority of Abu Hurairah ﷺ by Al-Bukhari (534) and Muslim (615), Abu Dawood (402), At-Tirmidhi (157), An-Nasa'i (500), Ibn Majah (677), Ahmad (7205), Malik (29) and Ad-Darimi (1207).

and then through Nubia and its main city is Dongola. It then passes through Aswan, after which it passes through the lands of Egypt. It then goes a little way beyond Egypt and splits into two parts near a village on its shoreline; this village is known as Shattanawf. Then the westerly flow takes it through Rasheed and pours into the briny sea. As for the easterly flow, it also divides into two flows at Jawjar. The western flow passes through the western side of Dimyat and pours into the sea, while the eastern flow passes through Ushmoon Tannah, where it pours into a lake east of Dimyat. This lake is known as Lake Tinnees or Lake Dimyat. The distance between its starting point and its end point is a vast one and this is why it is such a calm river. Ibn Seena said, "It has characteristics which no other river on Earth has; these include the fact that measured from its source to its end-point, it is the longest river. In addition, it flows through rocks and sands, but it contains no moss or mire. Also, it does not cause the rocks and stones over which it flows to become green and this is due to its purity, sweetness and calmness. [And of that the increase in the days of a decrease of other rivers, and the decrease in the days of increase and its plenty.] As for the claim made by some, that its source is in an elevated place seen by some people and that they saw there a great horror, beautiful maidens and strange things and that whoever sees it is unable to speak after that, all of these are superstitions of chroniclers and liars.

'Abdullah Ibn Lahi'ah reported on the authority of Qais Ibn Al-Hajjaj, who reported from someone else that he said: When 'Amr Ibn Al-'As ⬥ conquered Egypt, its people came to him during the month of Ba'unah, which is one of the months of the Coptic calendar, and said to him, "O, Commander! There

is a religious custom relating to this Nile of ours and it will not
flood without it." He said to them, "And what is that?" "When
twelve nights of the month have passed, we go to a virgin slave
who is living with her parents and taking care of them, then
we decorate her with jewels and the finest clothes and throw
her into the Nile." 'Amr ﷺ said, "This is not a part of Islam
and Islam eradicates what came before it." So they celebrated
Ba'unah (with sacrificing a virgin) and the Nile did not flood –
neither a little nor a lot." According to another narration, "They
celebrated the three months of Ba'unah, Abeeb and Misra and
it did not flood, which caused them to consider migration. "So
'Amr ﷺ wrote to 'Umar Ibn Al-Khattab ﷺ and informed him
about this. He wrote back to him, saying "You were right in
what you said. Truly, Islam eradicates what preceded it." He
sent a slip of paper inside his letter and wrote to 'Amr, "I have
sent you a slip of paper inside my letter, so throw it in the Nile."
When 'Umar's letter reached 'Amr Ibn Al-'As ﷺ, he took the
slip and opened it, and there was in it, "From the slave of Allah,
'Umar Ibn Al-Khattab, the Commander of the Faithful, to the
Nile of Egypt: Now, if you used to flood before of your own
accord, then don't flood! If it was Allah, the Subduer, Who
made you flow, then I ask Allah to make you flow." He threw
the slip into the Nile. They woke up on Saturday morning, and
Allah had made it flow (and it rose) sixteen cubits in one night.
Allah cut off this custom of the people of Egypt right up to this

day." [1]

As for the Euphrates, its source is in northern Arzan Ar-Room and it passes close to Malatyah and then it passes through Sumayaat. Then it passes through southern Ilbeerah and then it turns east, toward Balls and Ja'bar Fortress. Then it flows toward Ar-Raqqah, then it flows to the northern side of Ar-Rahbah and then to 'Aanah, then to Heet and then to Al-Koofah. Then it goes out to the empty spaces of Iraq and pours into broad, shallow bodies of water, i.e., lakes and large rivers, which are well-known, flow out from them and toword Ar-Raqqah, then it flows and pours into the Sea of Al-Basrah.

As for Saihan, it is said that it is also known as Saihoon. It begins in the lands of the Romans and it flows from the north and west to the south and east. It is to the west of the course of Jaihan and it is smaller in size than it. It is in the land of the Armenians, which are today known as the lands of Sees (Sisiyah). At the start of the Islamic State, it was in the hands of the Muslims. But when the Fatimids conquered the lands of Egypt and occupied Ash-Sham and its garrison was unable to protect it from its enemies, Nicephorus the Armenian conquered these lands, i.e., the lands of Sees (Sisiyah) – that was in the year 300 A.H. and they still control them up to our time. And it is Allah Whom we should ask that they be returned to us, by His Power and Strength. Then Saihan and Jaihan combine at

---

(1) Abu Ash-Shaikh in *Al-'Azamah* (941) and Ibn 'Asakir in *Tareekh Dimashq* (13/135). Translator's note: This story is rejected on a number of levels; Firstly, the person Ibn Al-Hajjaj reported from where is unknown, secondly, the text of the story is inconsistent with Islamic practice and, thirdly, there is no historical evidence that it was ever the practice of the Copts to cast a virgin into the Nile – either before or after they became Christians.

Azanah and become one river. Then they pour into the Sea of Rome (the Mediterranean) between Iyas and Tarasoos.

As for Jaihan, which is also known as Jaihoon, and by the common people as Jahan, its source is in the lands of Rome and it flows into the land of Sees (Sisiyah) from north to south and it is similar in size to the Euphrates. Then it combines with Saihan and they become one river, which flows into the sea at Iyas and Tarasoos. And Allah knows better.

Section Pertaining to the Explanation of All Creation – On Land and in the Sea

Allah, Most High, says, ﴾ Allah is He Who raised the heavens without any pillars that you can see. Then, He *istawa* (rose above) the Throne (really in a manner that suits His Majesty). He has subjected the sun and the moon (to continue going round)! Each running (its course) for a term appointed. He regulates all affairs, explaining the *Ayat* (proofs, evidences, verses, lessons, signs, revelations, etc.) in detail, that you may believe with certainty in the meeting with your Lord. And it is He Who spread out the Earth, and placed therein firm mountains and rivers and of every kind of fruits He made *zawjain ithnain* (two in pairs – may mean two kinds or it may mean: of two sorts, e.g. black and white, sweet and sour, small and big, etc.) He brings the night as a cover over the day. Verily, in these things, there are *Ayat* (proofs, evidences, lessons, signs, etc.) for people who reflect. And in the Earth are neighboring tracts, and gardens of vines, and green crops (fields, etc.), and date-palms, growing out two or three from a single stem root, or otherwise (one stem root for every palm), watered with the same water, yet some of them We make more excellent than others to eat. Verily, in these things, there are *Ayat* (proofs, evidences, lessons, signs) for the people who understand.❩ (*Soorah Ar-Ra'd* 13:2-4)

He, Most High, says, ❨ Is not He (better than your gods) Who created the heavens and the Earth, and sends down for you water (rain) from the sky, whereby We cause to grow wonderful gardens full of beauty and delight? It is not in your ability to cause the growth of their trees. Is there any *ilah* (god) with Allah? Nay, but they are a people who ascribe equals (to Him)! Is not He (better than your gods) Who has made the Earth as a fixed abode, and has placed rivers in its midst, and has placed firm mountains therein, and has set a barrier between the two seas (of salt and sweet water). Is there any *ilah* (god) with Allah? Nay, but most of them know not. ❩ (*Soorah An-Naml* 27:60,61)

He, Most High, says, ❨ He it is Who sends down water (rain) from the sky; from it you drink and from it (grows) the vegetation on which you send your cattle to pasture. With it He causes to grow for you the crops, the olives, the date-palms, the grapes, and every kind of fruit. Verily! In this is indeed an evident proof and a manifest sign for people who give thought. And He has subjected to you the night and the day, the sun and the moon; and the stars are subjected by His Command. Surely, in this are proofs for people who understand. And whatsoever He has created for you on this Earth of varying colours [and qualities from vegetation and fruits, etc. (botanical life) and from animal (zoological life)]. Verily! In this is a sign for people who remember. ❩ (*Soorah An-Nahl* 16:10-13)

So Allah, Most High, has mentioned the things that He has created in the Earth, such as the mountains, the trees, fruits, the plains, and the rugged surfaces. He has mentioned the types of things that He created, such as the inorganic materials (minerals, etc.), the living creatures in the countryside, in the desert and in the seas. All of these prove His Greatness, His Power, His Wisdom and His Mercy toward His creation and He has made for every moving creature the provision that they require day and night, in summer and in winter, in the morning and in the evening, as Allah, Most High, says, ❴ And no moving creature is there on Earth but its provision is due from Allah. And He knows its dwelling place and its deposit. All is in a Clear Book.❵ (*Soorah Hood* 11:6)

Chapter: What Pertains to the Creation of the Heavens and the Signs They Contain

We have already stated that the creation of the Earth took place before the creation of the heaven, as Allah, Most High, says, ❨ He it is Who created for you all that is on Earth. Then He *Istawa ila* the heaven and made them seven heavens and He is the Knower of everything. ❩ (*Soorah Al-Baqarah* 2:29)

He, Most High, says, ❨ Say: "Do you verily disbelieve in Him Who created the Earth in two days and you set up rivals with Him Who is the Lord of all that exists." He placed therein firm mountains from above it, and He blessed it, and measured therein its sustenance in four Days equal for all those who ask. Then He rose over (*istawa ila*) the heaven when it was smoke, and said to it and to the Earth: "Come both of you willingly or unwillingly." They both said: "We come willingly." Then He completed and finished their creation (as) seven heavens in two days and He made in each heaven its affair. And We adorned the nearest (lowest) heaven with lamps (stars) to be an adornment as well as to guard. Such is the decree of Him, the

Almighty, the All-Knowing. 》 (*Soorah Fussilat* 41:9-12)

He, Most High, says, 《 Are you more difficult to create or is the heaven that He constructed. He raised its height, and has perfected it. Its night He covers and He brings out its forenoon. And after that He spread the Earth. 》 (*Soorah An-Nazi'at* 79: 27-30)

We have explained His Words: 《 And after that He spread the Earth 》 by saying that the Arabic word *dahya* (spreading) does not mean *khalq* (creation); it was after the creation of the heaven.

He, Most High, says, 《 Blessed be He in Whose Hand is the dominion; and He is Able to do all things. Who has created death and life that He may test you which of you is best in deed. And He is the Almighty, the Oft-Forgiving. Who has created the seven heavens one above the other; you can see no fault in the creation of the Most Gracious. Then look again. Can you see any rifts? Then look again and yet again, your sight will return to you humiliated and worn out. And indeed We have adorned the nearest heaven with lamps, and We have made such lamps (as) missiles to drive away the Shayatin, and have prepared for them the torment of the blazing Fire. 》 (*Soorah Al-Mulk* 67:1-5)

He, Most High, says, 《 (He is the) Cleaver of the daybreak. He has appointed the night for resting, and the sun and the moon for reckoning. Such is the measuring of the Almighty, the All-Knowing. It is He Who has set the stars for you, so that you may guide your course with their help through the darkness of the land and the sea. We have (indeed) explained in detail Our Signs for people who know. 》 (*Soorah Al-An'am* 6:96-97)

He, Most High, says, 《 Indeed, your Lord is Allah, Who

created the heavens and the Earth in six days, and then He rose over *(istawa)* the Throne. He brings the night as a cover over the day, seeking it rapidly, and (He created) the sun, the moon, the stars subjected to His command. Surely, His is the creation and commandment. Blessed is Allah, the Lord of all that exists.❭ (*Soorah Al-A'raf* 7:54). And the Verses on this subject are extremely numerous and we have spoken about all of them in our *Tafseer*.

What is meant is that He, Most High informs us about the creation of the heavens and its great vastness and elevation, that it is the ultimate in beauty, splendor, perfection and brilliance, as He, Most High, says, ❬ By the heaven full of *hubuk* (full of beauty, grace, magnificence and perfection). ❭ (*Soorah Adh-Dhariyat* 51:7) That is, the beautiful creation.

He, Most High, says, ❬ Who has created the seven heavens one above the other; you can see no fault in the creation of the Most Gracious. Then look again. Can you see any rifts. Then look again and yet again, your sight will return to you humiliated and worn out. ❭ (*Soorah Al-Mulk* 67:3-4) That is, humiliated from trying to see any defect, imperfection or flaw in it. The Arabic word *haseer* means exhausted and weak; even if one looked until one's sight became feeble, fatigued and weakened, one would not find any defect in it, nor any fault, because Allah, Most High, had ordained its creation and adorned its sky with the stars.

Al-Bukhari said in the *Book of the Beginning of Creation*: Qatadah said, "❬ And indeed We have adorned the nearest heaven with lamps. ❭ (*Soorah Al-Mulk* 67:5) The creation of these stars was for three purposes: as decoration of the sky, as missiles to hit the devils, and as signs to guide travelers. So, if anybody tries to find a different interpretation, he is mistaken, he will lose his reward and has taken on a task about which he has no knowledge." This was Qatadah's clear statement regarding the Words of Allah, Most High: ﴿ And indeed We have adorned the nearest heaven with lamps and We have made such lamps (as) missiles to drive away the *shayateen* (devils). ﴾ (*Soorah Al-Mulk* 67:5)

He, Most High, says, ﴿ It is He Who has set the stars for you, so that you may guide your course with their help through the darkness of the land and the sea ﴾ (*Soorah Al-An'am* 6:97) So whoever assigns any other purpose to them, i.e. such as the knowledge of (Divine) ordainments, taking their movements as evidence and comparisons between their orbits and claims that this is proof that certain Earthly events will take place, is mistaken. This is because most of what they say on this subject contains nothing but conjecture, lies and false claims. Allah mentioned that He created seven heavens one above another. But scholars have differed as to whether or not the spaces between them are piled up together or whether there are spaces between them. In fact, the latter is the correct opinion.

In the *Saheehain* it is reported on the authority of Anas ﷺ in the *hadeeth* of *Al-Isra`* that he said: In the lowest heaven he (Prophet Muhammad ﷺ) found Adam ﷺ and Gabriel said to the Prophet ﷺ, "He is your father; greet him." The Prophet ﷺ greeted him and Adam ﷺ returned his greeting and said, "Welcome, Oh, my son! O, what a good son you are!" And then he ascended to the second heaven. Likewise, he reported that the same thing happened in the third, fourth, fifth, sixth and seventh heavens." This proves that they are separated from each other, because he said that they ascended until they reached the second heaven and sought entrance, upon which it was said, "Who is this?..." [1] up to the end of the *hadeeth*. So this proves what we have said. And Allah knows better.

Ibn Hazm, Ibn Al-Muneer, Abul Faraj Ibn Al-Jawzi and other scholars have reported that there is a consensus among scholars that the heavens are spherical and what lends weight to that is His Saying: ﴿ They all float, each in an orbit ﴾ (*Soorah Ya Seen* 36:40) *Al-Hasan* said, "They revolve." Ibn 'Abbas ⸱ said, "In an orbit, like the turning of a spinning mill." They said, This is proven by the fact that the sun sets every night and then it rises at the end of it from the east, as Umayyah Ibn Abis-Salt said in *Al-Bahr Al-Kamil*:

The sun rises at the end of every night,

Red and rosy is the place at which it rises.

According to the *hadeeth* narrated by Al-Bukhari on the authority of Abu Dharr ⸱: The Messenger of Allah ﷺ said to Abu Dharr ⸱ as the sun set, "Do you know where it (the sun) goes (at the time of sunset)?" I replied, "Allah and His Messenger know better." He said, "It goes (i.e. travels) till it prostrates itself underneath the Throne and takes the permission to rise again, and it is permitted and then (a time will come when) it will be about to prostrate itself but its prostration will not be accepted, and it will ask permission to go on its course but it will not be permitted, but it will be ordered to return whence it has come and so it will rise in the West. And that is the interpretation of the Statement of Allah: ﴿ And the sun runs its fixed course for a term (decreed). That is the Decree of (Allah) the Almighty, the All-Knowing ﴾ (*Soorah Ya Seen* 36:38)"

---

(1) Narrated by Al-Bukhari in the Book of *Tawheed* (7517) and Muslim (162).

When this is known, then it (will be realized that) this is a *hadeeth* which does not contradict what we have mentioned regarding the rotation of the heavenly bodies, according to the most well-known two opinions. There is not evidence of the spherical shape of the Throne, as some have claimed, we have already proven the falseness of their opinion. Nor does it prove that it (the sun) ascends to a place above the heavens from our direction until it prostrates beneath the Throne. Rather, it sets out of our sight and continues in its course. There is nothing in the revealed Scripture to invalidate it, rather that which proves it and requires it is in perception, like eclipses. This is because, if it follows its course until it reaches the middle of it – so that it is the time of the middle of the night, for example – then it will be at its furthest point from the Throne and likewise, it will be at its closest point at the time of setting from our direction. When it is in the place of its prostration, it seeks permission from the Lord as it rises from the East and permission is granted to it and it appears from the direction of the East.

And when it is the time which Allah wills for its setting from the direction of the West, it prostrates according to its custom and seeks permission to rise, according to its custom, but it will not be permitted to do so and so it prostrates again, then asks permission, but is denied, then it prostrates a third time, but it is denied and this goes on throughout the night, as we have said in the *Tafseer*. Then it will say, "O Lord! The dawn is nigh and the distance is far." Then it will be said to it, "Return from whence you came." And so it will rise from the West. Then, when the people see it, they will all believe and that is (the meaning of) the Words of Allah, Most High: ❴ When no soul which had not believed previously or earned good though its belief will benefit thereby and the sun runs its fixed course for a term (decreed). ❵ (*Soorah Ya Seen* 36:38).

It was said that this means until the time at which it has been commanded to rise from the West. It was also said that the word *mustaqarr* means the place in which it prostrates beneath the Throne. And it was also said that it means the end of its course, which is the end of the world. And it was reported on the authority of 'Abdullah Ibn 'Abbas ﷺ that he recited, ❨ And the sun runs without a *mustaqarr* for it ❩. That is, it does not stop; based on this recitation, it would mean that it prostrates while moving in its course. This is why Allah, Most High, says, ❨ It is not for the sun to overtake the moon, nor does the night outstrip the day. They all float, each in an orbit. ❩ (*Soorah Ya Seen* 36:40) That is, the sun cannot overtake the moon and rise in its domain; neither can the moon overtake the sun and rise in its domain. Likewise, the night cannot precede the day. Rather, when the day has gone, the night comes after it, following on its heels, as the Messenger of Allah ﷺ said, "When the night approaches from here and the day departs from here and the sun sets, the fasting person should break his fast." [1] It is accepted that time is divided into night and day and there is nothing between them. This is why Allah, Most High, says, ❨ Allah merges the night into the day (i.e. the decrease in the hours of the night are added in the hours of the day), and merges the day into the night (i.e. the decrease in the hours of day are added in the hours of night), and has subjected the sun and the moon, each running its course for a term appointed. ❩ (*Soorah Luqman* 31:29).

That is, He merges this into that; He takes from the length of this and adds to the shortness of that and they become equal, just as at the start of the spring season, the nights before that

_____

(1) Narrated on the authority of 'Umar Ibn Al-Khattab ﷺ by Al-Bukhari (1954), Muslim (1100), Abu Dawood (2351), At-Tirmidhi (698), Ahmad (193) and Ad-Darimi (1700).

are long and the days short. But the nights continue to shorten and the days to lengthen, until they are equal – and that is at the beginning of spring. Then the days begin to lengthen and the nights get shorter, until they also become equal at the beginning of the autumn. Then the nights begin to lengthen and the days to shorten, until the end of the autumn. Then the days begin to lengthen slowly and the nights begin to shorten slowly, until they become equal at the start of the spring, as we said previously. That is what happens every year. This is why Allah says, ❴ His is the alternation of night and day. Will you not then understand? ❵ (*Soorah Al-Mu'minoon* 23:80) That is, the disposal of all that is in His Hands; the Judge, Who is not contradicted and is not opposed. And this is why He says in three Verses, when speaking of the heavens, the stars, the night and the day, ❴ Such is the measuring of the Almighty, the All-Knowing ❵ (*Soorah Al-An'am* 6:96) That is, the Almighty, Who has subjugated all things and to Whom all things have submitted and so He is not opposed and He cannot be overcome. He is the Knower of all things and He has appointed a measure for everything, according to a rule which does not change and cannot be disturbed.

So the bodies that are in the sky include those that constantly move and they are known as *mutahayyirah* [1] by the scholars of *tasyeer*; [2] and most of this knowledge is correct, unlike the "science" of (astrological) rulings, most of which is false and without any evidence to support its claims. These are seven in number and they are: the moon, which is in the lowest heaven, *'Utarid* (Mercury), which is in the second, *Az-Zuhrah*

---

(1) *Mutahayyirah*:Wandering stars; they were known as such because they seemed to stray irregularly across the sky. At times they are seen moving from East to West, and at others, from West to East.

(2) *Tasyeer*: The science of calculating the movements of heavenly bodies.

(Venus), which is in the third, the sun, which is in the fourth, *Al-Mirreekh* (Mars), which is in the fifth, *Al-Mushtari* (Jupiter) and *Zuhal* (Saturn) in the seventh. The other planets are known as the fixed stars and they are, according to them, in the eighth heaven, which is known in the language of many of the later scholars as *Al-Kursi*. Others deny this saying, all of the planets are in the lowest heaven and there is no objection to the view that some of them are above others. It might be said that there is evidence for this in the Words of Allah, Most High: ❨ And indeed We have adorned the nearest heaven with lamps, and We have made such lamps (as) missiles to drive away the *Shayateen* (devils) ❩ *(Soorah Al-Mulk* 67:5), and in the Words of Him, Most High: ❨ Then He completed and finished from their creation (as) seven heavens in two days and He made in each heaven its affair. And We adorned the nearest (lowest) heaven with lamps (stars) to be an adornment as well as to guard (from the devils by using them as missiles against the devils). Such is the Decree of Him the Almighty, the All-Knowing ❩ *(Soorah Fussilat* 41:12). So Allah selected the lowest heaven from among the heavens to be adorned with heavenly bodies, and if this proves that they (the planets) are adornments, then so be it. If not, then there is no objection to what the others say. And Allah knows better. According to them, the seven heavens, indeed, the eight, turn with all the fixed stars that they contain, while the wandering stars move in an orbit contrary to it, from the West to the East. So the moon completes its orbit in a month and the sun completes its orbit in a year. If there is no disparity between the two courses and their movements are similar, then the extent of the fourth heaven is twelve times greater than that of the lowest heaven. *Zuhal* (Saturn) – which is in the seventh heaven – completes its orbit in thirty years. Based on this, the extent of the seventh heaven will be three hundred and sixty times greater than that of the Earth.

The scholars have spoken about the masses of these stars and their orbits and movements and they have enlarged on these things until they have crossed over into the "science" of *Al-Ahkam* and the "knowledge" of Earthly events derived from it and matters of which most of them have no knowledge. The Greeks, who resided in Syria many years before the time of the Messiah ﷺ, had spoken at great length about such matters and it would require a lengthy discussion to explain all of it. It was they who built the city of Damascus and made seven gates for it and at each gate they built a temple representing each of the planets. They would worship each of them in the appropriate temple and make supplications to them which have been passed down from them by more than one historian and by others. The author of the book *As-Sirr Al-Maktoom Fee Mukhatabat Ash-Shams Wal-Qamar Wan-Nujoom* (The Hidden Secret in the Address to the Sun, the Moon and the Stars) – but they are superstitions to which none should pay any heed. And that is fairy tale, and people did not care of it. They were also recorded by some of the scholars of the Harnanis, the philosophers of ancient Harran. They were pagans, who worshipped the seven stars and they were a sect from among the Sabians. [1] This is why Allah, Most High, says, ﴾ And from among His Signs are

---

[1] Harnanis: Or Harranis; later Muslim writers (after the 'Abbasid Caliph Al-Ma'mun 832-833 C.E.) described them as people who worshipped planets, idols, stars and lived in the city of Harran, in south-east Turkey. It was said that Al-Ma'moon, passing through Harran on his way to a campaign against Byzantium, forced the Harranians to convert to either to Islam or one of the "religions of the book", meaning Judaism, Christianity, or Sabianism. The people of Harran identified themselves with the Sabians in order to fall under the protection of Islam. Sabians were mentioned in the Qur'an, but those were a group of Gnostic Mandaeans living in southern Iraq who were extinct at the time of Al-Ma'moon.

the night and the day, and the sun and the moon. Prostrate not to the sun or to the moon, but prostrate to Allah, Who created them, if you (really) worship Him ﴾. (*Soorah Fussilat* 41:37) And He informs us that the hoopoe said to Sulaiman (Solomon ﷺ), when informing him about Bilqees, the Queen of Saba', in Yemen and her armies and supporters, ﴿ "I found a woman ruling over them, and she has been given all things that could be possessed by any ruler of the Earth, and she has a great throne. I found her and her people worshipping the sun instead of Allah, and *Shaitan* (Satan) has made their deeds fair-seeming to them, and has barred them from (Allah's) Way, so they have no guidance., *Al-La* (this word has two interpretations: (i) Satan has barred them from Allah's Way so that they do not worship (prostrate before) Allah, or (ii) so that they may worship (prostrate before) Allah, Who brings to light what is hidden in the heavens and the Earth, and knows what you conceal and what you reveal)." (*Tafseer At-Tabari,* Vol. 19, Page Allah, *La ilaha illa Huwa* (none has the right to be worshipped but He), the Lord of the Supreme Throne! ﴾ (*Soorah An-Naml* 27:23-26)

Because the most eminent of the visible bodies in the heavens and the Earth are the planets and the most eminent of them are the sun and the moon, Al-Khaleel Ibraheem ﷺ proved the futility of worshipping them; and that is in the Words of Allah, Most High: ﴿ When he saw the moon rising up, he said, 'This is my lord.' But when it set, he said, 'Unless my Lord guides me, I shall surely be among the erring people.' When he saw the sun rising up, he said, 'This is my lord. This is greater.' But when it set, he said, 'O, my people! I am indeed free from all that you join as partners in worship with Allah. Verily, I have turned my face toward Him Who has created the heavens and the Earth *Hanifan* (Islamic Monotheism, i.e. worshipping none but Allah, Alone) and I am not of *al-mushrikoon* (pagans, idolaters, etc,." ﴾ (*Soorah Al-An'am* 6:77-79) So he made clear, using decisive evidence, that worshipping any of these visible bodies, such as the planets, the moon and the sun does not benefit anyone at all, because all of them are created things, subject to Allah's Lordship, His Direction and made to follow their orbits and they cannot deviate from what has been created for them, unless it is ordained for them. This is the proof that they are subject to Allah's Lordship, created, made subservient and subjugated, which is why Allah, Most High, says, ﴾ And from among His Signs are the night and the day, and the sun and the moon. Prostrate not to the sun or to the moon, but prostrate to Allah Who created them, if you (really) worship Him. ﴿ (*Soorah Fussilat* 41:37) It has been authentically reported in the *Saheehain* regarding the eclipse prayer that the Messenger of Allah ﷺ said during a sermon one day, "Verily, the sun and the moon are two Signs from among Allah's Signs and they do not eclipse for the death of anyone, nor for his life." [1]

Al-Bukhari narrated in the *Book of the Beginning of Creation*, on the authority of Abu Hurairah ؓ from the Prophet ﷺ that he said, "The sun and the moon will be rolled up on the Day of Resurrection." [2]

These traditions prove that the sun and the moon are from among Allah's creations, which He created for the purposes that He designed and then He does with them as He wills. And to Him belongs the argument that eliminates falsehood and is incontrovertible.

When this is known, (it becomes clear that) all of the wandering and fixed stars which are in the heaven are creations of Allah, as

---

(1)   Narrated by Al-Bukhari (1044) and Muslim (901), on the authority of 'A'ishah (may Allah be pleased with her).

(2)   Narrated by Al-Bukhari (3200).

He, Most High, says, ❨ And He made in each heaven its affair. And We adorned the nearest (lowest) heaven with lamps (stars) to be an adornment as well as to guard (from the devils by using them as missiles against the devils). Such is the Decree of Him the All-Mighty, the All-Knower. ❩ (*Soorah Fussilat* 41:12)

As for what many of the scholars of *tafseer* have said regarding the story of Haroot and Maroot, that *Az-Zuhrah* was a woman whom they attempted to seduce, but she refused unless they agreed to teach her the greatest Name, which they did and she spoke it and ascended to the heaven and became a planet, I believe that this is from among the *Isra'eeliyyat* and even though it may have been narrated by Ka'b Al-Ahbar and passed on from him by a group from among the *Salaf*, who related it as a story from the Children of Isra'eel.

Section Regarding What Has Been Said About the Galaxy and Rainbows

Abul Qasim At-Tabarani narrated on the authority of 'Abdullah Ibn 'Abbas ﷺ that Heraclius wrote to Mu'awiyah ﷺ and said, "If there remains among them anything of Prophethood, then he will inform me about whatever I ask them." So he wrote to him, asking him about the galaxy and about rainbows and about a place on which the sun has not shone except for one hour. When the messenger reached Mu'awiyah with the letter, he said, "This is a thing about which I did not think that I would be asked before today." He asked, "Who can answer this?" It was said, "'Abdullah Ibn 'Abbas." So Mu'awiyah ﷺ folded up Heraclius' message and sent it to 'Abdullah Ibn 'Abbas ﷺ and he ('Abdullah Ibn 'Abbas ﷺ) wrote (back) to him, "The rainbow is a protection for the people of the Earth from flooding and the galaxy is the door to the heaven, from which the Earth is separated. As for the place on which the sun has not shone except for an hour of the daytime, it is that which lies beneath the sea that was parted for the Children of Isra'eel." [1] This has an authentic chain of narrators up to 'Abdullah Ibn 'Abbas ﷺ.

Allah, Most High, says, ﴿ Verily, in the creation of the heavens and the Earth, and in the alternation of night and day, and the ships which sail through the sea with that which is of use to mankind, and the water (rain) which Allah sends down from the sky and makes the Earth alive therewith after its death, and the moving (living) creatures of all kinds that He has scattered therein, and in the veering of winds and clouds which are held between the sky and the Earth, are indeed *Ayat* (proofs, evidences, signs, etc.) for people of understanding. ﴾ (*Soorah Al-Baqarah* 2:164)

Imam Ahmad narrated on the authority of Yazeed Ibn Haroon, who in turn reported on the authority of Ibraheem Ibn Sa'd, who reported from his father, who in turn reported on the authority of one of the Shaikhs of Banu Ghifar that he said, "I heard the Messenger of Allah ﷺ says, 'Verily, Allah creates the cloud and He speaks in the best way and laughs in the best way,.." [2]

Malik narrated on the authority of 'Abdullah Ibn Az-Zubair that whenever he heard thunder, he would stop speaking and then he would say, "Glory be to Him Whose praises the thunder glorifies, as do the angels from fear of Him." [3]

---

(1) Narrated by At-Tabarani in *Al-Mu'jam Al-Kabeer* (10/244). Al-Haithami said in *Majma' Az-Zawa'id* (15524), "It was narrated by At-Tabarani and its narrators are reliable."

(2) This is an authentic *hadeeth* narrated by Imam Ahmad (23174).

(3) Narrated by Imam Malik in *Al-Muwatta'* (*Book 56, Number 56.11.26*)

Imam Ahmad narrated on the authority of Abu Hurairah ﷺ that the Messenger of Allah ﷺ said, "Your Lord said, 'If My slaves were to obey Me, I would send down rain to them at night and I would send down the sun upon them during the daytime and I would never let them hear the sound of thunder,." [1]

---

and by Al-Bukhari in *Al-Adab Al-Mufrad* (724) and others. It was declared authentic by the *muhaqqiq* (verifier) of *Tafseer Ibn Katheer*.

(1)   Narrated by Imam Ahmad in his *Musnad* (2/359).

Chapter: Mention of the Creation of the Angels and Their Attributes

Allah, Most High, says, ❨ Allah bears witness that *La ilaha illa Huwa* (none has the right to be worshipped but He), and the angels, and those having knowledge (also give this witness); (He is always) maintaining His creation in Justice. *La ilaha illa Huwa* (none has the right to be worshipped but He), the All-Mighty, the All-Wise. ❩ (*Soorah Ale 'Imran* 3:18).

He, Most High, says, ❨ But Allah bears witness to that which He has sent down (the Qur'an) unto you (O, Muhammad), He has sent it down with His Knowledge, and the angels bear witness. ❩ (*Soorah An-Nisa'* 4:166)

IIc, Most High, says, ❨ And they say: 'The Most Beneficent (Allah) has begotten a son (or children).' Glory to Him! They (those whom they call children of Allah, i.e. the angels, 'Eesa [Jesus] son of Maryam [Mary] and 'Uzair [Ezra], etc.) are but honored slaves. They speak not until He has spoken, and they act on His Command. He knows what is before them, and what is behind them, and they cannot intercede except for him with whom He is pleased. And they stand in awe for fear of Him. And if any of them should say: 'Verily, I am an *ilah* (a god) besides Him (Allah),' such a one We should recompense with Hell. Thus We recompense the *zalimoon* (polytheists, wrongdoers, etc.) ❩ (*Soorah Al-Anbiya'* 21:26-29)

He, Most High, says, ❨ Nearly the heavens might rent asunder from above them (by His Majesty), and the angels glorify the praises of their Lord, and ask for forgiveness for those on the Earth, verily, Allah is the Oft-Forgiving, the Most Merciful. ❩ (*Soorah Ash-Shoora* 42:5)

He, Most High, says, ❨ Those (angels) who bear the Throne (of Allah) and those around it glorify the praises of their Lord, and believe in Him, and seek forgiveness for those who believe (in the Oneness of Allah) (saying): 'Our Lord! You comprehend all things in mercy and knowledge, so forgive those who repent and follow Your Way, and save them from the torment of the blazing Fire! Our Lord! And make them enter the *'Adn* (Eden) Paradise (everlasting Gardens) which you have promised them, and to the righteous among their fathers, their wives, and their offspring! Verily, You are the Almighty, the All-Wise,. ❩ (*Soorah Ghafir* 40:7,8)

He, Most High, says, ❨ All praises and thanks be to Allah,

the (only) Originator (or the [only] Creator) of the heavens and the Earth, Who made the angels messengers with wings - two or three or four. He increases in creation what He wills. Verily, Allah is Able to do all things. ⟫ (*Soorah Fatir* 35:1)

He, Most High, says, ⟨ And (remember) the Day when the heaven shall be rent asunder with clouds, and the angels will be sent down, with a grand descending. The sovereignty on that Day will be the true (sovereignty), belonging to the Most Beneficent (Allah), and it will be a hard Day for the disbelievers (those who disbelieve in the Oneness of Allah (Islamic Monotheism). ⟫ (*Soorah Al-Furqan* 25:25,26)

He, Most High, says, ⟨ O, you who believe! Ward off from yourselves and your families a Fire (Hell) whose fuel is men and stones, over which are (appointed) angels stern (and) severe, who disobey not, (from executing) the Commands they receive from Allah, but do that which they are commanded. ⟫ (Soorah At-Tahreem 66:6)

The Verses which mention the angels are numerous; Allah describes them as being strong in worship and in physical form. They are of comely appearance and huge in size and they take on many forms, as He, Most High, says, ⟨ And when Our Messengers came to Loot (Lot), he was grieved on their account and felt himself straitened for them (lest the townspeople should approach them to commit sodomy with them). He said, 'This is a distressful day.' And his people came rushing toward him, and since aforetime they used to commit crimes (sodomy, etc.)⟫ (*Soorah Hood* 11:77,78)

We mentioned in the *Tafseer* what more than one scholar said that the angels appeared in the form of handsome men as a test and a trial, so that the evidence would be established against the people of Lot ﷺ and Allah will inflict upon them the seizure of Allah, the Almighty, Most Competent. Likewise, Gabriel ﷺ used to come to the Prophet ﷺ in different forms; sometimes he would come to him in the form of Dihyah Ibn Khaleefah Al-Kalbi, [1] sometimes in the form of a Bedouin man, [2] sometimes in his true form. [3] He has six hundred wings and the distance between each wing is like the distance between the East and the West. The Prophet ﷺ saw him in this form on two occasions: once, when he was descending from the heaven to the Earth and once, at *Sidrah Al-Muntaha*, [4] which is near to *Jannah Al-Ma'wa*. [5] And this is mentioned in the Words of Allah, Most High: ❴ He has been taught (this Qur'an) by one mighty in power (Jibrael [Gabriel]), *dhu mirrah* (free from any defect in body and mind), *fastawa* (then he [Jibrael] rose and became stable) (*Tafseer At-Tabari*) while he (Jibrael) was in the highest part of the horizon. Then he (Jibrael) approached and came closer. ❵ (*Soorah An-Najm* 53:5-8). That is, Gabriel ﷺ, as we reported on the authority of more than one of the Companions, including 'Abdullah Ibn Mas'ood, Abu Hurairah, Abu Dharr and 'A'ishah (may Allah be pleased with all of them). ❴ And was at a distance of two bows' length or (even) nearer, So did (Allah) convey the Inspiration to His slave. ❵ (*Soorah An-Najm* 53:9,10) That is, to the slave of Allah, Muhammad ﷺ. Then He says, ❴ And indeed he (Muhammad) saw him (Jibrael) at a second descent (i.e. another time) near *Sidrah Al-Muntaha* (the Lote-tree of the Utmost Boundary [beyond which none can pass]) ❵ (*Soorah An-Najm* 53:13,14). The reference in all

---

(1)   See: *Saheeh Al-Bukhari* (3634) and *Saheeh Muslim* (2451).

(2)   See: *Saheeh Muslim* (8).

(3)   See: *Saheeh Muslim* (177).

(4)   *Sidrah Al-Muntaha*: The Farthest Lote-tree.

(5)   *Jannah Al-Ma'wa*: The Garden of Refuge.

these is to Gabriel صلى and we have mentioned in the *ahadeeth* of *Al-Isra'* in *Soorah Subhan* [1] that *Sidrah Al-Muntaha* is in the seventh heaven. In another narration, it is mentioned that it is in the sixth heaven. That is, its trunk and its branches are in the seventh heaven. ﴿ When that covered the Lote-tree which did cover it ﴾ *(Soorah An-Namj* 53:16). It was said that it was covered by the Light of the Lord, the Almighty, the All-Powerful. It was also said that it was covered by golden moths. It was also said that it was covered by numerous different colors, without limit. It was also said that it was covered by the angels, like ravens. It was also said that it was covered by the Light of Allah, Most High, and no one can describe it, because of its beauty and its splendor.

There is no contradiction between these sayings, because all of them are possible at one time.

Sufyan Ath-Thawri, Shu'bah and Abul-Ahwas narrated on the authority of Simak Ibn Harb, who reported from Khalid Ibn 'Ar'arah that Ibn Al-Kawwa' asked 'Ali Ibn Abi Talib ؏ about *Al-Bait Al-Ma'moor* and he said: "It is a mosque in the seventh heaven, which is known as *Ad-Durah*, opposite the *Ka'bah* from above. Its sacredness in the heaven is like the sacredness of the House on Earth. Every day, seventy thousand angels pray in it and they never return to it." [2]

Others said that in every heaven there is a House which is filled with angels, who come there in order to worship. They visit it in shifts, just as the people of the Earth visit the Sacred House in order to perform Hajj every year and to perform *'Umrah* at all times and to make *tawaf* and offer prayers.

---

(1) *Soorah Al-Isra'*.

(2) Narrated by Al-Baihaqi in *Ash-Shu'ab* (3/437). It also has support in the *Saheehain, Al-Bukhari* (3207) and *Muslim* (164).

The name of the House which is in the heaven is *Bait Al-'Izzah* and the name of the angel who leads the angels in it is Isma'eel According to this, the seventy thousand angels who enter *Bait Al-Ma'moor* every day and they do not return to it again – i.e., they will never return to it until the end of time – are from the inhabitants of the seventh heaven alone. This is why Allah, Most High, says, ❨And none can know the hosts of your Lord but He❩ (*Soorah Al-Muddaththir* 74:31)

Imam Ahmad narrated on the authority of Abu Dharr ﷺ that he said: The Messenger of Allah ﷺ said, "Verily, I see what you do not see and I hear what you do not hear. The heaven cried out and it was entitled to cry out. There is no place larger than the space of four fingers which does not have a prostrating angel on it. If you knew what I know, you would laugh little and weep much, and you would not take pleasure in women on your beds – you would go out to the heights and raise your voices to Allah, the Almighty, the All-Powerful." Abu Dharr ﷺ said, "By Allah, I wished that I was a firm supported tree." [1]

Al-Hafiz Abul-Qasim At-Tabarani narrated on the authority of Jabir Ibn 'Abdullah ﷺ that he said: The Messenger of Allah ﷺ said, "There is not in the seven heavens the space of a foot, or even a finger joint, or a hand which does not have a prostrating angel or a bowing angel in it. When the Day of Resurrection comes, they will all say, 'We would not have worshipped You as You deserve to be worshipped if we had not done so without ascribing partners to you.'" [2]

These two narrations prove that there is no place in the seven

---

(1) A sound (*hasan*) *hadeeth*, narrated by Ahmad (21005), At-Tirmidhi (2312), Ibn Majah (4190), Al-Hakim in *Al-Mustadrak* (4/622, No. 8724) in a *mawqoof* form.

(2) Narrated by At-Tabarani in *Al-Mu'jam Al-Kabeer* (2/184, no. 1751).

heavens which is not occupied by the angels engaged in all kinds of worship. Some of them are continuously standing, others are continuously bowing and others are continuously prostrating. Others are involved in other forms of worship and Allah knows better what they are. They are continuously occupied in worship, glorification and remembrance of Allah; deeds which Allah has commanded them to do and they have places near to their Lord. Allah, Most High, says, ❨ There is not one of us (angels) but has his known place (or position); Verily, we (angels), we stand in rows for the prayers (as you Muslims stand in rows for your prayers); Verily, we (angels), we are those who glorify (Allah's praises, i.e. offer prayers) ❩ (*Soorah As-Saffat* 37:164-166)

The Prophet ﷺ said: "Why don't you draw yourselves up in rows as angels do in the presence of their Lord?" The Companions said, "Messenger of Allah, how do the angels draw themselves up in rows in the presence of their Lord?" He ﷺ said, "They make the first row complete and keep close together in the row. " [1]

He said: "We have been favoured over the rest of the mankind in three matters: the earth has been made as a mosque (i.e. a place in which to pray) for us and its dust has been made a means of purification for us and our ranks (in prayer) have been made like those of the angels." [2]

Thus they will come on the Day of Resurrection in front of their Lord, the All-Powerful, in ranks, as Allah, Most High, says, ❨ And your Lord comes with the angels in rows ❩ (*Soorah*

---

(1)   Narrated on the authority of Jabir Ibn Samurah ﷺ by Muslim (430), Abu Dawood (661), An-Nasa'i (816), Ibn Majah (992) and Ahmad (20519).

(2)   Narrated on the authority of Hudhaifah Ibn Al-Yaman ﷺ by Muslim (522).

Al-Fajr 89:22)

They will stand in rows before their Lord, the Almighty, the All-Powerful on the Day of Resurrection, as He, Most High, says, ❨ The Day that *Ar-Rooh* and the angels will stand forth in rows, none shall speak except him whom the Most Beneficent (Allah) allows, and he will speak what is right ❩ (*Soorah An-Naba'* 78:38) What is meant by *Ar-Rooh* here is mankind, according to 'Abdullah Ibn 'Abbas ؏, Al-Hasan and Qatadah. It was also said that it means a group of angels resembling mankind in appearance. This was also said by 'Abdullah Ibn 'Abbas ؏, Mujahid, Abu Salih and Al-A'mash. It was also said that it refers to Jibrael. This was the opinion of Ash-Sha'bi, Sa'eed Ibn Jubair and Ad-Dahhak. It was also said that it refers to an angel who is known as *Ar-Rooh*, who is responsible for all mankind. 'Ali Ibn Abi Talhah reported on the authority of 'Abdullah Ibn 'Abbas ؏ [1] that he said regarding the Words of Allah, Most High: ❨ The Day that *Ar-Rooh*... will stand forth ❩ that it is one of the greatest of the angels in form. A great thing has been mentioned in the description of Jibrael ؏ in the Words of Allah, Most High: ❨ He has been taught by One Mighty in power ❩ (*Soorah An-Najm* 53:5). The scholars said that so great is his strength that he lifted up the cities of the people of Loot ؏ – and they were seven in number – with all of their inhabitants; they numbered four hundred thousand, in addition to their livestock and other animals. He also lifted up all the cities of the surrounding lands and their buildings, etc. He lifted all of these on the tip of one of his wings until it was as high as the clouds in the sky, so that the angels heard the barking of dogs and the crowing of their cockerels. Then he turned them upside-down – and that is the One Mighty in

---

(1) According to scholars of *hadeeth*, 'Ali Ibn Abi Talhah did not hear from 'Abdullah Ibn 'Abbas ؏.

Power. As for His Saying: ❨ *Dhu Mirrah* ❩, it means: handsome in form, splendid and radiant, as Allah, Most High, says in another Verse: ❨ Verily, this is the Word of a most honorable messenger. ❩ (*Soorah Al-Haqqah* 69:40), i.e. Jibrael عليه السلام and the word ❨ honorable ❩ here means beautiful in appearance. His Saying: ❨ one mighty in power ❩ means that he possesses great strength and enormous power. ❨ With the Lord of the Throne ❩ means that he has a high status and elevated station, next to Allah, the Lord of the Glorious Throne. ❨ Obeyed there ❩ means Jibrael is obeyed by the heavenly host (i.e. the angels). ❨ And trustworthy ❩ means great trust has been placed in him by Allah, which is why he was the ambassador between Allah and His Prophets (peace be upon them all), descending to them with Revelation containing true information and just laws. He used to come to the Messenger of Allah ﷺ and he would descend to him in a number of different forms, as we mentioned earlier. He saw in him in the form in which Allah created him on two occasions. He has six hundred wings, according to the narration of Al-Bukhari, on the authority of Talq Ibn Ghannam, who reported on the authority of Za'idah Ash-Shaibani that he said, "I asked Zirr about the Words of Allah: ❨ And was at a distance of two bows' length or less. So did He convey the Inspiration to His slave. ❩ (*Soorah An-Najm* 53:9,10) and he said, "'Abdullah ('Abdullah Ibn Mas'ood رضي الله عنه) informed us that Muhammad ﷺ saw Jibrael عليه السلام and he had six hundred wings."[1]

Imam Ahmad narrated on the authority of Abu Wa'il, who reported on the authority of 'Abdullah رضي الله عنه that he said, "The Messenger of Allah ﷺ saw Jibrael عليه السلام in his (original) form and he had six hundred wings and each wing filled the horizon and pearls and precious stones of all colors fell from his wings, in

---

(1)   Narrated by Al-Bukhari (4857).

a manner that only Allah knows." [1]

In the *Saheehain* it was reported on the authority of Masrooq that he said, "I was with 'A`ishah and I said, 'Does not Allah say, ❴ And indeed he (Muhammad ﷺ) saw him in the clear horizon (toward the East) ❵ (*Soorah At-Takweer* 81:23) and, ❴ And indeed he (Muhammad ﷺ) saw him at a second descent (another time) ❵ (*Soorah An-Najm* 53:13)' She said, 'I was the first of this nation to ask the Messenger of Allah ﷺ about this and he said, 'That refers to none other than Jibrael عليه السلام.' " [2] He did not see him in the form in which Allah created him except on two occasions: he saw him descending from the heaven to the Earth, the greatness of his size filling what lies between the heaven and the Earth.

Al-Bukhari narrated on the authority of 'Abdullah Ibn 'Abbas ؓ that he said, "The Messenger of Allah ﷺ said to Jibrael عليه السلام, 'Will you not visit us more than you do?' Upon which Allah revealed: ❴ And we (angels) descend not except by the Command of your Lord (O, Muhammad). To Him belongs what is before us and what is behind us ❵ " (*Soorah Maryam* 19:64)

Al-Bukhari narrated on the authority of 'Abdullah Ibn 'Abbas ؓ that he said, "The Messenger of Allah ﷺ was the most generous of people and he was at his most generous during the month of Ramadan, when Jibrael عليه السلام met him. Jibrael ؓ used to meet him on every night of Ramadan till the end of the month. The Prophet used to recite the Holy Qur'an to Jibrael, and when Jibrael met him, he used to be more generous than a

---

(1)   This is a sound (*hasan*) tradition narrated by Imam Ahmad (3905, 4382).

(2)   Narrated by Al-Bukhari (3235) and Muslim (177) and the wording is that of the latter.

fast wind (which brings rain and welfare)." [1]

One of the attributes of Israfeel – who is one of the bearers of the Throne – is that he will blow the trumpet by the Command of his Lord three times. The first trump is the trump of terror, the second will be the trump of swooning and the third will be the trump of Resurrection. The trumpet is a horn on which he will blow. Every circle of it is like the distance between the heaven and the Earth. And in it there is a place in which the souls of the slaves are placed when Allah commands the blowing of the trumpet. When it is blown, the souls will come out of it and the Lord, the All-Powerful will say, "By My Might and My Power, let every soul return to the body which it inhabited during its earthly life." They will enter the bodies in the graves and they will enter them, as poison enters a person who has been stung. Then the bodies will come to life and the graves will split open over them and they will emerge from them and hasten to the gathering place.

This is why the Messenger of Allah ﷺ said, "How can I live a life of ease when the bearer of the horn has put it to his lips and raised his forehead anticipating to hear the call, so when he is ordered to blow, he will blow." The Companions said, "What should we say (supplicate) O, Messenger of Allah?" He replied: "Say, 'Sufficient is Allah for us and He is the best of Guardians, we put our trust in Allah, our Lord'." [2]

Al-Hafiz Abul-Qasim At-Tabarani narrated on the authority of 'Abdullah Ibn 'Abbas ﷺ that he said: Change only this While the Messenger of Allah ﷺ was with Jibrael ﷺ in a secluded place, the horizon of the heaven split and Israfeel ﷺ

---

(1)   Narrated by Al-Bukhari (1902).

(2)   Narrated by Ahmad (11299) and graded authentic, due to supporting narrations.

approached, coming close to the Earth and swayed and then an angel stood before the Prophet ﷺ and said, "O, Muhammad! Verily, Allah commands you to choose between (being) a slave-prophet and a king-prophet." He said, "Gabriel ﷺ signed to me with his hand to be humble and I knew that he was advising me and so I said, 'A slave-prophet.' Then that angel ascended to the heaven and I said, 'O, Gabriel! I wanted to ask you about this, but I saw in your expression something which deterred me from asking the question. So who was that, O, Gabriel?' He said, "That was Israfeel ﷺ. On the day that Allah created him, He created him in front of Him, with his feet together and he did not raise his gaze. Between him and the Lord were seventy lights and every time one of them came near to him, it would burn out. In front of him is a tablet and whenever Allah commands something in the heaven or the Earth, it is raised up to the tablet and it strikes his forehead and he looks. If it is one of my responsibilities, then it commands me to do it; if it is one of Meeka'eel's responsibilities, then it commands him to do it and if it is one of the Angel of Death's responsibilities, then it commands him to do it.' I said, 'O, Gabriel! And what are your responsibilities?' He said, 'For the wind and the armies.' I said, 'And what are Meeka'eel's responsibilities?' He said, 'For the plants and the rain." I said, 'And what are the responsibilities of the Angel of Death?' He said, 'For taking the souls; I thought that he had descended for no other reason than to begin the Hour (of Resurrection) and what you saw in me was only fear of the start of the Hour." [1] This *hadeeth* is *ghareeb* from this

---

(1) Narrated by At-Tabarani in *Al-Mu'jam Al-Kabeer* (11/379, No. 12061). Al-Haithami said in *Majma' Az-Zawa'id* (9/19), "It was narrated by At-Tabarani and in its chain is one Muhammad Ibn Abi Laila; he was declared trustworthy by some, but he had a poor memory. All of the other narrators in the chain are trustworthy." The author said that the text of the *hadeeth* is *ghareeb*.

source.

In *Saheeh Muslim*, it is reported on the authority of 'A`ishah that when the Messenger of Allah ﷺ stood up at night to pray, he would say, "O, Allah, the Lord of Jibrael, Michael and Israfeel, the Creator of the heavens and the Earth, Knower of the unseen and the seen! You judge between Your slaves in those matters in which they disagree. Guide me with Your permission in the divergent views (which the people hold) about Truth, for it is You Who guides whom You will to the Straight Path." [1]

Imam Ahmad said: Abul-Yaman told us: Ibn 'Ayyash told us on the authority of 'Umarah Ibn Ghaziyyah Al-Ansari that he heard Humaid Ibn 'Ubaid, the freed slave of Banu Mu'alla say: I heard Thabit Al-Bunani reporting on the authority of Anas Ibn Malik ﷺ, who reported from the Messenger of Allah ﷺ that he said to Gabriel عليه السلام, "Why do I never see Michael عليه السلام laughing?" Jibrael عليه السلام replied, "Michael has not laughed since the Fire was created." [2] So these angels, who have been clearly mentioned in the Qur'an and authentic *ahadeeth*, are those who are mentioned in the Prophetic supplication: "O, Allah, the Lord of Jibrael, Michael and Israfeel..." [3] So Jibrael عليه السلام descends with guidance to the Messengers, in order that they might convey it to the nations. Michael عليه السلام is charged with responsibility for the rain and the plants, from both of which sustenance is created in this (earthly) abode. He has assistants who do as he orders them to do, by Allah's Command. They distribute the winds and the clouds, in according to the Will of the Lord, the All-Powerful.

---

(1) Narrated by Muslim (770).

(2) Narrated by Imam Ahmad (12930); it was declared to be *hasan* due to other supporting narrations.

(3) The *takhreej* has already been given.

As for the Angel of Death, his name is not made clear in the Qur'an or in the authentic *ahadeeth*, though it has been given as 'Izra'eel in some traditions – and Allah knows better.

Allah, Most High, says, ❨ Say: 'The angel of death, who is set over you, will take your souls, then you shall be brought to your Lord'." ❩ (*Soorah As-Sajdah* 32:11). He has helpers who extract the soul of the slave from the body until it reaches the throat, whereupon, the Angel of Death takes it in his hand; and when he takes it, he does not leave it in his hand for more than the blink of an eye before it is taken by his helpers and cast into shrouds befitting it, as made clear in the explanation of the Words of Allah, Most High: ❨ Allah will keep firm those who believe, with the word that stands firm in this world (i.e. they will keep on worshipping Allah alone and none else) and in the Hereafter. ❩ (*Soorah Ibraheem* 14:27)

Then they ascend with it. If it was a righteous soul, the gates of the Heaven are opened for it, but if it was not righteous, they remain closed to it and it is thrown down to the Earth. Allah, Most High, says, ❨ He is the Irresistible, Supreme over His slaves, and He sends guardians (angels guarding and writing all of one's good and bad deeds) over you, until when death approaches one of you, Our Messengers (the Angel of Death and his assistants) take his soul, and they never neglect their duty. Then they are returned to Allah, their *Mawla* (True Master [God], the Just Lord [to reward them]). Surely, His is the Judgment and He is the Swiftest in taking account. ❩ (*Soorah Al-An'am* 6:61,62)

We mentioned in the *hadeeth* of the trumpet, on the authority of Abu Hurairah ☀, who reported from the Messenger of Allah ☀, in a long *hadeeth*, that he said, "Allah will command Israfeel to blow on the trumpet and make the trump of swooning and he will do so, upon which the inhabitants of the heavens and the inhabitants of the earth will swoon, except those whom Allah wills. Then while they are lying still, the Angel of Death will come to Allah, the Omnipotent, the Almighty, the All-Powerful and he will say, 'O, my Lord! The inhabitants of the heavens and the earth have died, except those whom You willed.' Then Allah – Who knows better who remains – will say, 'Who remains?' The Angel of Death will reply, 'You, the Ever-Living, Who does not die, remain and the bearers of Your Throne remain, as do Gabriel and Michael and I (also) remain.' Then Allah will say, 'Let Gabriel and Michael die.' Then Allah will make His Throne speak and it will say, 'O, my Lord! Shall Gabriel and Michael die?' Allah will answer, "Silence! For I have ordained death for everyone who is beneath My Throne.' So they will both die and then the Angel of Death will come to the Omnipotent, the Almighty, the All-Powerful and he will say, 'O, my Lord! Gabriel and Michael have died." Then Allah – Who knows better who remains – will say, 'Now who remains?' He will say, 'You, the Ever-Living, Who does not die, remain, the bearers of Your Throne remain and I remain.' Then Allah will say, 'Let the bearers of My Throne die.' So they will die and Allah will command the Throne and it will seize the trumpet from Israfeel. Then the Angel of Death will come to Allah and say, 'O, my Lord! The bearers of the Throne have died.' Then Allah – Who knows better who remains – will say, 'Who remains?' The Angel of Death will reply, 'You, the Ever-living, Who does not die, remain and I remain.' Then Allah will say, 'You are one of My creation; I have created you for what I willed, so die.' Then he will die and when none remains, except Allah, the One, the Irresistible, the (Indivisible) One, the Self-Sufficient, Who does not beget, nor was He begotten and Who has no equal, He will be the Last, just as He was the First…"

This was narrated by At-Tabarani, Ibn Jareer and Al-Baihaqi. [1]

Among the angels whose names have been mentioned in the Qur'an are Haroot and Maroot. There are numerous sayings pertaining to them reported from the *Salaf* and many traditions have been reported concerning their story and their affairs, but most of them are *Isra'eeliyyat*.

Among the angels whose names are given in the *ahadeeth* are Munkar and Nakeer (peace be upon them both). Their names have been mentioned numerous times regarding the questions in the grave and we have recorded them with Allah's Words: ﴿ Allah will keep firm those who believe, with the word that stands firm in this world (i.e. they will keep on worshipping Allah, Alone, and none else) and in the Hereafter and Allah will cause to go (further) astray those who are *zalimoon* (polytheists and wrongdoers, etc.), and Allah does what He wills. ﴾ (*Soorah Ibraheem* 14:27) They are responsible for the trial of the grave and have been charged with the responsibility of questioning the inhabitant of the grave about his Lord and his Religion and his Prophet and they test the righteous and the sinners. They have black faces and blue eyes and they have fangs; their physical forms are disturbing and their voices are terrifying. May Allah protect us from the punishment of the grave and make us steadfast with steady speech. Ameen.

Al-Bukhari has narrated on the authority of 'Urwah that 'A'ishah, the wife of the Prophet ﷺ, informed him that she said to the Prophet ﷺ, "Have you encountered a day harder than the Day (of the Battle) of Uhud?" The Prophet ﷺ replied,

---

(1)   Narrated by At-Tabarani in *Al-Ahadeeth At-Tiwal* (36), by Ibn Jareer in his *Tafseer* (24/30), by Al-Baihaqi in *Al-Ba'th An-Nushoor* (668 and 669) and by As-Suyooti in *Ad-Durr Al-Manthoor Fit-Tafseer Bil-Ma'thoor* (7/257).

"Your tribes have troubled me a lot, and the worst trouble was the trouble on the day of 'Aqabah, when I presented myself to Ibn 'Abd Yalil Ibn 'Abd Kulal and he did not respond to my demand. So I departed, overwhelmed with extreme sorrow, and proceeded on and could not relax till I found myself at Qarn Ath-Tha'alib where I lifted my head toward the sky to see a cloud shading me unexpectedly. I looked up and saw Gabriel in it. He called me saying, 'Allah has heard your people's saying to you and what they have replied back to you. Allah has sent the Angel of the Mountains to you so that you may order him to do whatever you wish to these people.' The Angel of the Mountains called and greeted me and then said, 'O Muhammad! Order what you wish. If you like, I will let Al-Akhshabain (i.e. the two mountains) fall on them.' The Prophet ﷺ said, 'No, but I hope that Allah will let them beget children who will worship Allah, Alone, and will worship none besides Him'." [1]

Section on the Categories of Angels

The angels (peace be upon them) are divided into various categories, according to the responsibilities which Allah has ordained for them. Among them are the bearers of the Throne, as mentioned earlier. Others include the Archangels, who are around the Throne and they are the most honored of the angels, along with the bearers of the Throne; and they are the angels closest to Allah, as He, Most High, says, ❨ The Messiah will never be proud to reject to be a slave to Allah, nor the angels who are near (to Allah). ❩ (*Soorah An-Nisa'* 4:172)

Also among them are Jibrael and Michael (peace be upon

---

(1)   Narrated by Al-Bukhari (3231) and Muslim (1795).

them both). Allah has mentioned regarding them that they seek forgiveness for the Believers in their absence, as Allah, Most High, says, ❴ Those (angels) who bear the Throne (of Allah) and those around it glorify the praises of their Lord, and believe in Him, and seek forgiveness for those who believe (in the Oneness of Allah) (saying): 'Our Lord! You comprehend all things in mercy and knowledge, so forgive those who repent and follow Your Way, and save them from the torment of the blazing Fire! Our Lord! And make them enter the *'Adn* (Eden) Paradise (everlasting gardens) which you have promised them, and to the righteous among their fathers, their wives, and their offspring! Verily, You are the Almighty, the Most Wise. And save them from (the punishment, because of what they did of) the sins, and whomsoever You save from (the punishment, because of what they did of) the sins (i.e. excuse them) that day, him verily, You have taken into mercy.' And that is the supreme success. ❵ (*Soorah Ghafir* 40:7-9)

And because of their pure natures, they love those who possess this attribute and it has been authentically reported in the *hadeeth* on the authority of the truthful one and the one who is believed (i.e. Muhammad ﷺ), "When the slave supplicates on behalf of his brother in his heart, the angel says, 'Ameen; and for you be the same'." [1]

Also among them are the inhabitants of the seven heavens; they abide there in constant worship, night and day, morning and evening, as Allah, Most High, says, ❴ They (i.e. the angels) glorify His Praises night and day (and) they never slacken (in doing so). ❵ (*Soorah Al-Anbiya'* 21:20)

The custodian of Paradise is an angel whose name is Ridwan;

---

(1) Narrated by Muslim (2732), Abu Dawood (1534), Ibn Majah (2895), Ahmad (27010), on the authority of Abu Ad-Darda' ﷺ.

this has been clearly reported in a number of *ahadeeth*. [1]

Also among them are those responsible for the Fire and they are *Az-Zabaniyyah*. In front of them are nineteen angels. The custodian of the Fire is Malik and he is in charge of all of the guardians. It is they who are referred to in the Words of Allah, Most High: ❨ And those in the Fire will say to the keepers (angels) of Hell, 'Call upon your Lord to lighten for us the torment for a day'!" ❩ (*Soorah Ghafir* 40:49)

Allah, Most High, says, ❨ And they will cry: 'O Malik (keeper of Hell)! Let your Lord make an end of us." He will say: 'Verily, you shall abide forever.' Indeed We have brought the truth (Muhammad ﷺ with the Qur'an) to you, but most of you have a hatred for the truth. ❩ (*Soorah Az-Zukhruf* 43:77,78)

Al-Walibi reported on the authority of 'Abdullah Ibn 'Abbas ؓ regarding the Words of Allah, Most High: ❨ For each (person), there are *mu'aqqibat* in succession, before and behind him. They guard him by the Command of Allah. Verily! Allah will not change the good condition of a people as long as they do not change their state of goodness themselves (by committing sins and by being ungrateful and disobedient to Allah). But when Allah wills a people's punishment, there can be no turning back of it, and they will find besides Him no protector.❩ (*Soorah Ar-Ra'd* 13:11) that he said that the *mu'aqqibat* by the Command of Allah are the angels. 'Ikrimah reported on the authority of 'Abdullah Ibn 'Abbas ؓ that he said regarding the Words of Allah: ❨ They guard him by the Command of Allah. ❩, The angels guard him from in front of him and from behind him and when Allah's Ordainment comes, they leave him. Mujahid

---

(1) See: *Musnad Ash-Shihab* (2/130). In *Ad-Durr Al-Manthoor Fit-Tafseer Bil-Ma'thoor* (355/8), As-Suyooti attributed it to Ad-Daraqutni, on the authority of Anas ؓ.

said, "Every slave has an angel charged with protecting him during his sleep and his wakefulness from the jinn and mankind and harmful creatures. And nothing can come to him intending to harm him without an angel saying, "Behind you!" – Unless Allah wills that it should afflict him, in which case it will do so. Also among them are the angels entrusted with protecting the deeds of the slaves, as Allah, Most High, says, ﴾ (Remember) that the two receivers (recording angels) receive (each human being after he or she has attained the age of puberty), one sitting on the right and one on the left (to note his or her actions). Not a word does he (or she) utter, but there is a watcher by him ready (to record it). ﴿ (*Soorah Qaf* 50:17,18)

Allah, Most High, says, ﴾ But verily, over you (are appointed angels in charge of mankind) to watch you. *Kiraman* (honorable) *Katibeen* writing down (your deeds). They know all that you do. ﴿ (*Soorah Al-Infitar* 82:10-12)

So Allah made them honorable in their being and in their behavior. A part of their honorableness is demonstrated in the *hadeeth* narrated in the books of authentic *ahadeeth* and in the *Sunan* [1] and *Masaneed* [2] on the authority of a number of the Companions ﷺ, who reported from the Messenger of Allah ﷺ that he said, "The angels do not enter a house in which there is a picture or in which there is a dog or in which there is a person in a state of *janabah*. [3]" [4] In the narration of 'Asim Ibn

---

(1) *Sunan*: Collections of *ahadeeth* arranged according to subject matter.

(2) *Masaneed*: Collections of *ahadeeth* arranged according to their *asaneed* (chains of narrators).

(3) *Janabah*: Ritual impurity.

(4) With the addition of the words: "or where there is a person in a state of *janabah*," this is a weak narration. It was narrated by Abu Dawood (227), by An-Nasa'i (261), by Ahmad (1292) and by Ibn Hibban in his *Saheeh* (5/4, No. 1205). As for the *hadeeth* narrated on the authority of 'Abdullah

Damrah, who reported on the authority of 'Ali Ibn Abi Talib ﷺ, is the addition "or urine." [1] In the narration of Rafi', on the authority of Abu Sa'eed Al-Khudri ﷺ, in a *marfoo'* form, it was stated: "The angels do not enter a house in which there is a picture or a statue." [2] And in the narration of Mujahid on the authority of Abu Hurairah ﷺ, in a *marfoo'* form, it was stated: "The angels do not enter a house in which there is a dog or a statue." [3] In a narration on the authority of Abu Hurairah ﷺ it was stated that he said: The Messenger of Allah ﷺ said, "The angels do not accompany travelers who have with them a dog or a bell." [4] It was narrated by Zurarah Ibn Awfa, who reported on the authority of the Messenger of Allah ﷺ that he said, "The angels do not accompany travelers who have with them a bell." [5] Al-Bazzar narrated on the authority of Abu Hurairah ﷺ that he said: The Messenger of Allah ﷺ said, "Verily, the angels of Allah know the children of Adam," and I think he said, "and they know their deeds, so if they see a slave performing an act of obedience to Allah, they speak of it among themselves and they name it and say, 'So-and-so has succeeded this night. So-and-so has been saved this night.' But if they see a slave committing an act of disobedience to Allah, they speak of it among themselves and they name it and say, 'So-and-so is

---

Ibn 'Abbas ﷺ, which states that: "Angels do not enter a house in which there is a dog or a picture," it was narrated by Muslim (3929).

(1)   This is an extremely weak *hadeeth*. It was narrated by Imam Ahmad ﷺ and it contains in its chain of narrators one 'Amr Ibn Khalid, who is a liar.

(2)   This is an authentic *hadeeth* narrated by Imam Ahmad (11448), Malik (1801) and At-Tirmidhi (2805).

(3)   This *hadeeth* is authentic in meaning; it was narrated by Abu Dawood (4158) and At-Tirmidhi (2806).

(4)   Narrated by Muslim (2113), Abu Dawood (2555), At-Tirmidhi (1703), Ahmad (7512) and Ad-Darimi (2676).

(5)   An authentic *hadeeth* narrated by Ahmad (8772).

destroyed this night'." [1]

Al-Bukhari narrated on the authority of Abu Hurairah ﷺ that he said: The Messenger of Allah ﷺ said, "The angels keep on descending from and ascending to the heaven in turn, some at night and some by day, and all of them assemble together at the time of the *Fajr* and '*Asr* prayers. Then those who have stayed with you overnight ascend unto Allah, Who asks them, and He knows the answer better than they, 'How have you left My slaves?' They reply, 'We have left them praying as we found them praying'." [2] This is the wording in the *Book of the Beginning of Creation*.

What is meant is that every person has two protecting angels, one before him and the other behind him. They protect him from Allah's Command, by Allah's Command. And there are two recording angels, one on his right and one on his left; and the recording angel on the right commands the angel on the left. The one on the right records his good deeds, while the one on the left records his bad deeds. When the angel on the left intends to record a bad deed, the angel on the right says to him, "Give him a respite, that haply, he may repent or seek forgiveness." If he performs a good deed, the angel on the right records it without hesitation, as Allah, Most High, says, ﴾(Remember) that the two receivers (recording angels) receive (each human being after he or she has attained the age of puberty), one sitting on the right and one on the left (to note his or her actions). Not a word does he (or she) utter, but there is a watcher by him ready (to record it). ﴿ (*Soorah Qaf* 50:17,18)

---

(1)　This was mentioned by Al-Haithami in *Majma' Az-Zawa'id* (10/226) and he said of it, "Narrated by Al-Bazzar; it contains (in its chain of narrators) people whom I do not know."

(2)　Narrated by Al-Bukhari (3223).

As for the *hadeeth* narrated by Imam Ahmad on the authority of 'Abdullah Ibn Mas'ood ✿, in which he said: The Messenger of Allah ✿ said, "There is not a single one of you but has his *qareen* from among the jinn and his *qareen* (companion) from among the angels." They said, "And you also, Messenger of Allah?" He replied, "Yes, I also, but Allah has helped me against him so that he does not command me except in that which is true and good." [1] It is possible that this *qareen* from the angels is unlike the *qareen* that protects mankind. He is only charged with guiding and directing him by Allah's Permission to the way of goodness and the path of righteousness. Likewise, the *qareen* from among the devils has been charged to spare no effort in causing confusion and misguidance. The one who is protected is the one whom Allah, the Almighty, the All-Powerful protects – and Allah is the One from Whom protection is sought.

Al-Bukhari narrated on the authority of Abu Hurairah ✿ that he said: The Messenger of Allah ✿ said, "Every Friday the angels take their stand at every gate of the mosques to write the names of the people chronologically (i.e. according to the time of their arrival for the Friday prayer) and when the *Imam* sits (on the pulpit) they fold up their scrolls and get ready to listen to the sermon." [2] Al-Bukhari narrated in this from this source and it is narrated in the *Saheehain* from another source. [3]

Allah, Most High, says, ❴ And recite the Qur'an in the early dawn (i.e. the morning prayer). Verily, the recitation of the Qur'an in the early dawn is ever witnessed (attended by the angels in charge of mankind of the day and the night). ❵ (*Soorah Al-Isra'* 17:78)

---

(1)   Narrated by Muslim (2814) and Imam Ahmad (3770).

(2)   Narrated by Al-Bukhari (3211).

(3)   Narrated by Al-Bukhari (929) and Muslim (850).

Al-Bukhari narrated on the authority of Abu Hurairah
👐 from the Prophet 👐 that he said, "A prayer performed in
congregation is twenty-five times more superior in reward to
a prayer performed by a single person. The angels of the night
and the angels of the day are assembled at the time of the *Fajr*
prayer." Abu Hurairah 👐 added, "If you wish, you can recite:
❨ And recite the Qur'an in the early dawn (i.e. prayer. Verily,
the recitation of the Qur'an in the early dawn is ever witnessed
(attended by the angels in charge of mankind of the day and the
night). ❩ (*Soorah Al-Isra'* 17:78)

Al-Bukhari narrated, on the authority of Abu Hurairah 👐,
that he said: The Messenger of Allah 👐 said, "When a man
calls his wife to his bed (to have sexual relations with her) and
she refuses and causes him to sleep in anger, the angels curse
her till morning." [1]

It has been narrated in the *Saheehain* that the Messenger of
Allah 👐 said, "When the *Imam* says *Ameen* (in the prayer),
says *Ameen*, because if anyone's *ta'meen* (saying *Ameen*)
coincides with that of the angels, all of his previous sins will
be for given." [2]

Imam Ahmad narrated, on the authority of Abu Hurairah 👐
or on the authority of Abu Sa'eed Al-Khudri 👐, – Al-A'mash
(one of the narrators) was unsure which of them it was – said:
The Messenger of Allah 👐 said, "Verily, Allah has angels
who travel throughout the earth in addition to the recorders
of mankind and when they find people remembering Allah,
the Almighty, the All-Powerful, they call out to one another,
'Come to the object of your desire!' And they take them up to
the lowest heaven. Their Lord asks then, and He knows better

---

(1)   Narrated by Al-Bukhari (3237).

(2)   Narrated by Al-Bukhari (780) and Muslim (781).

than them, 'What are My slaves saying?' They say: 'They are glorifying, magnifying, praising and extolling You.' He asks, 'Have they seen Me?' They say, 'No, by Allah, they have not seen You.' He asks, 'And how would it be if they saw Me?' They say, 'They would be even more fervent and devoted in their praise and worship.' He asks, 'What are they asking me for?' They say, 'They ask You for Paradise.' He asks, 'And have they seen it?' They say, 'No, by Allah, Lord, they have not seen it.' He asks, 'And how would it be if they saw it?' They say: 'They would be even more eager for it and they would beseech You even more earnestly.' He asks, 'And what do they seek My protection from?' They say, 'From the Fire of Hell.' He asks, 'Have they seen it?' They say, 'No, by Allah, they have not seen it.' He asks, 'And how would it be if they saw it?' They say: 'They would be even more afraid and anxious to escape it.' Allah says: 'You are My witnesses that I have forgiven them.' One of the angels says: 'So-and-so is not really one of them; he came (to the gathering) for some other reason.' Allah says, 'They were all in the gathering, and one of them will not be excluded (from forgiveness)'." [1]

Imam Ahmad narrated on the authority of Abu Hurairah ☼, that he said: The Messenger of Allah ﷺ said, "Whoever relieves a believer from a hardship in this life, Allah will relieve him from a hardship on the Day of Resurrection. Whosoever brings ease to a believer who is in difficulty, Allah will bring ease to him in both this life and the next. Whosoever conceals the shortcomings of a Muslim, Allah will conceal his shortcomings in this world and the next. Allah will always help a servant as long as that servant helps his brother. And whoever follows a path by which he seeks knowledge, Allah will make easy for him a path to Paradise. Those people who assemble in a house from among the houses

---

(1) This is an authentic *hadeeth* narrated by Imam Ahmad (7376).

of Allah (mosques) and recite the Book of Allah and learn and teach the Qur'an, tranquility will descend upon them and mercy will cover them and the angels will surround them. Allah makes a mention of them in the presence of those near Him, and he who is slow-paced in doing good deeds, his (exalted) lineage will not make him go faster." [1]

Imam Ahmad narrated from 'Abdullah Ibn Mas'ood ﷺ that the Messenger of Allah ﷺ said: "Verily, Allah has angels who travel in the earth. They convey to me the peace greetings (*salam*) from my *Ummah*." [2]

Likewise, when a slave leaves his house and says, "*Bismillahi Tawakkaltu 'Alallahi Wa La Hawla Wa La Quwwata Illa Billah* (In the Name of Allah, I have placed my trust in Allah and there is no strength and no power except in Allah)," the angel says to him, "Your needs shall be fulfilled, you shall be saved from difficulties and hardships. Satan, hearing these words, leaves him." [3]

The *ahadeeth* in which the angels are mentioned are numerous and we have mentioned from them what Allah has made easy for us, all praise be to Him.

Section Regarding the Superiority of Angels Over Mankind

People have differed regarding the superiority of the angels

---

(1) Narrated by Ahmad (7379) and Muslim (2699).

(2) This is an authentic *hadeeth* narrated by Imam Ahmad (4198).

(3) This is an authentic *hadeeth* narrated by Abu Dawood (5095) and At-Tirmidhi (3426), on the authority of Anas Ibn Malik ﷺ.

over mankind, holding a number of diverse opinions: Most of what has been written relating to this issue is recorded in the books of the rationalists and the disagreements therein with the *Mu'tazilites* and those who agreed with their opinions. The oldest discourse that I have seen relating to this issue is that mentioned by Al-Hafiz Ibn 'Asakir in his *Tareekh*, in the biography of Umayyah Ibn 'Amr Ibn Sa'eed Ibn Al-'As, in which it was stated that he attended a gathering held by 'Umar Ibn 'Abdul-Aziz and found with him a group of people. 'Umar said, "There is no one more noble in Allah's Sight than a noble person from the children of Adam." And he cited as evidence for his claim the Words of Allah, Most High: ﴿ Verily, those who believe (in the Oneness of Allah and in His Messenger, Muhammad [peace be upon him] including all obligations ordered by Islam) and do righteous good deeds, they are the best of creatures. ﴾ (*Soorah Al-Bayyinah* 98:7) Umayyah Ibn 'Amr Ibn Sa'eed agreed with him in this, but 'Irak Ibn Malik said, "There is none more noble in Allah's Sight than His angels: they perpetually serve Him and they are His messengers to his Prophets." He cited as evidence for his claim the Words of Allah, Most High: ﴿ "Your Lord did not forbid you this tree save you should become angels or become of the immortals." ﴾ (*Soorah Al-A'raf* 7:20) 'Umar Ibn 'Abdul-Aziz said to Muhammad Ibn Ka'b Al-Qurazi, "What do you say, Abu Hamzah?" He said, "Allah has honored Adam and created him with His Hand and He breathed into him of His Spirit and caused the angels to prostrate before him and He created from his progeny the Prophets, the Messengers and those whom the angels visit." 'Umar Ibn 'Abdul-Aziz agreed with this judgment, but he cited evidence other than that cited by Muhammad Ibn Ka'b and he declared the use of Allah's Words: ﴿ Verily, those who believe (in the Oneness of Allah and in His Messenger, Muhammad [peace be upon him] including all obligations ordered by Islam) and do righteous good deeds… ﴾ as evidence for man's superiority to be weak, because the Verse is not exclusive to mankind; Allah has described the angels as having faith in His Words: ﴾ And they (the angels) believe in Him. ﴿ (*Soorah Ghafir* 40:7) and also the jinn: ﴾ And indeed when we heard the Guidance (this Qur'an), we believed therein (Islamic Monotheism) ﴿ (*Soorah Al-Jinn* 72:13) and: ﴾ And of us some are Muslims (who have submitted to Allah, after listening to this Qur'an). ﴿ (*Soorah Al-Jinn* 72:14)

Chapter: Mention of the Creation of the Jinn and the Story of Satan

Allah, Most High, says, ❨ He created man (Adam) from sounding clay like the clay of pottery. And the jinn did He create from a smokeless flame of fire. Then which of the Blessings of your Lord will you both (jinn and men) deny? ❩ (*Soorah Ar-Rahman* 55:14-16)

He, Most High, says, ❨ And indeed, We created man from sounding clay of altered black smooth mud. And the jinn, We created aforetime from the smokeless flame of fire. ❩ (*Soorah Al-Hijr* 15:26,27)

'Abdullah Ibn 'Abbas ☙, 'Ikrimah, Mujahid, Al-Hasan and a number of others said that the meaning of the Words of Allah, Most High: ❨ from a smokeless flame of fire ❩ (*Soorah Ar-Rahman* 55:15) is: from the tip of the flame, or in another narration, from the purest and best part of it. We have mentioned previously by way of Az-Zuhri, on the authority of 'Urwah, who reported on the authority of 'A'ishah that she said: The Messenger of Allah ﷺ said: "The angels were created from light, the jinn were created from a smokeless fire and Adam was created from what has been described (in the Qur'an) to you (i.e. from clay)." [1]

Many of the scholars of *tafseer* said that the jinn were created before Adam ﷺ and that the *hinn* [2] and the *binn* lived in the Earth before mankind and Allah sent the jinn against them and they killed them, drove them out of it and exterminated them. And they inhabited it after them, because of what they had done. As-Suddi said in his *Tafseer* on the authority of 'Abdullah Ibn 'Abbas, on the authority of Murrah, who reported on the authority of 'Abdullah Ibn Mas'ood and on the authority of some of the Companions of the Messenger of Allah ﷺ, that they said that when Allah had completed the creation as He willed, He ascended (*istawa*) over the Throne and He appointed Iblees over the dominion of the earthly heaven. He belonged to a tribe of the angels known as the jinn. They were called the jinn because they were the guardians of *Al-Jannah* (Paradise). In addition to his dominion of the earthly heaven, Iblees was a guardian and the idea grew in his heart that Allah had favored only him above all of the angels. Ad-Dahhak mentions, on the authority of 'Abdullah Ibn 'Abbas ﷺ, that when the jinn caused corruption in the Earth committed bloodshed, Allah sent Iblees against them with an army of angels and they killed them and expelled them from the land to islands in the seas.

Muhammad Ibn Ishaq reported, on the authority of 'Abdullah Ibn 'Abbas ﷺ, that he said that the name of Iblees before he committed the act of disobedience (to Allah) was 'Azazeel and he was one of the inhabitants of the Earth and one of the strongest of the angels in formulating legal judgments and the

---

(1) Narrated by Muslim (2996) and Imam Ahmad (24826).

(2) *Hinn*: The weakest and lowest of the jinn.

greatest of them in knowledge. He hailed from a tribe known as the Jinn.

Al-Hasan Al-Basri said: "He was not of the angels for even the blink of an eye. His origin was the jinn, just as Adam's origin was human." Shahr Ibn Hawshab and others said that Iblees was of the jinn whom the angels expelled and they captured some of them and took them to the heaven. This was narrated by Ibn Jareer At-Tabari.

They said that when Allah willed to create Adam ﷺ in order that he might be on the Earth along with his progeny who came after him and created his body from it, Iblees – whose name at that time was 'Azazeel and who was the leader of the jinn and the most fervent of them in worshipping Allah – went around and inside his body and when he found that it was hollow, he realized that he was a creation who could not be controlled and he said, "If I gain mastery over you, I will certainly destroy you, but if you gain mastery over me, I will disobey you." Then, when Allah blew into him of His Spirit, as we shall see, and commanded the angels to prostrate before him, Iblees became filled with extreme envy and refused to prostrate before him. He said, "I am better than he; You created me from fire and You created him from clay." So he disobeyed the command and opposed the Lord, the Almighty, the All-Powerful and he committed a sin by his words and was withdrawn from the Mercy of his Lord and removed from the high position that he had occupied due to his worship. He had resembled the angels but he was not of the same species as them, because he was created from fire, while they were created from light. He had been deceived by his nature and returned to his fiery origin: ﴿So the angels prostrated themselves, all of them, except Iblees (Satan) he was proud and was one of the disbelievers.﴾ (*Soorah*

Sad 38:73,74)

So Iblees was sent down from the heavenly host and he was prohibited from ever entering it again. As a result, he went down to the Earth wretched, humbled, disgraced and expelled, with the threat (or promise) of the Fire for him and those of the jinn and mankind who follow him. In spite of this, he exerts all of his efforts to misguide the children of Adam, by every means and every way, as Allah, Most High, says, ◀ (Iblees) said, 'See? This one whom You have honored above me, if You give me respite (keep me alive) to the Day of Resurrection, I will surely seize and mislead his offspring (by sending them astray), all but a few!' (Allah) said, 'Go, and whosoever of them follows you, surely! Hell will be the recompense of you (all) an ample recompense. And *Istafziz* (literally means: befool them gradually) those whom you can among them with your voice (i.e. songs, music, and any other call for Allah's disobedience), make assaults on them with your cavalry and your infantry, mutually share with them wealth and children (by tempting them to earn money by illegal ways usury, etc., or by committing illegal sexual intercourse, etc.), and make promises to them. But Satan promises them nothing but deceit. Verily! My slaves (i.e. the true believers of Islamic Monotheism), you have no authority over them. And All-Sufficient is your Lord as a Guardian'." ▶ (*Soorah Al-Isra'* 17:62-65) And we shall relate the story in detail when we mention the creation of Adam ﷺ.

Allah, Most High, says in *Soorah Al-Jinn*, ◀ Say (o, Muhammad): 'It has been revealed to me that a group (from three to ten in number) of jinn listened (to this Qur'an). They said, 'Verily! We have heard a wonderful Recital (this Qur'an)! It guides to the Right Path, and we have believed therein, and we shall never join (in worship) anything with our Lord

(Allah). And exalted be the Majesty of our Lord, He has taken neither a wife, nor a son (nor offspring nor children). And that the foolish among us (i.e. Iblees) or the polytheists among the jinn used to utter against Allah that which was wrong and not right. And verily, we thought that men and jinn would not utter a lie against Allah. And verily, there were men among-mankind who took shelter with the masculine among the jinn, but they (the jinn) increased them (mankind) in sin and disbelief. And they thought as you thought, that Allah will not send any Messenger (to mankind or jinn). And we have sought to reach the heaven; but found it filled with stern guards and flaming fires. And verily, we used to sit there in stations, to (steal) a hearing, but anyone who listens now will find a flaming fire watching him in ambush. And we know not whether evil is intended for those on Earth, or whether their Lord intends for them a Right Path. There are among us some that are righteous, and some the opposite; we are groups each having a different way (religious sect, etc.). And we think that we cannot escape (from the punishment of) Allah on Earth, nor can we escape (from the punishment) by flight. And indeed when we heard the Guidance (this Qur'an), we believed therein (Islamic Monotheism), and whosoever believes in his Lord shall have no fear, either of a decrease in the reward of his good deeds or an increase in punishment for his sins. And of us some are Muslims (who have submitted to Allah, after listening to this Qur'an), and of us some are *al-qasitoon,* (disbelievers, those who have deviated from the Right Path)." And whosoever has embraced Islam (i.e. has become a Muslim by submitting to Allah), then such have sought the Right Path. And as for the *qasitoon* (disbelievers who deviated from the Right Path), they shall be the firewood for Hell, If they (the non-Muslims) had believed in Allah, and went on the Right Way (i.e. Islam) We should surely have bestowed on them water (rain) in abundance. That We might try them thereby. And whosoever turns away from the Reminder of his Lord (i.e. this Qur'an, and practices not its laws and orders), He will cause him to enter in a severe torment (i.e. Hell). ‍ *(Soorah Al-Jinn* 72:1-17)

We have given the explanation of this *Soorah* and the complete story at the end of *Soorah Al-Ahqaf* and we mentioned *ahadeeth* relating to it there. We said that this group was from among the jinn of Naseebeen [1] – or according to other narrations, from the jinn of Busra – and they passed by the Messenger of Allah ‍ when he was standing in prayer with his Companions ‍ at Batn Nakhlah, in Makkah and they stood and listened to his recitation. Then the Prophet ‍ met with them for a whole night and they asked him about things that he had enjoined upon them and things that he had forbidden to them. They also asked him about provision (for the Afterlife) and he said to them: "Every bone on which the name of Allah is recited is your provision. The time it will fall in your hand it would be covered with flesh, and the dung of (the camels) is fodder for your animals." [2]

The Prophet ‍ forbade Muslims from performing *istinja'* [3] with these (things), saying, "For these are the provision of your brothers, the jinn." [4]

Scholars have disagreed regarding whether the believing jinn would enter Paradise, or whether the reward for their obedience would only be that they were not punished in the

---

(1) Naseebeen: A town on the upper reaches of the Euphrates.

(2) Narrated by Muslim (450), At-Tirmidhi (3258) and Imam Ahmad (4138).

(3) *Istinja'*: Wiping the private parts after answering the call of nature.

(4) Narrated by At-Tirmidhi (18, 29), An-Nasa'i (34) and Imam Ahmad (20251).

Fire. According to one opinion (the correct one) they would enter Paradise, based on the generality of the Words of Allah, Most High, ❨ But for him who (the true believer of Islamic Monotheism who performs all the duties ordained by Allah and His Messenger Muhammad, and keeps away (abstains) from all kinds of sin and evil deeds prohibited in Islam and) fears the standing before his Lord, there will be two Gardens (i.e. in Paradise). Then which of the Blessings of your Lord will you both (jinn and men) deny?" ❩ (*Soorah Ar Rahman* 55:46,47)

Al-Bukhari narrated, on the authority of Abu Sa'eed Al-Khudri ﷺ, that the Prophet ﷺ said: "I observe that you like sheep and the wilderness. So whenever you are with your sheep or in the wilderness and you want to pronounce the *azan* for the prayer, raise your voice, for whoever hears the *azan*, whether a human being, a jinn or any other creature, will be a witness for you on the Day of Resurrection." Abu Sa'eed added, "I heard it (this narration) from the Messenger of Allah." [1]

As for the disbelievers among the jinn, some of them are *shayateen* and their leader is Iblees, the enemy of Adam ﷺ, the father of the mankind and he and his progeny have been given the opportunity to gain ascendancy over Adam ﷺ and his progeny. Allah, the Almighty, the All-Powerful pledges to protect those of them who have faith in Him, believe in His Messengers, obey His Laws, as He, Most High, says, ❨ Verily! My slaves (i.e. the true believers in Islamic Monotheism), you have no authority over them. And All-Sufficient is your Lord as a Guardian. ❩ (*Soorah Al-Isra'* 17:65)

And He, Most High, says, ❨ And indeed Iblees did prove true his thought about them, and they followed him, all except

---

(1)   Narrated by Al-Bukhari (609), An-Nasa'i (644), Ibn Majah (723) and Ah-mad (10912).

a group of true believers (in the Oneness of Allah). And he (Iblees) had no authority over them, except that We might test him, who believes in the Hereafter from him who is in doubt about it. And your Lord is a *Hafiz* over everything. (Knower of everything i.e. He keeps record of each and every person as regards deeds, and then He will reward them accordingly). ﴾ (*Soorah Saba'* 34:20,21)

He, Most High, says, ﴿ O, Children of Adam! Let not *Shaitan* deceive you, as he got your parents (Adam and Hawwa' [Eve]) out of Paradise, stripping them of their raiments, to show them their private parts. Verily, he and *qabeeluhu* (his soldiers from the jinn or his tribe) see you from where you cannot see them. Verily, We made the *Shayateen awliya'* (protectors and helpers) for those who believe not. ﴾ (*Soorah Al-A'raf* 7:27) What is meant is that Allah has granted him respite and delayed his punishment until the Day of Resurrection, as a trial and a test for His slaves, as He, Most High, says, ﴿ And he (*Iblees*) had no authority over them, except that We might test him, who believes in the Hereafter from him who is in doubt about it. And your Lord is a *Hafiz* over everything. (Knower of everything i.e. He keeps record of each and every person as regards deeds, and then He will reward them accordingly). ﴾ (*Soorah Saba'* 34:21)

So Iblees – may Allah's curse be upon him – is alive now, given respite until the Day of Resurrection, according to the evidence of the Qur'an and he has a throne over the surface of the sea. He sits on it and sends forth his legions to spread evil and trials among the mankind. Allah, Most High, says, ﴿ Ever feeble indeed is the plot of *Shaitan* ﴾ (*Soorah An-Nisa'* 4:76)

The proof that the throne of Iblees is on the sea is the *hadeeth* narrated by Imam Ahmad, on the authority of Jabir Ibn

'Abdullah ﷺ, who said: The Messenger of Allah ﷺ said: "The throne of Iblees is on the sea and he sends his legions every day to spread discord among the people and the greatest of them in rank in Iblees' sight is the one who causes the greatest discord among the people." [1]

Imam Ahmad narrated, on the authority of Jabir Ibn 'Abdillah ﷺ, that he said: I heard the Messenger of Allah ﷺ saying: "The throne of Iblees is over the sea and he sends his legions every day to spread discord among the people and the greatest of them in his sight is the one who spreads the most discord." [2]

Imam Muslim narrated, on the authority of Jabir Ibn 'Abdullah ﷺ from the Prophet ﷺ, that he said: "Iblees places his throne upon water; he then sends detachments (for creating dissension); the nearer to him in rank are those who are the greatest in creating discord. One of them comes and says: 'I did such-and-such.' And he says: 'You have done nothing.' Then one amongst them comes and says: 'I did not spare so-and-so until I caused discord between a husband and his wife.' The devil goes near him and says: 'You have done well.' Al-A'mash said, 'He then embraces him'." [3]

And we have already mentioned this *hadeeth* in explanation of the Words of Allah, Most High: ❨ that by which they cause separation between a man and his wife ❩ (*Soorah Al-Baqarah* 2:102) That is, the magic that is learnt from the devils among the mankind and the jinn leads to the separation of those between whom there exists the greatest intimacy and love; this

---

(1) This is an authentic *hadeeth* narrated by Imam Ahmad (14400) and all of the men in its chain are trustworthy.

(2) This is an authentic *hadeeth* narrated by Imam Ahmad (14699) and the men in its chain are trustworthy.

(3) Narrated by Muslim (2813).

is why Satan thanks the efforts of the one who causes this. So the one whom Allah rebukes, Satan praises; the one who invokes Allah's anger, Satan is pleased with him – may Allah's Curse be upon him. Allah has revealed the *Mu'awwidhatain* (i.e. *Soorah Al-Falaq* and *Soorah An-Nas*) [1] as a means of repelling all manners of evil and its causes and objectives, in particular,

Soorah An-Nas, which sates, ❴ Say, 'I seek refuge with (Allah,) the Lord of the mankind, the King of the mankind, The *Ilah* (God) of the mankind, from the evil of the whisperer (the devil who whispers evil into the hearts of people) who withdraws (from his whispering in one's heart after one remembers Allah), who whispers in the breasts of the mankind, of jinn and men."❵ (*Soorah An-Nas* 114:1-6)

In *Saheeh Al-Bukhari*, it is reported, on the authority of Safiyyah Bint Huyayyi (may Allah be pleased with her), that the Messenger of Allah ﷺ said, "Verily, Satan circulates in the human mind as blood circulates in it." [2]

Allah, Most High, says, ❴ But *Shaitan* made him forget to mention it to his Lord (or Satan caused [Yoosuf عليه السلام] to forget the remembrance of his Lord [Allah] so as to ask for His Help, instead of others). ❵ (*Soorah Yoosuf* 12:42) That is, when Yoosuf said to the wine-pourer, ❴ "Mention me to your lord (i.e. your king, so as to get me out of the prison)." ❵ (*Soorah*

---

(1)   Narrated by Ahmad in his *Musnad* (No. 16983) with an authentic chain of narrators, on the authority of 'Abdullah Ibn 'Abbas Al-Juhani ﷺ, who said that the Messenger of Allah ﷺ said to him, "O 'Abdullah Ibn 'Abbas! Shall I inform you about the best thing with which to seek protection with Allah?" He said, "Certainly." The Messenger of Allah ﷺ said, "Say, 'I seek refuge with the Lord of the daybreak' and 'I seek refuge with the Lord of the mankind'."

(2)   Narrated by Al-Bukhari (2038).

Yoosuf 12:42) – the wine-pourer forgot to mention him to his lord (the king) and this forgetfulness was from Satan, as a result of which Yoosuf remained in prison for a number of years more. This is why He says after it, ❨ Then the man who was released (one of the two who were in prison), now at length remembered and said... ❩ (*Soorah Yoosuf* 12:45)

Imam Ahmad narrated, on the authority of Abu Hurairah ﷺ, that he said: The Messenger of Allah ﷺ said: "When any of you is in the mosque Satan comes to him and beguiles him with his whisperings as a man entices his riding beast and when it is quiet, he hobbles it or bridles it." Abu Hurairah ﷺ said, "And you people see that: as for the one that is hobbled, you see him inclining this way and that and he does not remember Allah, while as for the one who is bridled, he opens his mouth, but he does not mention Allah, the Almighty, the All-Powerful." [1] Imam Ahmad alone narrated this.

Imam Ahmad narrated, on the authority of 'Abdullah Ibn 'Abbas ﷺ, that he said: A man came to the Prophet ﷺ and said, "O Messenger of Allah! I speak to myself about something which I would rather fall down from the sky than discuss (with another)." The Prophet ﷺ said, "*Allahu Akbar* (Allah is Greatest)! All praise and thanks be to Allah, Who has reduced the guile of Satan to mere whispering..." [2]

Al-Bukhari narrated, on the authority of Abu Hurairah ﷺ, that he said: The Messenger of Allah ﷺ said: "Satan comes to one of you and says, 'Who created this?' and, 'Who created this?' Until he says, 'Who created your Lord?' So, when he inspires

---

(1)   This is an authentic *hadeeth* narrated by Imam Ahmad (8170) and the men in its chain are trustworthy.

(2)   This is an authentic *hadeeth* narrated by Imam Ahmad (2098) and Abu Dawood (5112).

such a question, one should seek refuge with Allah and give up such thoughts." [1]

Allah, Most High, says, ❰ Verily, those who are *al-muttaqoon* (pious, God-fearing), when an evil thought comes to them from *Shaitan*, they remember (Allah), and (indeed) they then see (aright). ❱ (*Soorah Al-A'raf* 7:201)

He, Most High, says, ❰ And say: 'My Lord! I seek refuge with You from the whisperings (suggestions) of the *Shayateen*." And I seek refuge with You, My Lord, lest they may attend (or come near) me." ❱ (*Soorah Al-Mu'minoon* 23:97,98)

Allah, Most High, says, ❰ And if an evil whisper comes to you from *Shaitan* then seek refuge with Allah. Verily, He is the All-Hearing, All-Knowing. ❱ (*Soorah Al-A'raf* 7:200)

He, Most High, says, ❰ So when you want to recite the Qur'an, seek refuge with Allah from *Shaitan*, the outcast (the accursed one). Verily, He has no power over those who believe and put their trust only in their Lord (Allah). His power is only over those who obey and follow him (Satan), and those who join partners with Him (Allah) (i.e. those who are *Mushrikoon* – polytheists). ❱ (*Soorah An-Nahl* 16:98-100)

Imam Ahmad and the compilers of the *Sunan* narrated on the authority of Abul-Mutawakkil, who reported on the authority of Abu Sa'eed Al-Khudri ﷺ, that he said: The Messenger of Allah ﷺ used to say, "I seek refuge with Allah, the All-Hearing, the All-Knowing from the accursed Satan, from his urging, from his inspiration and from his utterances." [2]

---

(1) Narrated by Al-Bukhari (3276) and Muslim (134).

(2) An authentic *hadeeth* narrated by Imam Ahmad (11081), Abu Dawood (775), At-Tirmidhi (242) and Ad-Darimi (1239).

Al-Bukhari narrated, on the authority of 'Adiyy Ibn Thabit that he said: Sulaiman Ibn Surad ﷺ said: Two men were insulting each other in the presence of the Prophet ﷺ and we were sitting with them. One of the two abused his companion furiously and his face became red. The Prophet ﷺ said, "I know a word (sentence) the saying of which will cause him to relax if this man says it. Only if he said, 'I seek refuge with Allah from Satan, the outcast'." So they said to that (furious) man, "Don't you hear what the Prophet is saying?" He said, "I am not mad." [1]

Imam Ahmad narrated, on the authority of 'Abdullah Ibn 'Umar ﷺ, that the Messenger of Allah ﷺ said, "None of you should eat with his left hand nor should he drink with his left hand, because Satan eats with his left hand and drinks with his left hand." [2]

Imam Ahmad narrated, on the authority of Abu Ziyad At-Tahhan that he said: I heard Abu Hurairah ﷺ say (that he heard) from the Prophet ﷺ that he saw a man drinking whil standing and he said to him, "Vomit (it out)." The man said, "Why?" He said, "Would it please you that a cat should drink with you?" He said, "No." The Prophet ﷺ said, "Then (you should know that) the one who is more evil than that has drunk with you – Satan." [3]

Imam Ahmad narrated, on the authority of Ibn Az-Zubair, that he asked Jabir ﷺ: Did you hear the Prophet ﷺ say, "When a man enters his house and mentions Allah when he enters and when he eats, the devil says, 'There is no place for you to sleep

---

(1) Narrated by Al-Bukhari (6115).

(2) This is an authentic *hadeeth* narrated by Imam Ahmad (5490) and by Muslim (2020).

(3) This is an authentic *hadeeth* narrated by Imam Ahmad (7943).

and no dinner for you here.' But if he enters and he does not mention Allah's name as he enters, he (Satan) says, 'You have found a place to spend the night.' And if he does not mention Allah's name when he eats, he (Satan) says, 'You have found a place to spend the night and dinner.' He (Jabir ⚭) said, 'Yes'." [1]

Al-Bukhari narrated on the authority of 'Abdullah Ibn 'Umar ⚭ that he said, "When the (upper) edge of the sun appears (in the morning), do not perform a prayer till the sun appears in full, and when the lower edge of the sun sets, do not perform a prayer till it sets completely. You should not seek to pray at sunrise or sunset, for the sun rises between the two sides of the head of the devil." [2]

And in the *Sunan* it was reported that the Messenger of Allah ﷺ forbade that anyone should sit between the sun and the shade. He said, "It is the sitting place of Satan." [3]

This is why Allah, Most High, says, ❲ The shoots of its fruit-stalks are like the heads of *Shayatin.* ❳ (*Soorah As-Saffat* 37:65) When the women witnessed the handsomeness of Yoosuf ﷵ ❲No man is this! This is none other than a noble angel❳ (*Soorah Yoosuf* 12:31).

Al-Bukhari narrated on the authority of Jabir Ibn 'Abdillah ⚭ from the Prophet ﷺ that he said, "When night falls, then keep your children close to you, for the devils spread out then. An hour later you can let them free; and close the gates of

---

(1) This is an authentic *hadeeth* narrated by Imam Ahmad (14319).

(2) Narrated by Al-Bukhari (3273).

(3) This is an authentic *hadeeth* narrated by Ibn Majah (3722), without the words, "It is the sitting place of Satan." This addition is in *Musnad Al-Imam Ahmad* (14995). In addition, some traditions have been reported from the *Salaf* from among the Companions ⚭ and others. See *Ibn Abi Shaibah* (5/268).

your house (at night), and mention Allah's name thereupon, and cover your utensils, and mention Allah's name thereupon, (and if you do not have something to cover your utensils) you may put something across it (e.g. a piece of wood, etc.)." [1]

Al-Bukhari narrated on the authority of 'Abdullah Ibn 'Abbas ﷺ that he said, "If anyone of you has when having sexual relation with his wife, he should say: 'In the Name of Allah: O Allah! Protect us from Satan and prevent Satan from approaching our offspring You are going to give us,' and if he begets a child (as a result of that relation) Satan will not harm it." [2]

Al-Bukhari narrated on the authority of Abu Hurairah ﷺ that the Messenger of Allah ﷺ said, "Satan ties three knots at the back of the head of each of you, and he breathes the following words at each knot, 'The night is, long, so keep on sleeping.' If that person wakes up and recites the praises of Allah, then one knot is undone, and when he performs ablution the second knot is undone, and when he prays, all the knots are undone, and he gets up in the morning lively and gay, otherwise he gets up dull and gloomy." [3]

Al-Bukhari narrated on the authority of Abu Hurairah ﷺ that he said: The Messenger of Allah ﷺ said: "When the call for the prayer is pronounced, Satan takes to his heels, passing wind with noise. When the call for prayer is finished, he comes back. When the *iqamah* is pronounced, he again takes to his heels, and after its completion, he returns again to interfere between the (praying) person and his heart, saying to him. 'Remember this or that thing,' till the person forgets whether he has offered

---

(1) Narrated by Al-Bukhari (3280).

(2) Narrated by Al-Bukhari (3283).

(3) Narrated by Al-Bukhari (3269).

three or four *rak'at*: so if one forgets whether he has prayed three or four *rak'at*, he should perform two prostrations of *sahw* (i.e. forgetfulness)." [1]

Ahmad narrated on the authority of 'Ata' Ibn As-Sa'ib, who reported on the authority of Anas ﷺ that he said, "Stand close together in the ranks (in prayer), because Satan stands in the spaces." [2]

Al-Bukhari narrated on the authority of Abu Sa'eed Al-Khudri ﷺ that he said: The Messenger of Allah ﷺ said, "If somebody intends to pass in front of you while you are praying, prevent him; should he insist, prevent him again; if he insists again, fight with him (i.e. prevent him violently e.g. by pushing him violently), because such a person is (like) a devil." [3]

Imam Ahmad narrated on the authority of Abu Sa'eed Al-Khudri ﷺ that the Messenger of Allah ﷺ stood up to offer the *Fajr* prayer and he (Abu Sa'eed ﷺ) was standing behind him.

He recited and became confused in his recitation. When the prayer was over, he said, "If only you could have seen me and Iblees I grabbed him and kept on trying to strangle him until I felt the coldness of his saliva on these two fingers, the thumb and the one next to it. Were it not for the prayer of my brother Sulaiman (Solomon), he would have been tied to one of the pillars of the mosque this morning, and the children of Al-Madinah would have played with him. Whoever among you can prevent anyone from coming between him and the *qiblah*, let him do so." [4]

---

(1)   Narrated by Al-Bukhari (3285).

(2)   Narrated by Imam Ahmad (12162).

(3)   Narrated by Al-Bukhari (3274).

(4)   Narrated by Imam Ahmad (11371).

Muslim narrated on the authority of Abu Ad-Darda' ﷺ that he said: The Messenger of Allah ﷺ stood praying and we heard him say, "I seek refuge with Allah from you." Then he repeated three times, "I curse you with the curse of Allah." Then he stretched out his hand as though he was taking hold of something. When he finished the prayer, we said, 'O, Messenger of Allah! We heard you say something during the prayer which we have not heard you say before, and we saw you stretch out your hand.' He replied, 'Allah's enemy Iblees came with fire to put it in my face, so I said three times, 'I seek refuge in Allah from you.' Then I said three times, 'I curse you with the full curse of Allah.' But he did not retreat. Then I intended to seize him. I swear by Allah that had it not been for the supplication of my brother Sulaiman ﷺ, he would have been bound, and made an object of sport for the children of the people of Al-Madinah'." [1]

Allah, Most High, says, ❴ Let not then this (worldly) present life deceive you, nor let the chief deceiver (Satan) deceive you about Allah. ❵ (*Soorah Luqman* 31:33)

He, Most High, says, ❴ Surely, *Shaitan* is an enemy to you, so take (treat) him as an enemy. He only invites his *hizb* (followers) that they may become the dwellers of the blazing Fire. ❵ (*Soorah Fatir* 35:6) So Satan spares no effort to hinder and confuse a person in all of his affairs, all of his activities and all of his inactive moments, as Al-Hafiz Abu Bakr Ibn Abi Ad-Dunya wrote in his book entitled: *Masa'id Ash-Shaitan* (The Afflictions of Satan); and in it are numerous benefits.

In the *Sunan* of Abu Dawood, it is reported that the Messenger of Allah ﷺ used to say in his supplication, "I seek refuge with You from Satan's attempts to struggle with me, play with me

---

and corrupt my religion and my mind at the time of death." [1]

At-Tirmidhi, An-Nasa'i, Ibn Hibban (in his *Saheeh*) and Ibn Abi Hatim (in his *Tafseer*) narrated on the authority of 'Abdullah Ibn Mas'ood ﷺ that he said: The Messenger of Allah ﷺ said, "Verily, Satan has an effect on the son of Adam, and the angel also has an effect. As for the effect of Satan, it is by his threatening him with evil repercussions and rejecting the truth. As for the effect of the angel, it is by his promise of a good end and believing in the truth. Whoever finds the latter, let him know that it comes from Allah and let him thank Allah for it. Whoever finds the former, let him seek refuge (with Allah) from Satan." Then he recited, ﴿ Satan threatens you with poverty and orders you to commit *fahsha'* (sins, immorality, lewdness etc.); whereas Allah promises you forgiveness from Himself and bounty, and Allah is All-Sufficient for His creations' need, All-Knower. ﴾ (*Soorah Al-Baqarah* 2:268) [2]

Al-Bukhari narrated on the authority of Abu Hurairah ﷺ that the Messenger of Allah ﷺ said, "Whoever says, *La ilaha illallahu wahdahu la shareeka lahu, lahul-mulku wa lahul-hamdu wa huwa 'ala kulli shay'in qadeer* (None has the right to be worshipped except Allah, Alone, without partners, to Him belongs the Dominion and to Him belong all praise and thanks, and He has power over all things [i.e. He is Omnipotent])," one hundred times in a day, he will have the reward of manumitting ten slaves, and one-hundred good deeds will be written in his account, and one-hundred bad deeds will be wiped off or erased from his account. On that day he will be protected from the morning till evening from Satan; and nobody will be superior to him except one who has done more than that which he has

---

(1)   Narrated by Abu Dawood on the authority of Abu Yusr ﷺ (1552).

(2)   Narrated by At-Tirmidhi (2988).

done. Al-Bukhari narrated on the authority of Abu Hurairah ﷺ that he said: The Messenger of Allah ﷺ said: "When any human being is born, Satan touches him at both sides of the body with his two fingers, except 'Eesa the son of Maryam, whom Satan tried to touch but failed, for he touched the covering of the placenta instead." [1]

Al-Bukhari narrated on the authority of 'A'ishah (may Allah be pleased with her) that she said, "I asked the Prophet ﷺ about one's looking here and there during the prayer. He replied, 'It is what Satan steals from the prayer of any one of you'." [2]

Al-Bukhari narrated on the authority of 'Abdullah Ibn Abi Qatadah, who reported on the authority of his father ﷺ that he said: The Messenger of Allah ﷺ said: "A good dream is from Allah, and a bad or evil dream is from Satan; so if any one of you has a bad dream of which he gets afraid, he should spit on his left side and should seek refuge with Allah from its evil, for then it will not harm him." [3]

Imam Ahmad narrated on the authority of Abu Hurairah ﷺ that he said: The Messenger of Allah ﷺ said: "None of you should point to his brother with his weapon (sword, spear, arrow, dagger, etc.), because none of you knows, perhaps Satan may cause him (to hurt his brother) and as a result, he would fall into a pit of Fire." [4]

Allah says, ❨ And indeed We have adorned the nearest heaven with lamps, and We have made such lamps (as) missiles to drive away the *Shayateen*, and have prepared for them the torment of the blazing Fire ❩ (*Soorah Al-Mulk* 67:5).

---

(1)   Narrated by Al-Bukhari (3286).

(2)   Narrated by Al-Bukhari (3289).

(3)   Narrated by Al-Bukhari (3292).

(4)   This is an authentic *hadeeth* narrated by Ahmad (27432) and by Al-Bukhari (7072) and Muslim (2617).

He, Most High, says, informing us about the jinn (that they said), ❨ And we have sought to reach the heaven, but found it filled with stern guards and flaming fires. And verily, we used to sit there in stations, to (steal) a hearing, but anyone who listens now will find a flaming fire watching him in ambush. ❩ (*Soorah Al-Jinn* 72:8,9)

Al-Bukhari narrated on the authority of Abu Hurairah ﷺ that he said: Verily, the Prophet of Allah ﷺ said, "When Allah decrees some order in the heaven, the angels flutter their wings indicating complete surrender to His saying which sounds like chains being dragged on rock. ❨ Until fear is banished from their hearts, they say, 'What is it that your Lord has said?' They say: 'The truth. And He is the Most High, the Most Great.' ❩ (*Soorah Saba'* 34.23) Then the stealthy listeners (devils) hear this command, and these stealthy listeners are like this, one over the other." (Sufyan, a sub-narrator demonstrated this by holding his hand upright and separating the fingers.) "A stealthy listener hears a word which he will convey to the one below him and the second will convey it to the one below him till the last of them will convey it to the magician or foreteller. Sometimes a flame (fire) may strike the devil before he can convey it, and sometimes he may convey it before the flame (fire) strikes him, whereupon the magician adds to that word a hundred lies. The people will then say, 'Did not he (i.e. the magician) tell such-and-such a thing on such-and-such a date?' So that magician is said to have told the truth because of the statement which has been heard from the heavens." [1]

Allah, Most High, says, ❨ And whosoever turns away (blinds himself) from the remembrance of the Most Beneficent (Allah) (i.e. the Qur'an and worship of Allah), We appoint for him a *Shaitan* to be a *qareen* (an intimate companion) to him. And verily, they (the devils) hinder them from the Path (of Allah),

---

(1)   Narrated by Al-Bukhari (4800).

but they think that they are guided right! Till, when (such a one) comes to Us, he says (to his *qareen* [devil companion]), Would that between me and you were the distance of the two easts (or the east and west).' The worst (type of) companion (indeed)! 》 (*Soorah Az-Zukhruf* 43:36-38)

He, Most High, says, 《 And We have assigned them (devils) intimate companions (in this world), who have made fair-seeming to them what was before them (evil deeds which they were doing in the present worldly life and disbelief in the Reckoning and the Resurrection, etc.) and what was behind them (denial of the matters in the coming life of the Hereafter as regards punishment or reward, etc.) 》 (*Soorah Fussilat* 41:25)

Imam Ahmad narrated on the authority of 'Abdullah Ibn 'Abbas ﷺ that he said: The Messenger of Allah ﷺ said: "There is no one among you who has not had a *qareen* from among the devils appointed for him." They said, "Even you, Messenger of Allah?" He said, "Yes, but Allah has helped me against him and he has embraced Islam." [1]

Imam Ahmad narrated on the authority of Abu Hurairah ﷺ that the Prophet ﷺ said, "Verily, the believer emaciates his devil as one of you emaciates his camel on a journey." [2]

Imam Ahmad narrated on the authority of Saburah Ibn Abi Fakih ﷺ that he said: I heard the Messenger of Allah ﷺ say: "Verily, Satan lays in wait for the son of Adam ﷺ at (a number of) paths: he lays in wait for him at the path of Islam and says: 'Will you embrace Islam and abandon your religion and the religion of your forefathers?' But he disobeys him and embraces Islam. So he lays in wait for him at the path of *hijrah* (migration in Allah's Cause) and says, 'Will you migrate and abandon your land and your sky?' But the similitude of the

---

(1)   Narrated by Ahmad (2319) and the men in its chain are trustworthy.

(2)   This is an authentic *hadeeth* narrated by Ahmad (8717).

muhajir (migrate) is that of a horse in his strength and stamina. But he disobeyes him and migrates. Then he lays in wait for him at the path of *jihad*, which is to struggle with one's self and one's wealth, and he says: 'Will you fight and be killed, after which your wife will be married and your wealth divided?' But he disobeyes him and performes *jihad*." The Messenger of Allah 變 said, "So if anyone of them (the sons of Adam عليه السلام) does that, it will be his right upon Allah that He will admit him to Paradise. If he is killed, it will be his right upon Allah that He will admit him to Paradise. If he is drowned, it will be his right upon Allah that He will admit him to Paradise. And if his riding beast breaks his neck, it will be his right upon Allah that He will admit him to Paradise." [1]

Imam Ahmad narrated on the authority of 'Abdullah Ibn 'Umar ﷺ that he said: The Messenger of Allah 變 did not use to neglect these supplications in the morning and the evening: "O Allah! I ask You to pardon me in the life of this world and in the Hereafter. O Allah! I ask You to pardon me and grant me wellbeing in my Religion, my worldly affairs, my family and my property. O Allah! Cover up my deficiencies and calm my fears. O Allah! Protect me from my front, from behind, from my right, from my left and from above me. I seek refuge with Your Majesty from being snatched from below." Wakee' said it means to sink down. [2]

---

(1)   This is an authentic *hadeeth* narrated by Imam Ahmad (15528).

(2)   This is an authentic *hadeeth* narrated by Imam Ahmad (4770). It was also narrated by Abu Dawood (5074) and by An-Nasa'i in an abbreviated form (5530), Ibn Majah (3871), Ibn Hibban in his *Saheeh* (3/241, No. 961) and Al-Hakim in *Al-Mustadrak* (1/698, No. 1902).

Chapter: What Has Been Said Regarding the Creation of Adam عليه السلام

Allah, Most High, says, ❨ And (remember) when your Lord said to the angels: "Verily, I am going to place (mankind) generations after generations on Earth," they said, "will You place there those who will make mischief and shed blood while we glorify You with praises and thanks (Exalted be You above all that they associate with You as partners) and sanctify You." He (Allah) said, "I know that which you do not know." And He taught Adam all the names (of everything), then He showed them to the angels and said, "Tell Me the names of these if you are truthful." They said, "Glory be to You, we have no knowledge except what you have taught us. Verily, it is You, the All-Knower, the All-Wise." He said, "O Adam! Inform them of their names," and when he had informed them of their names, He said, "Did I not tell you that I know the *ghaib* (unseen) in the heavens and the Earth and I know what you reveal and what you have been concealing? And (remember) when We said to the angels: 'Prostrate yourselves before Adam. And they prostrated except Iblees; he refused and was proud and was one of the disbelievers (disobedient to Allah). And We said, 'O Adam! Dwell you and your wife in the Paradise and eat both of you freely with pleasure and delight of things therein wherever you will, but come not near this tree or you both will be of the *zalimoon* (wrong-doers).' Then the *Shaitan* made them slip therefrom (Paradise), and got them out from that in which they were. We said, 'Get you down, all, with enmity between yourselves. On Earth will be a dwelling place for you and an enjoyment for a time.' Then Adam received from his Lord of the Words. And his Lord pardoned him (accepted his repentance). Verily, He is the One Who forgives (accepts repentance), the Most Merciful. We said, 'Get down all of you from this place (the Paradise), then whenever there comes to you Guidance from Me, and whoever follows My Guidance, there shall be no fear on them, nor shall they grieve. But those who disbelieve and belie Our *Ayat* (proofs, evidences, Verses, lessons, signs, revelations, etc.) such are the dwellers of the Fire, they shall abide therein forever'." (*Soorah Al-Baqarah* 2:30-39)

Likewise, He, Most High, says, ❰ O mankind! We have created you from a male and a female, and made you into nations and tribes, that you may know one another. Verily, the most honorable of you with Allah is that (believer) who has *taqwa* (i.e. one of the *muttaqoon* (pious). Verily, Allah is All-Knowing, Aware of all things. ❱ (*Soorah Al-Hujurat* 49:13)

He, Most High, says, ❰ It is He Who has created you from a single person (Adam), and (then) He has created from him his wife (Hawwa), in order that he might enjoy the pleasure of living with her. When he had sexual relations with her, she became pregnant and she carried it about lightly. Then, when it became heavy, they both invoked Allah, their Lord (saying):

'If You give us a *saleh* (good in every aspect) child, we shall indeed be among the grateful. 》 (*Soorah Al-A'raf* 7:189)

He, Most High, says, 《 And (remember) when We said to the angels: 'Prostrate Adam," they prostrated except Iblees. He said, Shall I prostrate to one whom You created from clay?' (Iblees) said, 'See? This one whom You have honored above me, if You give me respite (keep me alive) to the Day of Resurrection, I will surely seize and mislead his offspring (by sending them astray) all but a few!' (Allah) said, 'Go, and whosoever of them follows you, surely, Hell will be the recompense of you (all) – an ample recompense. And *Istafziz* (literally means: befool them gradually) those whom you can among them with your voice (i.e. songs, music, and any other call for Allah's disobedience), make assaults on them with your cavalry and your infantry, mutually share with them wealth and children (by tempting them to earn money by illegal ways usury, etc., or by committing illegal sexual intercourse, etc.), and make promises to them.' But Satan promises them nothing but deceit. "Verily, My slaves (i.e. the true believers of Islamic Monotheism), you have no authority over them. And All-Sufficient is your Lord as a Guardian'. 》 (*Soorah Al-Isra'* 17:61-65)

He, Most High, says, 《 (Allah) said, 'Get you down (from the Paradise to the Earth), both of you together, some of you are an enemy to some others. Then if there comes to you guidance from Me, then whoever follows My Guidance shall neither go astray, nor fall into distress and misery'. 》 (*Soorah Ta Ha* 20:123)

Allah, Most High, says that He addressed the angels, saying 《 "Verily, I am going to place generations after generations on Earth." 》 (*Soorah Al-Baqarah* 2:30)

He apprised them of the reason why He had created Adam صلى الله عليه وسلم and his progeny, who would follow each other in succeeding generations, as He, Most High, says, ❴And makes you inheritors of the Earth, generations after generations.❵ (*Soorah An-Naml* 27:62) He informed them of this by way of praise for the creation of Adam صلى الله عليه وسلم and his progeny and He informed them of this great event before it took place. The angels asked, with the intention of acquiring knowledge and seeking wisdom, not as some ignorant people have supposed, in order to express disagreement or to belittle the children of Adam صلى الله عليه وسلم or display envy toward them: ❴ They said, "Will You place therein those who will make mischief therein and shed blood?" ❵ (*Soorah Al-Baqarah* 2:30) It was said by Qatadah that they knew that this would happen because of what they had observed of the behavior of the *binn* and the jinn before Adam صلى الله عليه وسلم.

As for the Words of Allah, Most High, ❴ I know that which you do not know ❵ (*Soorah Al-Baqarah* 2:30), the meaning is: I know better the greater good that there is in the creation of them, which you do not know. That is, there will be among them Prophets, Messengers, those who accept the truth without hesitation, martyrs and righteous folk. Then He made clear to them Adam's superiority over them in knowledge, saying, ❴ And He taught Adam all the names (of everything). ❵ (*Soorah Al-Baqarah* 2:31)

'Abdullah Ibn 'Abbas رضي الله عنه said, "They are these names with which the mankind is acquainted, such as humans, animals, earth, plains, seas, mountains, camels, donkeys and other things." Mujahid said, "He taught him the names of the plate and the pot and even the terms for breaking wind."

Mujahid also said, "He taught him the name of every animal, every bird and everything."

Al-Bukhari and Muslim narrated on the authority of Anas Ibn Malik ﷺ, who reported from the Messenger of Allah ﷺ that he said, "On the Day of Resurrection the believers will assemble and say, 'Let us ask somebody to intercede for us with our Lord.' So they will go to Adam ﷺ and say, 'You are the father of all the people; and Allah created you with His Own Hands, and ordered the angels to prostrate to you, and taught you the names of all things.' [1] He recorded the *hadeeth* in full.

❴ Then He showed them to the angels and said, 'Tell Me the names of these if you are truthful'." ❵ (*Soorah Al-Baqarah* 2:31)

Al-Hasan Al-Basri said, "When Allah wanted to create Adam ﷺ, the angels said, 'Our Lord will not create a creation except that we are more knowledgeable than it.' Thus they were put to trial and that was why Allah said, ❴ '…if you are truthful.'❵ (*Soorah Al-Baqarah* 2:31)

❴ They (angels) said, 'Glory be to You, we have no knowledge except what you have taught us. Verily, it is You, the All-Knowing, Most Wise'." ❵ (*Soorah Al-Baqarah* 2:32) That is, no one can encompass anything from Your Knowledge, except what You have taught; You are far above that. This is as Allah says, ❴ And they will never compass anything of His Knowledge except that which He wills. ❵ (*Soorah Al-Baqarah* 2:255)

❴ He said, 'O, Adam! Inform them of their names,' and when he had informed them of their names, He said, 'Did I not tell you that I know the *ghaib* (unseen) in the heavens and the Earth, and I know what you reveal and what you have been concealing'?" ❵ (*Soorah Al-Baqarah* 2:33) That is, I know the

---

[1]   Narrated by Al-Bukhari (4476) and Muslim (193).

secrets just as I know the apparent things. It was also said that His Words: ❲ "and I know what you reveal…" ❳ refer to their saying, ❲ "Will You place therein those who will make mischief therein and shed blood, - while we glorify You with praises and thanks (Exalted be You above all that they associate with You as partners) and sanctify You." ❳ (*Soorah Al-Baqarah* 2:30). This was what they did openly.

As for His Words: ❲ "and what you have been concealing?" ❳ (*Soorah Al-Baqarah* 2:33), what is referred to here is the saying of Iblees, when he concealed within his heart arrogance and belief in his superiority over Adam عليه السلام. This was said by Sa'eed Ibn Jubair, Mujahid, As-Suddi, Adh-Dhahhak and Ath-Thawri; and it was the preferred opinion of Ibn Jareer At-Tabari.

❲ And (remember) when We said to the angels: 'Prostrate yourselves before Adam.' And they prostrated except Iblees, he refused and was proud. ❳ (*Soorah Al-Baqarah* 2:34) This is a great honor bestowed by Allah on Adam عليه السلام, when He created him with His Hand and breathed into him His Spirit, as He, Most High, says, ❲ "So, when I have fashioned him completely and breathed into him (Adam) the soul which I created for him, then fall (you) down prostrating yourselves unto him."❳ (*Soorah Al-Hijr* 15:29) So these were four honors: His creation of him with His Hand, His breathing into him of His Spirit, His command to the angels to prostrate before him and His teaching him the names of (all) things.

In another Verse, He says, ❲ And surely, We created you (your father Adam) and then gave you shape (the noble shape of a human being), then We told the angels, 'Prostrate to Adam,' and they prostrated, except Iblees, he refused to be of those who prostrated. (Allah) said, 'What prevented you (O, Iblees,) that you did not prostrate, when I commanded you?' Iblees said, 'I am better than he (Adam), You created me from fire, and him You created from clay'." ⟩ (*Soorah Al-A'raf* 7:11,12) Al-Hasan Al-Basri said, "Iblees used *qiyas* (analogy) and he was the first one to do so." This statement has an authentic chain of narrations. Ibn Seereen said, "The first to use *qiyas* was Iblees, and the sun and moon would not be worshipped if not for *qiyas*." Both of these statements were reported by Ibn Jareer At-Tabari.

The meaning of this is that he compared himself with Adam المعلا and considered that he was superior to Adam المعلا, and thus refused to prostrate him, in spite of the fact that he and all of the angels had been commanded to do so. But analogy in the presence of evidence is invalid. In addition, it is in itself, invalid, because mud is more beneficial than fire: mud has the qualities of wisdom, forbearance, patience and assurance and mud is where plants grow, flourish, increase, and provide good. To the contrary, fire has the qualities of burning, recklessness and hastiness.

In addition, Allah honored Adam المعلا by creating him with His Hand and breathing into him His Spirit. This is why He commanded the angels to prostrate before him, as He says, ⟨ And (remember) when your Lord said to the angels: 'I am going to create a man (Adam) from sounding clay of altered black smooth mud'." ⟩ – up to the Words of Allah, Most High: ⟨ And verily, the curse shall be upon you till the Day of Recompense (i.e. the Day of Resurrection). ⟩ (*Soorah Al-Hijr* 15:28-35) He deserved this from Allah, Most High, because he insisted that Adam المعلا was inferior to him and belittled him, while claiming that he himself was superior to him, in sheer opposition to the Command of Allah and in defiance of the truth.

In *Soorah Al-Kahf*, Allah says, ❨ He disobeyed the Command of his Lord. Will you then take him (Iblees) and his offspring as protectors and helpers rather than Me while they are enemies to you? What an evil is the exchange for the *zalimoon* (polytheists, and wrongdoers, etc.) ❩ (*Soorah Al-Kahf* 18:50) That is, he abandoned obedience to Allah, deliberately, obstinately and arrogantly refusing to comply with His Command. Iblees was deceived by his fiery nature and substance into believing that he was superior to Adam عليه السلام because of him having been created from fire, when he should have known better. Imam Muslim narrates in his *Saheeh*, on the authority of 'A'ishah (may Allah be pleased with her), who reported from the Messenger of Allah ﷺ that he said: "The angels were created from light, the jinn were created from a smokeless flame of fire, and Adam عليه السلام was created from what has been described to you." [1]

'Abdullah Ibn Mas'ood ﷺ, 'Abdullah Ibn 'Abbas ﷺ a group of the Companions ﷺ, Sa'eed Ibn Al-Musayyib and others said that Iblees was the leader of the angels in the earthly heaven. In one narration attributed to 'Abdullah Ibn 'Abbas ﷺ, he said that his name was 'Azazeel, while in another narration, it was ascribed to him that he said that his name was Al-Harith. An-Naqqash said that his agnomen was Abu Kardoos. 'Abdullah Ibn 'Abbas ﷺ said: "He was from one of the tribes of the angels which was known as *Al-Jinn*. They were the guardians of the Gardens and he was the most eminent of them and the greatest of them in knowledge. He had four wings, but Allah transformed him into a curse." In *Soorah Sad*, He says, ❨ (Remember) when your Lord said to the angels: 'Truly, I am going to create man from clay.' So when I have fashioned him and breathed into him (his) soul created by Me, then you fall down prostrate him. So the angels prostrated themselves, all of them: except Iblees.

---

(1)   The *takhreej* for this has already been given.

He was proud and was one of the disbelievers. (Allah) said, 'O, Iblees (Satan)! What prevents you from prostrating yourself the one whom I have created with My both Hands? Are you too proud (to prostrate Adam), or are you one of the high exalted?" (Iblees [Satan]) said, "I am better than he; You created me from fire, and You created him from clay.' (Allah) said, 'Then go down from here, for verily, you are an outcast. And verily, My Curse is on you until the Day of Recompense.' (Iblees [Satan]) said, 'My Lord! Give me then respite till the Day the (dead) are resurrected.' (Allah) said, "Verily, you are of those allowed respite till the Day of the time appointed.' (Iblees [Satan]) said, 'By Your Might, then I will surely mislead them all, except Your chosen slaves among them (the faithful, obedient, true believers of Islamic Monotheism).' (Allah) said, 'The Truth is, and the Truth I say, that I will fill Hell with you (Iblees) and those of them (mankind) that follow you, together'." 》 (*Soorah Sad* 38:71-85)

He, Most High, says in *Soorah Al-A'raf,* 《 (Iblees) said, 'Because You have sent me astray, surely I will sit in wait against them (human beings) on Your Straight Path. Then I will come to them from before them and behind them, from their right and from their left, and You will not find most of them as thankful ones (i.e. they will not be dutiful to You)'." 》 (*Soorah Al-A'raf* 7:16,17) That is, because You have sent me astray, I will wait in ambush for them at every opportunity and I will come to them from every direction. So the successful person is the one who disobeys him (Satan) and the wretched person is the one who obeys him.

Scholars of *tafseer* have disagreed regarding the angels who were ordered to prostrate to Adam ﷺ: were they all of the angels, as seems to be proven by the generality of the Verses?

This is the opinion of the majority of scholars. Or is the reference to the angels of the Earth, as narrated by Ibn Jareer At-Tabari by way of Ad-Dahhak, who reported on the authority of 'Abdullah Ibn 'Abbas ﷺ? But its chain of narrators is interrupted and in its wording there is something objectionable, though some of the later scholars preferred it. However, it is apparent from the wordings that the former is correct and this is proven by the *hadeeth*: "And He made His angels prostrate him." [1] And this is also general – and Allah knows better.

The meaning of His Words: ❲ Go down from here (i.e. Paradise) ❳ (*Soorah Al-A'raf* 7:18) is: "Get out of here." This is an evidence that he was in heaven and was ordered to go down from it; to leave his position and status which he had achieved through his worship and his similarity to the angels in obedience and worship. All this was taken away from him because of his arrogance, his envy and his disobedience to his Lord, and he was sent down to the Earth, disgraced and expelled.

Allah, Most High, commanded Adam ﷺ to live with his wife in Paradise, saying, ❲ And We said, 'O, Adam! Dwell you and your wife in Paradise and eat both of you freely with pleasure and delight of things therein wherever you will, but come not near this tree or you will both be of the *zalimoon* (wrongdoers). ❳ (*Soorah Al-Baqarah* 2:35) In *Soorah Al-A'raf*, He, Most High, says, ❲ (Allah) said (to Iblees), "Get out from this (Paradise) disgraced and expelled. Whoever of them (mankind) will follow you, then surely I will fill Hell with you all. And O, Adam! Dwell you and your wife in Paradise, and eat thereof as you both wish, but approach not this tree otherwise you both will be of the *zalimoon* (unjust and wrongdoers)." ❳

---

(1)   The *takhreej* of this *hadeeth* has already been given.

(*Soorah Al-A'raf* 7:18,19)

The context of these Verses necessitates that the creation of Hawwa' (Eve) was before Adam ﷺ entered Paradise, as He, Most High, says, ﴾ And We said, 'O, Adam! Dwell you and your wife in Paradise'." ﴿ (*Soorah Al-Baqarah* 2:35) But As-Suddi related from Abu Saleh and Abu Malik, on the authority of 'Abdullah Ibn 'Abbas ﷺ and from Murrah, on the authority of 'Abdullah Ibn Mas'ood ﷺ and from people among the Companions ﷺ that they said that Iblees was removed from Paradise and Adam was made to live in Paradise and he used to walk therein alone, having no wife with whom to live. Then he slept for a short while and awoke to find a woman sitting at his head. Allah had created her from his rib. He asked her, "Who are you?" And she said, "I am a woman." He asked her, "Why were you created?" She said, "So that you might live with me." The angels said to him, in order to find out the extent of his knowledge, "What is her name, Adam?" He said, "Hawwa (Eve)." They said, "Why is she called Hawwa'?" He replied, "Because she was created from something *hayy* (i.e. living)." [1]

Corroboration for this is found in the Words of Allah, Most High: ﴾ O, mankind! Be dutiful to your Lord, Who created you from a single person (Adam), and from him (Adam) He created his wife (Hawwa), and from them both He created many men and women ﴿ (*Soorah An-Nisa'* 4:1)

In the *Saheehain* on the authority of Abu Hurairah ﷺ, who reported from the Prophet ﷺ that he said: "I advise you to take care of the women, for they are created from a rib and the most crooked portion of the rib is its upper part; if you try to straighten it, it will break, and if you leave it, it will remain

---

(1)   Narrated by Ibn Jareer (4/224).

crooked, so I urge you to take care of the women." [1] This is the wording of Al-Bukhari.

Scholars of *tafseer* have differed regarding the meaning of the Words of Allah, Most High: ❴ but come not near this tree ❵ (*Soorah Al-Baqarah* 2:35) It was said that it was a grapevine, while Ath-Thawri reported on the authority of Abu Husain, who reported on the authority of Abu Malik that he said, "❴ but come not near this tree ❵ it was a date palm. Ibn Juraij reported on the authority of Mujahid that it was a fig tree and Qatadah and Ibn Juraij concurred with this.

These are minor differences of opinion; in fact, Allah has left obscure the precise nature of the tree – and if there was any benefit for us in His mentioning it, He would have done so. This is also the case with regard to other matters which have been left undefined in the Qur'an.

The only real difference that they mentioned was regarding whether or not the Garden that Adam ﷺ entered was in heaven or on the Earth. This is a difference of opinion which must be clarified and settled.

The majority of scholars hold (the view) that it was (located) in heaven and that it was *Jannat Al-Ma'wa* (the Garden of Refuge), based on the apparent meaning of the Verses and *ahadeeth*, as in the Words of Him, Most High: ❴ And We said, 'O, Adam! Dwell you and your wife in the Paradise'." ❵ (*Soorah Al-Baqarah* 2:35) The wording here indicates that what is referred to is a specific Paradise and that is *Jannat Al-Ma'wa*.

Muslim narrated in his *Saheeh* on the authority of Hudhaifah

---

(1)   Narrated by Al-Bukhari (5186) and Muslim (1468).

that he said: The Messenger of Allah ﷺ said: "Allah will gather the people and the believers will stand till the Garden will be brought near them. They will come to Adam and say, 'O, our father! Open for us the Garden., He would say, 'Did anything turn you out of the Garden other than the sin of your father, Adam'?" [1] And he narrated the *hadeeth* in full. In this there is strong and clear evidence that it is *Jannat Al-Ma'wa*, but there is room for argument.

Others said that the Garden in which Adam ﷺ resided was not *Jannat Al-Khuld*,[2] because he was enjoined therein not to eat from that tree and because he slept therein, in addition to which he was removed from it and Iblees entered it. All of these things negate the possibility that it could be *Jannat Al-Ma'wa*. This opinion was related on the authority of Ubayy Ibn Ka'b ﷺ, 'Abdullah Ibn 'Abbas ﷺ, Wahb Ibn Munabbih and Sufyan Ibn 'Uyainah.

This opinion is (from) the text of the Torah, which is in the hands of the People of the Scripture and among those who related the disagreement in this matter were Abu Muhammad Ibn Hazm in *Al-Milal Wan-Nihal*, Abu Muhammad Ibn 'Atiyyah in his *Tafseer*, Abu 'Eesa Ar-Rummani in his *Tafseer* – and he related from the *first jumhoor* (earliest school of thought) – Abul-Qasim Ar-Raghib and Al-Qadi Al-Mawardi in his *Tafseer*: he said: "They disagreed regarding the Garden in which they (i.e. Adam ﷺ and Eve) had resided, holding two opinions in the matter: one of them declared that it was *Jannat Al-Ma'wa*, while the other held that it was a Garden which Allah had prepared for them and which He had made an abode of trial; they said that this was not *Jannat Al-Khuld*, which He

---

(1) Narrated by Muslim (195).

(2) *Jannat Al-Khuld*: The Eternal Garden.

had made as the abode of recompense. Those who said this disagreed as to its location: one opinion held that it was in the heaven, because Allah sent them down from it. This was the opinion of Al-Hasan. The other opinion stated that it was on the Earth, because Allah tried them therein, by forbidding them to eat from the tree, while allowing them to eat from the others. This was the opinion of Ibn Yahya. This took place after Iblees was commanded to prostrate Adam عليه السلام – and Allah knows better regarding the truth of this.

This is what he said and it implies three opinions; and I sense from his words that he was undecided in the matter. Abu 'Abdullah Ar-Razi related four opinions in his *Tafseer* regarding this question: three which were recorded by Al-Mawardi and the fourth was *waqf*, i.e., refusal or inability to arrive at a conclusion as to which is the strongest. But he preferred the first opinion. And Allah knows better.

❨ Then *Shaitan* (Satan) made them slip therefrom. ❩ (*Soorah Al-Baqarah* 2:36) That is, from Paradise ❨ and got them out from that in which they were. ❩ (*Soorah Al-Baqarah* 2:36) That is, from the ease, plenty and happiness (of Paradise) to the abode of toil, exertion and difficulty. This was because of what Satan had whispered to them and made them seem attractive to their hearts, as Allah, Most High, says, ❨ Then *Shaitan* (Satan) whispered suggestions to them both in order to uncover that which was hidden from them of their private parts (before); he said, "Your Lord did not forbid you this tree save you should become angels or become of the immortals'." ❩ (*Soorah Al-A'raf* 7:20)

He said that Allah only forbade them from eating from this tree because by doing so they would become angels or immortals. That is, if you both eat from it, you will become thus.

❨ And he (*Shaitan* [Satan]) swore to them both. ❩ (*Soorah Al-A'raf* 7:21) That is, he swore to them that he was speaking the truth with regard to his claim concerning the tree. ❨ Then *Shaitan* (Satan) whispered to him, saying : 'O, Adam! Shall I lead you to the Tree of Eternity and to a kingdom that will never waste away'?" ❩ (*Soorah Ta Ha* 20:120) That is, shall I guide you to a tree which, if you eat from it, you will attain eternity in the ease in which you are now and you will continue in a kingdom that will never end? But this was deception, falsehood and the exact opposite of the truth.

❨ So he misled them with deception. Then, when they tasted of the tree, that which was hidden from them of their shame (private parts) became manifest to them and they began to stick together the leaves of Paradise over themselves (in order to cover their shame). ❩ (*Soorah Al-A'raf* 7:22) This is like His Words: ❨ Then they both ate of the tree, and so their private parts appeared to them, and they began to stick on themselves the leaves from Paradise for their covering. Thus did Adam disobey his Lord, so he went astray. ❩ (*Soorah Ta Ha* 20:121) Eve ate from the tree before Adam ﷺ and it was she who urged Adam ﷺ to eat from the tree. And Allah knows better.

This is understood from the *hadeeth* narrated by Al-Bukhari on the authority of Abu Hurairah ﷺ, who reported from the Prophet ﷺ that he said "But for the Children of Isra'eel, meat would not decay, and but for Hawwa (Eve), wives would never betray their husbands." [1]

Ibn Abi Hatim narrated on the authority of Ubayy Ibn Ka'b ﷺ that he said, "Allah created Adam ﷺ as a tall man, with abundant hair on his head, as if he was a tall date palm. When

---

(1)   Narrated by Al-Bukhari (2330).

he tasted the (fruit from) tree, his clothing fell from him and the first thing that appeared from him was his genitals and when he looked at them, he began to run through the Garden, his hair was caught by a tree and he struggled with it. Then the Most Beneficent, the Almighty, the All-Powerful called him, saying, 'O, Adam! Are you fleeing from Me?' When he heard the Words of the Most Beneficent, he said, 'O, My Lord! No! But (I ran) out of embarrassment (at my naked state)'." [1]

Ath-Thawri reported on the authority of 'Abdullah Ibn 'Abbas ﷺ that he said regarding the Words of Allah, Most High, ﴾ They began to stick together the leaves of Paradise over themselves (in order to cover their shame). ﴿ (*Soorah Al-A'raf* 7:22) – "The leaves were those of the fig tree." The *isnad* is authentic up to him. But it appears as if it was taken from the People of the Scripture and the apparent meaning of the Verse necessitates a more general meaning. But if we accept it, it does no harm – and Allah knows better.

﴾ (Allah) said, 'Get down, one of you an enemy to the other (i.e. Adam, Hawwa, and *Shaitan*, etc.). On Earth will be a dwelling place for you and an enjoyment - for a time'." ﴿ (*Soorah Al-A'raf* 7:24) This address is to Adam ﷺ, Eve and Iblees. It was also said that a serpent was with them and they were commanded to go down from Paradise while they were in a state of mutual hostility and warfare. The inclusion of the serpent with them is supported by the authentic *hadeeth* narrated from the Messenger of Allah ﷺ, in which it was stated that he ordered the killing of serpents, saying, "We have not made peace with them since we (first) fought with them." [2]

---

(1) Ibn Hajar ascribed it in *Fath Al-Bari* (6/367) to Ibn Abi Hatim and he said that its chain of narrators is *hasan* (sound).

(2) This *hadeeth* is *hasan-saheeh* and it was narrated by Abu Dawood (5248) and Ahmad (7319).

As for His Words in *Soorah Ta Ha*: ﴿ (Allah) said, 'Get you down (from Paradise to the Earth), both of you, together, some of you are an enemy to others'." ﴾ (*Soorah Ta Ha* 20:123), it is a command to Adam ﷺ and Iblees and their respective offspring that they will remain in a state of mutual hostility forever; and Adam ﷺ was followed by Eve, while Iblees was followed by the serpent.

It was also said that it was a command to all of them in the dual form, like the Words of Him, Most High: ﴿ And (remember) Dawood (David) and Sulaiman (Solomon), when they gave judgment in the case of the field in which the sheep of certain people had pastured at night and We were witness to their judgment. ﴾ (*Soorah Al-Anbiya'* 21:78)

But the correct opinion is that because the judge is not passing judgment except between two sides, the claimant and the defendant, Allah says, ﴿ and We were witness to their judgment.﴾ (*Soorah Al-Anbiya'* 21:78)

As for the repetition of the sending down in *Soorah Al-Baqarah* in His Words: ﴿ Then *Shaitan* made them slip therefrom (Paradise) and got them out from that in which they were. We said, 'Get you down, all, with enmity between yourselves. On Earth will be a dwelling place for you and an enjoyment for a time.' Then Adam received Words from his Lord. And his Lord pardoned him (accepted his repentance). Verily, He is the One Who forgives (accepts repentance), the Most Merciful. We said, 'Get down all of you from this place (Paradise), then whenever there comes to you Guidance from Me, and whoever follows My Guidance, there shall be no fear on them, nor shall they grieve. But those who disbelieve and belie Our *Ayat* (proofs, evidences, Verses, lessons, signs, revelations, etc.) such are the dwellers of the Fire, they shall abide therein forever'." ﴾

(*Soorah Al-Baqarah* 2:36-39) Some of the scholars of *tafseer* said that what is meant by the first reference of being sent down is the sending down from Paradise to the earthly heaven, while the second is from the earthly heaven to the Earth.

But this is weak, because He says regarding the first (sending down), ❨ Then *Shaitan* made them slip therefrom (Paradise) and got them out from that in which they were. We said, 'Get you down, all, with enmity between yourselves. On Earth will be a dwelling place for you and an enjoyment for a time'." ❩ (*Soorah Al-Baqarah* 2:36), which proves that they were sent down to the Earth in the first sending down. And Allah knows better.

What is correct is that He repeated it in words, but in reality, it only took place once and He linked to each mention a *hukm* (ruling, verdict): to the first was attached the enmity between them and with the second He made it conditional upon them that whoever followed His Guidance – which He would reveal to them after that – would be happy, while whoever rejected it would be wretched. There are other examples of this manner of speaking in the Qur'an.

Al-Hakim narrated in his *Mustadrak* on the authority of 'Abdullah Ibn 'Abbas ﷺ that he said, "Adam ﷺ did not reside in Paradise for longer than the time between the *'Asr* prayer and the setting of the sun." [1] Then he said, "It is authentic, according to the criteria for acceptance stipulated by Al-Bukhari and Muslim, though it was not narrated by them."

In *Saheeh Muslim*, it is reported on the authority of Abu Hurairah ﷺ that he said: The Messenger of Allah ﷺ said: "The

---

(1) Narrated by Al-Hakim in *Al-Mustadrak* (2/591, No. 3993) and he declared it to be authentic – Az-Zahabi concurred with this.

best day on which the sun rises is Friday: on that day Adam صلى الله عليه وسلم was created; on it he was admitted to Paradise and on it he was sent out of it." [1]

As for the Words of Allah, Most High: ❪ Then Adam received Words from his Lord. And his Lord pardoned him (accepted his repentance). Verily, He is the One Who forgives (accepts repentance), the Most Merciful. ❫ (*Soorah Al-Baqarah* 2:37), it was said that those Words were His Saying: ❪ "Our Lord! We have wronged ourselves. If You forgive us not, and bestow not upon us Your Mercy, we shall certainly be of the losers." ❫ (*Soorah Al-A'raf* 7:23) This was narrated on the authority of Mujahid, Sa'eed Ibn Jubair, Abul-Aliyah, Ar-Rabee' Ibn Anas, Al-Hasan, Qatadah, Muhammad Ibn Ka'b , Khalid Ibn Ma'dan, 'Ata Al-Khurasani and 'Abdur-Rahman Ibn Zaid Ibn Aslam.

Al-Hakim narrated in *Al-Mustadrak* on the authority of 'Abdullah Ibn 'Abbas رضي الله عنه regarding the Words of Allah, Most High: ❪ Then Adam received from his Lord Words and his Lord pardoned him (accepted his repentance). ❫ (*Soorah Al-Baqarah* 2:37) that he said, "Adam صلى الله عليه وسلم said, 'O, my Lord! Did You not create me with Your Hand?' It was said to him, 'Certainly.' Adam صلى الله عليه وسلم said, 'And You breathed into me Your Spirit?' It was said to him, 'Certainly.' He continued, 'I sneezed and You said, 'Allah have mercy on you.' And Your Mercy preceded Your Anger?' It was said to him, 'Certainly.' Adam صلى الله عليه وسلم said, 'And You ordained upon me that I should do this?' It was said to him, 'Certainly.' Adam صلى الله عليه وسلم then said, 'Tell me then, if I turn to You in repentance, will You return me to Paradise?' He said, 'Yes'." Then Al-Hakim said that the *isnad* is authentic, though Al-Bukhari and Muslim did not narrate it.

---

(1)   Narrated by Muslim (854).

Mention of How Adam Defeated Moosa (Peace be Upon Them Both) in an Argument

Al-Bukhari narrated on the authority of Abu Hurairah ﷺ from the Prophet ﷺ that he said, "Moosa ﷺ argued with Adam ﷺ and said to him (Adam), 'You are the one who got the people out of Paradise by your sin, and thus made them miserable.' Adam ﷺ replied, 'O, Moosa! You are the one whom Allah selected for His Message and for His direct Speech. Yet you blame me for a thing which Allah had ordained for me before He created me'?" The Messenger of Allah ﷺ added, "So Adam overcame Moosa ﷺ by this Argument." [1]

Imam Ahmad narrated on the authority of Abu Hurairah ﷺ from the Prophet ﷺ that he said, "Adam ﷺ argued with Moosa ﷺ. Moosa ﷺ said, 'O, Adam! It is you whom Allah created with His Hand and breathed into you His Spirit. You led mankind astray and caused them to be removed from Paradise.' Adam ﷺ said, It was you, Moosa, who was chosen by Allah for His direct Speech; and yet you blame me for a deed which I did not do. Allah ordained for me before He created the heavens and the earth'?" The Messenger of Allah ﷺ added, "Thus Adam ﷺ defeated Mooosa." Imam Ahmad narrated on the authority of Abu Hurairah ﷺ from the Prophet ﷺ that he said, "Adam ﷺ met Moosa ﷺ and he said, 'You are Adam, whom Allah created with His Hand and before whom He made His angels prostrate and He made you to reside in Paradise, then you did what you did?' He said, 'You are Moosa, to whom Allah spoke directly and whom He chose for His Message and to whom He revealed the Torah. Then (tell me), did I come first, or was it the Reminder (i.e. the Revelation)?' Moosa ﷺ said, 'No, it

---

(1)   Narrated by Al-Bukhari (4738).

was the Reminder.' Thus Adam ﷺ defeated Moosa ﷺ." [1]

Imam Ahmad narrated on the authority of Abu Hurairah ﷺ that he said: The Messenger of Allah ﷺ said, "Adam ﷺ argued with Moosa ﷺ and Moosa ﷺ said to Adam ﷺ, 'O, Adam! It is you who caused your progeny to enter the Fire.' Adam ﷺ said, 'O, Moosa! Allah chose you to receive His Message and to hear His direct Speech and He revealed to you the Torah. Did you find (therein) that I would descend (to Earth)?' He said, 'Yes.' Thus Adam ﷺ defeated him." [2]

The understanding of the people toward this *hadeeth* has differed:

A group from among the *Qadariyyah* rejected it because of the affirmation of *Qadar* implicit in it.

A group from among the *Jabariyyah* cited it, as it appeared to them that when he said, "So Adam defeated Moosa," he did so using his own Scripture against him. The reply to this will be given later.

Others said that he only argued with him because he rebuked him for a sin for which he had repented – and a person who has repented of a sin is like a person who is without sin.

It was also said that he only argued with him because he (Adam) is older (and therefore wiser) than he (Moosa). It was also said that it was because he (Adam) is his (Moosa') father. It was said that it was because they are both in two different Revelations. It was said that it was because they are both in the abode of *Al-Barzakh* and responsibility for them had ended, according to their claim.

---

(1)   Narrated by Imam Ahmad (9664).

(2)   Narrated by Imam Ahmad (7579).

The Ahadeeth Related to the Creation of Adam السّلَام

Imam Ahmad reports from Abu Moosa that the Prophet ﷺ said: "Allah created Adam from a handful taken from all parts of the Earth, and so the Children of Adam came out according to the colors of the Earth. Among them there is the white, the red, the black, and what is in between, and there is the filthy and the pure, and the soft and the hard and what is in between."[1]

He also reported it from Qasamah bin Zuhair: I heard Al-Ash'ari say: Allah's Messenger ﷺ said: "Allah created Adam from a handful (of dust) taken from all parts of the Earth, and so the Children of Adam came out according to the colors of the Earth. Among them there is the white, the red, the black, and what is in between, and there is the soft and the hard and what in is between, and there is the filthy and the pure and what is in between."[2]

Imam Ahmad reports from Anas that the Prophet ﷺ said: "When Allah created Adam, He left him alone for as long as He willed to leave him alone, so Iblees began circling around him. Once he saw that he was hollow. He realized that he was a creation that could not control itself."[3]

Ibn Hibban reports in his *Saheeh* from Anas ibn Malik that Allah's Messenger ﷺ said: "When the soul was blown into Adam and it reached its head, he sneezed and said, 'All praise is due to Allah, Lord of the Worlds,' so He, blessed and exalted

---

(1)   *Saheeh*: Ahmad (No. 19085).

(2)   *Saheeh*: Ahmad (No. 19145).

(3)   *Saheeh*: Ahmad (No. 12130).

is He, replied, 'May Allah have mercy on you'."[1]

Al-Hafiz Abu Ya'la reports from Abu Hurairah that Allah's Messenger ﷺ said: Allah created Adam from dust, then he made him mud. Then, he left him until he became black mud. He created and fashioned him. Then, He left him until he became dry clay like pottery."

He said: Iblees would pass by him and say, "You have been created for a great purpose." Then, Allah blew into him from Ilis soul. The first part that his soul passed through was his eyes and his nose causing him to sneeze, and Allah showed him mercy. Allah said, "May your Lord have mercy on you." Then Allah said, "O Adam, go to this group (of angels) and say to them *as-salaam 'alaikum* and see how they respond'?" He went and greeted them to which they responded. *"Wa 'alaika al-salam wa rahmatullah wa barakaatuh."* He said, "O Adam, this is your greeting and the greeting of your offspring." Adam said, "O Lord, and what are my offspring?" He said, "Choose one of My Hands, O Adam." He said, "I choose the right hand of my Lord, and both of My Lord's Hands are right." He opened His Hand and all his offspring who were to be were displayed in the Hand of the Most Merciful. There were men among them whose faces were light, and the light of one man in particular impressed Adam. He said, "O my Lord, who is this?" He said, "This is your son, Dawood." He said, "O my Lord, how long a lifespan have you given him." He said, "I have given him sixty (years)." He said, "Then give him from my age so that he may have a full one hundred years." Allah did so and called a witness to that. When the lifespan of Adam ran out, Allah sent to him the Angel of Death. Adam said, "Do I not have forty years of life left?" The angel asked him, "Did you not

---

(1)   *Saheeh*: Ibn Hibbaan: 14/37, No. 6165.

give it to your son, Dawood?" but he denied that and likewise his offspring denied (things) as well, and just as he forgot, his offspring also forgot.[1]

At-Tirmidhi reports from Abu Hurairah that he said: Allah's Messenger☀ said: When Allah created Adam, He wiped his back and every being that He was going to create up to the Day of Resurrection fell from his back. He placed between the eyes of everyone of them a flash of light, then presented them to Adam, who asked, "My Lord, who are these?" He said, "These are your offspring." Upon seeing a man among them whose light between his eyes impressed him, he asked, "My Lord, who is this?" He said, "This is a man from one of the last nations of your offspring called Dawood." He asked, "My Lord, how long a lifespan have you granted him?" He said, "Sixty years." He said, "My Lord, give him another forty years from my lifespan." When Adam's lifespan drew to an end and the Angel of Death came to him, he asked, "Are there not forty years of my life remaining?" He said, "Did you not give them to your son Dawood?" He said: Adam denied and his offspring (likewise) denied; Adam forgot and so his offspring (likewise) forgot; and Adam sinned and his offspring (likewise) sinned.[2]

Al-Bukhari reports from Abu Hurairah that the Prophet ☀ said: Allah created Adam with a height of sixty cubits. Then he said, "Go and greet that group of angels with *salaam* and see how they respond to you, for that shall be your greeting and the

---

(1) Abu Ya'laa reports it in his *Musnad*, 11/453, No. 6580; Al-Haithami states in *Al-Majma'* (8/197), "Abu Ya'laa reported it, and it contains Ismaa'eel ibn Raafi'. Al-Bukhari said he is "reliable (*thiqah*), mediocre in narration (*muqaarib al-hadeeth*)," while the majority declared him weak. The remainder of the narrators are from the narrators of the *Saheeh*."

(2) *Hasan Saheeh*: At-Tirmidhi: *Book of Tafseer of the Qur'an*: Ch. Concerning *Soorah Al-A'raaf*, No. 3076.

greeting of your offspring." He said, "*As-salaam 'alaikum*" to which they replied, "*As-salaam 'alaika wa rahmatullah.*" So they added in reply to him, "*wa rahmatullah.*" All those who enter Paradise will have Adam's form; and the creation have not ceased to diminish in size (from his time) until now.[1]

Imam Malik ibn Anas reports in his *Muwatta'* that 'Umar ibn Al-Khattab was asked about this Verse, "And (remember) when your Lord brought forth from the Children of Adam, from their backs, their seed and made them testify as to themselves (saying), 'Am I not your Lord?' They said: 'Yes! We testify'." (*Al-A'rāf* 7:172)

'Umar ibn Al-Khattaab said: I heard Allah's Messenger ﷺ being asked about it and he said, "When Allah created Adam, peace be upon him, He wiped his back with His Right Hand and brought out his offspring." He said, "I created these for Paradise, and they will do the deeds of the People of Paradise." A man asked, "O Messenger of Allah, then what is the purpose of working?" Allah's Messenger ﷺ said, "When Allah creates a slave for Paradise, He causes him to do the deeds of the People of Paradise, until when he dies on one of the deeds of the People of Paradise, he enters Paradise. When Allah creates a slave for the Fire, He causes him to do the deeds of the People of the Fire until when he dies on one of the deeds of the People of the Fire, he enters the Fire."[2]

All these *Ahadeeth* demonstrate that Allah brought out the offspring of Adam from his back like specks of dust. He then divided them into two groups, the People of the Right Hand

---

(1) Al-Bukhari: *Book of the Hadiths of the Prophets*: Ch. The Creation of Adam, Allah's salutations be on him, and his offspring, No. 3326.

(2) *Saheeh Li Ghairih*: Malik: *Kitaab Al-Jaami'*: Ch. Prohibition of Rejecting Predestination, No. 1661.

(*Ahl Al-Yameen*) and the People of the Left Hand (*Ahl Al-Shimaal*), and He said, "These are for Paradise and I do not care, and these are for the Fire and I do not care."[1]

As for taking witnesses against them or making them verbally acknowledge His Oneness, this is not mentioned in the authentic *Ahadeeth*. Therefore, to interpret the Verse in *Soorah Al-A'raaf* to be referring to these reports is questionable, as we explained there,[2] and we mentioned the *Ahadeeth* and *athaar* in full with their chains of narrations and their wordings. Therefore, whoever would like to verify the matter should refer to it there. And Allah knows best.

As for the *hadeeth* reported by Imam Ahmad from Ibn 'Abbas that the Prophet ﷺ said, "Allah took the covenant from Adam's back in Na'maan the Day of 'Arafah,[3] and brought forth from his loins all his offspring whom He has created and He scattered them before Him. He then spoke to them directly. He said, 'Am I not your Lord?' They said: 'Yes! We testify,' lest you should say on the Day of Resurrection, 'Verily, we were unaware of this'." (*Al-A'raaf* 7:172).[4] This *hadeeth* has a good, strong chain of narrations meeting the criterion of Muslim.

Anas ibn Malik reports that the Prophet ﷺ said, "A man from the People of the Fire will be asked on the Day of Resurrection, 'If you had all that is in the earth, would you ransom yourself with it?' He will say, 'Yes.' He will say, 'I wanted from you that which is easier than that. I took a covenant from you in

---

(1)   *Saheeh*: Ahmad (No. 17207).

(2)   in his *Tafseer*.

(3)   The printed edition of *Musnad Ahmad* states, "*Na'maan*, meaning: 'Arafah." Na'maan is the name of a place near 'Arafah on the path between Makkah and Tā'if, cf. *Mir'aat Al-Mafaateeh*, 1/212.

(4)   *Saheeh*: Ahmad (No. 2451).

the back of Adam to not associate partners with Me, yet you insisted on associating partners with Me."[1] Al-Bukhari and Muslim report it via Shu'bah. [2]

Imam Ahmad reports that Abu Hurairah said: Allah's Messenger ﷺ said, "When the son of Adam recites a (Verse of) prostration and prostrates, Satan leaves him and weeps, saying, 'Woe to me, the son of Adam was ordered to prostate and has done so, so he shall have Paradise, while I was ordered to prostrate but I disobeyed, so I shall have the Fire'."[3]

Once Adam was made to dwell in Paradise in which he dwelled, regardless of whether it is in the Heaven or the Earth – as there is a difference of opinion which was mentioned earlier – he and his wife Hawwa, peace be upon them, would eat from it in abundance and from wherever they liked. However, when they ate from the tree from which they had been prohibited, they were stripped of their garments and sent down to the Earth. We have also mentioned the different opinions about the place where he came down.

They also disagreed about the length of time that he spent in Paradise. One view is that it was just part of a day by the length of the days of this world. And we mentioned the *hadeeth* reported by Muslim on the authority of Abu Hurairah that the Prophet ﷺ said, "He created Adam on the last hour on the day of Friday."[4]

We also mentioned the *hadeeth* that on that day "He created

---

(1) *Saheeh*: Ahmad (No. 11880).

(2) Al-Bukhari: Book of the *Ahadeeth* of the Prophets: Ch. Creation of Adam ﷺ and His Offspring, No. 3334; Muslim, No. 2805.

(3) *Saheeh*: Ahmad (No. 9420).

(4) Muslim: No. 2789.

Adam and on that day he was sent out from there."[1]

The Story of Adam's Two Sons: Qabeel (Cain) and Habeel (Abel)

Allah ﷻ said, "And recite to them the story of the two sons of Adam in truth; when each offered a sacrifice, it was accepted from the one but not from the other. The latter said to the former, 'I will surely kill you.' The former said, 'Verily, Allah accepts only from those mindful of Him. If you do stretch your hand against me to kill me, I shall never stretch my hand against you to kill you, for I fear Allah; the Lord of the Worlds. Verily, I intend to let you draw my sin on yourself as well as yours, then you will be one of the dwellers of the Fire, and that is the recompense of the wrongdoers. But his soul enticed him to murder his brother; he murdered him and became one of the losers. Then Allah sent a crow who scratched up the ground to show him how to cover the dead body of his brother. He said: 'Woe to me! Am I not even able to be as this crow and cover the dead body of my brother?' Then he became one of the remorseful." (*Al-Mā'idah* 5:27-31)

Al-Suddee has reported from Ibn 'Abbas, Ibn Mas'ood, and a group of the Companions that Adam would marry off the male offspring of every pregnancy with the female of another. Habeel had wanted to marry the (twin) sister of Qabeel, and he was older than Habeel. The sister of Habeel was more beautiful (than Qābeel's sister), so he wanted to keep her from his brother.[2] Adam, peace be upon him, ordered him to marry

---

(1)   Ibid.

(2)   The version of this narration mentioned in *Tafseer At-Tabaree* states that the sister of Qabeel was more beautiful and so it was he who refused to marry off his sister. What is mentioned here might be a typographical error.

her to him but he refused. Therefore, he ordered them both to make an offering while Adam went off to Makkah to perform *Hajj*. Upon departure, he requested the heavens to guard his sons but they refused. He asked the earths and the mountains but they refused, but Qabeel agreed to guard them.

When he had left, they both made their offering. Habeel offered a fat lamb as he was an owner of sheep, while Qabeel made an offering of a bundle of crops taken from those of his crops that were of poor quality. A fire came down and consumed the offering of Habeel but left the offering of Qabeel. He became angry and said, "I will kill you so that you cannot marry my sister." He responded, "Allah only accepts from those mindful of Him."

When he threatened to kill him, he said, "If you do stretch your hand against me to kill me, I shall never stretch my hand against you to kill you, for I fear Allah; the Lord of the Worlds." This indicates his good character and his fear of Allah, Most High. He refrained from responding to his brother with an evil like the one he intended. This is as has been reported in the two *Saheehs* that Allah's Messenger ﷺ said, "When two Muslims meet one another with their swords, then both the killer and the killed are in the fire." They said, "O Messenger of Allah, one was a killer, but what of the one killed?" He replied, "He was keen to kill his companion."[1]

He said, ﴾"Verily, I intend to let you draw my sin on yourself as well as yours, then you will be one of the dwellevs of the fire, and that is the recompeuse of the *Zalimoon*. (*Al-Ma'idah* 5:29)"﴿ meaning, I want you to bear the sin of killing me along with your past sins before that. This was stated by Mujahid, Al-Suddi, ibn Jareer, and others.

---

(1)   Al-Bukhari (No. 31), Muslim (No. 2888).

It does not mean that the sins of a person killed pass on to the killer simply by virtue of his killing him as some people might understand. Ibn Jareer has cited a consensus that this is not the case.

As for the *hadeeth* quoted by some who have no knowledge from the Prophet ﷺ that he said, "The killer has not left the killed with a sin."[1] it is without basis, and it is not known in any of the books of *hadeeth* with an authentic or fair chain of narrations, nor even a weak chain of narrations. However, it might happen in some cases that on the Day of Resurrection, the killed one will seek justice from his killer and the good deeds of the killer will be insufficient to compensate for this injustice. In that case, the sins of the killed one will be transferred to the killer, as is established in the *Saheeh* concerning all injustices,[2] murder being among the greatest of them, and Allah knows best. We have addressed all of this in *Tafseer*, and to Allah belongs all praise.

Imam Ahmad, Abu Dawood, and At-Tirmidhi report from Sa'd ibn Abi Waqqaas when the *fitnah* befell 'Uthman ibn. 'Affaan, Sa'd said, "I bear witness that Allah's Messenger ﷺ said, 'There shall occur a *fitnah* in which the one sitting is better than the one standing, the one standing will be better than the one walking, and the one walking will be better than the one running'." He said, "What if he enters my house and stretches out his hand to kill me?" He said, "Be like the son of Adam."[3]

---

(1) It is without basis as the author has mentioned in *Fayt ul-Qadeer* (4/506), Al-Munaawi attributes it to Al-Bazzaar in his *Musnad* on the authority of Abu Hurayrah.

(2) The author is referring to the *hadeeth* of 'the bankrupt person' reported by Muslim: Book: Right ions of Prayer and Mannerism. Chapter: Impermissibly of Oppression, No. 2581.

(3) *Saheeh*: Ahmad (No. 1612) and At-Tirmidhi (No. 2194) report it from

As for the other (son), Imam Ahmad reports that Ibn Mas'ood said: Allah's Messenger ﷺ said, "No soul shall be killed wrongly except that a share of sin for its blood belongs to the original son of Adam, for he was the first person to introduce murder."[1]

At Mount Qasiyoon, north of Damascus, there is a cavern known as the Cavern of Blood which is popularly believed to be the place where Qabeel killed Habeel. This is something that the people learned from the People of the Book, and Allah alone knows how true It is.

Allah, Most High, says, ❨ "Then Allah sent a crow who scratched up the ground to show him how to cover the dead body of his brother. He said: 'Woe to me! Am I not even able to be as this crow and cover the dead body of my brother?' Then he became one of the remorseful."❩ (*Al-Ma'idah* 5:31) Some have mentioned that when he killed him, he carried him on his back for a year, others have said a hundred years. He remained like that until Allah sent two crows – As-Suddi reports with his *isnād* to the Companions that they were brothers – who fought with one another. One killed the other, and so he started digging a grave for him. He pushed him into it, buried him, and covered him up. When he saw him doing that, he said, "Woe to me! Am I not even able to be as this crow and cover the dead body of my brother?" Then he became one of the remorseful. So he did as the crow did; he covered up his brother by burying him.

Mujahid has stated that Qabeel received immediate punishment the day he killed his brother. His shin became stuck to his thigh, and his face became pointed toward the sun wherever it went. This was an exemplary punishment for him

---

Sa'd; Abu Dawood (No. 4256) reports it on the authority of Abu Bakrah.

(1) *Saheeh*: Ahmad (No. 3623).

for his sin and for his jealousy of his own full brother.

It is reported in the *hadeeth* from Allah's Messenger ﷺ that he said, "There is no sin more fitting that Allah should mete out punishment for it in advance in this world along with what He has stored up for its perpetrator in the Hereafter than transgression and severing the ties of kinship."

Mention of the Death of Adam and His Advice to His Son, Sheeth عليه السلام

The meaning of "Sheeth" is: "Gift of Allah". His parents named him thus because they were blessed with him after the death of Habeel.

'Abdullah Ibn Al-Imam Ahmad reported on the authority of 'Utayy – who was the son of Dhamrah As-Sa'di – that he said, "I saw an old man speaking in Al-Madinah and I asked about him and they said, 'This is Ubayy Ibn Ka'b رضي الله عنه.' He (Ubayy) said, "When death approached Adam عليه السلام, he said to his sons, "O, my sons! I long for the fruits of Paradise." So they went out to search for something for him. While they were searching, they were met by the angels, who had with them Adam's shrouds, embalming fluid and digging tools from Allah, from

Paradise. They said, "O, sons of Adam! what do you intend and what is it that you seek?" They answered, "Our father is ill, and he longs for the fruits of Paradise." The angels said, "Return, for the time has come for your father to die." So they all came and Eve recognized them. She clung to Adam ﷺ and he said, "Leave me! For I surely came before you. Let me be alone with the angels of my Lord, the Most Glorified, Most High." Then they took out his soul, gave his body a bath, shrouded the body, embalmed it and dug a grave for him and offered his funeral prayer and lowered him in the grave and closed the grave over him with earth. Then they said, "O, sons of Adam! This is to be your tradition." Its *isnad* is authentic. [1]

Ibn 'Asakir narrated on the authority of 'Abdullah Ibn 'Abbas ﷺ that the Messenger of Allah ﷺ said, "The angels said, *"Allahu Akbar* (Allah is Greatest)" over Adam ﷺ four times; and Abu Bakr said, *"Allahu Akbar"* over Fatimah four times; and 'Umar said, *"Allahu Akbar"* four times over Abu Bakr; and Suhaib said, *"Allahu Akbar"* four times over 'Umar." [2] Ibn 'Asakir said, "It was also narrated by others on the authority of Maimoon, who reported it on the authority of 'Abdullah Ibn 'Umar ﷺ.

Scholars have offered different opinions as to where he was buried; The most favored opinion is that Adam ﷺ was buried near mountain in India where he had descended from Paradise. It was also said that he was buried near Mount Qubais in Makkah. And it was said that when it was the time of the Great Flood, Nooh carried the bodies of Adam and Eve in a casket and

---

(1)   Narrated by Ahmad in his *Musnad* (20734).

(2)   Narrated by Ibn 'Asakir in a *marfoo'* form (7/458) it contains in its *isnad* one Muhammad Ibn Ziyad Al-Yashkuri, who used to fabricate *ahadeeth*. It was also narrated by Al-Hakim in *Al-Mustadrak*, but according to Adh-Dhahabi and Ad-Daraqutni, its *isnad* also contains unacceptable narrators.

buried them in *Bait Al-Maqdis* (Jerusalem). This was related by Ibn Jareer At-Tabari. They also disagreed regarding his lifespan – peace be upon him: We have previously referred to the *hadeeth* reported on the authority of 'Abdullah Ibn 'Abbas ⬥ and Abu Hurairah ⬥ in a *marfoo'* form, in which it was stated that: "His lifespan was ordained in *Al-Lawh Al-Mahfooz* (the Preserved Tablet) to be a thousand years." [1]

This is not contradicted by what is written in the Torah, which states that he lived for nine hundred and thirteen years, because this saying of theirs is discredited and rejected, since it contradicts the truth which is in our hands, that being preserved from the one who was protected from error. In addition, it is possible to reconcile this saying of theirs with what is narrated in the *hadeeth* – if it is correct – may refer to the period of his life on Earth, after he was sent down from Paradise, that being nine hundred and thirty solar years, which, in lunar years, would be equivalent to nine hundred and fifty-seven years. To this is added the forty-three years which he spent in Paradise, prior to being sent down to Earth, according to what was said by Ibn Jareer and others. This would make a total of a thousand years.

What Has Been Mentioned About Idrees ﷺ

Allah, Most High, says, ❴ And mention in the Book (the Qur'an) Idrees (Enoch). Verily, he was a man of truth (and) a

---

(1) This narration is raised to the level of *hasan* by other supporting narrations; it was narrated by Ahmad (2270) on the authority of 'Abdullah Ibn 'Abbas ⬥.

Prophet and We raised him to a high station. ❭ (*Soorah Maryam* 19:56,57)

So Idrees ﷺ has been praised by Allah and He described him as being a Prophet and a man of truth. He is also known as Idress and he was a direct ancestor of the Messenger of Allah ﷺ, according to what has been said by more than one scholar of genealogy. He was the first of the sons of Adam ﷺ to be granted Prophethood after Adam ﷺ and Sheeth ﷺ.

Ibn Ishaq said that he was the first person to write with a pen. He lived for three hundred and eight years of Adam's life. A group of people said that it was he who was referred to in the *hadeeth* reported on the authority of Mu'awiyah Ibn Al-Hakam As-Sulami ﷺ, who reported that when he asked the Messenger of Allah ﷺ about writing in the sand, he said, "There was a Prophet who wrote in the sand, so if they do it as he did, that is permissible." [1]

With regard to Allah's saying: ❲ We raised him to a high station ❳ (*Soorah Maryam* 19:57), according to what has been authentically reported in the *Saheehain* [2] in the *hadeeth* of *Al-Isra'*, the Messenger of Allah ﷺ visited him in the fourth heaven.

Al-'Awfi reported on the authority of 'Abdullah Ibn 'Abbas ﷺ that he said regarding the Words of Allah, Most High: ❲ We raised him to a high station ❳ (*Soorah Maryam* 19:57), "He was raised to the sixth heaven and he died there." Ad-Dahhak said likewise. But the *hadeeth* in which it is stated that he is in the fourth heaven, which is agreed upon by Al-Bukhari and

---

(1)   Narrated by Muslim (537), Abu Dawood (930), An-Nasa'i (1218) and Ahmad (23255).

(2)   Narrated by Al-Bukhari (3207) and Muslim (162).

Muslim, is more correct and it is the opinion of Mujahid and others.

Some have claimed that Idrees did not live before Nooh, rather, they say that he lived during the time of the Children of Isra'eel.

Al-Bukhari said, "It was mentioned on the authority of 'Abdullah Ibn Mas'ood ﷺ and 'Abdullah Ibn 'Abbas ﷺ that Ilyas (Elias) was Idrees.[1] They drew support for this claim from the *hadeeth* of Adh-Dhuhri, on the authority of Anas ﷺ regarding *Al-Isra'*, in which it was stated that when the Prophet ﷺ passed by him, he said, "Welcome, pious brother and pious Prophet!" He did not say as Adam ﷺ and Ibraheem ﷺ had said, "Welcome, pious Prophet and son!" They said, "If he was a direct descendant of him, he would have said as they did."

But this does not necessarily prove their case, because it might be that the narrator did not remember it precisely, or he may have said it by way of indulgence and humility and he did not address him as a father as Adam, the father of the mankind and Ibraheem, the *Khaleel,* of the Most Beneficent and the greatest of the *Ulul-'Azm* [2] – after Muhammad (may the Blessings and Peace of Allah be upon them all).

---

(1) Narrated by Al-Bukhari in a *mu'allaq* form in the Book of the *Ahadeeth* of the Prophets.

(2) *Ulul-'Azm*: They are Nooh, Ibraheem, Moosa, 'Eesa and Muhammad (peace be upon them all). 'Abdullah Ibn 'Abbas said that *Ulul-'Azm* means: The Possessors of Resoluteness and Patience.

The Story of Nooh ﷺ

He is Nooh, son of Lamak, son of Mattooshlakh, the son of Khanookh (i.e. Idrees), son of Yard, son of Mahla'eel, son of Qainan, son of Anush, son of Sheeth, son of Adam, the father of the mankind ﷺ.

He was born a hundred and twenty-six years after the death of Adam ﷺ, according to what Ibn Jareer and others have mentioned.

According to the history of the People of the Scripture, the period between the birth of Nooh ﷺ and the death of Adam ﷺ was a hundred and forty six years. But in fact, the time span between them was ten centuries, as Al-Hafiz Abu Hatim Ibn Hibban said in his *Saheeh*, on the authority of Abu Umamah ﷺ, who reported that a man said, "O, Messenger of Allah! Was Adam a Prophet?" The Prophet ﷺ said, "Yes; and he was spoken to (by Allah)." The man then asked, "And how long was there between him and Nooh ﷺ?" The Prophet ﷺ replied, "Ten centuries." [1] I say: This is in accordance with the criteria

---

(1) This is an authentic *hadeeth* narrated by Ibn Hibban in his *Saheeh* (14/69, No. 6190).

for acceptance stipulated by Muslim, though it was not narrated by him or by Al-Bukhari.

It was reported on the authority of 'Abdullah Ibn 'Abbas رضي الله عنهما that he said, "Between Adam علیه السلام and Nooh علیه السلام was a period of ten centuries – during which all of the people followed Islam (i.e. submission to Allah)." [1]

If what is meant by a *qarn* (century) is a hundred years, as appears to be the case for many people, then between them is a period of a thousand years, without doubt. But this does not negate the possibility that it could be longer, in view of what 'Abdullah Ibn 'Abbas specified, which was Islam, since there might be other later centuries between them, during which the people did not follow Islam. But the *hadeeth* of Abu Umamah رضي الله عنه proves that the period is restricted to ten centuries and 'Abdullah Ibn 'Abbas added the additional information that all of them followed Islam.

But if the meaning of a *qarn* is a generation of mankind, as in the Words of Allah, Most High: ﴿ And how many generations have We destroyed after Nooh! ﴾ (*Soorah Al-Isra'* 17:17) and the Words of Him, Most High: ﴿ Then, after them, We created other generations ﴾ (*Soorah Al-Mu'minoon* 23:42) and His Words: ﴿ And many generations in between ﴾ (*Soorah Al-Furqan* 25:38)' and His Words: ﴿ And how many a generation (past nations) have We destroyed before them ﴾ (*Soorah Maryam* 19:74).

The Prophet ﷺ said: "The best of people are my generation," [2]

---

(1) This was narrated by Al-Hakim (3654) and he declared it authentic. Adh-Dhahabi concurred with this.

(2) Narrated by Al-Bukhari (6429), Muslim (2533), At-Tirmidhi (3859), Ibn Majah (2362) and Ahmad (3583), on the authority of 'Abdullah Ibn Mas'ood رضي الله عنه.

the generation. before Nooh lived long lives and based on this, the time between Adam المِلَا and Nooh المِلَا would be thousands of years. And Allah knows better.

In short, Allah, Most High, only sent Nooh المِلَا when idols and *Tawagheet* [1] had come to be worshipped and the people had begun to err and commit acts of disbelief. He, Most High, then sent him as a mercy for the slaves; and he was the first Messenger sent to the inhabitants of the Earth, as the people of *Al-Mawqif* will say to him on the Day of Resurrection. [2]

Allah has told his story, the response of his people, the punishment of the Flood which descended on those who disbelieved in him and how Allah saved him and his companions aboard the ship (Ark) in several places in the Qur'an.

In *Soorah Al-A'raf*, He says, ﴿ Indeed, We sent Nooh (Nooh) to his people and he said, 'O, my people! Worship Allah! You have no other *ilah* (God) but He. (*La ilaha ill-Allah*: none has the right to be worshipped but Allah). Certainly, I fear for you the torment of a Great Day!' The leaders of his people said, 'Verily, we see you in plain error.' (Nooh) said, 'O, my people! There is no error in me, but I am a Messenger from the Lord of the *'Alameen* (mankind, jinn and all that exists)! I convey unto you the Messages of my Lord and give sincere advice to you. And I know from Allah what you know not. Do you wonder that there has come to you a reminder from your Lord through a man from amongst you, that he may warn you, so that you may fear Allah and that you may receive (His) Mercy?' But they belied him, so We saved him and those along with him in

---

(1) *Tawagheet*: (sing. is *Taghoot*) Those who call to the worship of other than Allah or who are worshipped besides Allah and they accept and are pleased with that worship.

(2) The *takhreej* for this will be given later.

the ship, and We drowned those who belied Our *Ayat* (proofs, evidences, Verses, lessons, signs, revelations, etc.). They were indeed a blind people. 》(*Soorah Al-A'raf* 7:59-64).

He, Most High, says in *Soorah Yoonus*, 《 And recite to them the news of Nooh. When he said to his people: 'O, my people, if my stay (with you), and my reminding (you) of the *Ayat* of Allah is hard on you, then I put my trust in Allah. So devise your plot, you and your partners, and let not your plot be in doubt for you. Then pass your sentence on me and give me no respite. But if you turn away (from accepting my doctrine of Islamic Monotheism, (i.e. to worship none but Allah), then no reward have I asked of you; my reward is only from Allah and I have been commanded to be one of the Muslims (those who submit to Allah's Will)'." 》(*Soorah Yoonus* 10:71,72)

He, Most High, says in *Soorah As-Saffat*, 《 And indeed Nooh (Nooh) invoked Us, and We are the Best of those who answer (the request). And We rescued him and his family from the great distress (i.e. drowning). And, his progeny, them We made the survivors (i.e. Shem, Ham and Japheth). And left for him (a goodly remembrance) among generations to come in later times: *Salamun* (peace) be upon Nooh (from Us) among the *'Alameen* (mankind, jinn and all that exists)!" Verily, thus We reward the *Muhsinoon* (those who do good - see v. 2:112). Verily, he (Nooh) was one of Our believing slaves. Then We drowned the other (disbelievers and polytheists, etc.) 》(*Soorah As-Saffat* 37:75-82)

He, Most High, says in *Soorah Bara'ah* (*At-Tawbah*), 《 Has not the story reached them of those before them? - The people of Nooh, 'Ad and Thamood, the people of Ibraheem, the dwellers of Madyan (Midian) and the cities overthrown (i.e. the people to whom Loot [Lot] preached), to them came their Messengers with clear proofs. So it was not Allah Who wronged them, but they used to wrong themselves 〉 (*Soorah At-Tawbah* 9:70) His story has already been mentioned in *Soorah Yoonus* and *Soorah Hood*.

In *Soorah Subhan* (*Al-Isra'*), He, Most High, says, ﴾ O, offspring of those whom We carried (in the ship) with Nooh! Verily, he was a grateful slave. 〉 (*Soorah Al-Isra'* 17:3) And He, Most High, also said in the same *Soorah*, ﴾ And how many generations have We destroyed after Nooh! And Sufficient is your Lord as Knower of all things and Beholder of the sins of His slaves. 〉 (*Soorah Al-Isra'* 17:17)

He, Most High, says in *Soorah Qaf*, ﴾ Denied before them (i.e. these pagans of Makkah who denied you, O, Muhammad,) the people of Nooh, and the dwellers of Rass, and Thamood, and 'Ad, and Fir'awn (Pharaoh), and the brethren of Loot (Lot), And the dwellers of the Wood, and the people of Tubba'; all of them denied (their) Messengers, so My Threat took effect.〉 (*Soorah Qaf* 50:12-14)

He, Most High, says in *Soorah At-Tahreem* ﴾ Allah sets forth an example for those who disbelieve, the wife of Nooh and the wife of Loot. They were under two of our righteous slaves, but they both betrayed their (husbands by rejecting their doctrine) so they (Nooh and Loot) benefited them (their respective wives) not against Allah, and it was said, 'Enter the Fire along with those who enter'!" 〉 (*Soorah At-Tahreem* 66:10)

As for the details of what befell him at the hands of his people, it is taken from the Qur'an and the *Sunnah* and the traditions. We have previously mentioned a report on the authority of 'Abdullah Ibn 'Abbas ﷺ that he said, "Between Adam الﻌﻠﻴﻪ and Nooh الﻌﻠﻴﻪ was a period of ten centuries, during which all of the people followed Islam." This was narrated by Al-Bukhari.[1] We mentioned that the meaning of *qarn* is "generation" or a hundred years.

Then, after those righteous generations, it happened that the people of that time reverted to idol worship and the reason for that was narrated by Al-Bukhari, on the authority of 'Abdullah Ibn 'Abbas ﷺ, in the *tafseer* of the Words of Allah, Most High: ❴ And they have said, 'You shall not leave your gods, nor shall you leave *Wadd*, nor *Suwa'*, nor *Yaghooth*, nor *Ya'ooq*, nor *Nasr* (names of the idols)'. ❵ (*Soorah Nooh* 71:23), in which he said, "These were names of righteous men from among the people of Nooh and when they died Satan incited their people to (prepare) and place idols at the places where they used to sit, and to call those idols by their names. The people did so, but the idols were not worshipped till those people (who initiated them) had died and the origin of the idols had become obscure, whereupon people began worshipping them." 'Abdullah Ibn 'Abbas ﷺ added, "These idols, which had been worshipped by the people of Nooh المسلم, later became the idols which the Arabs worshipped." 'Ikrimah said likewise, as did Ad-Dahhak, Qatadah and Muhammad Ibn Ishaq.

It has been confirmed in the *Saheehain* from the Messenger of Allah ﷺ that when Umm Salamah ﷺ and Umm Habeebah ﷺ mentioned the church which they saw in Abyssinia in which there were pictures, the Messenger of Allah ﷺ said, "If any religious man dies amongst those people they will build a place of worship at his grave and make these pictures in it. They will be the worst creature in the sight of Allah on the Day of Resurrection." [2]

---

(1)   The *takhreej* for this narration has already been given.

(2)   Narrated by Al-Bukhari (427) and Muslim (528).

And what is meant is that when the corruption spread on the earth and the scourge of worshipping idols became widespread therein, Allah sent His slave and His Messenger, Nooh to call them to the worship of Allah, Alone, without partners and to forbid them from worshipping other than Him. He was the first Messenger sent by Allah to the people of the Earth, as confirmed in the *Saheehain*, on the authority of Abu Hurairah , who reported from the Prophet that he said, in the *hadeeth* of *Ash-Shafa'ah* (the Intercession), "They will go to him and say, 'O, Adam! You are the father of all mankind, and Allah created you with His Own Hands, and ordered the angels to prostrate for you, and made you live in Paradise. Will you not intercede for us with your Lord? Don't you see in what (miserable) state we are, and to what condition we have reached?' On that, Adam will reply, 'My Lord is so Angry, as He has never been before and will never be in the future; (besides), He forbade me (to eat from) the tree, but I disobeyed (Him), (I am worried about) myself! Myself! Go to somebody else; go to Nooh.' They will go to Nooh and say, 'O, Nooh! You are the first amongst the Messengers of Allah to the people of the Earth, and Allah named you a thankful slave. Do you not see in what a (miserable) state we are and to what condition we have reached? Will you not intercede for us with your Lord?' Nooh will reply, 'Today my Lord has become so Angry, as He has never been before and will never be in the future. Myself! Myself!" [1] And he mentioned the *hadeeth* in its entirety. He also related it in the story of Nooh .

When Allah sent Nooh , he called upon them to worship only Allah, Alone, without partners and not to worship any idols or graven images or any *Taghoot* with Him and to acknowledge His Oneness and the fact that none has the right

_____

(1) Narrated by Al-Bukhari (3340 and 4712) and Muslim (194).

to be worshipped but He. There is no lord but He, just as He commanded the Messengers who came after him – all of whom were from his progeny – to do, as He, Most High, says, ❨ And his progeny, them We made the survivors (i.e. Shem, Ham and Japheth). ❩ (*Soorah As-Saffat* 37:77)

He said regarding him (Nooh 🕮🕮🕮) in *Soorah Ibraheem*, ❨ and We placed in their offspring Prophethood and Scripture.❩ (*Soorah Ibraheem* 57:26) That is, every Prophet who came after Nooh 🕮🕮🕮 is from his progeny and likewise Ibraheem 🕮🕮🕮.

Allah, Most High, says, ❨ He said, "O, my people! Verily, I am a plain warner to you, that you should worship Allah, Alone, be dutiful to Him, and obey me. He (Allah) will forgive you for your sins and grant you a respite to an appointed term. Verily, the term of Allah when it comes, cannot be delayed, if you but knew.' He said, 'O, my Lord! Verily, I have called my people night and day (i.e. secretly and openly to accept the doctrine of Islamic Monotheism). But all my calling added nothing but to (their) flight (from the truth). And verily, every time I called unto them that You might forgive them, they thrust their fingers into their ears, covered themselves up with their garments, and persisted (in their refusal), and magnified themselves in pride. Then verily, I called to them openly (aloud); then, verily: I proclaimed to them in public and I have appealed to them in private. I said (to them), 'Ask forgiveness from your Lord; Verily, He is Oft-Forgiving; He will send rain to you in abundance and give you increase in wealth and children and bestow on you gardens and bestow on you rivers. What is the matter with you, (that you fear not Allah [His punishment] and) you hope not for reward (from Allah or you believe not in His Oneness), while He has created you in (different) stages (i.e. first a *nutfah*, then an *'alaqah* and then a *mudhghah'*. ❩

(*Soorah Nooh* 71:2-14)

So Allah mentioned that Nooh عليه السلام called them to Allah in every possible way, both night and day, in secret and in public, sometimes through encouragement and at other times through intimidation. But all of this did not succeed with them. On the contrary, most of them persisted in their wrong-doing, tyranny and idol worship and they displayed enmity towards him at all times, belittling him and those who believed him. They threatened them with stoning and expulsion and they inflicted harm on them and tried their utmost to frustrate them in matters pertaining to their Religion: ﴿ The leaders of his people said, "Verily, we see you in plain error." (Nooh) said, 'O, my people! There is no error in me, but I am a Messenger from the Lord of the *'Alameen* (mankind, jinn and all that exists)'!" ﴾ (*Soorah Al-A'raf* 7:60,61). That is, I am not as you claim, a person who is astray; rather, I am following sound guidance, a Messenger from the Lord of the worlds, i.e. He Who says to a thing, "Be!" And it is: ﴿ "I convey unto you the Messages of my Lord and give sincere advice to you. And I know from Allah what you know not." ﴾ (*Soorah Al-A'raf* 7:62) This is the nature of the Messenger, that he is an eloquent adviser and the most knowledgeable of people regarding Allah, the Almighty, the All-Powerful.

Among the things that they said to him was this: ﴿ "We see you but a man like ourselves, nor do we see any following you but the meanest among us and they (too) followed you without thinking. And we do not see in you any merit above us, in fact we think you are liars." ﴾ (*Soorah Hood* 11:27) They were astonished at the idea that a human being should be a Messenger and they belittled those who followed him, holding them to be the most humble and despised people among them.

It has been said that they were the commonest among the people and the weakest of them, as Heraclius said, "They (i.e. the humble and weak) are the followers of the Messengers." [1] And this was only because there was nothing to prevent them from following the truth.

As for His Words: ﴾ without thinking ﴿ (*Soorah Hood* 11:27), the meaning is that simply because you preached to them, they followed the first thing that came to their minds, without thinking and without reflecting. This accusation which they made against them is in fact a thing for which they deserve praise – may Allah be pleased with them – because evident truth does not require reflection or thought or contemplation. On the contrary, it requires that one follows it and submits to it wherever it appears, which is why the Messenger of Allah ﷺ said, when praising *As-Siddeeq*, "Every person whom I called to Islam hesitated, except Abu Bakr, for he did not hesitate for a moment." [2] For this reason, the people also swiftly gave their pledge of allegiance to him on the Day of *As-Saqeefah*, [3] without contemplation and without reflection, because his superiority over all others was clearly apparent to the Companions 🙂. This is why when the Messenger of Allah wanted to write a document regarding the subject of the Caliphate, he abandoned it, saying, "Allah and the Believers will reject anyone except Abu Bakr 🙂." [4] As for what the disbelievers among the people of Nooh 🕊 said to him and those who believed in him, ﴾ "And

---

(1) Narrated by Al-Bukhari (7), Muslim (1723) and Imam Ahmad (2366).

(2) Narrated by Ibn Hisham in his *Seerah* (2/91).

(3) The Day of As-Saqeefah: As-Saqeefah means The Shelter. On the day of the Prophet's death, the Muslims gathered together in a shelter belonging to Banu Sa'idah to choose a Caliph. The name of the house is used as shorthand for the event, or the gathering, which was a crucial turning point in the history of Islam.

(4) Narrated by Muslim (2387) and Ahmad (24589).

we do not see in you any merit above us." ❯ (*Soorah Hood* 11:27) – it means: We do not see that you and your followers have any virtuous status above us in your physical appearance, your character, your provisions, or your condition, since you accepted this religion of yours.

❮ "In fact we think you are liars." He said, "O, my people! Tell me, if I have a clear proof from my Lord, and a Mercy has come to me from Him, but that (Mercy) has been obscured from your sight, shall we compel you to accept it (Islamic Monotheism) when you have a strong hatred for it?" ❯ (*Soorah Hood* 11:27-28) This is an expression of courteousness and gentleness in his address to them, when calling them to the truth, as He, Most High, says, ❮ And speak to him mildly, perhaps he may accept admonition or fear Allah. ❯ (*Soorah Ta Ha* 20:44)

He, Most High, says, ❮ Invite (mankind, O, Muhammad,) to the Way of your Lord (i.e. Islam) with wisdom (i.e. with the Divine Inspiration and the Qur'an) and fair preaching, and argue with them in a way that is better. ❯ (*Soorah An-Nahl* 16:125)

This is apparent in Nooh's words to them: ❮ "Oh, my people! Tell me, if I have a clear proof from my Lord, and a Mercy has come to me from Him," ❯ (*Soorah Hood* 11:28) The "Mercy" referred to is Prophethood and the Message. ❮ "But that (Mercy) has been obscured from your sight." ❯ (*Soorah Hood* 11:28) That is, you did not understand it and you were not guided to it, ❮ "Shall we compel you to accept it?" ❯ (*Soorah Hood* 11:28) That is, shall we coerce you and force you to believe in it? ❮ "When you have a strong hatred for it?" ❯ (*Soorah Hood* 11:28) That is, I have no means to make you do so in such circumstances. ❮ "And o, my people! I ask of you no wealth for it, my reward is from none but Allah." ❯ (*Soorah Hood* 11:29)

That is, I do not require any payment from you for conveying to you that which will benefit you in your earthly life and in your Afterlife. I do not seek that from anyone except Allah, Whose Reward is better for me and more lasting than what you might give to me.

❴ "I am not going to drive away those who have believed. Surely, they are going to meet their Lord, but I see that you are a people who are ignorant." ❵ (*Soorah Hood* 11:29) It is as if they had requested him to send those people away from him and promised him that they would join him if he did so. But he refused their request and said, ❴ "Surely, they are going to meet their Lord." ❵ (*Soorah Hood* 11:29) and so I fear that if I send them away, they will complain of me to Allah, the Almighty, the All-Powerful.

❴ "And I do not say to you that with me are the Treasures of Allah, nor that I know the *ghaib* (unseen); nor do I say I am an angel." ❵ (*Soorah Hood* 11:31) That is, on the contrary, I am a slave and a Messenger. I do not possess anything of Allah's Knowledge, except that which He has informed me and I have no ability to do anything except that which Allah has enabled me to do. Nor do I possess the power to benefit or inflict harm, except as Allah wills. ❴ "And I do not say of those whom your eyes look down upon…" ❵ (*Soorah Hood* 11:31). That is, Nooh's followers. ❴ "that Allah will not bestow any good on them. Allah knows what is in their inner-selves (as regards belief, etc.). In that case, I should, indeed be one of the *zalimoon* (wrongdoers, oppressors, etc.)." ❵ (*Soorah Hood* 11:31). That is, I will not testify against them that they will not be rewarded by Allah on the Day of Resurrection. Allah knows better regarding them and He will recompense them for what is in their hearts; if what is in them is good, then He will reward them with goodness and if it is evil, He will recompense them with evil, as He, Most High, says in another *Soorah,* ❨ "They said, 'Shall we believe in you, when the meanest (of the people) follow you?' He said, 'And what knowledge have I of what they used to do? Their account is only with my Lord, if you could (but) know. And I am not going to drive away the believers. I am only a plain warner.' ❩ (*Soorah Ash-Shu'ara'* 26:111-115)

A long time passed and the arguments between him and them continued, as Allah, Most High, says, ❨ And indeed We sent Nooh to his people, and he stayed among them a thousand years less fifty years (inviting them to believe in the Oneness of Allah [Monotheism], and discard the false gods and other deities), and the Deluge overtook them while they were *zalimoon* (wrongdoers, polytheists, disbelievers, etc.) ❩ (*Soorah Al-'Ankaboot* 29:14) That is, throughout all this extended period of time, none but a few of them believed. Every time a generation passed away, they would advise those who came after them not to believe in him and to contest him and oppose him. When a man's son reached maturity and understood his words, he would advise him in any discussions they had never to believe in Nooh 🕮 for as long as he lived.

Their nature prevented them from believing and following the truth, which is why Nooh 🕮 said, ❨ "and they will beget none but wicked disbelievers." ❩ (*Soorah Nooh* 71:27) – and that is why they said, ❨ They said, O, Nooh! You have disputed with us and much have you prolonged the dispute with us, now bring upon us what you threaten us with, if you are of the truthful.' He said, 'Only Allah will bring it (the punishment) on you, if He will, and then you will escape not.' ❩ (*Soorah Hood* 11:32,33) That is, only Allah, the Almighty, the All-Powerful is able to do that, for it is He Who is capable of doing anything, and nothing is difficult for Him; rather, it is He Who says to a thing, "Be!" and it is. ❨ "And my advice will not profit you, even if I wish to give you good counsel, if Allah's Will is to keep you astray. He is your Lord and to Him you shall return." ❩ (*Soorah Hood* 11:34) That is, if Allah wants to put anyone to trial (i.e. make him go astray), no one will be able to guide him. It is He Who guides whom He wills, and causes to go astray whom He wills and He does what He intends (or wills). He is the Almighty, the Most Wise, the Knower of who deserves to be guided and who deserves to be led astray and to Him belong the most far-reaching Wisdom and the most irrefutable argument.

❨ And it was inspired to Nooh: 'None of your people will believe except those who have believed already'. ❩ (*Soorah Hood* 11:36) This was said as a consolation to him, in light of what they had done to him. ❨ And it was inspired to Nooh: "None of your people will believe except those who have believed already. So be not sad because of what they used to do'. ❩ (*Soorah Hood* 11:36) It was a consolation to Nooh ﷺ regarding his people to know that none of them would believe except those who had already believed. That is, let it not grieve you what has passed, for victory is near and the tidings are wonderful.

❨ "And construct the ship under Our Eyes and with Our Inspiration, and address Me not on behalf of those who did wrong; they are surely to be drowned." ❩ (*Soorah Hood* 11:37) When Nooh ﷺ despaired of their ever-becoming righteous and successful and considered that there was no good in them and that they continued to harm him, to oppose him and to belie him with all the means at their disposal, including words and deeds, he invoked Allah's Anger against them and Allah answered his invocation. He, Most High, says, ❨ And indeed Nooh invoked Us, and We are the Best of those who answer (the request). And We rescued him and his family from the great distress (i.e. drowning) ❩ (*Soorah As-Saffat* 37:75,76)

He, Most High, says, ❨ Then he invoked his Lord (saying): 'I have been overcome, so help (me)'! ❩ (*Soorah Al-Qamar* 54:10). So their sins of disbelief and iniquity and the invocation of their Prophet combined against them and at that point, Allah commanded him to build the Ark.

Allah, Most High, informed him that when His Punishment – which could not be rescinded from the evildoing people – descended on them, He would not be able to ask Allah about them again, because he might be afflicted by feelings of pity toward his people, when he saw with his own eyes the punishment inflicted on them, for being informed about something is not the same as seeing it with one's own eyes. This is why He says, ❨ "And construct the ship under Our Eyes and with Our Inspiration, and address Me not on behalf of those who did wrong; they are surely to be drowned. And as he was constructing the ship, whenever the chiefs of his people passed by him, they made a mockery of him. ❩ (*Soorah Hood* 11:37,38) That is, they mocked him, regarding it as unlikely that what he had promised them would in fact, befall them. ❨ "He said, 'If you mock at us, so do we mock at you likewise for your mocking." ❩ (*Soorah Hood* 11:38) That is, it is we who will mock you. We are amazed at your continuing disbelief and stubbornness, which demands the infliction of punishment on you. ❨ "And you will know who it is on whom will come a torment that will cover him with disgrace and on whom will fall a lasting torment." ❩ (*Soorah Hood* 11:39) It was their nature to stubbornly disbelieve and vehemently oppose him in the life of this world and likewise in the Hereafter, for they will deny also that any Messenger came to them, as narrated by Al-Bukhari, on the authority of Abu Sa'eed Al-Khudri 𐎀, who said: The Messenger of Allah 𐎀 said, "Nooh 𐎀𐎀 and his people will come and Allah, the Almighty, the All-Powerful will say, 'Did you convey (the Message)?' He will reply, 'Yes, my Lord!' Then He will ask his people, 'Did he convey (the Message) to you?' But they will answer, 'No, no Prophet came to us.' Allah will then ask Nooh 𐎀𐎀, 'Who will bear witness on your behalf?' He will reply, 'Muhammad and his people.' They will bear witness that he conveyed (the Message)." And that is the meaning of the Words of Allah, Most High: ﴿ Thus We have made you (true Muslims - real believers of Islamic Monotheism, true followers of Prophet Muhammad 𐎀 and his *Sunnah* [legal ways], a *wasat* [and the best] nation, that you be witnesses over mankind and the Messenger [Muhammad 𐎀] be a witness over you. ﴾ (*Soorah Al-Baqarah* 2:143) The word *wasat* means just; and this nation will bear witness to (the truth of) the testimony of its truthful Prophet, who is believed.

Allah, Most High, says, ﴿ (Nooh) said, 'O, my Lord! Help me because they deny me.' So We inspired him (saying): 'Construct the ship under Our Eyes and under Our Revelation (guidance).' ﴾ (*Soorah Al-Mu'minoon* 23:26,27) That is, according to Our Command to you and in Our Sight, we shall supervise your construction of it and We shall instruct you as to the correct manner of doing so. ﴿ Then, when Our Command comes, and the *tannoor* (oven) gushes forth water, take on board of each kind two (male and female), and your family, except those thereof against whom the Word has already gone forth. And address Me not in favor of those who have done wrong. Verily, they are to be drowned. ﴾ (*Soorah Al-Mu'minoon* 23:27)

Then Allah instructed him that when His Command was enacted and His Punishment was inflicted, he should carry male and female pairs of every animal and all living creatures, including those which are eaten and others, in order that their progeny might survive. He was also instructed to carry his family with him; that is, the members of his household, except those regarding whom the Word had already gone forth. That is, those who had disbelieved, because the irrevocable invocation against them had already been put into effect and the infliction of the Punishment had already been sanctioned upon them and that was irreversible. Allah could not be appealed regarding them once the great Punishment had been inflicted upon them, as we have explained previously. According to the majority of scholars, what is meant by the *tannoor* is the face of the earth, i.e. water gushes forth from every place on earth, even the "ovens" which are the places of fire. As for the Words of Allah, Most High: ❨ (So it was) till then there came Our Command and the *tannoor* (oven) gushed forth (water like fountains from the earth). We said, "Embark therein, of each kind two (male and female), and your family, except him against whom the Word has already gone forth, and those who believe. And none believed with him, except a few." ❩ (*Soorah Hood* 11:40) This was a command that when the affliction (i.e. the flood) started, he should carry a male and female of every species on board the Ark.

❨ "And your family, except him against whom the Word has already gone forth." ❩ (*Soorah Hood* 11:40) That is, those disbelievers upon whom the invocation was effected, including his son, Yam, who was drowned as we shall see.

❨ "And those who believe." ❩ (*Soorah Hood* 11:40). That is, carry in the ship those of your people who believe in you.

Allah, Most High, says, ❰ "And none believed with him, except a few." ❱ (*Soorah Hood* 11:40) This was in spite of the long period of time and the fact that he remained among them and the urgent exhortations he made to them night and day, propounding to them teachings, with courteousness, sometimes using threats and warnings and other times using encouragement and promises.

Allah, Most High, says, ❰ And when you have embarked on the ship, you and whoever is with you, then say, 'All praise and thanks be to Allah, Who has saved us from the people who are *zalimoon* (i.e. oppressors, wrong-doers, polytheists, those who join others in worship with Allah, etc.). And say: "My Lord! Cause me to land at a blessed landing-place, for You are the Best of those who bring to land." ❱ (*Soorah Al-Mu'minoon* 23:28,29) He commanded him to praise and thank his Lord for providing him with this ship and for saving him therewith; for granting him victory over his people and relieving his heart of those who opposed him and belied him, as He, Most High, says, ❰ And Who has created all the pairs and has appointed for you ships and cattle on which you ride, in order that you may mount firmly on their backs, and then may remember the Favor of your Lord when you mount thereon, and say: 'Glory to Him who has subjected this to us, and we could never have it (by our efforts).' And verily, to Our Lord we indeed are to return!" ❱ (*Soorah Az-Zukhruf* 43:12-14)

Likewise, he was commanded to invoke Allah at the start of the events, so that he might receive goodness and blessings and that his end might be a laudable one. He, Most High, said to His Messenger (Muhammad) 鑾, when he migrated (from Makkah to Al-Madinah), ❰ And say (O, Muhammad), "My Lord! Let my entry (to the city of Al-Madinah) be good, and likewise my exit (from the city of Makkah) be good. And grant me from You an authority to help me (or a firm sign or a proof)." 》 (*Soorah Al-Isra'* 17:80)

Nooh carried out these instructions: 《 And he (Nooh) said, "Embark therein, in the Name of Allah will be its moving course and its resting anchorage." 》 (*Soorah Hood* 11:41) That is, begin the voyage by invoking Allah's Name and end it in the same way. 《 "Surely, my Lord is Oft-Forgiving, Most Merciful." 》 (*Soorah Hood* 11:41). That is, and (He is) the Owner of a painful Punishment – although He is the Oft-Forgiving, Most Merciful – His Punishment cannot be rescinded from the sinning people; thus it was sanctioned for the people of the Earth who disbelieved and worshipped other than Him.

Allah, Most High, says, 《 So it (the ship) sailed with them amid the waves like mountains. 》 (*Soorah Hood* 11:42). This was because Allah, Most High, sent rain from the sky, the like of which the earth had not known before and has not seen since; it was like the mouths of waterskins (pouring forth). And He commanded the earth to bring forth water from all directions, as Allah says, 《 Then he invoked his Lord (saying): "I have been overcome, so help (me)!" So We opened the gates of heaven with water pouring forth. And We caused the earth to gush forth with springs. So the waters (of the heaven and the earth) met for a matter predestined. And We carried him on a (ship) made of planks and nails. 》 (*Soorah Al-Qamar* 54:10-13) 《 Floating under Our Eyes. 》 (*Soorah Al-Qamar* 54:14) That is, under Our Protection, Our Watch, Our Guard and Our Observation. 《 a reward for him who had been rejected! 》 (*Soorah Al-Qamar* 54:14) Allah, Most High, says, 《 Verily! When the water rose beyond its limits (Nooh's Flood), We carried you (mankind) in the floating 》(*Soorah Al-Haqqah* 69:11). That is, in the floating ship 《 That We might make it a remembrance for you, and the keen ear (person) may (hear and) understand it 》 (*Soorah Al-Haqqah* 69:12)

A number of scholars of *tafseer* said that the water rose fifteen cubits above the highest mountain on Earth; this was what was said by the People of the Scripture. It was also said that it rose eighty cubits and that it covered the whole of the Earth, the length and breadth of it, its plains, its rugged ground, its mountains, its deserts and its sands. No living thing remained on the face of the Earth, whether great or small.

《 And it was said, "O, earth! Swallow up your water," and, "O, sky! Withhold (your rain)." And the water was diminished and the Decree (of Allah) was fulfilled (i.e. the destruction of the people of Nooh. And it (the ship) rested on Mount Judi, and it was said "Away with the people who are *zalimoon* 》(*Soorah Hood* 11:44). That is, when Allah had dealt with the inhabitants of the Earth and none of those who had worshipped others besides Allah, the Almighty, the All-Powerful remained, Allah commanded the earth to swallow its water and He commanded the sky to stop raining. 《 And the water was diminished 》 - That is, it decreased from what it had been. 《 And the Decree (of Allah) was fulfilled. 》 That is, that which Allah had previously ordained, due to His All-Encompassing Knowledge was inflicted upon them. 《 And it was said "Away with the people who are *zalimoon.* 》 (*Soorah Hood* 11:44) And also Allah, Most High, says: 《 Because of their sins they were drowned, then weve made to enter the Fire. And they towund none to to help them instead of Allah. And Nooh said: "My Lord! Leave not one of the disbelievers on the early If you leave them, they will mislead your slaves, and they will beget none but wicked disbelievers.⟫ (*Soorah An-Nooh* 71:25-27) Allah, Most High answered his supplication, all praise and thanks are due to Him and all grace proceeds from Him and not a single one of them remained.

Then He, Most High, says, ⟪ It was said, "O, Nooh! Come down (from the ship) with peace from Us and blessings on you and on the people who are with you (and on some of their offspring), but (there will be other) people to whom We shall grant their pleasures (for a time), but in the end a painful torment will reach them from Us." ⟫ (*Soorah Hood* 11:48) This was a command to Nooh 牒 when the water subsided from the face of the earth and it became possible to travel across it and to dwell in it. So he disembarked from the ship, which had come to rest after its long journey, on the upper portion of a mountain in Al-Jazeerah, which is well-known. We have already spoken of it when we discussed the creation of the mountains. ⟪ With peace from Us and blessings ⟫. That is, disembark in safety, with blessings upon you and upon the nations that will be born afterwards. That is, from your progeny, for Allah did not allow any of the Believers who were with him to produce offspring, aside from Nooh 牒.

Allah, Most High, says, ⟪ And, his progeny, them We made the survivors. ⟫ (*As-Saffat* 37:77) So everyone on the face of the earth today, from all races of mankind, descended from Nooh's three sons. And they are Shem, Ham and Jephe. Imam Ahmad narrated on the authority of Abu Hurairah 牒 that he said: The Prophet 牒 passed by some people from among the Jews who were fasting the day of *'Ashoorah*, and he said to them, "What is this fast?" This is the day on which Allah saved Moosa 牒 and the Children of Isra'eel from being drowned; and on that day, He drowned Fir'awn. And on this day, the ship landed on Mount Joodi. Nooh ﷺ and Moosa ﷺ fasted in order to give thanks to Allah, the Almighty, the All-Powerful." The Prophet ﷺ said, "I have more claim over Moosa ﷺ and more right to fast on this day (than you)." Then he said to his Companions ﷺ, "If anyone of you has been fasting since this morning, let him complete his fast and if anyone of you has taken lunch with his family, let him complete the rest of the day." [1] This *hadeeth* is supported by a narration in the *Saheeh*. [2] But the *ghareeb* part is the mention of Nooh ﷺ also. And Allah knows better.

As for what has been said by many ignorant people, that they ate from the leftovers of their provisions and from grains which they had brought with them and they ground them that day and applied *ithmid* to their eyes in order to strengthen their sight, because it had become cut off by the bright light, after having been confined in the darkness of the ship, none of this is authentic. It is only mentioned in incomplete traditions narrated from the Children of Isra'eel. They are not to be relied on and they should not be followed. And Allah knows better.

A number of ignorant people from Persia and India have

---

(1) Narrated by Imam Ahmad (8500). In its *isnad* is one Abu Ja'far, who has been condemned as "weak" by a number of scholars, while others declared him to be trustworthy. (In such cases, it is the practice of the scholars to act upon the negative report, since a scholar might declare a person trustworthy because he has heard nothing negative about him, another scholar might know something (negative) about him which the other scholar does not know). There is also one 'Abdus-Samad, who has been declared weak by scholars. In addition, his father is unknown to the scholars. Another person in the chain is Shabeel, who was known to make mistakes.

(2) Narrated by Al-Bukhari (2004), on the authority of 'Abdullah Ibn 'Abbas ﷺ and by Muslim (1130), but neither of these two narrations mentions Nooh ﷺ.

denied that the flood took place, while others among them have accepted it and they said, "It was only in the land of Babylon and it did not reach us." They said, "We have continued to inherit the land from generation to generation from the time of Adam عَلَيْهِ السَّلَام until our time."

What Has Been Mentioned About the Character of Nooh عَلَيْهِ السَّلَام

Allah, Most High says, ❴ Verily, he was a grateful slave. ❵ (*Soorah Al-Isra`* 17:3) It was said that he used to thank Allah for his food, his drink and all of his affairs.

Imam Ahmad narrated on the authority of Anas Ibn Malik رَضِيَ اللهُ عَنْهُ that he said: The Messenger of Allah ﷺ said, "Verily, Allah is pleased with the slave when he eats his food and thanks Him for it and when he drinks his beverage and thanks Him for it."[1] Muslim, At-Tirmidhi and An-Nasa'i narrated likewise from the *hadeeth* of Abu Usamah رَضِيَ اللهُ عَنْهُ. [2]

It is clear that a grateful person is the one who performs all acts of obedience, including those of the heart, verbal ones and physical ones, because gratitude is expressed by all of them, as the poet says in *Al-Bahr At-Taweel*:

"You generous people have benefitted from three things from me,

My hand, my tongue and heart."

---

(1) This is an authentic *hadeeth* narrated by Imam Ahmad (11758).

(2) Narrated by Muslim (2734), At-Tirmidhi (1816) and An-Nasa`i (4/202, No. 6899)

His Advice to His Son

Imam Ahmad narrated on the authority of 'Abdullah Ibn 'Amr ﷺ that he said: We were with the Messenger of Allah ﷺ when a Bedouin man came to him wearing a flowing cloak, decorated with brocade and he ﷺ said, "Verily, this companion of yours has humiliated ever horseman who is the son of a horseman (or he said: wants to humiliate ever horseman who is the son of a horseman) and he has elevated every herdsman, who is the son of a herdsman." 'Abdullah ﷺ said: Then the Messenger of Allah ﷺ took hold of the edges of his cloak and said, "I do not see upon you the garments of a person who is not endowed with intelligence." Then he said, "When death approached the Prophet of Allah, Nooh صلى الله عليه وسلم, he said to his son, 'I will convey to you my advice: I order you to do two things and I forbid you to do two things. I order you to believe that *La ilaha Illallah* (none has the right to be worshipped except Allah), because if the seven heavens and the seven earths were placed in one hand and *La ilaha illallah* was placed in the other hand, *La ilaha illallah* would outweigh them. And if the seven heavens and the seven earths were a dark circle, it would be filled by *La Ilaha illallah*. Glory and praise be to Allah, because in it are the connections to everything and through it all creation is sustained. I forbid you to commit *shirk* (ascribe partners to Allah) and to commit *kibr*., Either 'Abdullah or someone else said, "O, Messenger of Allah! As for *shirk*, we know what it is, but what is *kibr*? Is it that one of us should have a pair of fine shoes with fine straps on them?" He ﷺ said, "No." The questioner asked, "Is it that one of us should have a fine garment which he wears?" He ﷺ said, "No." The questioner asked, "Is it that one of us has a camel which he rides?" The Prophet 🕊️ said, "No." The questioner then asked, "Is it that one of us has companions who sit around him?" The Messenger of Allah 🕊️ replied, "No." 'Abdullah 🕊️ or another person said, "O, Messenger of Allah! Then what is *kibr*?" He 🕊️ replied, "Ignorance of the truth and displaying contempt toward people." [1] The *isnad* of this *hadeeth* is authentic, though Al-Bukhari and Muslim did not narrate it.

As for his grave, Ibn Jareer and Al-Azraqi narrated on the authority of 'Abdur-Rahman Ibn Sabit or another of the *Tabi'oon* in a *mursal* [2] form, that Nooh 🕊️ was buried within the precincts of the Sacred Mosque (in Makkah).

This is stronger and more reliable than what has been said by many of the later scholars, who claimed that he is in a town, in a place known today as Kark Nooh. In that place is a mosque which has been built because of these claims. And Allah knows better.

---

(1)   This is an authentic *hadeeth* narrated by Imam Ahmad (2/170, No. 6547).

(2)   *Mursal*: A chain of narrators which does not include a Companion 🕊️.

The Story of Hood عليه السلام

He is Hood, son of Shalakh, son of Arfakhshad, son of Sam, son of Nooh عليه السلام. It was said that Hood عليه السلام is 'Abir, the son of Shalakh, the son of Arfakhshad, the son of Sam, the son of Nooh عليه السلام. This was reported by Ibn Jareer At-Tabari.

He belonged to a tribe known as 'Ad, son of 'Aws, son of Sam, son of Nooh عليه السلام. They were Arabs living in the winding sand tracts (Al-Ahqaf), which is a mountain of sand in Yemen, between Oman and Hadhramawt, in a land looking out upon the sea, which is known as Ash-Shihr. The name of their valley was Mugheeth. They lived a great deal in tents which had huge poles, as Allah, Most High, says, ﴿ Did you (Muhammad,) not see (think) how your Lord dealt with 'Ad (people), of Iram, with lofty poles?. ﴾ (Soorah Al-Fajr 89:6,7) That is, 'Ad Iram, who were the first 'Ad. As for the second 'Ad, they came later, as we shall make clear in its place. The first 'Ad were 'Ad ﴿ of Iram, with lofty poles, The like of which were not created in the land? ﴾ (Soorah Al-Fajr 89:7,8) That is, the like of the tribe. It was also said that it means: the like of whose poles, but the correct opinion is the former, as we made clear in the Tafseer.

The Arabs were known before Isma'eel ﷺ as *Al-'Arab Al-'Aribah* and they consisted of numerous tribes, including: 'Ad, Thamood, Jurhum, Tasm, Jadees, Ameem, Madyan, Imlaq, Abil, Jasim, Qahtan, Banu Yaqtun and others.

As for the Arabised Arabs, they were of the progeny of Isma'eel, the son of Ibraheem *Al-Khaleel* (peace be upon them both). Isma'eel, was the first to speak eloquent, classical Arabic and he learned the speech of the Arabs from the tribe of Jurhum, who camped near his mother, Hajar, in the Sacred Precincts, as we shall make clear in its place, if Allah wills. But Allah made him able to speak with the utmost eloquence and powers of elucidation and the Messenger of Allah ﷺ was likewise articulate in it.

What is meant is that 'Ad – the first 'Ad – were the first to worship idols after the Great Flood. Their idols were three: Sadd, Samood and Hara. Allah sent to them their brother, Hood ﷺ and he called them to Allah, as He, Most High, says after mentioning the people of Nooh ﷺ and their case in *Soorah Al-A'raf*, ﴾ And to 'Ad (people, We sent) their brother Hood. He said, "O, my people! Worship Allah! You have no other *ilah* (god) but Him. (*La ilaha illallah*: none has the right to be worshipped but Allah). Will you not fear (Allah)?" The leaders of those who disbelieved among his people said, "Verily, we see you in foolishness and verily, we think you are one of the liars." (Hood) said, "O, my people! There is no foolishness in me, but (I am) a Messenger from the Lord of the *'Alameen* (mankind, jinn and all that exists)! I convey unto you the Messages of my Lord, and I am a trustworthy adviser (or well-wisher) for you. Do you wonder that there has come to you a Reminder (and an advice) from your Lord through a man from amongst you that he may warn you? And remember that He

made you successors after the people of Nooh and increased
you amply in stature. So remember the graces (bestowed upon
you) from Allah, so that you may be successful." They said,
"You have come to us that we should worship Allah, Alone and
forsake that which our fathers used to worship. So bring us that
wherewith you have threatened us if you are of the truthful."
(Hood) said, "Torment and wrath have already fallen on you
from your Lord. Dispute you with me over names which you
have named – you and your fathers, with no authority from
Allah? Then wait, I am with you among those who wait." So
We saved him and those who were with him by a Mercy from
Us, and We cut the roots of those who belied Our *Ayat* (proofs,
evidences, verses, lessons, signs, revelations, etc.), and they
were not believers 》 (*Soorah Al-A'raf* 7:65-72)

He, Most High, says, ﴾ They said, "O, Hood! No evidence
have you brought us, and we shall not leave our gods for your
(mere) saying! And we are not believers in you. All that we
say is that some of our gods (deities) have seized you with
evil (madness)." He said, "I call Allah to witness and bear you
witness that I am free from that which you ascribe as partners
in worship with Him (Allah). So plot against me, all of you,
and give me no respite. I put my trust in Allah, my Lord and
your Lord! There is not a moving (living) creature but He has
grasp of its forelock. Verily, my Lord is on the Straight Path
(the truth)." 》 (*Soorah Hood* 11:53-56)

He, Most High, says in *Soorah Qad Aflahal-Mu'minoon* (*Al-
Mu'minoon*) after the story of Nooh's people: ﴾ Then, after
them, We created another generation. And We sent to them a
Messenger from among themselves (saying), "Worship Allah!
You have no other *ilah* (god) but Him. Will you not then be afraid
(of Him i.e. of His Punishment because of worshipping others

besides Him)?" And the chiefs of his people, who disbelieved and denied the Meeting in the Hereafter, and to whom We had given the luxuries and comforts of this life, said, "He is no more than a human being like you, he eats of that which you eat, and drinks of what you drink. If you were to obey a human being like yourselves, then verily! You indeed would be losers. Does he promise you that when you have died and have become dust and bones, you shall come out alive (resurrected)? Far, very far is that which you are promised. There is nothing but our life of this world! We die and we live! And we are not going to be resurrected! He is only a man who has invented a lie against Allah, but we are not going to believe in him." He said, "O my Lord! Help me because they deny me." He (Allah) said, "In a little while, they are sure to be regretful." So *As-Saihah* (punishment - awful cry, etc.) overtook them with justice, and We made them as rubbish of dead plants. So away with the people who are *zalimoon* (polytheists, wrongdoers, disbelievers in the Oneness of Allah, disobedient to His Messengers, etc.) ﴾ (*Soorah Al-Mu'minoon* 23:31-41).

He, Most High, says in *Soorah Ha Meem As-Sajdah* (*Fussilat*), ﴿ As for 'Ad, they were arrogant in the land without right, and they said, "Who is mightier than us in strength?" See they not that Allah, Who created them was mightier in strength than they? And they used to deny Our *Ayat*! So We sent upon them furious wind in days of evil omen (for them) that We might give them a taste of disgracing torment in this present worldly life, but surely the Punishment of the Hereafter will be more disgracing, and they will never be helped. ﴾ (*Soorah Fussilat* 41:15,16)

We will relate the purport of the story gathered from these threads, along with what can be added to it from the traditions.

We have already mentioned that they were the first of the nations to worship idols after the Great Flood and this is clear from His Words regarding them, ❨ And remember that He made you successors after the people of Nooh, and increased you amply in stature." ❩ (*Soorah Al-A'raf* 7:69) That is, He made them the strongest people in their time, in physique, power and bravery.

In *Soorah Al-Mu'minoon*, He says, ❨ Then, after them, We created another generation. ❩ (*Soorah Al-Mu'minoon* 23:31) They were the people of Hood, according to the correct view.

Others said that they were Thamood, based on the Words of Allah, Most High, ❨ So *As-Saihah* (punishment - awful cry, etc.) overtook them with justice, and We made them as rubbish of dead plants. ❩ (*Soorah Al-Mu'minoon* 23:41) They said, "They are the people of Saleh عليه السلام, for it is they who were destroyed by *As-Saihah*. ❨ And as for 'Ad, they were destroyed by a furious, violent wind. ❩ (*Soorah Al-Haqqah* 69:6) This saying of theirs does not rule out the possibility that they were overcome by a combination of *As-Saihah* and the furious, violent wind, as we shall show in the story of the people of Madyan, the Dwellers of the '*Aykah* (Wood). For a combination of punishments were inflicted on them, in addition to which, there is no dispute regarding the fact that 'Ad lived before Thamood.

What is meant is that 'Ad were alienated, disbelieving Arabs, who were arrogant and defiantly determined to worship idols and so Allah sent to them a man from among them, to call upon them to believe in Allah, Most High, and to sincerely devote their worship to Him alone. But they belied him, opposed him and belittled him, as a result of which, Allah seized them with the Seizing of the Almighty, (Who is) Most Able to carry out what he Wills.

When he commanded them to worship Allah, urged them to obey Him and seek forgiveness from Him and promised them that if they did so, they would receive a goodly reward in the life of this world and in the Hereafter, while threatening them with punishment in the life of this world and in the Hereafter, should they violate these injunctions, ﴾ The leaders of those who disbelieved among his people said, "Verily, we see you in foolishness," ﴿ (*Soorah Al-A'raf* 7:66) That is, this thing to which you call us is foolishness in comparison with our worship of these idols, from which we seek victory and sustenance. And in addition to this, we believe that you are lying in your claim to be a Messenger sent by Allah.

﴾ (Hood) said, "O, my people! There is no foolishness in me, but (I am) a Messenger from the Lord of the *'Alameen* (mankind, jinn and all that exists)!. ﴿ (*Soorah Al-A'raf* 7:67) That is, the matter is not as you think, nor as you believe: ﴾ "I convey unto you the Messages of my Lord, and I am a trustworthy adviser (or well-wisher) to you." ﴿ (*Soorah Al-A'raf* 7:68) And conveying the Message requires that the conveyor be free from untruthfulness and that he makes no addition, nor any omission when delivering the Message. His delivery of the Message must also be eloquent, succinct, comprehensive and unarguable, and contain no ambiguity, no contradiction and no confusion.

But in spite of his delivery of the Message in this manner and his advising his people to the utmost of his ability – and in spite of his compassion toward them and his intense desire that they be guided – he did not seek any reward or payment from them, rather, he devoted himself sincerely to Allah in his call to (believe in) Him and his advice to His creation. He only sought recompense from the One Who sent him. This is because the good things in this life and in the Hereafter are in Allah's Hands and at His Command; that is why he said, ‹ "O, my people! I ask of you no reward for it (the Message). My reward is only from Him Who created me. Will you not then understand?" › (*Soorah Hood* 11:51) That is, you have no minds with which to distinguish (truth from error) and understand that I am inviting you to the clear truth to which your innate nature – in which He created you – bears witness; and that is the Religion of truth, with which Allah sent Nooh صلى الله عليه وسلم and He destroyed those who opposed him. Now I am calling you to (believe in) Him and I do not ask any reward from you for it. Rather, I seek that from Allah, in Whose Hand is harm and benefit and this is why a Believer said in *Soorah Ya Seen*, ‹ "Obey those who ask no wages of you (for themselves), and who are rightly guided. And why should I not worship Him (Allah, Alone), Who has created me and to Whom you shall be returned." › (*Soorah Ya Seen* 36:21,22)

Among the things that the people of Hood صلى الله عليه وسلم said to him was, ‹ "O, Hood! No evidence have you brought us, and we shall not leave our gods for your (mere) saying! And we are not believers in you. All that we say is that some of our gods (deities) have seized you with evil (madness)." He said, "I call Allah to witness and bear you witness that I am free from that which you ascribe as partners in worship." › (*Soorah Hood* 11:53,54) That is, you have not produced any supernatural miracle which would bear witness for you of the truth of what you have brought. And we are not a people who will abandon the worship of our idols simply because on your words, when you have brought no proof. We do not think that you are anything but an insane person in what you claim. You have only been seized with this (madness) because some of our deities have become angry with you and afflicted your mind with madness. That is apparent from their words: ‹ All that we say is that some of our gods (deities) have seized you with evil (madness)." He said, "I call Allah to witness and bear you witness that I am free from that which you ascribe as partners in worship with Him (Allah). So plot against me, all of you, and give me no respite." ❭ (*Soorah Hood* 11:54,55) This was a challenge from him to them, a declaration of his innocence of any complicity in the worship of their idols and a statement of his contempt for them. It is also a clear assertion that they can neither benefit nor harm and that they are simply inanimate objects. If they can, as you claim, help, benefit and harm, then here I stand, declaring myself innocent of them and cursing them: ❴ "So plot against me, all of you, and give me no respite." ❵ (*Soorah Hood* 11:55) That is, you people and your idols together, with all of the resources at your disposal and all of the power at your command, do not grant me a respite of a single hour, or even the blink of an eye, because I do not care about you and I do not even think of you, nor even look at you. ❴ "I put my trust in Allah, my Lord and your Lord! There is not a moving (living) creature but He has grasp of its forelock. Verily, my Lord is on the Straight Path (the truth)." ❵ (*Soorah Hood* 11:56) That is, I put my faith and trust in Allah and I am supported by Him and confident of His Protection, which does not misguide those who seek it and have trust in it. So I do not care about any creature besides Him and I do not put my trust in anyone but Him, and I do not worship anyone besides him.

This alone is a decisive proof that Hood ﷺ was the slave of Allah and His Messenger; the people were ignorant and astray in their worship of other than Allah because they were unable to inflict any harm on him and this proves the truthfulness of what he brought to them and the falsity of what they followed and the immorality of their beliefs. It is precisely this evidence which Nooh ﷺ cited before him in His Words, ❴ And recite to them the news of Nooh, when he said to his people, "O my people, if my stay (with you) and my reminding (you) of the *Ayat* of Allah is hard on you, then I put my trust in Allah. So devise your plot, you and your partners, and let not your plot be in doubt for you. Then pass your sentence on me and give me no respite." ﴿ (*Soorah Yoonus* 10:71) He, Most High, says, ﴾ And the chiefs of his people, who disbelieved and denied the Meeting in the Hereafter, and to whom We had given the luxuries and comforts of this life, said, "He is no more than a human being like you, he eats of that which you eat and drinks of what you drink. If you were to obey a human being like yourselves, then verily, you indeed would be losers. Does he promise you that when you have died and have become dust and bones, you shall come out alive (resurrected)?" ﴿ (*Soorah Al-Mu'minoon* 23:33-35) They thought that the idea that Allah would send a Messenger was far-fetched and this specious argument was offered by many ignorant disbelievers in the past and present, as Allah, Most High, says, ﴾ Is it wonder for mankind that We have sent Our Inspiration to a man from among themselves (i.e. Prophet Muhammad ﷺ) (saying): "Warn mankind (of the coming torment in Hell)." ﴿ (*Soorah Yoonus* 10:2). This is why Hood علیه السلام said to his people, ﴾ "Do you wonder that there has come to you a Reminder from your Lord through a man from amongst you, that he may warn you, so that you may fear Allah and that you may receive (His) Mercy?" ﴿ (*Soorah Al-A'raf* 7:63). That is, it is not surprising, because Allah, Most High knows better regarding the selection of His Messengers.

He, Most High, says, ﴾ Does he promise you that when you have died and have become dust and bones, you shall come out alive (resurrected)? Far, very far is that which you are promised. There is nothing but our life of this world! We die and we live! And we are not going to be resurrected! He is only a man who has invented a lie against Allah, but we are not going to believe in him." 》 (*Soorah Al-Mu'minoon* 23:35-38). They expressed their belief that the promised Resurrection is far in the future and they rejected the idea that their bodies could be resurrected after they had become dust and bones. They said, "Far, far away is this promise. 〈 "There is nothing but our life of this world! We die and we live! And we are not going to be resurrected!" 》 (*Soorah Al-Mu'minoon* 23:37) That is, a people die and another people are born. This was the belief of the *Dahriyyah*, [1] as some of the ignorant people among the *zanadiqah* [2] say, "The wombs deliver and the earth swallows."

And he said to them, with regard to that concerning which he had warned them, 〈 "Do you build high palaces on every high place, while you do not live in them? And do you get for yourselves *masani'* (fine buildings) as if you will live therein for ever?" 》 (*Soorah Ash-Shu'ara'* 26:128,129) That is, do you build in every elevated place great and magnificent buildings, such as palaces and the like, building them for frivolous reasons, though you have no need of them? This was because they used to live in tents, as Allah, Most High, says, 〈 Did you (O, Muhammad,) not see (think) how your Lord dealt with 'Ad (people) of Iram, with lofty poles, the like of which were not created in the land? And (with) Thamood (people), who cut (hewed) out rocks in the valley (to make dwellings)? 》 (*Soorah Al-Fajr* 89:6-9) So 'Ad of Iram were the first 'Ad who used to live under huge poles, which supported their tents.

He, Most High, says, 〈 "And do you get for yourselves

---

(1) *Dahriyyah*: The belief that there is nothing save this abode in which one person passes away only to be replaced by another, and there is no Resurrection or Judgment. This was the view of the pagan Arabs who rejected the Resurrection.

(2) *Zanadiqah*: (sing. *zindeeq*) Atheists, freethinkers.

masani?" ❯ (*Soorah Ash-Shu'ara'* 26:129) It was said that *masani'* means palaces. It was said that it means pigeon towers. It is also said that it means water sources.

❮ "As if you will live therein for ever." ❯ (*Soorah Ash-Shu'ara'* 26:129) That is, it is your hope that you will abide in this earthly abode for a long time. ❮ "And when you seize, seize you as tyrants? So fear Allah, keep your duty to Him, and obey me. And keep your duty to Him, fear Him Who has aided you with all (good things) that you know. He has aided you with cattle and children and gardens and springs. Verily, I fear for you the punishment of a Great Day." ❯ (*Soorah Ash-Shu'ara'* 26:130-135).

Among the things they said to him was, ❮ "Have you come to us that we should worship Allah Alone and forsake that which our fathers used to worship. So bring us that wherewith you have threatened us if you are of the truthful." ❯ (*Soorah Al-A'raf* 7:70) That is, have you come to us (to ask us) to worship Allah, Alone, and to oppose our fathers and our forefathers and that which they followed? If you are truthful regarding what you have brought, then bring us the punishment that you promise, because we do not believe in you, we will not follow you and we do not believe you. As they said, ❮ "It is the same to us whether you preach or be not of those who preach. This is no more than the false tales and religion of the ancients, and we are not going to be punished." ❯ (*Soorah Ash-Shu'ara'* 26:136-138) The word in Verse 137 has been recited as *khalq* and *khuluq*. According to the former recitation, the meaning would be: What you have brought to us is no more than fabrication from you; and you have taken it from the books of the ancients. This was how it was explained by more than one of the Companions ﷺ and the *Tabi'oon*. And according to the second recitation, the meaning would be: This religion which we are following is no more than the religion of our fathers and our grandfathers and we will not change and we will continue to hold fast to it.

Both recitations are suited to their words, ❨ "and we are not going to be punished." ❩ (*Soorah Ash-Shu'ara'* 26:138)

He, Most High, says, ❨ (Hood) said, "Punishment and Wrath have already fallen on you from your Lord. Dispute you with me over names which you have named - you and your fathers, with no authority from Allah? Then wait, I am with you among those who wait." ❩ (*Soorah Al-A'raf* 7:71) That is, you have deserved because of these words ignominy and Anger from Allah; do you reject worship of Allah, Alone, without partners, in favor of the worship of idols, which you have carved out and called "gods" of your own accord and agreed upon – you and your forefathers – and Allah has revealed no authority for them? That is, He has sent down no evidence for your beliefs. If you refuse to accept the truth and insist on falsehood, it is all the same to you whether I forbid you to follow what you are following or not. So wait now for the Punishment of Allah which will befall you and that Punishment cannot be rescinded or prevented.

Allah, Most High, mentioned the story of their destruction in detail and in brief, as we said earlier, such as in His Words, ❨ So We saved him and those who were with him by a Mercy from Us, and We cut the roots of those who belied Our *Ayat* and they were not believers. ❩ (*Soorah Al-A'raf* 7:72)

His Words, ❨ And when Our Commandment came, We saved Hood and those who believed with him by a Mercy from Us, and We saved them from a severe punisment. Such were 'Ad (people). They rejected the *Ayat* of their Lord and disobeyed

His Messengers, and followed the command of every proud obstinate (oppressor of the truth, from their leaders). And they were pursued by a curse in this world and (so they will be) on the Day of Resurrection. No doubt! Verily, 'Ad disbelieved in their Lord. So away with 'Ad, the people of Hood. ❭ (*Soorah Hood* 11:58-60)

His Words, ❮ So *As-Saihah* (punishment - awful cry, etc.) overtook them with justice, and We made them as rubbish of dead plants. They said. The people of Salih were destroyed with awful cry ❭ (*Soorah Al-Mu'minoon* 23:41)

As for the details of their destruction, when Allah said, ❮ Then, when they saw it as a dense cloud coming towards their valleys, they said, "This is a cloud bringing us rain!" Nay, but it is that (punishment) which you were asking to be hastened! A wind wherein is a painful punishment! ❭ (*Soorah Al-Ahqaf* 46:24) – this was the beginning of the punishment which came to them, for they were suffering from a drought and so they requested rain (from their idols). They saw a cloud in the sky and thought that it was a rain of mercy (for them), but it was a deluge of punishment. This is why He, Most High, says, ❮ Nay, but it is that (punishment) which you were asking to be hastened! A wind wherein is a painful punishment! ❭ (*Soorah Al-Ahqaf* 46:24) That is, from the infliction of the Punishment and that is their saying, ❮ "So bring us that wherewith you have threatened us if you are of the truthful." ❭ (*Soorah Al-A'raf* 7:70) And there are other similar Verses in *Soorah Al-A'raf.*

He (Muhammad bin Ishaq bin Yasar) said, "And Allah sent the black cloud which Qail Ibn 'Itr chose (according to the *hadeeth* narrated by Imam Ahmad, on the authority of Al-Harith Al-Bakri), with the punishment it contained to 'Ad until it reached them at a valley known as Al-Mugheeth. When they saw it, they regarded it as a good sign and they said, "This is a cloud which will bring rain to us. But Allah said, ❨ Nay, but it is that (punishment) which you were asking to be hastened! A wind wherein is a painful punishment! Destroying everything by the Command of its Lord! So they became such that nothing could be seen except their dwellings! Thus do We recompense the people who are *Mujrimoon* (polytheists, disbelievers, sinners, etc.)! ❩ (*Soorah Al-Ahqaf* 46:24,25) That is, it destroys everything that it is commanded to destroy.

Muhammad Ibn Ishaq said, "The first person who saw it and realized that it was a wind was a woman from 'Ad, whose name was Mahd. When it became clear what was in it, she screamed and then fainted. When she regained consciousness, the people asked her, "What did you see, Mahd?" She said, "I saw a wind in it, like burning flames and in front of it were men, leading it. Allah imposed it on them ❨ for seven nights and eight days in succession ❩ (*Soorah Al-Haqqah* 69:7). It did not leave a single person from 'Ad alive." He (Ibn Ishaq) said, "Hood عليه السلام and those who believed in him were in an enclosed area. Nothing hit them or those with them except that which was gentle to the skin and pleasing to the soul. The wind passed over 'Ad, destroying all that was between the heaven and the earth and marking them with stones." Then he reported the rest of the story.

Imam Ahmad narrated a *hadeeth* in his *Musnad* on the authority of Al-Harith (i.e. Ibn Hassan, or it was said, Ibn Yazeed Al-Bakri) which resembles this story; he said, "I set out to complain to the Messenger of Allah ﷺ about Al-'Ala' Ibn Al-Hadrami and I passed by Ar-Rabazah, where I saw an old woman from Banu Tameem, who was alone in that area. She said to me, 'O, slave of Allah! I need to reach the Messenger of Allah to ask him for some of my needs, will you take me to him?' So I took her along with me to Al-Madinah and found the Mosque full of people. I also found a black flag raised high, while Bilal was holding a sword before the Messenger of Allah. I asked, 'What is the matter with the people?' They said, 'The Prophet 繁 intends to send 'Amr Ibn Al-'As (on a military expedition) somewhere.' So I sat down. When the Prophet 繁 went to his house, I asked for permission to see him, and he gave me permission. I entered and greeted him. He said, 'Was there a dispute between you and Banu Tameem?' I said, 'Yes. And we had been victorious over them. I passed by an old woman from Banu Tameem, who was alone, and she asked me to bring her to you, and she is at the door.' So he allowed her in and I said, 'O Messenger of Allah! What if you make a barrier between us and (the tribe of) Banu Tameem, such as the desert?' The old woman became angry and opposed me. So I said, 'My example is the example of a sheep that carried its own destruction. I carried this woman and did not know that she was an opponent. I seek refuge with Allah and His Messenger that I become like the emissary of 'Ad.' So the Prophet 繁 asked me about the emissary of 'Ad, having better knowledge in it, but he liked to hear the story again. I said, 'Once, 'Ad suffered from a famine and they sent an emissary (to get relief), whose name was Qail. Qail passed by Mu'awiyah Ibn Bakr and stayed with him for a month. Mu'awiyah supplied him with alcoholic drinks, and two female singers were singing for him. When the month ended, Qail went to the mountains of Tihamah and said, 'O, Allah! You know that I did not come here to cure an ill person or to ransom a prisoner. O, Allah! Give 'Ad water as You used to.' So black clouds came and he was called, 'Choose which one of them you wish (to go to 'Ad)!' So he pointed to one of the black clouds and he heard someone proclaiming from it,

'Take it, as ashes that will leave none in 'Ad!" And it has been
conveyed to me that the wind sent to them was no more than
what would pass through this ring of mine, but it destroyed
them'." Abu Wa'il said, "That is true. When a man or a woman
would send an emissary, they would tell him, 'Do not be like
the emissary of 'Ad (bringing disaster and utter destruction to
them instead of relief).' [1] At-Tirmidhi recorded it thus on the
authority of 'Abd Ibn Humaid, who narrated it on the authority
of Zaid Ibn Al-Hubab. [2]

'Abdullah Ibn Mas'ood, 'Abdullah Ibn 'Abbas (may Allah
be pleased with them both) and more than one *Imam* from
among the *Tabi'oon* said that it was a cold wind, which blew
severely. ﴾ Which Allah imposed on them for seven nights and
eight days in succession. ﴿ (*Soorah Al-Haqqah* 69:7) That is,
complete and successive days. It was said that the first of them
was a Friday and it was also said that it was a Wednesday. ﴾
So that you could see men lying overthrown (destroyed), as if
they were hollow trunks of date-palms! ﴿ (*Soorah Al-Haqqah*
69:7) Allah compared them with hollowed out trunks of date-
palms, which have no heads and this was because the wind
would come to one of them and pick him up and raise him into
the air, then it would invert him and drop him on the top of his
head and shatter it and he would remain like a body without
a head, as Allah, Most High, says, ﴾ Verily, We sent against
them a furious wind of harsh voice on a day of evil omen and
continuous calamity. ﴿ (*Soorah Al-Qamar* 54:19) That is, on a
day of evil omen for you and continuous punishment inflicted
upon you. ﴾ Plucking out men as if they were uprooted stems of
date-palms. ﴿ (*Soorah Al-Qamar* 54:20) Whoever says that the
day of evil omen and continuous calamity was a Wednesday

---

(1)   This *hadeeth* is *hasan* and it was narrated by Imam Ahmad (15524).

(2)   This *hadeeth* is *hasan* and it was narrated by At-Tirmidhi (3273).

and based on this understanding, consider it to be a day of evil omen, is in error and contradicted the Qur'an, because He, Most High says in another Verse, ❨ So We sent upon them furious wind in days of evil omen. ❩ (*Soorah Fussilat* 41:16) It is well known that they were eight consecutive days; and if they were themselves evil omens, then all of the seven days of the week included in them would be days of evil omen – and no one says this. What is meant is that they were days of evil omen for them.

He, Most High, says, ❨ And in 'Ad (there is also a sign) when We sent against them the barren wind. ❩ (*Soorah Adh-Dhariyat* 51:41) That is, which did not produce any good, because the wind alone does not scatter clouds or pollinate trees. Rather, it is barren and no good results from it, which is why Allah says, ❨ It spared nothing that it reached, but blew it into broken spreads of rotten ruins. ❩ (*Soorah Ad-Dhariyat* 51:42) That is, like a thing that is decayed and very old and from which no benefit whatsoever may be derived.

It has been confirmed in the *Saheehain* on the authority of 'Abdullah Ibn 'Abbas ﷺ that he reported from the Prophet ﷺ that he said, "I have been made victorious with the *Saba* (easterly wind), and the people of 'Ad were destroyed with the *Daboor* (westerly wind)." [1]

As for the Words of Him, Most High: ❨ And remember the brother of 'Ad, when he warned his people in *Al-Ahqaf* (the curved sand-hills in the southern part of the Arabian Peninsula). And surely, there have passed away warners before him and after him (saying): "Worship none but Allah; truly, I fear for you the punishment of a mighty Day." ❩ (*Soorah Al-Ahqaf* 46:21) So it is apparent that the 'Ad referred to here is the first

---

(1)   Narrated by Al-Bukhari (1035) and Muslim (900).

'Ad, because the context of the Verse is similar to the context of (the story of) the people of Hood عليه السلام and they were the first. It is also possible that the people mentioned in this story were the second 'Ad; and the evidence for this is in what we have mentioned and what we shall mention later in the *hadeeth* of 'A'ishah (may Allah be pleased with her).

As for the Words of Him, Most High: ❨ Then, when they saw it as a dense cloud coming toward their valleys, they said, "This is a cloud bringing us rain." ❩ (*Soorah Al-Ahqaf* 46:24), when 'Ad saw the cloud which was looming up in the sky, like a rain cloud, they thought that it was bringing them rain, but it was a cloud of punishment which they mistook for a cloud of mercy. They hoped that they would get something good from it, but they received the utmost evil from it. Allah, Most High, says, ❨ Nay, but it is that which you were asking to be hastened! ❩ (*Soorah Al-Ahqaf* 46:24). That is, the punishment; then He explained it in His Words: ❨ a wind wherein is a painful punishment. ❩ (*Soorah Al-Ahqaf* 46:24)

It is possible that the punishment which afflicted them from the furious and violent wind, which continued to afflict them for seven nights and eight days leaving not a single one of them, followed them even as they sought shelter in mountain caves and caverns, winding around them, expelling them, annihilating them and destroying their sturdily constructed houses and palaces over them. Just as they had been blessed with strength and power and said, "Who is greater in strength than we?" – Allah inflicted on them that which was greater in strength and more powerful than they – and that was the barren wind. It is possible that at the end, this wind raised up a cloud, which those who remained, thought was a cloud bearing mercy and abundant rain for them. But Allah sent it against them filled with sparks and fire, as more than one person has mentioned. This would be similar to that which afflicted the Companions of the Canopy from among the people of Madyan. A combination of a cold wind and a punishment of fire was inflicted on them – and that is the most severe punishment, consisting of different and opposing elements, accompanied by the cry which was mentioned in *Soorah Qad Aflaha* (*Soorah Al-Mu'minoon*). And Allah knows better. The apparent meaning of the Verse is that they saw an *'aridh* and what is understood from it linguistically is a cloud. Muslim narrated in his *Saheeh* on the authority of 'A'ishah (may Allah be pleased with her) that she said: Whenever the wind was stormy, the Messenger of Allah 🕊️ used to say: "O, Allah! I ask You for what is good in it, the good which it contains and the good of that which it was sent for. I seek refuge with You from what is evil in it, what evil it contains, and the evil of that which it was sent for." And when there was thunder and lightning in the sky, his color underwent a change, and he would pace in and out, backward and forward; and when the rain came, he felt relieved, and I would notice the (sign of relief) on his face. 'A'ishah (may Allah be pleased with her) asked him (about it) and he said, "It may be as the people of 'Ad said, when they saw a cloud formation coming to their valley, ﴾ "This is a cloud bringing us rain." ﴿ (*Soorah Al-Ahqaf* 46:24) [1]

---

(1)   Narrated by Muslim (899).

The Story of Saleh عليه السلام *, the Prophet of Thamood*

They were a well-known tribe, who were named Thamood after their ancestor, Thamood, the brother of Jadees; they were both sons of 'Abir, son of Iram, son of Sam, son of Nooh. They were Arabs from Al-'Aribah and they lived in Al-Hijr, which lies between Al-Hijaz and Tabook. The Messenger of Allah ﷺ passed by it [1] when he was going to Tabook with some of the Muslims, as we shall explain later. They came after the people of 'Ad and like them, they used to worship idols. So Allah sent to them a man from among them who was Allah's slave and Messenger: Saleh, son of 'Ubaid, son of Masikh, son of 'Ubaid, son of Hajir, son of Thamood, son of 'Abir, son

---

(1) Narrated by Al-Bukhari (3380), Muslim (2980) and Imam Ahmad (4547), on the authority of 'Abdullah Ibn 'Umar ﷺ.

of Iram, son of Sam, son of Nooh. He called upon them to worship Allah, Alone, without partners and to renounce their idols and rivals (to Allah); he called upon them not to ascribe any partners to Him. A group of them believed in him, but the majority of them disbelieved in him and attacked him, both physically and verbally and they tried to kill him. They killed the camel which Allah had made as a proof against them, Allah seized them with the Seizing of the Almighty, as He, Most High says in *Soorah Al-A'raf,* ❨ And to Thamood (people, We sent) their brother Salih. He said, "O, my people! Worship Allah! You have no other *ilah* (god) but Him. (*La ilaha Illallah*: none has the right to be worshipped but Allah). Indeed there has come to you a clear sign (the miracle of the coming out of a huge she-camel from the midst of a rock) from your Lord. This she-camel of Allah is a sign unto you; so you leave her to graze in Allah's earth, and touch her not with harm, lest a painful punishment should seize you. And remember when He made you successors after 'Ad (people) and gave you habitations in the land, you build for yourselves palaces in plains, and carve out homes in the mountains. So remember the graces (bestowed upon you) from Allah, and do not go about making mischief on the earth." The leaders of those who were arrogant among his people said to those who were counted weak - to such of them as believed, "Know you that Salih is one sent from his Lord?" They said, "We indeed believe in that with which he has been sent." Those who were arrogant said, "Verily, we disbelieve in that which you believe in." So they killed the she-camel and insolently defied the Commandment of their Lord and said, "O, Salih! Bring about your threats if you are indeed one of the Messengers (of Allah)." So the earthquake seized them and they lay (dead), prostrate in their homes. Then he (Salih) turned from them and said, "O, my people!

I have indeed conveyed to you the Message of my Lord, and have given you good advice but you like not good advisers." ﴿ (*Soorah Al-A'raf* 7:73-74). He, Most High, says in *Soorah Hood*, ﴾ And to Thamood (people, We sent) their brother Salih. He said, "O, my people! Worship Allah, you have no other *ilah* (god) but Him. He brought you forth from the earth and settled you therein, then ask forgiveness of Him and turn to Him in repentance. Certainly, my Lord is Near (to all by His Knowledge), Responsive." They said, "O, Salih! You have been among us as a figure of good hope (and we wished for you to be our chief), till this (new thing which you have brought; that we leave our gods and worship your God [Allah] Alone)! Do you (now) forbid us from the worship of what our fathers have worshipped? But we are really in grave doubt as to that which you invite us to (monotheism)." He said, "O, my people! Tell me, if I have a clear proof from my Lord, and there has come to me a Mercy (Prophethood, etc.) from Him, who then can help me against Allah, if I were to disobey Him? Then you increase me not but in loss. And O, my people! This she-camel of Allah is a sign to you, leave her to feed on Allah's earth, and touch her not with evil intention, lest a near torment will seize you." But they killed her. So he said, "Enjoy yourselves in your homes for three days. This is a promise (i.e. a threat) that will not be belied." So when Our Commandment came, We saved Salih and those who believed with him by a Mercy from Us, and from the disgrace of that Day. Verily, your Lord, He is the Strong, the Almighty. And *As-Saihah* (torment - awful cry, etc.) overtook the wrongdoers, so they lay (dead), prostrate in their homes, as if they had never lived there. No doubt! Verily, Thamood disbelieved in their Lord. So away with Thamood! ﴿ (*Soorah Hood* 11:61-68)

He, Most High, says in *Soorah Ash-Shu'ara'*, ﴾ Thamood

(people) belied the Messenger. When their brother Salih said to them: "Will you not fear Allah and obey Him? I am a trustworthy Messenger to you. So fear Allah, keep your duty to Him, and obey me. No reward do I ask of you for it (my Message of Islamic Monotheism), my reward is only from the Lord of the *'Alameen*. Will you be left secure in that which you have here? In gardens and springs and green crops (fields, etc.) and date-palms with soft spadix. And you carve houses out of mountains with great skill. So fear Allah, keep your duty to Him, and obey me. And follow not the command of *al-musrifoon* (i.e. their chiefs, leaders who were polytheists, criminals and sinners), who make mischief in the land, and reform not." They said, "You are only of those bewitched! You are but a human being like us. Then bring us a sign if you are of the truthful." He said, "Here is a she-camel; it has a right to drink (water), and you have a right to drink (water) (each) on a day, known. And touch her not with harm, lest the punishment of a Great Day seize you." But they killed her and then they became regretful. So the punishment overtook them. Verily, in this is indeed a sign, yet most of them are not believers. And verily! Your Lord, He is indeed the Almighty, the Most Merciful. ﴾ (*Soorah Ash-Shu'ara'* 26:141-159)

Allah frequently links in His Book the mention of 'Ad with that of Thamood, as in *Soorah Bara'ah* (*Soorah At-Tawbah*), *Soorah Ibraheem*, *Soorah Al-Furqan*, *Soorah Sad*, *Soorah Qaf*, *Soorah An-Najm* and *Soorah Al-Fajr*. It is said that the story of these two nations is not known to the People of the Scripture and that they were not mentioned in their Scripture, the Torah. But in the Qur'an there is evidence that Moosa ﷺ informed his people about them, as Allah says in *Soorah Ibraheem*, ﴾ And Moosa (Moses) said, "If you disbelieve, you and all on earth together, then verily, Allah is Rich (Free of all wants), Owner of all Praise. Has not the news reached you, of those before you, the people of Nooh, and 'Ad and Thamood? And those after them? None knows them but Allah. To them came their Messengers with clear proofs, but they put their hands in their mouths (biting them from anger) and said, Verily, we disbelieve in that with which you have been sent, and we are really in grave doubt as to that to which you invite us (i.e. Islamic Monotheism)." ⟫ (*Soorah Ibraheem* 14:8,9). It is apparent that these words are entirely those of Moosa ﷺ, which he addressed to his people. But because these two nations were from among the Arabs, their stories were not well documented and no attempt was made to record them, although they were well-known during the time of Moosa ﷺ. We have spoken in detail concerning all of this in the *Tafseer;* all praise and thanks be to Allah, from Whom proceeds all Grace.

What is intended now is to mention their story and their circumstances and how Allah saved His Prophet, Saleh ﷺ, and those who believed in him, and how He eradicated those who were guilty of injustice because of their disbelief, their arrogance and the opposition they displayed to their Messenger, Saleh ﷺ. We have already mentioned that they were Arabs and that they came after the people of 'Ad, but they did not pay heed to what had befallen them. This is why Saleh ﷺ said to them, ⟪ And to Thamood (people, We sent) their brother Salih. He said, "O, my people! Worship Allah! You have no other *ilah* (god) but Him. (*La ilaha Illallah*: none has the right to be worshipped but Allah). Indeed there has come to you a clear sign (the miracle of the coming out of a huge she-camel from the midst of a rock) from your Lord. This she-camel of Allah is a sign unto you; so you leave her to graze in Allah's earth, and touch her not with harm, lest a painful punishment should seize you. And remember when He made you successors after 'Ad (people) and gave you habitations in the land, you build for yourselves palaces in plains, and carve out homes in the mountains. So remember the graces (bestowed upon you) from Allah, and do not go about making mischief on the Earth." 》 (*Soorah Al-A'raf* 7:73,74) That is, He has only made you successors after them in order that you might pay heed to their fate and act in a manner contrary to their actions. He has permitted to you these lands, allowing you to build palaces in their plains. 《 "And you carve houses out of mountains with great skill." 》 (*Soorah Ash-Shu'ara'* 26:149) That is, you are proficient in building them, perfecting them and precisely executing (the building of) them, so respond to Allah's Blessing with gratitude, righteous deeds and worship Him, Alone, without ascribing partners to Him. Beware of opposing Him and refraining from His obedience, because the punishment for that is an evil one. This is why he warned them, saying, 《 "Will you be left secure in that which you have here, in gardens and springs and green crops (fields etc.) and date-palms with soft spadix?" 》 (*Soorah Ash-Shu'ara'* 26:146-148) That is, your provisions are numerous, luxurious and ripe. 《 "And you carve houses out of mountains with great skill. So fear Allah, keep your duty to Him, and obey me. And follow not the command of *al-musrifeen* (i.e. their chiefs, leaders who were polytheists, criminals and sinners), who make mischief in the land, and reform not." 》 (*Soorah Ash-Shu'ara'* 26:149-152). He also said to them, 《 "O, my people! Worship Allah, you have no other *ilah* (god) but Him. He brought you forth from the earth and settled you therein." 》 (*Soorah Hood* 11:61) That is, it is He Who created you and brought you forth from the earth and made you to populate it (i.e. He gave it to you, with all that it contains, such as crops and fruits), for He is the Creator and the Sustainer and it is He, Alone, without partners,

Who has the right to be worshipped. ❨ "Then ask forgiveness of Him and turn to Him in repentance." ❩ (*Soorah Hood* 11:61) That is, desist from what you now follow, and engage in worship of Allah, Alone, because He will accept it from you and pardon you for your sins. ❨ And to Thamood (people, We sent) their brother Salih. He said, "Oh, my people! Worship Allah, you have no other *ilah* (god) but Him. He brought you forth from the earth and settled you therein, then ask forgiveness of Him and turn to Him in repentance. Certainly, my Lord is Near (to all by His Knowledge), Responsive." They said, "O, Salih! You have been among us as a figure of good hope (and we wished for you to be our chief), till this (new thing which you have brought; that we leave our gods and worship your God [Allah] Alone)!" ❩ (*Soorah Hood* 11:61,62) That is, we had hoped that your mind was unimpaired before you said these words, that is your invitation to us to worship Allah, Alone, without partners and to abandon the rivals that we used to worship and desist from following the religion of our fathers and our grandfathers. This is why they said, ❨ "Do you (now) forbid us from the worship of what our fathers have worshipped? But we are really in grave doubt as to that which you invite us to (Monotheism).' He said, 'O, my people! Tell me, if I have a clear proof from my Lord, and there has come to me a Mercy (Prophethood, etc.) from Him, who then can help me against Allah, if I were to disobey Him? Then you increase me not but in loss." ❩ (*Soorah Hood* 11:62,63)

This was kindness and gentleness from him to them in his mode of expression and a beautiful manner of inviting them to goodness. That is, what do you think, if the matter is as I tell you and I invite you to it, what will be your excuse to Allah? What will save you when you stand before Him, when you ask me to refrain from inviting you to obey Allah? I am unable to do this, because it is an obligation upon me and if I abandon it, then no one from among you or from any other people can protect me from Him or help me. So I will continue to call you to Allah, Alone, with partners, until Allah judges between me and you.

They also said to him, ❨ "You are only of the *musahharoon!*" ❩ (*Soorah Ash-Shu'ara'* 26:153) That is, you are bewitched and you do not know what you are saying in your invitation to us to worship Allah, Alone, and to abandon the worship of rivals to Him. The majority of scholars are agreed upon this understanding, i.e. that '*musahharoon*' means bewitched. But it was also said that ❨ "of the *musahharoon*" ❩ means those who have lungs. So it is as if they were saying, "You are only a human being, possessing lungs." But the first explanation is more apparent, because they said after that, ❨ "You are but a human being like us." ❩ (*Soorah Ash-Shu'ara'* 26:154) and they said, ❨ "Then bring us a sign if you are of the truthful." ❩ (*Soorah Ash-Shu'ara'* 26:154) They asked him to produce some miracle which would prove the truth of what he brought to them. ❨ He said, "Here is a she-camel; it has a right to drink (water), and you have a right to drink (water) (each) on a day, known. And touch her not with harm, lest the punishment of a Great Day seize you." ❩ (*Soorah Ash-Shu'ara'* 26:155,156)

Scholars of *tafseer* have reported that Thamood gathered one day in their meeting place and Saleh ﷺ came to them and invited them to Allah and he reminded them, warned them, admonished them and commanded them, but they said to him, "If you bring forth for us from this rock," and they indicated a rock there, "a she-camel of such-and-such a description…" and they described and named, and became stubborn regarding it, insisting that it be in the tenth month of pregnancy, that it be tall and possessed of this attribute and that attribute. Prophet Saleh ﷺ said to them, "If I do as you ask, in the manner you have requested, will you have faith in what I have brought and believe in that with which I have been sent?" They said, "Yes." So he took their covenant and their agreement on that. Then he went to a place of prayer and prayed to Allah, the Almighty, the All-Powerful as much as Allah had ordained for him, then he invoked his Lord, the Almighty, the All-Powerful, asking Him to give what they had asked for. So Allah, the Almighty, the All-Powerful commanded that rock to split open and produce a huge camel, with a great hump, which was in the tenth month of pregnancy, as they had requested, or in accordance with the description they had given. When they saw with their own eyes a great thing, an amazing sight, (Allah's) overwhelming Ability (to do all things) and an irrefutable proof, a large number of them believed, but most of them continued in their disbelief, error and obstinacy. This is why Allah says, ❴ but they did wrong by them (i.e. Allah's Signs) ❵ (*Soorah Al-A'raf* 7:103) That is, they (i.e. most of them) rejected them and did not follow the truth in spite of them.

This is why Saleh ﷺ said to them, ❴ "This she-camel of Allah is a Sign unto you." ❵ (*Soorah Al-A'raf* 7:73) He attributed it to Allah, as a term of honor and veneration, as in the expressions "the House of Allah" and "the slave of Allah". ❴ "A sign for you (Jews)." ❵ (*Soorah Ali 'Imran* 3:13) That is, evidence of the truth of what I have brought to you. ❴ "leave her to feed on Allah's earth, and touch her not with evil, lest a near punishment will seize you." ❵ (*Soorah Hood* 11:64) They agreed to let the she-camel remain among them, grazing wherever it wished from their land and drinking the water at fixed times. When it drank the water, it would consume the water of the well that day and they knew their need for water from one day to the next. It was said that they used to drink its milk and that it was sufficient for all of them, which is why he said, ❨ "It has a right to drink (water), and you have a right to drink (water) (each) on a day, known." ❩ (*Soorah Ash-Shu'ara'* 26:155) This is why Allah, Most High, said (to Saleh عليه السلام), ❨Verily, We are sending the she-camel as a test for them. ❩ (*Soorah Al-Qamar* 54:27) That is as a test to see whether they will believe or disbelieve. And Allah knew better what they would do. ❨ So watch them (Salih) ❩ (*Soorah Al-Qamar* 54:27) That is, see what they will do ❨ and be patient. ❩ (*Soorah Al-Qamar* 54:27) That is, in the face of the harm they inflict, because news will come to you for sure. ❨ And inform them that the water is to be shared between (her and) them. Each one's right to drink being established (by turns) ❩ (*Soorah Al-Qamar* 54:28) But when this state of affairs had lasted for a long time, their elders gathered and agreed that they would kill this she-camel in order to be free of it and have their water all to themselves, and Satan made their deeds seem fair to them. Allah says, ❨ So they killed the she-camel and insolently defied the Commandment of their Lord, and said, 'O, Salih ! Bring about your threats if you are indeed one of the Messengers (of Allah)." ❩ (*Soorah Al-A'raf* 7:77)

Imam Ahmad narrated on the authority of 'Abdullah Ibn Zam'ah ﷺ that he said, "The Messenger of Allah ﷺ delivered a sermon and he mentioned the she-camel and he named the person who killed it; he said, "❨ When the most wicked man among them went forth (to kill the she-camel) ❩ (*Soorah Ash-Shams* 91:12): A violent, strong and imposing man, who was a leader among his people, went forth to (kill) the she-camel."[1] Al-Bukhari and Muslim narrated it from the *hadeeth* of Hisham. [2]

---

(1)   An authentic *hadeeth* narrated by Imam Ahmad (15790).

(2)   Narrated by Al-Bukhari (4942) and Muslim (2855).

Allah, Most High, says, ❨ So they killed the she-camel and insolently defied the Commandment of their Lord, and said, "O, Salih! Bring about your threats if you are indeed one of the Messengers (of Allah)." ❩ (*Soorah Al-A'raf* 7:77) In these words of theirs they combined extreme disbelief in a number of ways: One being that they disobeyed Allah and His Messenger ﷺ by doing what they had been firmly forbidden to do, which was to kill the she-camel which Allah had made a Sign for them. Another was that they were impatient for the imposition of Allah's Punishment upon them and they deserved it for two reasons: One of them is that it was ordained upon them in His Words, ❨ "And touch her not with evil, lest a near punishment will seize you." ❩ (*Soorah Hood* 11:64)

In one verse Allah says, ❨ great ❩ (*Soorah Ash-Shu'ara'* 26:156) and in another Verse, He says, ❨ painful ❩ (*Soorah Al-A'raf* 7:73) and both of them are true. The second is their impatience for it. Another was that they belied the Messenger ﷺ who had produced the irrefutable evidence of his Prophethood and his truthfulness and they knew this with certainty. But their disbelief, their error and their willfulness caused them to disbelieve in the truth and the infliction of the punishment on them.

Allah, Most High, says, ❨ But they killed her. So he said: "Enjoy yourselves in your homes for three days. This is a promise (i.e. a threat) that will not be belied." ❩ (*Soorah Hood* 11:65) It was said that when they went to kill the she-camel, the first person to attack her was Qudar Ibn Salif – may Allah curse him – and he hamstrung her and she fell to the ground. Then they rushed upon her with their swords and cut her up. When its calf saw this, it fled from them and climbed the highest mountain there and it let out three cries. This is why Saleh ﷺ

said to them, ❨ Enjoy yourselves in your homes for three days. ❩ (*Soorah Hood* 11:65) That is, three days, not including that day. But they also did not believe this certain promise of his. Instead, in the evening of that day, they planned to kill him and so they went out to him, in order to kill him, like the she-camel. ❨ They said, "Swear one to another by Allah that we shall make a secret night attack on him and his household." ❩ (*Soorah An-Naml* 27:49) That is, we shall attack him in his home, along with his family and we shall surely kill him, then we shall deny any knowledge of his killing, if we are asked about it by his kin. This is why they said, ❨ "and afterward we will surely say to his near relatives: 'We witnessed not the destruction of his household, and verily! We are telling the truth." ❩ (*Soorah An-Naml* 27:49)

Allah, Most High, says, ❨ So they plotted a plot, and We planned a plan, while they perceived not. Then see how was the end of their plot! Verily, We destroyed them and their nation, all together. These are their houses in utter ruin, for they did wrong. Verily, in this is indeed an *Ayah* (a lesson or a sign) for people who know. And We saved those who believed, and used to fear Allah, and keep their duty to Him ❩ (*Soorah An-Naml* 27:50-53) This was because Allah, Most High, sent a rock against those people who had tried to kill Saleh ﷺ which crushed them and killed them in advance of the rest of their people.

❨ And they lay prostrate in their homes ❩ (*Soorah Al-A'raf* 7:78) That is, motionless corpses, without souls.

And Allah, Most High, says, ❨ As if they had never dwelt there. ❩ (*Soorah Al-A'raf* 7:92) That is, as if they had never lived in their homes in comfort, with sustenance and wealth.

❨ No doubt! Verily, Thamood disbelieved in their Lord. So away with Thamood! ❩ (*Soorah Hood* 11:68) That is, the voice of *Al-Qadar* called to them.

Imam Ahmad said: 'Abdur-Razzaq told me: Ma'mar told me: 'Abdullah Ibn 'Uthman Ibn Khuthaim reported on the authority of Abuz-Zubair, who reported on the authority of Jabir that he said: When the Messenger of Allah ﷺ passed by Al-Hijr, he said, "Do not ask for signs, because the people of Saleh asked for them and it (i.e. the camel) used to arrive by this path and return by this path, but they defied the command of their Lord and killed it. It used to drink their water on one day and they would drink its milk on that day (and they would drink the water on the following day). But they killed it and the Cry took them and Allah destroyed all of them except for one man who was in Allah's Sanctuary." They said, "Who was he, Messenger of Allah?" He said, "He was Abu Righal; and when he went out from the Sanctuary, that which had befallen his people also befell him." This *hadeeth* conforms to the criteria for acceptance stipulated by Muslim, but it is not in any of the Six Books. And 'Abdur-Razzaq also said: Ma'mar said: Isma'eel Ibn Umayyah ﷺ informed me that the Prophet ﷺ passed by the grave of Abu Righal and he said, "Do you know who this is?" They replied, "Allah and His Messenger know better." He said, "This is the grave of Abu Righal, a man from Thamood. He was in Allah's Sanctuary and the Sanctuary protected him from Allah's Punishment. But when he left it, that which had befallen his people also befell him and he was buried here. A branch of gold was also buried with him." So the people used their swords and looked for the golden branch and found it.

'Abdur-Razzaq said: Ma'mar said: Az-Zuhri said: 'Abu

Righal was the father of (the tribe of) Thaqeef. But this narration is *mursal* from this source. It has been reported from another source in a *muttasil* (connected) form, as mentioned by Muhammad Ibn Ishaq in his *Seerah*.

❨ Then he (Salih) turned from them and said: "O, my people! I have indeed conveyed to you the Message of my Lord, and have given you good advice but you like not good advisers." ❩ (*Soorah Al-A 'raf* 7:79) This informs us that Salih ﷺ addressed his people after the destruction had befallen them and he had taken his departure from their place and was heading elsewhere; and he said to them, ❨ "O, my people! I have indeed conveyed to you the Message of my Lord, and have given you good advice .❩ (*Soorah Al-A 'raf* 7:79) That is, I strove to the utmost of my ability to guide you and I endeavored to do so by my words, my actions and my (sincere) intention: ❨ "but you like not good advisers." ❩ (*Soorah Al-A 'raf* 7:79) That is, your nature could not accept the truth and did not desire it. And this is why you reached the situation you are now in: a painful and continuous punishment which will afflict you forever. I have no ability to repel it from you. What was incumbent upon me was to convey the Message and that I have done, exerting myself to the utmost to that end. But Allah does as He wills.

The Prophet's Passage Through Wadi Al-Hijr in the Land of Thamood in the Year of the Battle of Tabook

Imam Ahmad narrated on the authority of 'Abdullah Ibn 'Umar ﷺ that he said: When the Messenger of Allah ﷺ camped with the people on the road to Tabook, he camped with them at Al-Hijr, which was near to the houses of Thamood and the people sought water from the wells from which Thamood used to drink and they made dough from them and prepared their cooking pots to cook meat. But the Messenger of Allah ﷺ ordered them to pour out the contents of the cooking pots and give the dough to the camels. Then he moved on with them and he camped with them near the well from which the she-camel used to drink and he forbade them from entering the houses of the people who had been punished, saying, "I fear that you might be afflicted by what afflicted them, so do not enter their dwellings." [1]

Imam Ahmad also narrated on the authority of 'Abdullah Ibn 'Umar ☬ that he said: When the Messenger of Allah ﷺ was at Al-Hijr, he said, "Do not enter the dwellings of those people who were punished, unless you are weeping; and if you are not weeping, then do not enter their dwellings, so that you will not be afflicted by a punishment similar to that which afflicted them." [2] Al-Bukhari and Muslim narrated it in the *Saheehain* from more than one source. [3]

Imam Ahmad narrated on the authority of 'Amr Ibn Sa'd ☬ that he said: At the time of the Battle of Tabook, the people hastened to enter the houses of the people of Al-Hijr; the Messenger of Allah ﷺ was informed of this and he called to the people, "Pray in congregation." 'Amr ☬ said: So I went to the Prophet ﷺ and found him holding onto his camel and he was saying, "Do not enter the dwellings of a people upon whom Allah's Wrath was visited." A man called out to him, "We are amazed at them, Messenger of Allah!" He said, "Shall I not

---

(1)   This is an authentic *hadeeth* narrated by Imam Ahmad (2/117, No. 5948).

(2)   This is an authentic *hadeeth* narrated by Imam Ahmad (2/174, No. 5418).

(3)   Narrated by Al-Bukhari (433) and Muslim (2980).

inform you of something more amazing than that? A man from among you informs you about what occurred before you and what will be after you, so be straight and stand shoulder-to-shoulder, because Allah does not care about your punishment and a people will come who will not protect themselves from anything." The *isnad* of this *hadeeth* is *hasan*, [1] but they (the compilers of the Authentic Six [2]) did not narrate it.

---

(1) This *hadeeth* is *hasan*; it was narrated by Imam Ahmad (4/227, No. 17568).

(2) The Authentic Six: In Arabic *As-Sihah As-Sittah*; refers to the *hadeeth* compilations of Al-Bukhari, Muslim, Abu Dawood, At-Tirmidhi, Ibn Majah and An-Nasa'i.

The Story of Ibraheem ﷺ

He is Ibraheem, son of Tarikh, son of Nahoor, son of Saroog, son of Raghu, son of Falagh, son of 'Abir, son of Shalakh, son of Kan'an, son of Arfakhshad, son of Sam, son of Nooh ﷺ. This is the text of the People of the Scripture in their Scripture. I have marked their ages under their names in Indian numerals from Al-Mudad [1] and we have already spoken of Nooh's age and so there is no need to repeat it here. It was *Al-Khaleel* ﷺ who was saved by Allah from the evils and misguidance (of his people), for Allah gave him his integrity and right-conduct in his early years and sent him as a Messenger and He took him as a *Khaleel* (Friend) during his adult years. Allah, Most High, says, ❴ And indeed We bestowed aforetime on Ibraheem (Ibraheem) his (portion of) guidance, and We were Well-Acquainted with him (as to his Belief in the Oneness of Allah, etc.) ❵ *(Soorah Al-Anbiya'* 21:51) That is, he was well qualified for that.

He, Most High, says, ❴ And (remember) Ibraheem when he said to his people, "Worship Allah (Alone), and fear Him, that

---

(1) Al-Mudad: One of the descendants of Nooh, who settled in Arabia.

is better for you if you did but know. You worship besides Allah
only idols, and you only invent falsehood. Verily, those whom
you worship besides Allah have no power to give you provision,
so seek your provision from Allah (Alone), and worship Him
(Alone), and be grateful to Him. To Him (Alone) you will be
brought back. And if you deny, then nations before you have
denied (their Messengers). And the duty of the Messenger is
only to convey (the Message) plainly. See they not how Allah
originates creation, then repeats it. Verily, that is easy for Allah.
Say, "Travel in the land and see how (Allah) originated creation,
and then Allah will bring forth (resurrect) the creation of the
Hereafter (i.e. resurrection after death). Verily, Allah is Able to
do all things." He punishes whom He wills, and shows mercy
to whom He wills, and to Him you will be returned. And you
cannot escape in the earth or in the heaven. And besides Allah
you have neither any *waliyy* (protector or guardian) nor any
helper. And those who disbelieve in the *Ayat* of Allah and the
Meeting with Him, it is they who have no hope of My Mercy,
and it is they who will (have) a painful torment. So nothing
was the answer of (Ibraheem's) people except that they said,
"Kill him or burn him." Then Allah saved him from the fire.
Verily, in this are indeed signs for a people who believe. And
(Ibraheem) said, "You have taken (for worship) idols instead of
Allah, and the love between you is only in the life of this world,
but on the Day of Resurrection, you shall disown each other
and curse each other and your abode will be the Fire; and you
shall have no helper.' So Loot (Lot) believed in him (Ibraheem's
Message of Islamic Monotheism). He (Ibraheem) said, "I will
emigrate for the sake of my Lord. Verily, He is the Almighty,
the Most Wise." And We bestowed on him (Ibraheem) Ishaq
(Isaac) and Ya'qoob (Jacob), and ordained among his offspring
Prophethood and the Book (i.e. the Tawrah [Torah] to Moosa

– Moses), the *Injeel* [Gospel] to 'Eesa [Jesus], the Qur'an [to Muhammad ﷺ], all from the offspring of Ibraheem, and We granted him his reward in this world, and verily, in the Hereafter he is indeed among the righteous. ﴾ (*Soorah Al-'Ankaboot* 29:16-27)

Then Allah, Most High mentioned his disputes with his father and his people as we shall mention, if Allah, Most High, wills. The first person he called to Allah was his father, who was one of those who worshipped idols, because he was the person with most right to his advice, as Allah, Most High, says, ﴾ And mention in the Book (the Qur'an) Ibraheem. Verily! He was a man of truth, a Prophet. When he said to his father, "O, my father! Why do you worship that which hears not, sees not and cannot avail you in anything? O, my father! Verily! There has come to me of knowledge that which came not unto you. So follow me. I will guide you to a Straight Path. O, my father! Worship not *Shaitan* (Satan). Verily! *Shaitan* has been a rebel against the Most Beneficent (Allah). O, my father! Verily! I fear lest a torment from the Most Beneficent (Allah) overtake you, so that you become a companion of *Shaitan* (in the Hellfire). (*Tafseer Al-Qurtubi*) He (his father) said, "Do you reject my gods, o, Ibraheem? If you stop not (this), I will indeed stone you. So get away from me safely before I punish you." Ibraheem said, "Peace be on you! I will ask Forgiveness of my Lord for you. Verily! He is unto me Ever Most Gracious. And I shall turn away from you and from those whom you invoke besides Allah. And I shall call on my Lord; and I hope that I shall not be unblessed in my invocation to my Lord." ﴾ (*Soorah Maryam* 19:41-48)

Allah, Most High, mentions the dispute and the argument between him and his father and describes how he invited his father to the truth using the kindest and most courteous expressions and the best advice; he explained to him the invalidity of worshipping idols and the sin that he was incurring by worshipping graven images, which cannot hear the supplications of those who worship them and cannot see where they are. So how can they avail them anything or do any good for them, such as sustaining them or helping them?

Then, alluding to the guidance and beneficial knowledge that Allah had given him, though he was younger than his father, he said, ❨ "O, my father! Verily! There has come to me of knowledge that which came not unto you. So follow me. I will guide you to a Straight Path." ❩ (*Soorah Maryam* 19:43) That is, a straight, clear, easy and true path, which will lead you to goodness in your religion and in your Hereafter. But when he presented this guidance to him and gave him this advice, he did not accept it and he did not act upon it. Instead, he threatened him and warned him to desist, saying, ❨ "Do you reject my gods, O, Ibraheem? If you stop not (this), I will indeed stone you." ❩ (*Soorah Maryam* 19:46) It was said that the Arabic verb *rajama* used in the Verse means to revile or curse and it was also said that it means to stone. [1] ❨ "So get away from me safely." ❩ (*Soorah Maryam* 19:46) That is, sever the relationship with me and prolong the separation. When he said this, Ibraheem عليه السلام said, ❨ "Peace be on you!" ❩ (*Soorah Maryam* 19:46) That is, nothing unpleasant will come to you from me and no harm will be inflicted on you by me; on the contrary, you are safe from me.

He added more kindness by saying, ❨ "I will ask Forgiveness of my Lord for you. Verily! He is unto me, Ever Most Gracious." ❩ (*Soorah Maryam* 19:47) 'Abdullah Ibn 'Abbas رضي الله عنه and others said it means: He is Kind to me, in that He has guided me to worship Him and sincere devotion to Him and this is why he said, ❨ And I shall turn away from you and from those whom

_____

(1)   Both meanings are linguistically valid.

you invoke besides Allah. And I shall call on my Lord; and
I hope that I shall not be unblessed in my invocation to my
Lord." 》 (*Soorah Maryam* 19:48) Ibraheem عليه السلام had asked
Allah to forgive him in his supplications, as he had promised
that he would. But when it became clear to him that he was
an enemy of Allah, he declared himself innocent of him, as
Allah, Most High, says, 《 And Ibraheem's invoking (of Allah)
for his father's forgiveness was only because of a promise he
(Ibraheem) had made to him (his father). But when it became
clear to him (Ibraheem) that he (his father) was an enemy to
Allah, he dissociated himself from him. Verily, Ibraheem was
Al-Awwah. (It has fifteen different meanings but the correct one
seems to be that he used to invoke Allah with humility, glorify
Him and remember Him much), and was forbearing. (*Tafseer
Al-Qurtubi*) 》 (*Soorah At-Tawbah* 9:114)

Al-Bukhari narrated on the authority of Abu Hurairah رضي الله عنه
from the Prophet ﷺ that he said, "Ibraheem will meet his
father, Azar on the Day of Resurrection whose face will be
dark and covered with dust (and Prophet Ibraheem عليه السلام will say
to him), "Did I not tell you not to disobey me?" His father
will reply, "Today I will not disobey you." 'Ibraheem will say:
"O, my Lord! You promised to not disgrace me on the Day of
Resurrection; and what will be more disgraceful to me than
cursing and dishonoring my father?" Then Allah will say (to
him), "I have forbidden Paradise for the disbelievers." Then
he will be addressed, "O, Ibraheem! Look! What is underneath
your feet?" He will look and there he will see a *Dheekh* (hyena-
or an animal) blood-stained, which will be caught by the legs
and thrown in the (Hell) Fire." [1] And this is how he narrated it
in the story of Ibraheem عليه السلام separately.

---

[1]   Narrated by Al-Bukhari (3350).

Allah, Most High, said, ❴ And (remember) when Ibraheem said to his father, Azar, "Do you take idols as *alihah* (gods)? Verily, I see you and your people in manifest error." ❵ (*Soorah Al-An'am* 6:74) This proves that Ibraheem's father's name was Azar and the majority of those with knowledge of genealogy, including 'Abdullah Ibn 'Abbas ⁂, hold that his father's name was Tarikh, while the People of the Scripture call him Tarikh. It was said that he was nicknamed Azar, that being the name of an idol that he used to worship.

Allah, Most High, says, ❴ Thus did we show Ibraheem the kingdom of the heavens and the earth that he be one of those who have Faith with certainty. When the night covered him over with darkness he saw a star. He said, "This is my lord." But when it set, he said, "I like not those that set." When he saw the moon rising up, he said, "This is my lord." But when it set, he said: "Unless my Lord guides me, I shall surely be among the erring people." When he saw the sun rising up, he said, "This is my lord. This is greater." But when it set, he said, "O, my people! I am indeed free from all that you join as partners in worship with Allah. Verily, I have turned my face towards Him Who has created the heavens and the Earth *Hanifan* (Islamic Monotheism, i.e. worshipping none but Allah Alone) and I am not of *al-mushrikoon*. His people disputed with him. He said, "Do you dispute with me concerning Allah while He has guided me, and I fear not those whom you associate with Allah in worship. (Nothing can happen to me) except when my Lord (Allah) wills something. My Lord comprehends in His Knowledge all things. Will you not then remember? And how should I fear those whom you associate in worship with Allah (though they can neither benefit nor harm), while you fear not that you have joined in worship with Allah things for which He has not sent down to you any authority. (So) which of the

two parties has more right to be in security? If you but knew."
It is those who believe (in the Oneness of Allah and worship
none but Him Alone) and confuse not their belief with *zulm*
(wrongdoing i.e. by worshipping others besides Allah), for
them (only) there is security and they are the guided. And that
was Our Proof which We gave Ibraheem (Ibraheem) against
his people. We raise whom We will in degrees. Certainly your
Lord is Most Wise, All-Knowing ﴾ (*Soorah Al-An'am* 6:75-83)

This was the position of debating with his people and an
explanation that the visible and luminous celestial bodies are
not deserving of worship besides Allah, the Almighty, the All-
Powerful, because they are created, subject to Allah's Lordship,
made, controlled, subservient. At times they rise and at other
times they set, so they are absent from this world, while the
Lord is never absent from anything and no secrets are kept from
Him. On the contrary, He is the Eternal, the Everlasting, Who
never disappears. None has the right to be worshipped but He
and there is no lord besides Him. So he first of all made clear to
them that the celestial bodies did not deserve to be worshipped.

It was said that it was the planet Venus and then he moved
on from it to the moon, which is brighter than it and of more
radiant beauty. Then he moved onto the sun, which is more
visible, brighter and more beautiful. And he made clear that
they are subservient, controlled, subject to Allah's Decree and
His Lordship, as He, Most High, says, ﴾ And from among His
Signs are the night and the day, and the sun and the moon.
Prostrate not to the sun, nor to the moon, but prostrate to Allah,
Who created them, if you (really) worship Him. ﴿ (*Soorah
Fussilat* 41:37) This is why He says, ﴾ When he saw the sun
rising up, he said, "This is my lord. This is greater." But when
it set, he said, "O, my people! I am indeed free from all that you

join as partners in worship with Allah. Verily, I have turned my face toward Him Who has created the heavens and the Earth *Hanifan* (Islamic Monotheism, i.e. worshipping none but Allah Alone) and I am not of *al-mushrikoon*." His people disputed with him. He said, "Do you dispute with me concerning Allah while He has guided me, and I fear not those whom you associate with Allah in worship. (Nothing can happen to me) except when my Lord (Allah) wills something. My Lord comprehends in His Knowledge all things. Will you not then remember?" ﴾ (*Soorah Al-An'am* 6:78-80) That is, I care not about the deities that you worship besides Allah, because they do not benefit anything and they do not hear or understand anything. Rather, they are subject to Allah's Lordship and subservient to Him, like the celestial bodies, and other similar things. Or they are created and fashioned.

He, Most High, says in *Soorah As-Saffat,* ﴿And, verily, among those who followed his (Nooh's) way (Islamic Monotheism) was Ibraheem. When he came to his Lord with a pure heart (attached to Allah, Alone, and none else, worshipping none but Allah, Alone, true Islamic Monotheism, pure from the filth of polytheism). When he said to his father and to his people, "What is it that which you worship? Is it false *alihah* (gods) other than Allah that you seek? Then what do you think about the Lord of the *'Alameen*?" Then he cast a glance at the stars (to deceive them) and he said, "Verily, I am sick (with plague)." He did this trick to remain in their temple of idols to destroy them and not to accompany them to the pagans' feast. So they turned away from him and departed (for fear of the disease). Then he turned to their *alihah* (gods) and said, "Will you not eat (of the offering before you)? What is the matter with you that you speak not?" Then he turned upon them, striking (them) with (his) right hand. Then they (the worshippers of idols) came, toward him, hastening. He said, "Worship you that which you (yourselves) carve, while Allah has created you and what you make?" They said, "Build for him a building (it is said that the building was like a furnace) and throw him into the blazing fire!" So they plotted a plot against him, but We made them the lowest. 》(*Soorah As-Saffat* 37:82-98)

Allah, Most High, informs us about Ibraheem عليه السلام, His *Khaleel*, and He tells us that he rebuked his people for worshipping idols and he scorned them in front of them and belittled them, saying, 《 "What are these images, to which you are devoted?" 》(*Soorah Al-Anbiya'* 21:52) That is, with which you seclude yourselves and to which you submit. This is why they said, 《 "We found our fathers worshipping them." 》(*Soorah Al-Anbiya'* 21:53) They had no evidence except the practices of their fathers and their grandfathers and the idol-worship in which they used to take part. 《 He said, "Indeed you and your fathers have been in manifest error." 》(*Soorah Al-Anbiya'* 21:54) This is like His Words, 《 When he said to his father and to his people, "What is it that which you worship? Is it false *alihah* (gods) other than Allah that you seek? Then what do you think about the Lord of the *'Alameen*?" 》(*Soorah As-Saffat* 37:85-87) Qatadah said that it means: What do you think that He will do with you if you meet him and you have been worshipping (false deities) other than Him? He said to them, 《 He said, "Do they hear you when you call (on them)? Or do they benefit you or do they harm (you)?" They said, "Nay, but we found our fathers doing so." 》(*Soorah Ash-Shu'ara'* 26:72-74) They admitted to him that they (the idols) did not hear supplications and that they could neither harm nor benefit and that the only thing which caused them to worship these idols was the fact that they were following the example of their ancestors and those like them in error, such as their fathers and the ignorant, which is why he said to them, ❰ "Do you observe that which you have been worshipping, you and your ancient fathers? Verily! They are enemies to me, save the Lord of the *'Alameen* ❱ (*Soorah Ash-Shu'ara'* 26:75-77). This is irrefutable evidence of the falseness of the divinity which they claimed for their idols, because he declared himself innocent of them and belittles them. If they had possessed the power to harm or affect him, they would have done so. ❰ They said, "Have you brought us the truth, or are you one of those who play about?" ❱ (*Soorah Al-Anbiya'* 21:55). They asked, 'This speech which you are saying to us and by which you belittle our gods and due to which you curse our fathers – is it the earnest truth, or are you simply playing with us?' ❰ He said, "Nay, your Lord is the Lord of the heavens and the earth, Who created them and of that I am one of the witnesses." ❱ (*Soorah Al-Anbiya'* 21:56). That is, on the contrary, I say this to you earnestly and truthfully; and your God is Allah, besides Whom none has the right to be worshipped. He is your Lord and the Lord of all things, the Originator of the heavens and the earth and their Creator, in a unique manner. So it is He Who deserves to be worshipped, Alone, without partners, and I bear witness to that. He said, ❰ "And by Allah, I shall plot a plan (to destroy) your idols after you have gone away and turned your backs." ❱ (*Soorah Al-Anbiya'* 21:57) He swore by Allah that he would plot against these idols which they worshipped after they had gone away to celebrate one of their pagan festivals. It has been mentioned that he said this to himself secretly. 'Abdullah Ibn Mas'ood المالا said, "Some of them heard him and they had an annual festival during which they used to sacrifice animals outside the city. His father called on him to accompany him to the festival, but he said, "I am sick," as Allah, Most High, says, ❰ Then he cast a glance at the stars (to deceive them) and he said, "Verily, I am sick (with plague. He did this trick to remain in their temple of idols to destroy them and not to accompany them to the pagans' feast)." ﴿ (*Soorah As-Saffat* 37:88,89) He resorted to dissimulation so that he could attain his objective, which was to humiliate their idols and support Allah's Religion of truth, by making clear the falseness of the idol-worship that they practiced – and those idols deserved to be broken and to be humiliated. So when they went out to attend their festival, leaving him behind in the city, ﴿ Then he turned to their *alihah* (gods). ﴾ (*Soorah As-Saffat* 37:91) That is, he went to them hastily and in secret and he found them in a great hall. In front of them, they had placed a variety of foods as offerings to them. and said in tones of mockery and ridicule, ﴿ Will you not eat (of the offering before you)? What is the matter with you that you speak not?" Then he turned upon them, striking (them) with (his) right hand ﴾ (*Soorah As-Saffat* 37:91-93).

He struck them with his right hand because it was stronger, more powerful, swifter and more irresistible – and he broke them with a *qaddoom*. [1] ﴿ So he broke them to pieces ﴾. That is, he smashed them all into rubble. ﴿ So he broke them to pieces, (all) except the biggest of them, that they might turn to it ﴾. It was said that he placed the *adz* in the hands of the large one, as an indication that it was envious that any of these smaller idols should be worshipped with it. When they returned from their festival and found what had befallen the objects of their worship, ﴿ They said, "Who has done this to our *alihah* (gods)? He must indeed be one of the wrongdoers." ﴾.

In this there was clear evidence for them, if they had but sense to realize, that if these idols which they used to worship

---

(1) *Qadoom* or *Qaddoom*: An *adz* or *adze*, which is a tool, used for smoothing rough-cut wood in hand-woodworking.

were truly gods, they would have defended themselves against anyone who wanted to harm them. But due to their ignorance, their lack of understanding, their great misguidance and their foolishness, they said, ❨ They said, "Who has done this to our *alihah* (gods)? He must indeed be one of the wrongdoers." They said, "We heard a young man talking about them who is called Ibraheem." ❩ (*Soorah Al-Anbiya'* 21:59,60) That is, saying bad things about them, belittling them and making light of them, so it must be he who has attacked them and broken them. According to 'Abdullah Ibn Mas'ood صلى الله عليه وسلم, it means they were reminded of his words: ❨ "And by Allah, I shall plot a plan (to destroy) your idols after you have gone away and turned your backs." ❩ (*Soorah Al-Anbiya'* 21:57) ❨ They said, "Then bring him before the eyes of the people, that they may testify." ❩ (*Soorah Al-Anbiya'* 21:61) That is to the Grand Assembly, for everyone to see, so that they may bear witness to his words, hear his speech and see for themselves the revenge that they would exact on him. This was *Al-Khaleel*'s main objective – to gather the people and to establish the proof against all of the idolaters of the falseness of their practices, as Moosa صلى الله عليه وسلم said to Fir'awn, ❨ "Your appointed meeting is the day of the festival, and let the people assemble when the sun has risen (forenoon)." ❩ (*Soorah Ta Ha* 20:59). Then, when they had assembled and brought him before them, as they had said, ❨ They said, "Are you the one who has done this to our gods, o, Ibraheem?" (Ibraheem) said, "Nay, this one, the biggest of them (idols) did it. Ask them, if they can speak!" ❩ (*Soorah Al-Anbiya'* 21:62,63) In saying this, he was hoping that they would acknowledge that these idols could not speak and that this idol would not say anything because it was inanimate and like any other inanimate object, incapable of speech.

❨ So they turned to themselves and said, "Verily, you are the *zalimoon* (wrongdoers)." ﴾ (*Soorah Al-Anbiya'* 21:64) That is they blamed themselves for abandoning them, without leaving anyone to protect them or guard them. ﴿ Then they bent their heads ﴾ (*Soorah Al-Anbiya'* 21:65) As-Suddi said that it means: Then they returned to the *fitnah* (i.e. their disbelief). Based on this, the meaning of their words ﴿ "Verily, you are the *zalimoon* (wrongdoers)" ﴾ would be: You are the wrongdoers in your worship of them (the idols). Qatadah said, "The people became confused and bowed their heads, then they said, ﴿ 'Indeed you (Ibraheem) know well that these (idols) speak not!' ﴾ (*Soorah Al-Anbiya'* 21:65) That is, you know full well, Ibraheem, that these idols do not speak, so how can you order us to ask them? At that point, *Al-Khaleel* إِلَيْه said to them, ﴿ "Do you then worship besides Allah things that can neither profit you, nor harm you? Fie upon you and upon that which you worship besides Allah! Have you then no sense?" ﴾ (*Soorah Al-Anbiya'* 21:66,67) This is like His Words: ﴿ Then they (the worshippers of idols) came toward him, *yaziffoon* ﴾ (*Soorah As-Saffat* 37:94) Mujahid said that it means: hastening. He said, ﴿ "Worship you that which you (yourselves) carve?" ﴾ (*Soorah As-Saffat* 37:95) That is, how can you worship idols which you yourselves have carved from wood and stone and shaped and fashioned as you wished? ﴿ "While Allah has created you and what you make!" ﴾ (*Soorah As-Saffat* 37:96) Regardless of whether the Arabic word *ma* used in the Verses is the indefinite pronoun signifying a verbal noun, or whether it means "that which" the meaning of the words is: You are created and these idols are created, so how can one creation worship another creation like it? Your worship of them is no more appropriate than their worship of you; the former is futile and invalid and so is the latter, since worship is neither useful nor obligatory except when it is worship of the Creator, Alone, without ascribing partners to Him. ﴿ They said,

"Build for him a building (it is said that the building was like a furnace) and throw him into the blazing fire. So they plotted a plot against him, but we made them the lowest!" 》 (*Soorah As-Saffat* 37:97,98) They desisted from arguing and debating when they were defeated and no argument and no sophism remained available to them. At that point, they resorted to force in order to support their foolishness and tyranny. But the Lord, the Almighty, the All-Powerful plotted against them and raised His Word, His Religion and His Proof, As He, Most High, says, ﴿ They said, "Burn him and help your *alihah* (gods), if you will be doing." We (Allah) said, "O, fire! Be you coolness and safety for Ibraheem!" And they wanted to harm him, but We made them the worst losers 》 (*Soorah Al-Anbiya'* 21:68-70) This was because they began to gather kindling from every place they could, to such an extent that, if a woman was sick, she would make a vow that if she recovered she would bring wood to burn Ibraheem الله. Then they made a hole in the ground and set it aflame, and it burned with huge sparks and immense flames. There had never been a fire like it. They put Ibraheem الله into a mangonel, at the suggestion of a nomadic Kurdish man from Persia, whose name was Hazan and who was the first person to build a mangonel. Allah caused the earth to swallow him up, and he will remain sinking into it until the Day of Resurrection. Then they shackled him and tied him in the bowl of the mangonel and he was saying, "*La ilaha illa Anta Subhanaka Lakal-Hamdu Wa Lakal-Mulku La Shareeka Lak* (None has the right to be worshipped but You. Glory be to You. All praise and thanks are due to You; to You belongs the dominion; and You have no partners)." Then, when Ibraheem الله was placed in bowl of the mangonel, tied and shackled and then cast into the fire from it, he said, "*Hasbunallahu Wa Ni'mal-Wakeel* (Sufficient for me is Allah, and He is the best Disposer of Affairs)." This is similar to what Al-Bukhari recorded from 'Abdullah Ibn 'Abbas رضي الله عنهما that Ibraheem علیه السلام said, "Sufficient for me is Allah and He is the best Disposer of Affairs," when he was thrown into the fire. Muhammad ﷺ said it when it was said to him, ﴿ Those (i.e. Believers) unto whom the people (hypocrites) said, "Verily, the people (pagans) have gathered against you (a great army), therefore, fear them." But it (only) increased them in faith, and they said, "Allah (Alone) is Sufficient for us, and He is the Best Disposer of affairs (for us)." So they returned with Grace and Bounty from Allah. No harm touched them; and they followed the good Pleasure of Allah. And Allah is the Owner of Great Bounty ﴾ (*Soorah Ali 'Imran* 3:173,174) [1]

It is narrated on the authority of 'Abdullah Ibn 'Abbas رضي الله عنهما and Sa'eed Ibn Jubair that they said: The keeper (angel) of the rain said, "When will I be commanded to send rain?" But the command of Allah was swifter. ﴿ We (Allah) said, "O, fire! Be you coolness and safety for Ibraheem!" ﴾ (*Soorah Al-Anbiya'* 21:69) 'Ali Ibn Abi Talib said that it means: Do not harm him.

'Abdullah Ibn 'Abbas رضي الله عنهما and Abul-'Aliyah said: If Allah had not said, ﴿ "and safety for Ibraheem!" ﴾ its coldness would have harmed Ibraheem علیه السلام."

Al-Bukhari narrated on the authority of Sa'eed Ibn Al-Musayyib, who reported on the authority of Umm Shareek that the Messenger of Allah ﷺ ordered the killing of the house gecko and he said, "It blew (the fire) on Ibraheem علیه السلام." [2]

Imam Ahmad narrated on the authority of Sa'ibah, the freed slave of Al-Fakih Ibn Al-Mugheerah that she said: I visited

---

(1)   Narrated by Al-Bukhari (4563).

(2)   Narrated by Al-Bukhari (3359).

'A'ishah (may Allah be pleased with her) and I saw a spear in her house and I said, "O, Mother of the Faithful! What are you doing with this spear?" She said, "This is for these house geckos; we kill them with it, because the Messenger of Allah ﷺ told us that: 'When Ibraheem ﷺ was thrown into the fire, there was no creature on the earth that did not (seek to) extinguish the fire except the house gecko; it blew (the fire) on him.' So the Messenger of Allah ﷺ ordered us to kill them." [1]

Mention of the Debate Between Ibraheem Al-Khaleel ﷺ and Those Who Wanted to Dispute With the Mighty, the All-Powerful in Garments of Greatness and Robes of Arrogance and So He Claimed Lordship, When He Was One of the Weak Slaves

Allah, Most High, says, ﴾ Have you not looked at him who disputed with Ibraheem about his Lord (Allah), because Allah had given him the kingdom? When Ibraheem said (to him), "My Lord (Allah) is He Who gives life and causes death." He said, "I give life and cause death." Ibraheem said, "Verily! Allah causes the sun to rise from the East; then causes it you to rise from the West." So the disbeliever was utterly defeated. And Allah guides not the people, who are *zalimoon* (wrongdoers, etc.) ﴿ (*Soorah Al-Baqarah* 2:258) Allah, Most High, mentions the debate between His *Khaleel* and the arrogant tyrant king, who claimed Lordship for himself; but *Al-Khaleel* invalidated his proof and made clear how great was his ignorance and the smallness of his intellect and the evidence silenced him and illuminated for him the right path.

The scholars of *tafseer* and others, such as the scholars of

---

(1)   This is an authentic *hadeeth* narrated by Imam Ahmad ﷺ.

lineage and those of traditions said that this king was the king of Babylon, whose name was Numrood, son of Kan'an, son of Koosh, son of Sam, son of Nooh, according to Mujahid. Others said that he was Numrood, son of Falah, son of 'Abir, son of Salih, son of Arfakhshad, son of Sam, son of Nooh ﷺ. This was also reported by Mujahid and others. He was one of the kings of the world, because the world was ruled by four kings, according to what has been narrated. They consisted of two Believers and two disbelievers; the two Believers were Dhul-Qarnain and Sulaiman and the two disbelievers were Numrood and Bukhtunassar. They mentioned that this king, Numrood, remained on the throne for four hundred years. He had become cruel, oppressive, tyrannical and arrogant and he had preferred the life of this world. When Ibraheem ﷺ called upon him to worship Allah, Alone, without partners, his ignorance and error and his personal desires caused him to deny the Creator and to dispute with Ibraheem ﷺ about it and claimed Lordship for himself. When *Al-Khaleel* said to him, ❨ "My Lord (Allah) is He Who gives life and causes death." He said, "I give life and cause death." ❩ (*Soorah Al-Baqarah* 2:258) Qatadah, As-Suddi and Muhammad Ibn Ishaq said that he meant that when two men are brought to him and he had decided to have them killed, then he ordered that one of them be killed and pardoned the other one, it would be as if he had given life to one and caused death to the other. But this was not a challenge to *Al-Khaleel*'s statement. Rather, it was a remark unrelated to the topic of discussion and it did not challenge or invalidate (Ibraheem's argument); it was simply a provocative statement and a deviation from the truth, because *Al-Khaleel* proved the existence of the Creator by the occurrence of these visible things, such as the granting of life to creatures and the bringing of death to them. For it is not possible that they brought themselves into existence; there must have been a Creator to bring them into existence and to subjugate them to man and to steer the heavenly bodies in their orbits and to direct the winds, the clouds and the rain and create these visible animals and then bring about their death. This is why Ibraheem المالا said, ❨ "My Lord (Allah) is He Who gives life and causes death." ❩ (*Soorah Al-Baqarah* 2:258) So if by his saying "I bring life and I cause death," this ignorant king meant that he was the doer of these visible events, then he was guilty of stubbornness and obstinacy. If he meant what was mentioned by Qatadah, As-Suddi and Ibn Ishaq, then he did not say anything related to the words of *Al-Khaleel*, since he had not challenged his speech and had not he countered the evidence.

Since the defeat of the king in this debate might be unclear to many of those people who attended it and others, he mentioned another proof, which made clear the existence of the Creator and the falseness of what Numrood claimed and the open defeat of him: ❨ "Verily! Allah causes the sun to rise from the East; then cause it you to rise from the West." ❩ (*Soorah Al-Baqarah* 2:258) That is, this sun is subjugated every day and caused to rise, in accordance with the subjugation of the One Who created it and controls and directs it and is Irresistible. And that is Allah, besides Whom none has the right to be worshipped, the Creator of everything. So if you are, as you claim, the one who gives life and causes death, then cause this sun to rise from the West, because, He Who gives life and causes death is the One Who does as He wills and He cannot be resisted or overcome. Rather, He overwhelms everything and everything submits to Him. So if you are as you claim, then do this. But if you cannot do it, then you are not as you claim. You and every other person knows that you are not able to do anything of this. Indeed, you are incapable and powerless to create a mosquito or to help yourself against it? So he made clear to him his error, his ignorance, the untruthfulness of his claim and the falseness of his behaviour and his bragging to the ignorant among his people. And there remained no argument for him to use against *Al-Khaleel* علیه السلام. Rather, he was defeated and silenced and this is why Allah says, ❴ So the disbeliever was utterly defeated. And Allah guides not the people, who are *zalimoon.* ❵ (*Soorah Al-Baqarah* 2:258)

The Story of Al-Khaleel's Migration to the Land of Ash-Sham, His Entry Into the Lands of Egypt and His Settling in the Holy Land

Allah, Most High, says, ❴ So Loot (Lot) believed in him (Ibraheem's Message of Islamic Monotheism). He (Ibraheem) said, "I will emigrate for the sake of my Lord. Verily, He is the Almighty, the Most Wise." And We bestowed on him (Ibraheem), Ishaq (Isaac) and Ya'qoob (Jacob), and ordained among his offspring Prophethood and the Book (i.e. the *Tawrah* [Torah]) (to Moosa [Moses]), the *Injeel* (Gospel) (to 'Eesa [Jesus]), the Qur'an (to Muhammad ﷺ), all from the offspring of Ibraheem), and We granted him his reward in this world, and verily, in the Hereafter he is indeed among the righteous. ❵ (*Soorah Al-'Ankaboot* 29:26,27)

He, Most High, says, ❴ And We rescued him and Loot (Lot) to the land which We have blessed for the *'Alameen*. And We bestowed upon him Ishaq (Isaac), and (a grandson) Ya'qoob (Jacob). Each one We made righteous. And We made them leaders, guiding (mankind) by Our Command, and We inspired in them the doing of good deeds, performing *salah* (*iqamatus-salah*) (prayers), and the giving of *zakah* and of Us (Alone) they were worshippers. ﴾ (*Soorah Al-Anbiya'* 21:71-73) When he abandoned his people for Allah's sake and migrated from them, his wife was barren and could not bear children and he had no sons. With him was his nephew, Lot ﷺ, son of Haran, son of Azar. But Allah, Most High, granted him after that righteous sons and granted Prophethood and Revelation to his progeny. Every Prophet sent after him was from his offspring and every Scripture sent down from the heaven to a Prophet after him was sent down to one of his descendants. This was an honor and a mark of esteem for him from Allah, when he abandoned his land, his family and his kin and migrated to a land where he could worship his Lord, the Almighty, the All-Powerful and where he could call the mankind to believe in Him. The land that he intended to migrate to was the land of Ash-Sham and it was this land that Allah referred to in His Words: ﴿ to the land which We have blessed for the *'Alameen.* ﴾ (*Soorah Al-Anbiya'* 21:71) This was said by Ubayy Ibn Ka'b, Abul-'Aliyah, Qatadah and others.

Al-Bukhari narrated on the authority of Abu Hurairah ﷺ that he said: Ibraheem ﷺ did not lie except for three lies; two of them for the sake of Allah when he said, ﴿ "Verily, I am sick (with plague)." ﴾ (*Soorah As-Saffat* 37:89) and he said, ﴿ "Nay, this one, the biggest of them (idols) did it." ﴾ (*Soorah Al-Anbiya'* 21:63) The (third was) that while Ibraheem ﷺ and Sarah (his wife) were going (on a journey) they passed by (the territory of) a tyrant. Someone said to the tyrant, "This man (i.e. Ibraheem ﷺ) is accompanied by a very charming lady." So, he sent for Ibraheem ﷺ and asked him about Sarah saying, "Who is this lady?" Ibraheem ﷺ said, "She is my sister." Ibraheem ﷺ went to Sarah and said, "O, Sarah!

There are no believers on the surface of the earth except you and I. This man asked me about you and I have told him that you are my sister, so do not contradict my statement." The tyrant then called Sarah and when she went to him, he tried to take hold of her with his hand, but (his hand became stiff and) he was confounded. He asked Sarah. "Pray to Allah for me, and I shall not harm you." So Sarah asked Allah to cure him and he got cured. He tried to take hold of her for the second time, but (his hand became stiff as or stiffer than before and) he was more confounded. He again requested Sarah, "Pray to Allah for me, and I will not harm you." Sarah asked Allah again and he became alright. He then called one of his guards (who had brought her) and said, "You have not brought me a human being but have brought me a devil." The tyrant then gave Hajar as a girl-servant to Sarah. Sarah came back (to Ibraheem ﷺ) while he was praying. Ibraheem ﷺ, gesturing with his hand, asked, "What has happened?" She replied, "Allah has spoiled the evil plot of the infidel (or immoral person) and given me Hajar for service." (Abu Hurairah ﷺ then addressed his listeners saying, "That (Hajar) was your mother, O, *Bani Ma'is-Sama'* (i.e. the Arabs, the descendants of Isma'eel ﷺ, Hajar's son)." [1] It was only narrated by Al-Bukhari from this source and it is in a *mawqoof* form.

Imam Ahmad narrated on the authority of Abu Hurairah ﷺ that he said: The Messenger of Allah ﷺ said, "Ibraheem did not tell any lies except three and all of them were in Allah's Cause. (They include) his saying, when he was invited to worship the idols of his people, ﴾ "Verily, I am sick (with plague)." ﴿ (*Soorah As-Saffat* 37:89), his saying, ﴾ "Nay, this one, the biggest of them (idols) did it." ﴿ (*Soorah Al-Anbiya'* 21:63) and his saying regarding Sarah, "She is my sister." He said: Prophet

---

(1)   Narrated by Al-Bukhari (3358).

Ibraheem عليه السلام emigrated with Sarah and entered a city where there was a king or a tyrant. (The king) was told that Ibraheem عليه السلام had entered accompanied by a woman who was one of the most charming women. So the king sent for Ibraheem عليه السلام and asked, "O, Ibraheem! Who is this lady accompanying you?" Ibraheem عليه السلام replied, "She is my sister." Then Ibraheem عليه السلام returned to her and said, "Do not contradict my statement, for I have informed them that you are my sister. By Allah, there are no true Believers on the earth except you and I," Then Ibraheem sent her to the king. When the king got to her, she got up and performed ablution, prayed and said, "O, Allah! If I have believed in You and Your Messenger, and have saved my private parts from everybody except my husband, then please do not let this pagan overpower me." On that, the king fell in a mood of agitation and started moving his legs. Abu Az-Zinad and Abu Salamah reported on the authority of Abu Hurairah رضي الله عنه that she said, "O, Allah! If he should die, the people will say that I have killed him." The king regained his power, and proceeded toward her but she got up again and performed ablution, prayed and said, "O, Allah! If I have believed in You and Your Apostle and have kept my private parts safe from all except my husband, then please do not let this pagan overpower me." The king again fell in a mood of agitation and started moving his legs. On seeing that state of the king, Sarah said, "O, Allah! If he should die, the people will say that I have killed him." The king got either two or three attacks, and after recovering from the last attack he said, "By Allah! You have sent a devil to me. Take her to Ibraheem and give Hajar to her." So she came back to Ibraheem and said, "Allah humiliated the pagan and gave us a slave-girl for service." [1] Ahmad was alone in narrating it from this source and it conforms to the conditions

---

(1)   This is an authentic *hadeeth* narrated by Imam Ahmad (8988).

for acceptance demanded by an authentic *hadeeth*. Al-Bukhari also narrated it in an abbreviated form on the authority of Abu Hurairah ﷺ. [1]

Some scholars have claimed that three women were granted Prophethood: Sarah, the mother of Moosa and Maryam, the mother of 'Eesa, – peace be upon them all. But the majority of scholars are of the opinion that they were *Siddeeqat* [2] – may Allah be pleased with them.

Then *Al-Khaleel* ﷺ returned from the land of Egypt to the land of good omens, i.e. the Holy Land, where he had formerly been. With him were livestock, slaves and a great amount of wealth. Hajar, the Egyptian Copt accompanied them. Then Loot ﷺ, following the command of *Al-Khaleel* ﷺ, went to live in the land of Al-Ghawr, which is more well-known as Ghawr Zaghar, taking with him a portion of the aforementioned wealth. He took up residence in the city of Sadoom (Sodom) which was the main city in those lands at that time. Its inhabitants were wicked and shameless disbelievers. Allah inspired *Al-Khaleel* ﷺ and told him to look at the landscape, north, south, east and west and He gave him the glad tidings that all of this land would be for him and his descendants until the end of time and that He would cause his progeny to be numerous, until they equalled the number of grains of sand on the Earth. These tidings are connected to this Islamic nation and they were not completely fulfilled except for it; this is supported by the words of the Prophet ﷺ, "Allah drew the ends of the world near one another for my sake. And I have seen its eastern and western ends. The dominion of my *Ummah* will reach those ends which

---

(1)   Narrated by Al-Bukhari (2217).

(2)   Siddeeqat: *Honest* and righteous women.

have been drawn near me." [1]

The Story of the Birth of Isma'eel عليه السلام *by Hajar*

The People of the Scripture said that Ibraheem عليه السلام asked Allah to grant him fine offspring and that Allah granted his request. According to what they said, when Ibraheem عليه السلام was in the land of Bait Ul-Maqdis for twenty years, Sarah said to Ibraheem عليه السلام, "Allah has not permitted me to bear children, so take my slave-girl, and haply, Allah will bless me with a son from her." Then, when she gave her to him, he had intimate relations with her, as a result of which, she became pregnant by him. They (the People of the Scripture) said that when she became pregnant, she became filled with a sense of her own importance and she became arrogant toward her mistress, Sarah. Sarah then became jealous of her and complained of her to Ibraheem عليه السلام and he said to her, "Do with her what you will." Hajar then became afraid and she fled and camped near a spring there. One of the angels said to her, "Be not afraid, for Allah will place goodness in this child which you have carried." And he commanded her to return and gave her the glad tidings that she would bear a son, whom she would call Isma'eel. He would be a powerful man, whose authority would extend over all men and every man's hand would act in obedience to him. He would rule all of the lands of his brothers. She thanked Allah, the Almighty, the All-Powerful for that.

These tidings only hold true for his son (i.e. descendant) Muhammad ﷺ, because it was through him that the Arabs gained ascendancy over all of the lands, from East to West, and

---

(1) Narrated by Muslim (2889), Abu Dawood (4252), At-Tirmidhi (2176), Ibn Majah (3952) and Imam Ahmad (21946).

Allah gave them beneficial knowledge and righteous deeds, the like of which were not given to any previous nation and this was only due to the honor of their Messenger ﷺ, the blessing of his Message, the success of his prophecies, the complete manner in which he delivered the Message and the general nature of his mission, to all of the people of the earth.

When Hajar returned, she gave birth to Isma'eel علیه السلام. It is said that she gave birth to him when Ibraheem علیه السلام was eighty-six years old and that was thirteen years before the birth of Ishaq علیه السلام. They said that when Isma'eel علیه السلام was born, Allah inspired in Ibraheem علیه السلام the glad tidings of Ishaq's birth from Sarah. On hearing these glad tidings, Ibraheem علیه السلام fell down to prostrate in thanks to Allah and Allah said to him, "I have answered your supplications by giving you Isma'eel and I have blessed him and increased him and advanced him greatly. From him will be born twelve great ones and I will make him the head of a great people. This was also glad tidings of the coming of this great (Muslim) nation and these twelve great ones are the twelve Righteous Caliphs of whom we were informed in the *hadeeth* of 'Abdul Malik Ibn 'Umair, on the authority of Jabir Ibn Samurah ﷺ, who reported from the Prophet ﷺ that he said, "There will be twelve Commanders." Then he spoke words which I did not understand and so I asked my father what he had said. He replied, "All (twelve) of them will be from Quraish." This was narrated by Al-Bukhari and Muslim in the *Saheehain*. [1] In another narration, he added, "This matter will continue." [2] And in still another narration, "Islam will continue to be powerful until there have been twelve Caliphs,

---

(1) Narrated by Al-Bukhari (7223) and Muslim (1821).

(2) Narrated by Imam Ahmad (20506). In this isnad is Simak Ibn Harb, who used to make lots of mistakes.

all of them from Quraish." [1]

These twelve include the four *Imams*, Abu Bakr, 'Umar, 'Uthman and 'Ali رضي الله عنهم and they also include 'Umar Ibn 'Abdil-'Azeez and among them are some from Banu Al-'Abbas. It does not mean that they will be twelve rulers in succession, rather, it means that they must come (as foretold). Neither is the reference to the twelve *Imams* believed in by the Shiites, of whom (according to their claim), the first is 'Ali Ibn Abi Talib and the last is the awaited *Imam*, who is (supposedly) hiding in a subterranean cavern and he is Muhammad Ibn Al-Hasan Al-'Askari, according to their claim. Among those twelve there are none more beneficial than 'Ali رضي الله عنه and his son, Al-Hasan Ibn 'Ali رضي الله عنهما, when he abandoned fighting and gave up the Caliphate to Mu'awiyah رضي الله عنه, thus extinguishing the fire of civil strife and stopping the wars between the Muslims. The other *Imams* (mentioned by them) had no rule over the (Islamic) nation in any matter. As for what is believed regarding the subterranean cavern, this is pure fantasy and there is no truth to it whatsoever and no evidence for it.

The Story of Ibraheem's Migration With His Son, Isma'eel, and His Mother, Hajar, to the Mountains of Faran, Which is the Land of Makkah, and His Building of the Ancient House

Al-Bukhari narrated on the authority of 'Abdullah Ibn 'Abbas رضي الله عنهما that he said, "The first lady to use a girdle was the mother of Isma'eel عليه السلام. She used a girdle so that she might hide her tracks from Sarah. Ibraheem brought her and her son, Isma'eel

---

(1)   Narrated by Muslim (1821) and Ahmad (20421).

صلى الله عليه وسلم while she was suckling him, to a place near the *Ka'bah*, under a tree on the spot of *Zamzam*, at the highest place in the mosque. During those days there was nobody in Makkah, nor was there any water. So he made them sit over there and placed near them a leather bag containing some dates, and a small waterskin containing some water, and set out homeward. Isma'eel's mother followed him, saying, "O, Ibraheem! Where are you going, leaving us in this valley where there is no person whose company we may enjoy, nor is there anything (to enjoy)?" She repeated that to him many times, but he did not look back at her. Then she asked him, "Has Allah ordered you to do so?" He said, "Yes." She said, "Then He will not neglect us," and she returned, while Ibraheem صلى الله عليه وسلم proceeded onward, and on reaching the mountain where they could not see him, he faced the *Ka'bah*, and raising both hands, invoked Allah saying the following prayers: ﴿ "O, our Lord! I have made some of my offspring dwell in a valley without cultivation, by Your Sacred House (the *Ka'bah* in Makkah) in order, our Lord, that they may offer prayer perfectly. So fill some hearts among men with love toward them, and (O, Allah) provide them with fruits, so that they may give thanks." ﴾ (*Soorah Ibraheem* 14.37) Isma'eel's mother went on suckling Isma'eel and drinking from the water (she had).

When the water in the waterskin had all been used up, she became thirsty and her child also became thirsty. she started looking at him (i.e. Isma'eel صلى الله عليه وسلم) tossing in agony; she left him, for she could not endure looking at him, and found that the mountain of As-Safa was the nearest mountain to her on that land. She stood on it and started looking at the valley keenly so that she might see somebody, but she could not see anybody. Then she descended from As-Safa and when she reached the valley, she tucked up her robe and ran in the valley like a person in distress and trouble, till she crossed the valley and reached Al-Marwah mountain where she stood and started looking, expecting to see somebody, but she could not see anybody. She repeated that (running between As-Safa and Al-Marwah) seven times.

The Prophet ﷺ said: This is the source of the tradition of the walking of people between them (i.e. As-Safa and Al-Marwah). When she reached Al-Marwah (for the last time) she heard a voice and she asked herself to be quiet and listened attentively. She heard the voice again and said, "O, (whoever you may be)! You have made me hear your voice; have you got something to help me?" And behold! She saw an angel at the place of *Zamzam*, digging the earth with his heel (or his wing), till water flowed from that place. She started to make something like a basin around it, using her hand in this way, and started filling her waterskin with water with her hands, and the water was flowing out after she had scooped some of it." The Prophet ﷺ added, "May Allah bestow Mercy on Isma'eel's mother! Had she let the *Zamzam* (flow without trying to control it) (or had she not scooped from that water) (to fill her water-skin), *Zamzam* would have been a stream flowing on the surface of the earth." The Prophet ﷺ further added, "Then she drank (water) and suckled her child. The angel said to her, "Do not be afraid of being neglected, for this is the House of Allah which will be built by this boy and his father, and Allah never neglects His people." The House (i.e. the *Ka'bah*) at that time was on a high place resembling a hillock, and when torrents came, they flowed to its right and left. She lived in that way till some people from the tribe of Jurhum or a family from Jurhum passed by her and her child, as they (i.e. the Jurhum people) were coming through the way of Kada'. They landed in the lower part of Makkah, where they saw a bird that had the habit of flying around water and not leaving it. They said, "This bird must be flying around water, though we know that there is no water in this valley." They sent one or two messengers who discovered the source of water, and returned to inform them of the water. So, they all came (toward the water). The Prophet ﷺ added: Isma'eel's mother was sitting near the water. They asked her, "Do you allow us to stay with you?" She replied, "Yes, but you will have no right to possess the water." They agreed to that. The Prophet ﷺ further said: Isma'eel's mother was pleased with the whole situation as she used to love to enjoy the company of people. So, they settled there, and later on they sent for their families who came and settled with them so that some families became permanent residents there. The child (i.e. Isma'eel عليه السلام) grew up and learned Arabic from them and (his virtues) caused them to love and admire him as he grew up, and when he reached the age of puberty they made him marry a woman from amongst them.

After Isma'eel's mother died, Ibraheem عليه السلام came after Isma'eel's marriage in order to see his family that he had left before, but he did not find Isma'eel عليه السلام there. When he asked Isma'eel's wife about him, she replied, "He has gone in search of our livelihood." Then he asked her about their way of living and their condition, and she replied, "We are living in misery; we are living in hardship and destitution," complaining to him. He said, "When your husband returns, convey my salutation to him and tell him to change the threshold of the gate (of his house)." When Isma'eel عليه السلام came, he seemed to have felt something unusual, so he asked his wife, "Has anyone visited you?" She replied, "Yes, an old man of so-and-so description came and asked me about you and I informed him, and he asked about our state of living, and I told him that we were living in hardship and poverty." On hearing that, Isma'eel عليه السلام

said, "Did he advise you anything?" She replied, "Yes, he told me to convey his salutation to you and to tell you to change the threshold of your gate." Isma'eel عليه السلام said, "It was my father, and he has ordered me to divorce you. Go back to your family." So, Isma'eel عليه السلام divorced her and married another woman from amongst them (i.e. Jurhum).

Then Ibraheem عليه السلام stayed away from them for a period as long as Allah wished and called on them again but did not find Isma'eel عليه السلام. So he came to Isma'eel's wife and asked her about Isma'eel عليه السلام. She said, "He has gone in search of our livelihood." Ibraheem عليه السلام asked her, "How are you getting on?" asking her about their sustenance and living. She replied, "We are prosperous and well-off (i.e. we have everything in abundance)." Then she thanked Allah. Ibraheem عليه السلام said, "What kind of food do you eat?" She said, "Meat." He said, "What do you drink?" She said, "Water." He said, "O, Allah! Bless their meat and water." The Prophet ﷺ added, "At that time they did not have grain, and if they had grain, he would have also invoked Allah to bless it." The Prophet ﷺ added, "If somebody has only these two things as his sustenance, his health and disposition will be badly affected, unless he lives in Makkah." The Prophet ﷺ added: Then Ibraheem عليه السلام said to Isma'eel's wife, "When your husband comes, give my salutations to him and tell him that he should keep firm the threshold of his gate." When Isma'eel عليه السلام came back, he asked his wife, "Did anyone call on you?" She replied, "Yes, a good-looking old man came to me," so she praised him and added. "He asked about you, and I informed him, and he asked about our livelihood and I told him that we were in a good condition." Isma'eel عليه السلام asked her, "Did he give you any piece of advice?" She said, "Yes, he told me to give his salutations to you and ordered that you should keep firm the threshold of your gate." On hearing that,

Isma'eel عليه السلام said, "It was my father, and you are the threshold (of the gate). He has ordered me to keep you with me."

Then Ibraheem عليه السلام stayed away from them for a period as long as Allah wished, and called on them afterward. He saw Isma'eel عليه السلام under a tree near *Zamzam*, sharpening his arrows. When he saw Ibraheem عليه السلام, he rose up to welcome him (and they greeted each other as a father does with his son or a son does with his father). Ibraheem عليه السلام said, "Oh, Isma'eel! Allah has given me an order." Isma'eel عليه السلام said, "Do what your Lord has ordered you to do." Ibraheem عليه السلام asked, "Will you help me?" Isma'eel عليه السلام said, "I will help you." Ibraheem عليه السلام said, "Allah has ordered me to build a house here," pointing to a hillock higher than the land surrounding it. The Prophet ﷺ added, Then they raised the foundations of the House (i.e. the *Ka'bah*). Isma'eel عليه السلام brought the stones and Ibraheem عليه السلام was building, and when the walls became high, Isma'eel عليه السلام brought this stone and put it for Ibraheem عليه السلام, who stood over it and carried on building, while Isma'eel عليه السلام was handing him the stones, and both of them were saying, "O, our Lord! Accept (this service) from us, Verily, You are the All-Hearing, the All-Knowing." The Prophet ﷺ added: Then both of them went on building and going round the *Ka'bah*, saying, ﴿ "O, our Lord ! Accept (this service) from us, Verily, You are the All-Hearing, the All-Knowing." ﴾ (*Soorah Al-Baqarah* 2:127). [1]

It has been confirmed in the *hadeeth* narrated by Al-Bukhari, on the authority of Abu Hurairah رضي الله عنه that he said: The Prophet ﷺ said, "Ibraheem did his circumcision with a *qaddoom* at the age of eighty." [2] A *qaddoom* is an implement (an *adz*). It was also said that it was a place. The wording of this *hadeeth* does

---

(1)   Narrated by Al-Bukhari (3364).

(2)   Narrated by Al-Bukhari (3356).

not negate the possibility that he was over eighty years of age. And Allah knows better.

The Story of the Sacrificial Offering

Allah, Most High, says, ❨ And he said (after his rescue from the fire), "Verily, I am going to my Lord. He will guide me! My Lord! Grant me (offspring) from the righteous." So We gave him the glad tidings of a forbearing boy. And, when he (his son) was old enough to walk with him, he said, "O, my son! I have seen in a dream that I am slaughtering you (offering you in sacrifice to Allah), so see what you think." He said, "O, my father! Do that which you are commanded, *In sha' Allah* (if Allah wills), you shall find me of *As-Sabireen* (one of the patient ones, etc.)." Then, when they had both submitted themselves (to the Will of Allah) and he had laid him prostrate on his forehead (or on the side of his forehead for slaughtering), and We called out to him, "O, Ibraheem! You have fulfilled the dream (vision)! Verily! Thus do We reward the *Muhsinoon* (those who do good)." Verily, that indeed was a manifest trial and We ransomed him with a great sacrifice (i.e. a ram); And We left for him (a goodly remembrance) among generations (to come) in later times. *Salamun* (peace) be upon Ibraheem!" Thus indeed do We reward the *Muhsinoon* (those who do good). Verily, he was one of Our believing slaves. And We gave him the glad tidings of Ishaq (Isaac), a Prophet from the righteous. We blessed him and Ishaq, and of their progeny are (some) that do right, and some that plainly wrong themselves. ❩ (*Soorah As-Saffat* 37:99-113)

Allah, Most High, informs us regarding His *Khaleel*,

Ibraheem إِلَيْهِ, that when he migrated from the lands of his people, he asked his Lord to grant him a righteous son and Allah gave him the glad tidings of a gentle boy, and that was Isma'eel إِلَيْهِ, because he was the first child born to *Al-Khaleel*, when he was eighty-six years of age. And there is no dispute on this point between the People of the Scripture, because he was his firstborn son.

As for Allah's saying: ❴ And, when he (his son) was old enough to walk with him ❵ (*Soorah As-Saffat* 37:102), it means when he became a young man and began to work as his father did. According to Mujahid, it means he became a young man, went on journeys and began to do what his father did, such as striving and working. At that time, Ibraheem إِلَيْهِ was shown in a dream that he was commanded to sacrifice this son of his.

In the *hadeeth* narrated on the authority of 'Abdullah Ibn 'Abbas رَضِيَ in a *marfoo'* form, he said, "The visions of the Prophets are Revelation." [1] It was also said by 'Ubaid Ibn 'Umair. [2]

This was a test from Allah, the Almighty, the All-Powerful, for His *Khaleel*, that he sacrifice his beloved son, who was born to him in his old age. This was after he had been commanded to leave Isma'eel إِلَيْهِ and his mother in a land of poverty, where there was no animals or people, no cultivation and no livestock. He obeyed Allah's Command to do this and left them there, trusting in Allah and depending on Him. And Allah made for them a relief and a way out (of their difficulties) and sustained them from whence they had not expected. Then, after all that, when Ibraheem إِلَيْهِ was commanded to sacrifice this son of

---

(1)   This was also reported by At-Tirmidhi in a *mu'allaq* form (3689).

(2)   Narrated by Al-Bukhari (138) and At-Tirmidhi (3689).

his, whom he had left alone, in accordance with the Command of his Lord, when he was his firstborn son and only child, he complied with that Command and hastened to obey his Lord. Then he submitted this to his son, in order that it should be more acceptable to his heart and easier for him, rather than seizing him by force and compelling him to submit to being sacrificed. ﴾ And, when he (his son) was old enough to walk with him, he said, "O, my son! I have seen in a dream that I am slaughtering you (offering you in sacrifice to Allah), so see what you think." ﴿ (*Soorah As-Saffat* 37:102) This gentle son hastened to do his father's bidding, saying, ﴾ "O, my father! Do that which you are commanded, *In sha' Allah* (if Allah wills), you shall find me of *As-Sabireen* (the patient ones, etc.)." ﴿ (*Soorah As-Saffat* 37:102) This reply displays the ultimate in right conduct, filial piety and obedience to the Lord of the slaves. Allah, Most High, says, ﴾ Then, when they had both submitted themselves (to the will of Allah), and he had laid him prostrate on his forehead (or on the side of his fore-head for slaughtering)﴿ (*Soorah As-Saffat* 37:103) It was said that this means: when they had submitted to Allah's Command and determined to carry it out, he placed him on his face. It was said that when he intended to sacrifice him, he placed him facedown so that he could slaughter him from behind, and not have to see his face at the time of slaughter, so that it would be easier for him. This was said by 'Abdullah Ibn 'Abbas رضي الله عنهما, Mujahid, Sa'eed Ibn Jubair, Qatadah and Ad-Dahhak. It was also said that he turned him on his side, the way one turns a sacrificial animal on its side, so that the side of his forehead was on the ground. ﴾ They had both submitted themselves ﴿, that is when Ibraheem عليه السلام had said, "*Bismillahi Wallahu Akbar* (in the Name of Allah and Allah is Greater)" and his son had said, "*Ashhadu Anla ilaha illallah* (I bear witness that none but Allah has the right to be worshipped),'' in preparation as for Allah's Saying: ❨ And We called out to him, "O, Ibraheem! You have fulfilled the dream (vision)!'' Verily! Thus do We reward the *Muhsinoon* (those who do good) ❩ (*Soorah As-Saffat* 37:104,105), it means that the goal in this test to which you have been subjected has been attained and you have shown yourself to be obedient and prepared to carry out Allah's Commands; just as you submitted your body to the fire, so you did not hesitate to submit your son to be sacrificed and spend your wealth for the sake of your guests. This is why Allah says, ❨ Verily, that indeed was a manifest trial ❩ (*Soorah As-Saffat* 37:106) That is, a clear test. As for His Saying: ❨ And We ransomed him with a great sacrifice ❩ (*Soorah As-Saffat* 37:107), it means: We made as a ransom for the sacrifice of his son, that which was easy for Allah, to be substituted for him and what has been widely reported from the majority of scholars is that it was a prime, white ram, with long horns, which he saw tied to an acacia tree at Thabeer (a mountain in Makkah).

It was mentioned in the *hadeeth* that it was a ram. This was narrated by Imam Ahmad, on the authority of Safiyyah Bint Shaibah, who said: A woman from Banu Saleem who was the midwife of most of the people in our household, informed me that the Messenger of Allah ﷺ sent for 'Uthman Ibn Talhah ﷺ. On one occasion she said: I asked 'Uthman, "Why did the Prophet ﷺ call you?'' He said: The Messenger of Allah ﷺ said to me, "I saw the horns of the ram when I entered the House (i.e. the *Ka'bah*) and I forgot to tell you to cover them up; cover them up, for there should not be anything in the House which could distract the worshipper.'' Sufyan said, "The horns of the ram remained hanging in the House until it was burned, and they were burned too.'' [1]

---

(1)   This is an authentic *hadeeth* narrated by Imam Ahmad (4/68, No. 2271).

The Story of the Birth of Ishaq

Allah, Most High, says, ❴ And We gave him the glad tidings of Ishaq (Isaac) a Prophet from the righteous. We blessed him and Ishaq (Isaac), and of their progeny are (some) that do right, and some that plainly wrong themselves. ❵ (*Soorah As-Saffat* 37:112,113) The glad tidings of his birth were brought by the angels to Ibraheem ﷺ and Sarah when they passed by them as they were heading for the cities of the people of Lot, in order to inflict destruction on them because of their disbelief and their wickedness and depravity, as will be explained in its place, if Allah wills.

Allah, Most High, says, ❴ Has the story reached you of the honored guests of Ibraheem? When they came in to him and said, "*Salam,* (peace be upon you)!" He answered, "*Salam* (peace be upon you)," and said, "You are a people unknown to me." Then he turned to his household, and brought out a fat (roasted) calf (as the property of Ibraheem was mainly cows) and placed it before them, (saying), "Will you not eat?" Then he conceived a fear of them (when they ate not). They said, "Fear not." And they gave him glad tidings of an intelligent son, having knowledge (about Allah and His Religion of True Monotheism). Then his wife came forward with a loud voice, she smote her face and said, "A barren old woman!" They said, "Even so says your Lord. Verily, He is the Most Wise, the All-Knowing." ❵ (*Soorah Adh-Dhariyat* 51:24-30) Allah, Most High, tells us that when the angels – who were three in number, Gabriel, Meekael and Israfeel – visited Al-*Khaleel* ﷺ, at first he thought that they were (human) visitors and he treated them as (honored) guests and roasted a fat calf from the best of his cattle for them. But when he presented it to them, he saw that they had no desire at all to eat. This is because angels have no strong need for food. He felt a sense of mistrust of them ❨ and conceived a fear of them. They said, "Fear not, we have been sent against the people of Loot (Lot)." ❩ (*Soorah Hood* 11:70) That is, to destroy them. Upon hearing this, Sarah laughed, being pleased that Allah's Wrath was to be visited upon them. She was standing waiting on the guests, as was the custom of the Arabs and others and when she laughed, being pleased at the news, Allah, Most High said, ❨ And We gave her glad tidings of Ishaq (Isaac) and after him, of Ya'qoob ❩ (*Soorah Hood* 11:71) That is, the angels gave her the glad tidings of that. ❨ Then his wife came forward with a loud cry ❩ (*Soorah Adh-Dhariyat* 51:29). That is, giving a loud cry of amazement. ❨ she smote her face ❩ (*Soorah Adh-Dhariyat* 51:29) As women do when they are surprised or amazed. ❨ "She said (in astonishment w+oe unto me! Shall I bear a child while I am an old woman, and here is my husband, an old man?" ❩ (*Soorah Hood* 11:72) That is, how can a person like me, who is advanced in years and also barren, give birth? ❨ and here is my husband, an old man? ❩. She was amazed that a child should be born to her while she was in this state and that is why she said, ❨ Verily! This is a strange thing!" They said: "Do you wonder at the Decree of Allah? The Mercy of Allah and His Blessings be on you, family (of Ibraheem). Surely, He (Allah) is Worthy of all praise, Most Glorious." ❩ (*Soorah Hood* 11:72,73) Ibraheem عليه السلام was also astonished, but very happy with these glad tidings, which strengthened him and gladdened his heart. ❨ (Ibraheem) said, "Do you give me glad tidings (of a son) when old age has overtaken me? Of what then is your news?" They (the angels) said, "We give you glad tidings in truth. So be not of the despairing ones." ❩

(*Soorah Al-Hijr* 15:54,55) They confirmed the truth of these glad tidings and informed them both ❨ of an intelligent son ❩ – and that was Ishaq 繠, the brother of Isma'eel 繠, a gentle son. Thus was he described by his Lord, as being one who kept his promises and was patient and forbearing. In another verse, He says, ❨ But We gave her glad tidings of Ishaq, and after him, of Ya'qoob. ❩ (*Soorah Hood* 11:71) Muhammad Ibn Ka'b Al-Qurazi and others cited this as evidence that Isma'eel 繠 was the sacrifice and that it would not be possible that Allah would order Ishaq 繠 to be sacrificed after the tidings of his birth and the birth of Ishaq's son, Ya'qoob 繠 had been given.

As for His Words: ❨ But We gave her glad tidings of Ishaq, and after him, of Ya'qoob ❩ (*Soorah Hood* 11:71), they are evidence that she would be happy with the birth of her son, Ishaq 繠 and after him, her grandson, Ya'qoob 繠; that is, he would be born during her lifetime and he would delight their hearts, just as her son had done. If this had not been written, there would have been no benefit in mentioning Ya'qoob 繠 and singling him out from among the progeny of Ishaq 繠. And since he was singled out for special mention, it proves that they would be happy at his birth, just as they were happy at the birth of his father before him. Allah, Most High, says, ❨ And We bestowed upon him Ishaq and Ya'qoob, each of them We guided, and before him We guided Nooh. ❩ (*Soorah Al-An'am* 6:84)

The Story of the Building of the Ancient House

Allah, Most High, says, ❨ And (remember) when the Lord of Ibraheem (i.e. Allah) tried him with (certain) Commands,

which he fulfilled, He (Allah) said (to him), "Verily, I am going
to make you a leader (Prophet) of mankind." (Ibraheem) said,
"And of my offspring (will You make leaders)?" (Allah) said,
"My Covenant (Prophethood, etc.) includes not *zalimoon*." And
(remember) when We made the House (the *Ka'bah* at Makkah)
a place of resort for mankind and a place of safety? And take you
(people) the *Maqam* (standing place) of Ibraheem (or the stone
on which Ibraheem stood while he was building the *Ka'bah*)
as a place of prayer (for some of your prayers, e.g. two *rak'ahs*
after the *tawaf* of the *Ka'bah* at Makkah). And We commanded
Ibraheem and Isma'eel that they should purify My House (the
Ka'bah at Makkah) for those who are circumambulating it, or
staying (*i'tikaf*), or bowing or prostrating themselves (there,
in prayer). And (remember) when Ibraheem said, "My Lord,
make this city (Makkah) a place of security and provide its
people with fruits, such of them as believe in Allah and the Last
Day." He (Allah) answered, "As for him who disbelieves, I
shall leave him in contentment for a while, then I shall compel
him to the punishment of the Fire, and worst indeed is that
destination!" And (remember) when Ibraheem and (his son)
Isma'eel were raising the foundations of the House (the *Ka'bah*
at Makkah), (saying), "Our Lord! Accept (this service) from
us. Verily! You are the All-Hearing, the All-Knowing. Our
Lord! And make us submissive unto You and of our offspring
a nation submissive unto You, and show us our *manasik* (all
the ceremonies of pilgrimage - *Hajj* and *'Umrah,* etc.), and
accept our repentance. Truly, You are the One Who accepts
repentance, the Most Merciful. Our Lord! Send amongst them
a Messenger of their own (and indeed Allah answered their
invocation by sending Muhammad [peace be upon him]),
who shall recite unto them Your Verses and instruct them in
the Book (this Qur'an) and *Al-Hikmah* (full knowledge of the

Islamic laws and jurisprudence or wisdom or Prophethood, etc.), and sanctify them. Verily! You are the Almighty, the Most Wise." ﴾ (*Soorah Al-Baqarah* 2:124-129). Allah, Most High, informs us concerning His slave, His Messenger, His Pure One and His *Khaleel*, the *Imam* of the *Hunafa'* [1] and the father of the Prophets إِلَيْهِ, that he built the Ancient House, which was the first mosque built for the generality of mankind to worship Allah. Allah guided him to the location in which it was to be built; and we have already narrated on the authority of the Commander of the Faithful, 'Ali Ibn Abi Talib رضي, and others that he was guided to it by Inspiration from Allah, the Almighty, the All-Powerful. We have already mentioned in the description of the creation of the heavens that the *Ka'bah*, is directly below *Al-Baitul-Ma'moor*, so that if it fell, it would fall upon it; and the same applies to the houses of worship in the seven heavens.

As some of the *Salaf* said, in every heaven there is a house in which the inhabitants worship Allah and they are like the *Ka'bah* for the people of the Earth. So Allah commanded Ibraheem إِلَيْهِ to build a house for Him, which would be for the inhabitants of the Earth, like those places of prayer for the angels of the heavens. Allah guided him to the place prepared for the building of the house, which had been selected for it since the creation of the heavens and the Earth, as confirmed in the *Saheeh*: "Verily, this city was made sacrosanct by Allah on the day of the creation of the heavens and the Earth and it will remain sacred by Allah's Command until the Day of Resurrection." [2] No information has come to us from an authentic source which would confirm that the House was

---

(1) *Hunafa'*: Those who profess the true Religion (Islamic Monotheism).

(2) Narrated by Al-Bukhari (1587) and Muslim (1353) and the wording is from the *hadeeth* of 'Abdullah Ibn 'Abbas رضي.

built before *Al-Khaleel* عليه السلام. Whoever relied for evidence on the Words of Allah: ❴ the site of the (Sacred) House ❵ (*Soorah Al-Hajj* 22:26), this is neither conclusive nor evident. Because what is meant is the place preordained by Allah – a location venerated by the Prophets from Adam عليه السلام until the time of Ibraheem عليه السلام.

Allah, Most High, says, ❴ Verily, the first House (of worship) appointed for mankind was that at *Bakkah* (Makkah), full of blessing, and a guidance for *'Alameen*. ❵ (*Soorah Ali 'Imran* 3:96). That is, the first House appointed for the generality of mankind for blessing and guidance was the House which was in Bakkah; it was said that Bakkah means Makkah and it was also said that Bakkah was the location of the *Ka'bah*. ❴ In it are manifest signs ❵ (*Soorah Ali 'Imran* 3:97). That is, it is the construction of Ibraheem عليه السلام, the father of the Prophets who came after him and the Imam of the *Hunafa'* from his sons, who followed his example and held fast to his *Sunnah*. This is why He says, ❴ the *Maqam* (place) of Ibraheem ❵ (*Soorah Ali 'Imran* 3:97). That is, the stone on which he stood when he raised the structure above his own height; his son placed this well-known stone for him to stand on, so that he would be tall enough when the building reached a height that was beyond his reach, as mentioned previously in the long *hadeeth* of 'Abdullah Ibn 'Abbas رضي الله عنهما. [1]

This stone was situated beside the wall of the *Ka'bah* in ancient times, until the time of 'Umar Ibn Al-Khattab رضي الله عنه; he moved it back a little from the House, so that it should not disturb the worshippers, as they circumambulated the House. 'Umar Ibn Al-Khattab رضي الله عنه was followed in this because his opinion had coincided with the Ordainments of his Lord in

---

(1)   The *takhreej* of this *hadeeth* has already been given a short while ago.

a number of matters, such as his saying to the Messenger of Allah ﷺ, "Were we to take *Maqam* Ibraheem as a place of prayer…" Then Allah revealed: ﴿ And take you (people) the *Maqam* (place) of Ibraheem (or the stone on which Ibraheem stood while he was building the Ka'bah) as a place of prayer ﴾ (*Soorah Al-Baqarah* 2:125). The footprints of *Al-Khaleel* عليه السلام had remained in the stone from the beginning of Islam and Abu Talib said in his well-known poem, "*Al-Qaseedah Al-Lamiyyah*":

And Thawr Cave and he who held fast with perseverance to his position,

And proved superior in piety in Hira' and remained there,

And by the House, the true House in the center of Makkah,

And by Allah, truly, Allah is not unaware,

And by the Black Stone, when they touch it,

When they surround it in the forenoon and the late afternoon,

And the place of Ibraheem is visible in the wet stone,

Of his feet, barefoot, without shoes.

This means that his noble feet were impressed in the stone, showing the prints of bare feet, without shoes. This is why Allah says, ﴿ And (remember) when Ibraheem and (his son) Isma'eel were raising the foundations of the House ﴾ (*Soorah Al-Baqarah* 2:127) That is, at the time when they said, ﴿ "Our Lord! Accept (this service) from us. Verily! You are the All-hearing, the All-Knowing." ﴾ (*Soorah Al-Baqarah* 2:127) They were at the highest levels of sincere devotion and obedience to Allah, the Almighty, the All-Powerful when they asked Allah, the All-Hearing, the All-Knowing to accept from them this great act of obedience and praiseworthy endeavor. ﴿ "Our Lord! And make us submissive unto You and of our offspring a nation submissive unto You, and show us our *Manasik* (all the ceremonies of pilgrimage - *Hajj* and *'Umrah,* etc.), and accept our repentance. Truly, You are the One Who accepts repentance, the Most Merciful." ﴾ (*Soorah Al-Baqarah* 2:128)

What is meant by this is that *Al-Khaleel* علي built the noblest of mosques in the noblest of locations, in an uncultivated valley and he supplicated on behalf of his family that they be blessed and given sustenance from the fruits, even though there was little water and no trees, cultivation or fruits. They asked Him to make it a Sacred Place, a Sanctuary and a place of safety for all time. Allah accepted their supplication – all praise and thanks be to Him – He gave *Al-Khaleel* علي what he had requested. Allah, Most High, says, ﴿ Have they not seen that We have made (Makkah) a sanctuary secure, and that men are being snatched away from all around them? ﴾ (*Soorah Al-'Ankaboot* 29:67) He says, ﴿ Have We not established for them a secure sanctuary (Makkah), to which are brought fruits of all kinds, a provision from Ourselves? ﴾ (*Soorah Al-Qasas* 28:57) Ibraheem علي asked Allah to send to them Messengers from among them. That is, from their race and speaking their eloquent language, full of sincere advice and admonishment, in order to complete upon them the two blessings of the life of this world and the Hereafter. Allah accepted this supplication from him and sent from among them a Messenger – and what a Messenger it was that was the Seal of His Prophets and His Messengers! He granted him a complete Religion that had never been given to anyone before him. His preaching was directed to all of the people of the earth, including people from all races, languages and descriptions and from all countries, cities and times, until the Day of Resurrection! This was one of the special attributes and privileges granted to him alone among the Prophets, due to his innate nobility, the completeness of the Message with which he was sent, the nobility of his location (i.e. Makkah), the eloquence of his speech, the complete solicitude that he displayed toward his people, his kindness, his compassion, his generous nature, his great birth and his fine beginning and end.

This is why Ibraheem, *Al-Khaleel* الخيال, as the builder of the *Ka'bah* for the inhabitants of the Earth, deserved to have an exalted position in the highest heaven, near *Al-Baitul-Ma'moor*, which is the *Ka'bah* for the inhabitants of the seventh heaven and that is a blessed house, which is entered by seventy thousand angels every day; therein they worship, never to return to it until the Day of Resurrection. We have already mentioned in the *Tafseer* of *Soorah Al-Baqarah* the description of his building of the House (of Allah) and the stories and traditions which contain plenty of information, so whoever wishes to know more should refer to the *Tafseer*, all praise and thanks be to Allah.

The edifice erected by *Al-Khaleel* الخيال remained for a long time, then after that, it was rebuilt by Quraish, who shortened the foundations of Ibraheem الخيال on the northern aspect, which faces Ash-Sham (Syria), as it is today. In the *Saheehain*, it is reported on the authority of 'A'ishah that the Messenger of Allah ﷺ said, "Do you know that when your people (Quraish) rebuilt the *Ka'bah*, they decreased it from its original foundation laid by Ibraheem?" I said, "O, Messenger of Allah! Why do you not rebuild it on its original foundation laid by Ibraheem?" He replied, "Were it not for the fact that your people are close to the pre-Islamic Period of Ignorance (i.e. they have recently become Muslims) I would have spent the treasure of the *Ka'bah* in Allah's Cause and I would have made its door near to the ground and included *Al-Hijr* in it." [1] It was also rebuilt

---

(1)   Narrated by Al-Bukhari (1583) and Muslim (1333).

by Ibn Az-Zubair – may Allah have mercy on him – during his time, according to what had been indicated by the Messenger of Allah ﷺ, based on the information given to him by his aunt, 'A'ishah, the Mother of the Believers, which she relayed from him ﷺ. When Al-Hajjaj killed him in the year 73 A.H., he wrote to 'Abdul Malik Ibn Marwan, who was the Caliph at that time. They thought that Ibn Az-Zubair had done it of his own accord and so Marwan ordered it to be returned to the way it had been before and so they demolished the wall that faced toward Ash-Sham and removed *Al-Hijr* from it, then they filled in the wall and put the stones inside the *Ka'bah*, raised its eastern door and blocked the western one completely, as one sees it today. Then, when they were informed that Ibn Az-Zubair had only this based on what 'A'ishah, the Mother of the Believers, had told him, they regretted what they had done and wished that they had left it as they had found it. Then during the era of Al-Mahdi Ibn Al-Mansoor, he sought the advice of Imam Malik Ibn Anas regarding the idea of returning it to the way Ibn Az-Zubair had rebuilt it, but he said to him, "I fear that the rulers will take it as a plaything." That is, whenever a new ruler comes to power, he will rebuild according to his own whim. And so it remained as it was up to the present day.

Mention of the Praise Heaped on Allah's Slave and Khaleel, Ibraheem, by Allah and His Messenger

Allah, Most High, says, ﴾ And (remember) when the Lord of Ibraheem (i.e. Allah) tried him with (certain) Commands, which he fulfilled. He (Allah) said (to him), "Verily, I am going to make you a leader (Prophet) of mankind." (Ibraheem) said,

"And of my offspring (to make leaders)." (Allah) said, "My Covenant (Prophethood, etc.) includes not the *zalimoon*." ❭ (*Soorah Al-Baqarah* 2:124). When he fulfilled the obligations enjoined on him by his Lord, He made him a leader of his people, who followed his example and his guidance. Ibraheem عليه السلام then asked Allah to let this leadership continue because of him and to let it remain within his lineage; and this thing which he asked for and craved was granted. Leadership was granted to him, but excepted from acquiring it were the wrongdoers; and those selected to receive it from his offspring were the scholars and those who performed righteous deeds. Allah, Most High says, ❬ And indeed, We sent Nooh and Ibraheem, and placed in their offspring Prophethood and Scripture, and among them there is he who is guided, but many of them are *fasiqoon* (rebellious, disobedient to Allah) ❭ (*Soorah Al-Hadeed* 57:26) So every Scripture sent down from the heaven to one of the Prophets who came after Ibraheem عليه السلام, *Al-Khaleel*, was sent to one of his offspring and his followers. This was an honor that was unique and without parallel and a rank and status without equal. From his loins were born two great sons: Isma'eel عليه السلام from Hajar and then Ishaq عليه السلام from Sarah. From the latter was born Ya'qoob عليه السلام, who was Isra'eel, from whom all of their tribes claim descent. Among them were Prophets and they were very numerous, so much so that it is impossible for us to know their exact number, except those whom He sent and selected to receive a Message, along with his Prophethood – and the last of them was 'Eesa عليه السلام, the son of Maryam, who was from Banu Isra'eel.

As for Isma'eel عليه السلام, from him descended the Arabs, including all of their diverse tribes, as we shall make clear later on, if Allah, Most High, wills. And there were no Prophets among his descendants except the Seal of the Prophets, Muhammad Ibn

'Abdullah Ibn 'Abdul-Muttalib Ibn Hashim Al-Qurashi, Al-Hashimi, Al-Makki (the Makkan), then Al-Madani (Madinite) – may Allah's Blessings and Peace be upon him. From this noble branch there was only this one dazzling, glittering and splendid jewel and the outstanding piece de resistance, who was the Leader of whom *Ahl ul-Jam'* are proud and whom the first and the last will envy on the Day of Resurrection.

It has been authentically reported from him ﷺ in *Saheeh Muslim* that he said, "(On the Day of Resurrection) I will occupy a position (so elevated) that all of creation will turn to me, even Ibraheem." [1] And he praised his father, Ibraheem ﷺ highly in this context. This saying of his proves that he (Ibraheem) is the best of creation after the Prophet ﷺ, in the Estimation of the Creator – both in the life of this world and in the Hereafter.

Al-Bukhari narrated on the authority of 'Abdullah Ibn 'Abbas ﷺ that he said: The Messenger of Allah ﷺ used to seek Refuge with Allah for Al-Hasan and Al-Husain and say, "Your forefather (i.e. Ibraheem) used to seek Refuge with Allah for Isma'eel and Ishaq by reciting the following: 'O, Allah! I seek Refuge with Your Perfect Words from every devil and from poisonous pests and from every evil, harmful, envious eye.'" [2]

Allah, Most High, says, ﴾ And (remember) when Ibraheem said, "My Lord! Show me how You give life to the dead." He (Allah) said, "Do you not believe?" He (Ibraheem) said, "Yes (I believe), but to be stronger in faith." He said, "Take four birds, then cause them to incline toward you (then slaughter them, cut them into pieces), and then put a portion of them

---

(1)   Narrated by Muslim (820).

(2)   Narrated by Al-Bukhari (3371), Abu Dawood (4737) and At-Tirmidhi (2060).

on every hill, and call them, they will come to you in haste. And know that Allah is Almighty, Most Wise." ﴾ (*Soorah Al-Baqarah* 2:260) Scholars of *Tafseer* said that there were reasons for this question, which we have explained in the *Tafseer* and we established them beyond doubt.

In short, we may say that Allah, the Almighty, the All-Powerful, answered his question and ordered him to take four birds – scholars differed as to the type of birds – but the objective was attained at all events – and He commanded him to slaughter them, remove their feathers, tear the birds to pieces and mix the pieces together. Then he was ordered to place parts of these mixed pieces on four hills. This he did and then he was ordered to call them, by his Lord's Permission. When he called them, Allah caused the pieces to fly to each other and each feather went to the body to which it belonged, until the bodies of the birds were joined together once more and he observed the Ability of the One Who says, "Be!" and it is. They came running to him, so that the matter should be even clearer to him than if they had come to him flying. It was said that he was ordered to take their heads in his hands and each bird came to him to collect its head from Ibraheem ﷺ and it became fixed to its body as it had been, thus proving that none has the right to be worshipped except Allah. Ibraheem ﷺ had known, with a certainty that admitted of no doubt, the Ability of Allah, Most High, to resurrect the dead, but he wanted to witness that for himself and progress from certain knowledge to eye-witness knowledge. So Allah agreed to his request and gratified his ultimate wish.

Allah, Most High, says, ﴾ O, People of the Scripture (Jews and Christians)! Why do you dispute about Ibraheem, while the *Tawrah* (Torah) and the *Injeel* (Gospel) were not revealed

till after him? Have you then no sense? Verily, you are those
who have disputed about that of which you have knowledge.
Why do you then dispute concerning that which you have
no knowledge? It is Allah Who knows, and you know not.
Ibraheem was neither a Jew nor a Christian, but he was a true
Muslim *Hanifan* (Islamic Monotheism – to worship none but
Allah, Alone) and he was not of *al-mushrikoon*. Verily, among
the mankind who have the best claim to Ibraheem are those
who followed him, and this Prophet (Muhammad ﷺ) and those
who have believed (Muslims). And Allah is the *Wali* (Protector
and Helper) of the Believers. ﴾ (*Soorah Ali 'Imran* 3:65-68)
Allah, Most High, rebukes the People of the Scripture, the Jews
and Christians, regarding each group's claim that Ibraheem عليه السلام
was an adherent of their religion. He declares him innocent
of that and made clear how ignorant they were and how little
intelligence they possessed in His Words: ﴿ While the *Tawrah*
(Torah) and the *Injeel* (Gospel) were not revealed till after him?
Have you then no sense? ﴾ (*Soorah Ali 'Imran* 3:65) So how
could he have followed your religion when what was legislated
for you was only legislated many long ages after him? This is
why He says, ﴿ Have you then no sense? ﴾ - up to His Words:
﴿ Ibraheem was neither a Jew nor a Christian, but he was a true
Muslim *Hanifan* (Islamic Monotheism – to worship none but
Allah, Alone) and he was not of *al-mushrikoon.* ﴾ (*Soorah Ali
'Imran* 3:65-67)

So He made clear that Ibraheem عليه السلام followed the true Religion
of Islamic Monotheism, which is to have sincere intention to
devote oneself to the worship of Allah, Alone, without partners
and to intentionally turn away from that which is false, in
favor of the truth, which contradicts Judaism, Christianity and
paganism. Allah, Most High, says, ﴿ And who turns away from
the religion of Ibraheem (i.e. Islamic Monotheism) except

him who befools himself? Truly, We chose him in this world and verily, in the Hereafter he will be among the righteous. When his Lord said to him, "Submit (i.e. be a Muslim)!" He said, "I have submitted myself (as a Muslim) to the Lord of the *'Alameen.*" And this (submission to Allah, Islam) was enjoined by Ibraheem upon his sons and by Ya'qoob, (saying), "O, my sons! Allah has chosen for you the (true) Religion, then die not except in the faith of Islam (as Muslims – Islamic Monotheism)." Or were you witnesses when death approached Ya'qoob? When he said unto his sons, "What will you worship after me?" They said, "We shall worship your *Ilah* (God – i.e. Allah), the *Ilah* (God) of your fathers, Ibraheem, Isma'eel, Ishaq, One *Ilah* (God), and to Him we submit (in Islam)." That was a nation who have passed away. They shall receive the reward of what they earned and you of what you earn. And you will not be asked of what they used to do. And they say, "Be Jews or Christians, then you will be guided." Say (to them, O, Muhammad), "Nay, (We follow) only the Religion of Ibraheem, *Hanifan* (Islamic Monotheism, i.e. to worship none but Allah, Alone), and he was not of *al-mushrikoon* (those who worshipped others along with Allah." Say (O, Muslims), "We believe in Allah and that which has been sent down to us and that which has been sent down to Ibraheem, Isma'eel, Ishaq, Ya'qoob, and to *Al-Asbat* (the twelve sons of Ya'qoob [Jacob]), and that which has been given to Moosa (Moses) and 'Eesa (Jesus), and that which has been given to the Prophets from their Lord. We make no distinction between any of them, and to Him we have submitted (in Islam)." So if they believe in the like of that which you believe, then they are rightly guided, but if they turn away, then they are only in opposition. So Allah will suffice you against them. And He is the All-Hearing, the All-Knowing. (Our *Sibghah* [Religion] is) the *Sibghah*

(Religion) of Allah (Islam) and which *Sibghah* (Religion) can be better than Allah's? And we are His worshippers. (*Tafseer Ibn Katheer*) Say (Muhammad to the Jews and Christians), "Dispute you with us about Allah while He is our Lord and your Lord? And we are to be rewarded for our deeds and you for your deeds. And we are sincere to Him in worship and obedience (i.e. we worship Him Alone and none else, and we obey His Orders)." Or say you that Ibraheem, Isma'eel, Ishaq, Ya'qoob and *Al-Asbat* (the twelve sons of Ya'qoob) were Jews or Christians? Say, "Do you know better or does Allah (knows better... that they all were Muslims)? And who is more unjust than he who conceals the testimony (i.e. to believe in Prophet Muhammad ﷺ when he comes, written in their Books) he has from Allah? And Allah is not unaware of what you do." ﴾ (*Soorah Al-Baqarah* 2:130-140) So Allah, the Almighty, the All-Powerful declared His *Khaleel* innocent of their claim, that he was a Jew or a Christian and made clear that he was only a *Haneef* – a Muslim and he was not one of the polytheists, which is why He says, ﴿ Verily, among mankind who have the best claim to Ibraheem are those who followed him ﴾ (*Soorah Ali 'Imran* 3:68) That is, those who followed his Religion and obeyed him during his lifetime and those who held fast to his Religion after them ﴿ and this Prophet ﴾ (*Soorah Ali 'Imran* 3:68). That is, Muhammad ﷺ, because Allah legislated for him the *Haneef* Religion, which He legislated for *Al-Khaleel* and He completed it for him, giving to him that which He had not given to any Prophet or Messenger before him, as He, Most High, says, ﴿ Say (o, Muhammad), "Truly, my Lord has guided me to a Straight Path, a right religion, the religion of Ibraheem, *Hanifan* (i.e. the true Islamic Monotheism – to believe in One God [Allah i.e. to worship none but Allah, Alone]) and he was not of *al-mushrikoon*." Say (O, Muhammad), "Verily, my *salah* (prayer), my sacrifice, my living and my dying are for Allah, the Lord of the _'Alameen_. He has no partner. And of this I have been commanded and I am the first of the Muslims." ❩ (_Soorah Al-An'am_ 6:161-163)

He, Most High, says, ❨ Verily, Ibraheem was an _Ummah_ (a leader having all the good righteous qualities), or a nation, obedient to Allah, _Hanifan_ (i.e. to worship none but Allah), and he was not one of those who were _al-mushrikoon_. (He was) thankful for His (Allah's) Graces. He (Allah) chose him and guided him to a Straight Path (Islamic Monotheism, neither Judaism nor Christianity). And We gave him good in this world, and in the Hereafter he shall be of the righteous. Then, We have inspired you (O, Muhammad, saying), "Follow the Religion of Ibraheem _Hanifan_ (Islamic Monotheism – to worship none but Allah) and he was not of the _mushrikoon_ ❩ (_Soorah An-Nahl_ 16:120-123).

Al-Bukhari narrated on the authority of 'Abdullah Ibn 'Abbas رضي الله عنهما that when the Prophet ﷺ saw the pictures in the House (of Allah), he would not enter it until he had ordered them to be erased; and he saw (pictures of) Ibraheem عليه السلام and Isma'eel عليه السلام, holding divining arrows in their hands. He said, "May Allah kill them! By Allah, they never cast lots with divining arrows."[1] It was not narrated by Muslim and in one of Al-Bukhari's wordings, it was written that he ﷺ said, "May Allah kill them! They knew full well that our _Shaikh_ (i.e. Ibraheem عليه السلام) never cast lots with them." [2]

As for His saying: ❨ an _Ummah_ ❩, a role model, an _Imam_, rightly-guided, a caller to goodness and one who should be followed, ❨ obedient to Allah ❩. That is, submissive to Him in

---

(1)   Narrated by Al-Bukhari (3352).

(2)   Narrated by Al-Bukhari (1601).

all his affairs and all his doings. ❨ *Hanifan* ❩ means sincerely devoted, while being informed. ❨ And he was not one of those who were *al-mushrikoon.* (He was) thankful for His (Allah's) Graces ❩ (*Soorah An-Nahl* 16:120,121). That is, he expressed his gratitude to Allah with all of his bodily organs, including his heart, his tongue and the actions of his limbs. ❨ He (Allah) chose him ❩. That is, Allah chose him for Himself, selected him to be a Messenger and took him as His *Khaleel.* He combined for him the goodness of the life of this world and of the Hereafter. And He, Most High, says, ❨ And who can be better in religion than one who submits his face (himself) to Allah (i.e. follows Allah's Religion of Islamic Monotheism); and he is a *Muhsin* (one who does good). And follows the Religion of Ibraheem *Hanifan.* And Allah did take Ibraheem (Ibraheem) as a *Khaleel* (an intimate friend) ❩ (*Soorah An-Nisa'* 4:125). Allah, Most High, encourages us to obey Ibraheem ﷺ, because he was upon the correct Religion and the Straight Path and he fulfilled all that was enjoined upon him by his Lord and He, Most High praised him in His Words: ❨ And of Ibraheem who fulfilled (or conveyed) all that (what Allah ordered him to do or convey) ❩ (*Soorah An-Najm* 53:37). This is why Allah took him as His *Khaleel.* And *khullah* (from which the word *khaleel* is derived) means great love, as someone said,

You have permeated (takhallalta) my soul,
And this is why the khaleel is called khaleel.

Likewise, the Seal of the Prophets and the Master of the Messengers, Muhammad ﷺ also attained this high rank, as confirmed in the *Saheehain* and in other collections, in the *hadeeth* of Jundub Al-Bajali, 'Abdullah Ibn 'Amr and 'Abdullah Ibn Mas'ood, who reported from the Messenger of

Allah ﷻ that he said, "O, people! Verily, Allah has taken me as a *Khaleel*, just as He took Ibraheem as a *Khaleel*." [1] And he also said in the last sermon that he gave: "O, people! If I were to take a *Khaleel* from among the people of the Earth, I would have taken Abu Bakr as a *Khaleel*, but (I,) your Companion, am Allah's *Khaleel*." [2] They both narrated it from the *hadeeth* of Abu Sa'eed Al-Khudri ﷺ.

Al-Hakim narrated in his *Mustadrak*, on the authority of Qatadah, who reported on the authority of 'Ikrimah, who in turn reported on the authority of 'Abdullah Ibn 'Abbas ﷺ that he said, "Do you reject that *Al-Khullah* should have been for Ibraheem ﷺ, that *Al-Kalam* (Allah's Speech) should have been for Moosa ﷺ and the vision for Muhammad ﷺ?" [3]

Allah mentioned him in many places in the Qur'an, praising him and lauding him; it was said that he was mentioned in thirty-five places, including fifteen mentions in *Soorah Al-Baqarah* alone. He is one the five *Ulul-'Azm*, [4] whose names have been specified from among the Prophets in two Verses in *Soorah Al-Ahzab* and *Soorah Ash-Shoora*; and they are the Words of Allah, Most High: ﴾ And (remember) when We took from the Prophets their covenant, and from you (O, Muhammad), and from Nooh, Ibraheem, Moosa and 'Eesa, son of Maryam (Mary). We took from them a strong covenant ﴿ (*Soorah Al-Ahzab* 33:7) and His Words: ﴾ He (Allah) has ordained for you the same Religion (Islam) which He ordained for Nooh, and

---

(1)   Narrated by Muslim (532, no. 2383), At-Tirmidhi (3655), Ibn Majah (93) and Ahmad (4110).

(2)   Narrated by Al-Bukhari (3654) and Muslim (2382).

(3)   This is an authentic *hadeeth*, narrated by Al-Hakim in Al-Mustadrak (1/133).

(4)   *Ulul-'Azm*: The Five Greatest Prophets: Nooh, Ibraheem, Moosa, 'Eesa and Muhammad (peace be upon them all).

that which We have inspired in you (O, Muhammad), and that which We ordained for Ibraheem, Moosa and 'Eesa saying you should establish the Religion (i.e. to do what it orders you to do practically) and make no divisions in it (the Religion) (i.e. various religious sects). 》 (*Soorah Ash-Shoora* 42:13) He is also the noblest of *Ulul-'Azm* after Muhammad 紫 and it is he whom he met in the seventh heaven, resting his back against *Al-Baitul-Ma'moor*, which is entered by seventy thousand angels every day, after which they never return to it again.

It is reported on the authority of Abu Hurairah 紫 that he said: Someone said, "O, Messenger of Allah! Who is the noblest of people?" He said, "The most pious and God-fearing of you." He (the questioner) said, "It is not about this that we ask you." He said, "Then it is Yoosuf, the Prophet of Allah, and the son of a Prophet of Allah, the son of a Prophet of Allah, the son of Allah's *Khaleel*." They said, "It is not about this that we ask you." He said, "Then you are asking about the descent of the Arabs. Those who were the best in the pre-lslamic period of ignorance will be the best in Islam provided they comprehend the religious knowledge." [1]

Al-Bukhari narrated on the authority of 'Abdullah Ibn 'Umar 紫 that the Prophet 紫 said, "The honorable, the son of the honorable, the son the honorable, the son of is Yoosuf, the son of Ya'qoob, the son of Ishaq, the son of Ibraheem." [2]

Allah, Most High, says, 《 And of Ibraheem who fulfilled (or conveyed) all that (what Allah ordered him to do or convey).》 (*Soorah An-Najm* 53:37) They scholars said that he fulfilled all that he was commanded to do and practiced all elements and branches of faith and he did not allow the pursuit of

---

(1)   Narrated by Al-Bukhari (3353).

(2)   Narrated by Al-Bukhari (3390).

highly important matters to cause them to neglect minor matters, and undertaking great obligations did not cause him to forget small ones.

'Abdur-Razzaq reported on the authority of 'Abdullah Ibn 'Abbas ⚶ that he said regarding the Words of Allah, Most High: ‹ And (remember) when the Lord of Ibraheem (i.e. Allah) tried him with (certain) Commands, which he fulfilled.› (*Soorah Al-Baqarah 2:124*), "Allah tried him with (acts of) purification: five (acts) in the head and five in the body. As for those in the head, they were: trimming the moustache, rinsing the mouth, the *siwak*, [1] sniffing water into the nose and parting the hair; and in the body they were: clipping the nails, shaving the pubic region, circumcision, plucking the armpit hair and washing away the traces of feces and urine with water." Ibn Abi Hatim narrated it. [2]

I say: And in the *Saheehain* it is reported on the authority of Abu Hurairah ⚶ that he said, "Five practices are characteristics of the *fitrah*: circumcision, shaving the pubic region, clipping the nails, cutting the moustache short and plucking the hair from the armpits." [3]

His Palace in Paradise

Al-Hafiz Abu Bakr Al-Bazzar said: It was reported on the authority of Abu Hurairah ⚶ that he said: The Messenger of Allah ﷺ said, "Verily, in Paradise there is a palace," The

---

(1) *Siwak*: A natural toothbrush made from the root of the arak tree.

(2) Narrated by Ibn Abi Hatim in the *Tafseer* (1/359).

(3) Narrated by Al-Bukhari (5889) and Muslim (257).

narrator said, "I think that he said it is made from pearl." He said: "In it there is no crack in it and no weakness. Allah has prepared it for His *Khaleel*, Ibraheem عليه السلام, to enjoy." Al-Bazzar said, "And Ahmad Ibn Jameel Al-Marwazi told us that An-Nadr Ibn Shumail told him that Hamad Ibn Salamah said that he reported it on the authority of Simak, who reported it on the authority of 'Ikrimah, who reported it on the authority of Abu Hurairah رضي الله عنه." And he said, "We are unaware of anyone narrating this *hadeeth* on the authority of Hamad Ibn Salamah except Yazeed Ibn Haroon, An-Nadr Ibn Shumail and others and he narrated it in a *mawqoof* form. I say that were it not for this defect, it would be in accordance with the conditions required of an authentic *hadeeth*. But the compilers of the *Saheeh* did not narrate it.

The Description of Ibraheem عليه السلام

Imam Ahmad narrated on the authority of Jabir Ibn 'Abdullah رضي الله عنه from the Messenger of Allah ﷺ that he said, "The Prophets were shown to me and I saw that Moosa was a man like the men of the tribe of Shanoo'ah. I saw 'Eesa, the son of Maryam, and observed that the person he most closely resembled was 'Urwah Ibn Mas'ood. I saw Ibraheem and I observed that the person he most closely resembled was your Companion (i.e. the Prophet ﷺ himself). I saw Gabriel عليه السلام and I observed that the person he most closely resembled was Dihyah." [1] Imam Ahmad was alone in narrating it from this source and with this wording.

---

(1)   This is an authentic *hadeeth* narrated by Imam Ahmad (14179).

Imam Ahmad also narrated on the authority of 'Abdullah Ibn 'Abbas ﷺ that he said: The Messenger of Allah ﷺ said, "I saw 'Eesa, the son of Maryam, Moosa and Ibraheem. As for 'Eesa, he had a reddish complexion and curly hair and a broad chest. As for Moosa, he was a large man." They asked him, "And (what about) Ibraheem?" He said, "Look at your Companion (meaning himself)." [1]

Al-Bukhari narrated that Mujahid said that when the people mentioned the *Dajjal* before Ibn 'Abbas and said that he would have the word *Kafir*, (i.e. disbeliever) or the letters *kaf, fa', ra'* (the root of the Arabic verb to disbelieve) written on his forehead, he said, "I heard Ibn 'Abbas saying, 'I did not hear this, but the Prophet ﷺ said, If you want to see Ibraheem, then look at your Companion (i.e. the Prophet himself) but Moosa was a curly-haired, brown man (who used to ride) a red camel, the reins of which were made of date-palm fibers. It is as if I were now looking down a valley." [2]

Mention of Ibraheem Al-Khaleel's Death And What is Said Regarding His Age

Ibn 'Asakir narrated numerous reports on the authority of more than one of the *Salaf*, regarding the traditions of the People of the Scripture describing how the Angel of Death came to Ibraheem علي<u></u>, and Allah knows best about their authenticity. It was said that he died suddenly and that Dawood علي<u></u> and Sulaiman علي<u></u> also died suddenly, but what has been said by the People of the Scripture and others contradicts this. They

---

(1) This is an authentic *hadeeth* narrated by Imam Ahmad (2692).

(2) Narrated by Al-Bukhari (3355).

said that Ibraheem ﷺ became ill and died when he was aged a hundred and seventy-five years. It was also said that he was aged ninety years at the time of his death and that he was buried in the cavern which was in the Hittite region of Hebron, near to his wife, Sarah, who was buried in the field of 'Afroon Al-Haith. His sons, Isma'eel ﷺ and Isaac ﷺ, undertook the task of burying him. There is also a report that provides evidence that he lived for two hundred years, according to Ibn Al-Kalbi.

Abu Hatim Ibn Hibban reported in his *Saheeh* on the authority of Abu Hurairah ؓ that he said, "Ibraheem circumcised himself with a *qaddoom* (adz) when he was hundred and twenty years old – and he lived for eighty years after that." [1]

Then Ibn Hibban said, "Mention of the refutation of the claim of those who asserted that this tradition is not *marfoo'*. We were informed by Muhammad Ibn 'Abdullah Ibn Al-Junaid that he said: We were told Qutaibah Ibn Sa'eed that he said: We were told by Al-Laith, who reported on the authority of Ibn 'Ajlan, who in turn reported on the authority of his father, who reported on the authority of Abu Hurairah ؓ from the Prophet ﷺ that he said, "Ibraheem circumcised himself when he was hundred and twenty years old and he lived for eighty years after that; and he circumcised himself with a *qaddoom* (adz)." [2]

I say: That which is in the *Saheeh* states that he circumcised himself when he had reached the age of eighty years, and in another narration, when he was eighty years old. And there is no contradiction in them regarding how long he lived afterward

---

(1)   This is an authentic *hadeeth* narrated by Ibn Hibban in his *Saheeh* (14/84, No. 6204).

(2)   Its chain of narrators is authentic, according to the conditions for acceptance stipulated by Muslim. It was narrated by Ibn Hibban in his *Saheeh* (14/86, No. 6250).

– and Allah knows better.

Mention of the Sons of Ibraheem, Al-Khaleel, (May the Choicest Prayers and Blessings of Allah Be Upon Them)

The first son born to him was Isma'eel الله‌السلام, who was born of Hajar, the Egyptian Copt. Then Ishaq الله‌السلام was born to him from Sarah, who was the daughter of his paternal uncle. Then after her, he married the Qantoora the daughter of Yaqtuna Al-Kan'aniyah. She bore him six children: Zamran, Yashan, Madyan, Ishbak, and Shuah. The sixth was not named. After her, he married Hajoon, the daughter of Ameen, who bore him five children: Kaisan, Sooraj, Umaim, Lootan and Nafis. This is how Abul-Qasim As-Suhaili reported it in his book '*At-Ta'reef Wal-I'lam*'.

Among the Great Events

That Occurred During the Lifetime of Ibraheem ﷺ, Al-Khaleel is the Story of the People of Lot ﷺ and the General Punishment That Befell Them

Loot ﷺ had parted company with his uncle, *Al-Khaleel* ﷺ, by his command and his permission and settled in the city of Sadoom (Sodom), in the land of Ghawr Zughar. It was the main city in the area and it contained land, workshops and villages which were attached to it. Its people included some of the most sinful and disbelieving people, harboring evil thoughts and wicked ideas. They practiced highway robbery and had illicit sex in their meeting places. There was no sin left that they did not indulge in. They committed sins which no man before them had committed, including: men having sexual relations with other men; abandoning the women whom Allah had created for His righteous slaves. Loot ﷺ called upon them to worship Allah, Most High, Alone, without ascribing partners to Him and forbade them from indulging in these unlawful deeds and vile, shameless acts. But they persisted in their error and transgression and continued in their debauchery and disbelief and so Allah ordained a punishment for them which could not be rescinded, the like of which they had never imagined or expected. He made them an example to all of mankind and a warning to all men of intelligence. This is why Allah, Most High, mentioned their story in a number of places in His Book, such as His Words in *Soorah Al-A'raf*: ❨And (remember) Loot, when he said to his people, "Do you commit the worst sin such as none preceding you has committed in the *'Alameen*? Verily, you practice your lusts on men instead of women. Nay, but you are a people transgressing beyond bounds (by committing great sins)." And the answer of his people was only that they said, "Drive them out of your town, these are indeed men who want to be pure (from sins)!" Then We saved him and his family, except his wife; she was of those who remained behind (in the punishment). And We rained down on them a rain (of stones). Then see what was the end of the *mujrimoon* (criminals, polytheists, sinners, etc.) ❩ (*Soorah Al-A'raf* 7:80-84)

He, Most High, says in *Soorah Hood*, ❨ And verily, there came Our Messengers to Ibraheem with glad tidings. They said, *Salam* (greetings or peace)!" He answered, "*Salam* (greetings or peace)!" And he hastened to entertain them with a roasted calf. But when he saw their hands went not toward it (the meal), he felt some mistrust of them, and conceived a fear of them. They said, "Fear not, we have been sent against the people of Loot." And his wife was standing (there) and she laughed (either, because the Messengers did not eat their food or for being glad for the destruction of the people of Loot. But We gave her glad tidings of Ishaq and after him, of Ya'qoob. She said (in astonishment), "woe unto me! Shall I bear a child while I am an old woman, and here is my husband, an old man?

Verily! This is a strange thing!" They said, "Do you wonder at the Decree of Allah? The Mercy of Allah and His Blessings be on you, O, family (of Ibraheem). Surely, He (Allah) is Most Praiseworthy, Most Glorious." Then when the fear had gone away from (the mind of) Ibraheem and the glad tidings had reached him, he began to plead with Us (Our Messengers) for the people of Loot. Verily, Ibraheem was, without doubt, forbearing, used to invoke Allah with humility, and was repentant (to Allah all the time, again and again). "O, Ibraheem! Forsake this. Indeed, the Commandment of your Lord has gone forth. Verily, there will come a torment for them which cannot be turned back." And when Our Messengers came to Loot, he was grieved on their account and felt himself straitened for them (lest the townpeople should approach them to commit sodomy with them). He said, "This is a distressful day." And his people came rushing toward him, and since aforetime they used to commit crimes (sodomy, etc.), he said, "O, my people! Here are my daughters (i.e. the daughters of my nation), they are purer for you (if you marry them lawfully). So fear Allah and degrade me not as regards my guests! Is there not among you a single right-minded man?" They said, "Surely you know that we have neither any desire nor are we in need of your daughters, and indeed you know well what we want!" He said, "Would that I had strength (men) to overpower you, or that I could betake myself to some powerful support (to resist you)." They (the Messengers) said, "O, Loot! Verily, we are the Messengers from your Lord! They shall not reach you! So travel with your family in a part of the night and let not any of you look back, but your wife (will remain behind), verily, the punishment which will afflict them will afflict her. Indeed, morning is their appointed time. Is not the morning near?" So when Our Commandment came, We turned (the towns of

Sodom in Palestine) upside down, and rained on them stones of baked clay, piled up; marked from your Lord, and they are not ever far from the *zalimoon.* ❭ (*Soorah Hood* 11:69-83)

He, Most High, says in *Soorah An-Naml,* ❬ And (remember) Loot! When he said to his people, "Do you commit *al-fahishah* (evil, great sin, every kind of unlawful sexual intercourse, sodomy, etc.) while you see (one another doing evil without any screen, etc.)? Do you approach men in your lusts rather than women? Nay, but you are a people who behave senselessly." There was no other answer given by his people except that they said, "Drive out the family of Loot from your city. Verily, these are men who want to be clean and pure!" So We saved him and his family, except his wife. We destined her to be of those who remained behind. And We rained down on them a rain (of stones). So evil was the rain of those who were warned.❭ (*Soorah An-Naml* 27:54-58)

He, Most High, says in *Soorah Adh-Dhariyat*, after relating the story of the guests of Ibraheem ﷺ and how they gave him the glad tidings of a son, ❬ (Ibraheem) said, "Then for what purpose have you come, o, Messengers?" They said, "We have been sent to a people who are *mujrimoon* (polytheists, sinners, criminals, disbelievers in Allah), to send down upon them stones of baked clay, marked by your Lord for the *musrifoon* (polytheists, criminals, sinners those who trespass Allah's set limits in evil-doing by committing great sins)." So We brought out from therein the Believers. But We found not there any household of the Muslims except one (i.e. Loot and his two daughters). And We have left there a sign (i.e. the place of the Dead Sea, well-known in Palestine) for those who fear the painful torment. ❭ (*Soorah Adh-Dhariyat* 51:31-37)

In *Soorah Al-Qamar*, He says, ❬ The people of Loot belied

the warnings. Verily, We sent against them a violent storm of stones (which destroyed them all), except the family of Loot, whom We saved in the last hour of the night, as a Favour from Us, thus do We reward him who gives thanks (by obeying Us). And he (Loot) indeed had warned them of Our Grasp, but they did doubt the warnings! And they indeed sought to shame his guests (by asking them to commit sodomy with them). So We blinded their eyes, "Then taste you My Torment and My Warnings." And verily, an abiding torment seized them early in the morning. "Then taste you My Punishment and My Warnings." And indeed, We have made the Qur'an easy to understand and remember, then is there any that will remember (or receive admonition)? ⟩ (*Soorah Al-Qamar* 54:33-40)

When Loot ﷺ called upon his people to worship Allah, Alone, without ascribing partners to Him and forbade them from committing the sins which Allah has described, they did not respond positively to his call, and not a single man from among them believed in him. Nor did they give up the sins that they had been forbidden from committing; instead, they continued as they had been, refusing to desist from their error and transgression and attempting to expel their Messenger from their midst. Their response to his address to them proved that they were a people without sense: ⟨ There was no other answer given by his people except that they said, "Drive out the family of Loot from your city. Verily, these are men who want to be clean and pure!" ⟩ (*Soorah An-Naml* 27:56) Thus they deemed the most commendable behavior to be blameworthy and requiring expulsion. Nothing compelled them to say this except their obduracy and stubbornness. Allah kept him and all of his family pure, except for his wife and He evacuated them from the city with the best evacuation and He left the rest of them to remain there. But after He had afflicted them with a stinking, fetid body of water, which had waves, but in reality, it was a blazing fire upon them and a burning heat and its water was salty and bitter. This was the repayment for the enormity and abomination which they had committed, which no people in this world had committed before them. This is why they were made an example and a warning to the people of the world. In addition to this, they used to practice highway robbery and betray their friends and they would utter and commit all sorts of evil words and deeds in their meeting places, to such an extent that it was said that they used to break wind in front of their companions in the meeting place and they would feel no shame or embarrassment toward them. It was also said that they used to commit the most shameful deeds in their gatherings and would not disdain to do so, nor did they pay heed to any warnings or advice given to them by those who possessed good sense. In their places and others, they were like animals, or even more astray. They refused to desist from what they were doing and they had no regrets for what they had done in the past. Nor did they show any desire to change in the future. So Allah seized them with a calamitous seizure. Among the things that they said to Loot ﷺ was, ❲ "Bring Allah's Punishment upon us if you are one of the truthful." ❳ (*Soorah Al-'Ankaboot* 29:29) So they requested of him the infliction of the painful punishment of which he had warned them. At that point, their noble Prophet ﷺ invoked Allah against them and asked the Lord of the Worlds and the *Ilah* (God) of the Messengers that He help him against the depraved people. So Allah was Jealous for his jealousness and Angry for his anger and He answered his supplication and sent His noble Messengers, His Mighty angels and they visited *Al-Khaleel*, Ibraheem ﷺ, and gave him the glad tidings of the birth of an intelligent son and they also informed him of the purpose for which they had come:

◀(Ibraheem) said, "Then for what purpose you have come, O, Messengers?" They said, "We have been sent to a people who arc *mujrimoon* to send down upon them stones of baked clay, marked by your Lord for the *musrifoon*." ▶ (*Soorah Adh-Dhariyat* 51:31-34)

He, Most High, says, ◀ Then, when the fear had gone away from (the mind of) Ibraheem and the glad tidings had reached him, he began to plead with Us (Our Messengers) for the people of Loot ▶ (*Soorah Hood* 11:74). This was because he hoped that they would repent to Allah, submit to Him and desist from their sinful ways.

This is why Allah, Most High, says, ◀ Verily, Ibraheem was, without doubt, forbearing, used to invoke Allah with humility, and was repentant (to Allah all the time, again and again). "O, Ibraheem! Forsake this. Indeed, the Commandment of your Lord has gone forth. Verily, there will come a punishment for them which cannot be turned back." ▶ (*Soorah Hood* 11:75,76) That is, desist from this and speak of something else, because their fate has been decided and their punishment, destruction and annihilation are inevitable. ◀ "Indeed, the Commandment of your Lord has gone forth." ▶. That is, He Whose Command cannot be rescinded, Whose Punishment cannot be turned back and Whose Judgement cannot be questioned, has given His Command: ◀ "Verily, there will come a punishment for them which cannot be turned back." ▶ (*Soorah Hood* 11:76)

The scholars of *tafseer* said that when the angels, i.e. Gabriel, Meeka'eel and Israfeel, departed from Ibraheem's presence, they continued until they reached the land of Sadoom (Sodom), where they assumed the form of handsome men, as a test from Allah, Most High, for the people of Loot 🕊️ and in order to establish the evidence against them. They sought hospitality with Loot صلى الله عليه وسلم and this was just before sunset. Loot صلى الله عليه وسلم feared that if he did not offer them hospitality, some other person from among his people would do so and he believed them to be human beings. ﴿ He was grieved on their account and felt himself straitened for them (lest the townspeople should approach them to commit sodomy with them). He said, "This is a distressful day." ﴾ (*Soorah Hood* 11:77) 'Abdullah Ibn 'Abbas رضى الله عنهما, Mujahid, Qatadah and Muhammad Ibn Ishaq said that it means a day of severe trial and tribulation. This was because he knew that he might not be able to defend them when night fell from what had befallen others at his peoples' hands. They had ordered him not to grant hospitality to anyone, but considered that it was unavoidable.

Qatadah stated that they arrived while he was working on the land and they sought hospitality from him. He was embarrassed before them and tried to persuade them to leave this town and seek shelter in another. He said to them, "O, people! I know not of any people on the face of the earth wickeder than the people of this city." Then he walked a little way, and then he repeated these words four times. He (Qatadah) said that they (the angels) had been commanded (by Allah) not to destroy them until their Prophet had borne witness to that effect.

As-Suddi said: The angels departed from Ibraheem's presence and headed for the people of Loot صلى الله عليه وسلم and they arrived there in the middle of the day. When they reached the River Sodom, they met the daughter of Loot صلى الله عليه وسلم, who was drawing water for her family. He had two daughters, the elder of whom was named Areetha, while the younger was named Daghootha. They said to her, "O, young girl! Do you know of any place where we can find accommodation?" She said, "Remain here! Do not enter (the city) until I come to you." She feared that some ill might befall them at the hands of her people and so she went to her father and said to him, "O, my father! Some young men are asking for you at the gates of the city; I have never seen more handsome faces of any men than theirs. Let not your people take them and dishonor them." His people had forbidden him from giving hospitality to any man, but he took them in secret and no one knew of their presence except his family. But his wife went out and informed his people of them, saying, "In Loot's house there are men, the like of whose beautiful faces I have never seen." Then his people came hastening angrily to him. Allah says, ❴ and since aforetime they used to commit crimes (sodomy, etc.) ❵ (*Soorah Hood* 11:78) That is, this was in addition to the many major sins they had committed. ❴ O, my people! Here are my daughters (i.e. the daughters of my nation), they are purer for you (if you marry them lawfully) ❵ (*Soorah Hood* 11:78) He forbade them from committing such indecent acts and bore witness that there was not a single right-minded and intelligent man among them, nor any good person; on the contrary, he averred that all of them were foolish, terribly debauched, arrogant disbelievers. This was just what the angels wanted to hear from him before they asked him about it. His people – may Allah's Curse be upon them – said, in answer to what their Prophet ﷺ had ordered them to do, ❴ "They said: Surely you know that we have neither any desire nor are we in need of your daughters, and indeed you know well what we want!" ❵ (*Soorah Hood* 11:79) They said – may Allah's Curse be on them "O, Loot! You know that we have no desire for women and verily, you know full well what we desire (i.e. men)." They addressed these wicked words to their noble Messenger and they did not fear the infliction of Allah's painful punishment. This is why Loot ﷺ said, ❴ "Would that I had strength (men) to overpower you, or that I could betake myself to some powerful support (to resist you)." 〉 (*Soorah Hood* 11:80) He wished that he had the strength to overcome them or the ability to resist them and kin to help him against them, in order to inflict on them the punishment they deserved for these words they had spoken. It is reported on the authority of Abu Hurairah ﷺ in a *marfoo'* form that he said, "We are more liable to be in doubt than Ibraheem when he said, 〈 "My Lord! Show me how You give life to the dead." . He (i.e. Allah) said, "Don't you believe then?" He (i.e. Ibraheem) said, "Yes, but (I ask) in order to be stronger in faith." 〉 (*Soorah Al-Baqarah* 2:260) May Allah send His Mercy on Loot! He wished to have a powerful support. If I were to stay in prison for such a long time, as Yoosuf did, I would have accepted the offer (of freedom without insisting on having my guiltlessness declared)." It is reported on the authority of Abu Hurairah ﷺ that he said, "May Allah have mercy on Lot; he wished that he could betake himself to some powerful support (to resist them). (Meaning Allah, the Almighty, the All-Powerful). Allah did not send a Prophet after him except that he was from the wealthy among his people." [1]

Allah, Most High, says, 〈 And the inhabitants of the city came rejoicing (at the news of the young men's arrival). (Loot) said, "Verily! These are my guests, so shame me not. And fear Allah and disgrace me not." They (the people of the city) said, "Did we not forbid you to entertain (or protect) any of the *'Alameen* (people, foreigners, strangers, etc. from us)?" (Loot) said, "These (the girls of the nation) are my daughters (to marry lawfully), if you must act (so)." 〉 (*Soorah Al-Hijr* 15:67-71)

He ordered them to have sexual relations with their women lawfully and warned them against continuing on the path they

---

(1)   This is an authentic *hadeeth* narrated by Imam Ahmad (2/332, No. 8761).

were following and the sins they were committing. But they did not cease and disregarded his words. Instead, the more he forbade them, the more strenuous became their efforts to reach the guests and the more excited they became. But they did not know the fate that had been decreed for them and to which they were heading. This is why Allah, Most High, says, swearing by the life of His Prophet, Muhammad ❨Verily, by your life (O, Muhammad), in their wild intoxication, they were wandering blindly ❩ (*Soorah Al-Hijr* 15:72) He, Most High, says, ❨ And he (Loot) indeed had warned them of Our Grasp, but they did doubt the warnings! And they indeed sought to shame his guests (by asking to commit sodomy with them). So We blinded their eyes, "Then taste you My Torment and My Warnings." And verily, an abiding punishment seized them early in the morning ❩ (*Soorah Al-Qamar* 54:36-38)

Scholars of *tafseer* and others have said that the Prophet of Allah, Loot ﷺ, tried to prevent his people from entering and resisted them; the door was locked and they were trying to open it and enter through it. Loot ﷺ warned them to desist and forbade them from behind the door, while they tried to force entry from outside. When the situation became straitened for him, he said, ❨ "Would that I had strength (men) to overpower you, or that I could betake myself to some powerful support (to resist you)." ❩ (*Soorah Hood* 11:80) That is, I would inflict the punishment on you. The angels said, ❨ "O, Loot! Verily, we are the Messengers from your Lord! They shall not reach you!" ❩ (*Soorah Hood* 11:81)

The scholars) said that Gabriel ﷺ attacked them and struck their faces with the edge of his wing and their sight was removed. Indeed, it was even said that their eyes were completely effaced, leaving no trace. They returned to their homes, feeling the walls and threatening the Messenger of Allah ﷺ and saying, "In the morning, we will deal with him." Allah, Most High, says, ❨ And they indeed sought to shame his guests (by asking to commit sodomy with them). So We blinded their eyes, "Then taste you My Punishment and My Warnings." And verily, an abiding punishment seized them early in the morning. ❩ (*Soorah Al-Qamar* 54:37,38) This was after the angels had approached Loot ﷺ and commanded him to travel in the latter part of the night with his family and they commanded them that none should look back, i.e. when they heard the sound of the punishment being inflicted on Loot's people. As for His Words: ❨ except your wife ❩ (*Soorah Hood* 11:81) if the word for "wife" is read in Arabic as *imra'atak*, then it is possible that the meaning is that his wife was excepted from the command: ❨ "So travel with your family in a part of the night." ❩ (*Soorah Hood* 11:81), as if it was being said, "except your wife, do not make the journey by night with her." It is also possible that it is from His Words: ❨ and let not any of you look back, except your wife ❩ (*Soorah Hood* 11:81) That is, she will certainly look back and that which will afflict them will afflict her also. This interpretation is strengthened by the recitation of the word "wife" in Arabic as *imra'atak*. However, the former is more apparent in meaning. And Allah knows better.

As for His Words: ❨ and We rained on them stones of baked clay, piled up ❩ (*Soorah Hood* 11:82) The word *sijjeel* is an Arabicised Persian word and it means forceful, hard and strong. ❨ Piled up ❩ that is, falling one upon another upon them from the sky. ❨ Marked ❩ that is, the stones were marked and sealed, all of them having the names of their victims written on them, as He, Most High, says, ❨ Marked by your Lord for the *musrifoon* (polytheists, criminals, sinners those who trespass Allah's set limits in evil-doings by committing great sins) 〉 (*Soorah Adh-Dhariyat* 51:34) and as He, Most High, says, 〈 And We rained on them a rain (of punishment). And how evil was the rain of those who had been warned 〉 (*Soorah Ash-Shu'ara'* 26:173) And He, Most High, says, 〈 And He destroyed the overthrown cities (of Sodom to which Prophet Loot was sent). So there covered them that which did cover 〉 (*Soorah An-Najm* 53:53,54) That is, he inverted them and dropped them face down and then covered them with a deluge of stones from *sijjeel*, which followed one upon another, each one of them marked with the name of the person among those present in the city upon whom it would fall and also upon those who were absent on journeys, those in distant lands and those who were isolated from it. It was said that the wife of Loot عليه السلام remained with her people and it was also said that she set out with her husband and her two daughters, but when she heard the shout and the falling of the city, she turned round toward her people, disobeying the Command of her Lord and said, "O, my people!" Then a rock fell on her and crushed her and she joined her people, since she followed their religion and she spied for them on the guests who stayed with Loot عليه السلام. Allah, Most High, says, 〈 Allah sets forth an example for those who disbelieve, the wife of Nooh and the wife of Loot. They were under two of our righteous slaves, but they both betrayed (their husbands) so they (Nooh and Loot) benefited them (their respective wives) not, against Allah, and it was said, "Enter the Fire along with those who enter!" 〉 (*Soorah At-Tahreem* 66:10). That is, betray them by not following their Religion; it does not mean that they used to commit adultery – Allah forbid that! Never! For Allah would not ordain for His Prophet that his wife should commit adultery, as 'Abdullah Ibn 'Abbas رضي الله عنه and other *Imams* among earlier and the later scholars said, "No wife of a Prophet ever committed adultery." [2] And whoever claimed otherwise has committed a grave error.

Allah made the location of this city into a putrid sea, whose water provides no benefit and neither do the lands surrounding it, due to their ruin, their badness and poor quality. Thus they became a lesson, a warning and a sign of Allah's Omnipotence, His Greatness and His Power in inflicting retribution on those who disobey His Command, belie His Messengers and follow their own lusts. These verses are also a proof of His Mercy towards His believing slaves, in that He saved them from being among those who were destroyed and He brought them out from darkness into light, as He, Most High, says, ❨ Verily, in this is an *Ayah* (proof or sign), yet most of them (polytheists, pagans, etc., who do not believe in the Resurrection) are not believers. And verily, your Lord! He is truly the Almighty, the Most Merciful ❩ (*Soorah Ash-Shu'ara'* 26:8,9)

And He, Most High, says, ❨ So *As-Saihah* (punishment - awful cry, etc.) overtook them at the time of sunrise; and We turned them (the towns of Sodom in Palestine) upside down and rained down on them stones of baked clay. Surely! In this are signs, for those who see (or understand or learn the lessons from the Signs of Allah). And verily, they (the cities) were right on the highroad (from Makkah to Syria i.e. the place where the Dead Sea is now). Surely! Therein is indeed a sign for the Believers ❩ (*Soorah Al-Hijr* 15:73-77) That is, those who look with a keen and intuitive eye at them, can see how Allah changed that land and its people and how He destroyed it and flooded it, after it had been populated and made prosperous, as

---

(2) Narrated by Ibn 'Asakir (14/636), on the authority of Ashras Al-Khurasani, in a *marfoo'* form, though in *Ad-Durr ul-Manthoor* (6/245), As-Suyooti ascribed it to Ibn Al-Mundhir and said that it is *mawqoof*, being a saying of 'Abdullah Ibn 'Abbas ﷺ.

narrated by At-Tirmidhi and others in a *marfoo'* form: "Fear the keen eye of the Believer, for verily, it looks with the Light of Allah." Then he recited, "❨ In this are signs, for those who see (or understand or learn the lessons from the Signs of Allah) ❩ (*Soorah Al-Hijr* 15:75)." [3]

As for His Saying: ❨ And verily, they (the cities) were right on the highroad (from Makkah to Syria i.e. the place where the Dead Sea is now) ❩ (*Soorah Al-Hijr* 15:76) it means they were on a road that is broad and well travelled and it is so until now, as He, Most High, says, ❨ Verily, you pass by them in the morning and at night; will you not then reflect? ❩ (*Soorah As-Saffat* 37:137,138)

Allah, Most High, says, ❨ So We brought out from therein the Believers. But We found not there any household of the Muslims except one (i.e. Loot and his two daughters). And We have left there a sign (i.e. the place of the Dead Sea, well-known in Palestine) for those who fear the painful punishment ❩ (*Soorah Adh-Dhariyat* 51:35-37). That is, We left it as a lesson and a warning for those who are afraid of the Punishment of the Hereafter; who fear the Most Merciful unseen and also fear the time when they will stand before their Lord (on the Day of Resurrection); who restrain their souls from evil desires and lusts, held back from committing those deeds which Allah has made unlawful, abandoned acts of disobedience and feared to resemble the people of Loot ﷺ. "Whoever imitates a people, he is one of them." [4] as someone said (in *Al-Bahr ut-Taweel*): Though you may not be the people of Loot themselves, still, the people of Loot are not that different from you.

(3) This is a weak *hadeeth* narrated by At-Tirmidhi (3127), on the authority of Abu Sa'eed Al-Khudri ﷺ.

(4) This *hadeeth* is *hasan-saheeh*; it was narrated by Abu Dawood on the authority of 'Abdullah Ibn 'Umar ﷺ.

The discerning and intelligent person, who fears his Lord fulfills what Allah, the Almighty, the All-Powerful has enjoined upon him and he accepts that to which the Messenger of Allah has guided him, such as lawful sexual relations with wives and slave-girls who possess beauty. He should beware of following every rebellious devil, for then he will merit punishment and he will be included in the Words of Allah, Most High: ❨ and they are not ever far from the *zalimoon* (polytheists, evil-doers, etc.) ❩ *(Soorah Hood 11:83)*

The Story of the People of Shu'aib

Allah, Most High, says in *Soorah Al-A'raf*, after relating the story of the people of Loot, ❨ And to (the people of) Madyan (Midian), (We sent) their brother Shu'aib. He said, "O, my people! Worship Allah! You have no other *ilah* (god) but Him (*La ilaha illallah* [none has the right to be worshipped but Allah]). Verily, a clear proof (sign) from your Lord has come unto you; so give full measure and full weight and wrong not men in their things, and do not commit mischief on the earth after it has been set in order, that will be better for you, if you are Believers. And sit not on every road, threatening, and hindering from the Path of Allah those who believe in Him and seeking to make it crooked. And remember when you were but few, and He multiplied you. And see what was the end of the *mufsidoon* (mischief-makers, corrupt people, liars). And if there is a party of you who believe in that with which I have been sent and a party who do not believe, be patient until Allah judges between us, and He is the Best of judges." The chiefs of those who were arrogant among his people said, "We shall certainly drive you out, O, Shu'aib and those who have believed with you from our town, or else you (all) shall return to our religion." He said, "Even though we hate it! We should have invented a lie against Allah if we returned to your religion, after Allah has rescued us from it. And it is not for us to return to it unless Allah, our Lord, should will. Our Lord comprehends all things in His Knowledge. In Allah (Alone) we put our trust. Our Lord! Judge between us and our people in truth, for You are the Best of those who give judgment." The chiefs of those who disbelieved among his people said (to their people), "If you follow Shu'aib, be sure then you will be the losers!" So the earthquake seized them and they lay (dead), prostrate in their homes. Those who belied Shu'aib became as if they had never dwelt there (in their homes). Those who belied Shu'aib, they were the losers. Then he (Shu'aib) turned from them and said, "O, my people! I have indeed conveyed my Lord's Messages unto you and I have given you good advice. Then how can I sorrow for the disbelieving people's (destruction)." 》 (*Soorah Al-A'raf* 7:85-93)

He, Most High, says in *Soorah Ash-Shu'ara'*, after relating their story, ﴾ The dwellers of *Al-Aikah* (near Madyan) belied the Messengers. When Shu'aib said to them, "Will you not fear Allah (and obey Him)? I am a trustworthy Messenger to you. So fear Allah, keep your duty to Him, and obey me. No reward do I ask of you for it (my Message of Islamic Monotheism), my reward is only from the Lord of the *'Alameen*. Give full measure, and cause no loss (to others). And weigh with a true and straight balance. And defraud not people by reducing their things, nor do evil, making corruption and mischief in the land. And fear Him Who created you and the generations of the men of old." They said, "You are only one of those bewitched! You are but a human being like us and verily, we think that you are one of the liars! So cause a piece of the heaven to fall on us, if you are of the truthful!" He said, "My Lord is the Best Knower of what you do." But they belied him, so the torment of the day of shadow (a gloomy cloud) seized them, indeed that was the torment of a Great Day. Verily, in this is indeed a sign, yet most of them are not believers. And verily! Your Lord, He is indeed the Almighty, the Most Merciful ⟩ (*Soorah Ash-Shu'ara'* 26:176-191).

The people of Madyan were Arab people and they dwelled in the city of Madyan, which was in the land of Mu'an, on the border of Ash-Sham, near to the region of Hijaz, and not far from the lake of the people of Loot عليه السلام – and they lived not long after them. Madyan was a tribe after whom the city was named. They were from the tribe of Madyan, son of Madyaan, son of Ibraheem *Al-Khaleel* عليه السلام and Shu'aib عليه السلام was their Prophet; he was the son of Meekeel Ibn Yashjan (Jokshan), according to Ibn Ishaq. He said, "In the Syriac language he was called Bathroon." But there is some doubt about this. It was also said that he was Shu'aib Ibn Yashjan Ibn Lawai (Levi) Ibn Ya'qoob (Jacob). It was also said that he was Shu'aib Ibn Thuwaib Ibn 'Abqa Ibn Madyan Ibn Ibraheem (Ibraheem). And it was said that he was Shu'aib Ibn 'Saifoor Ibn 'Abqa Ibn Thabit Ibn Madyan Ibn Ibraheem. Other genealogies have also been given for him.

In the *hadeeth* of Abu Dharr رضي الله عنه, which is in the *Saheeh* of Ibn Hibban, in the Chapter on Prophets and Messengers, the

Prophet ﷺ said, "Abu Dharr, four (of the Prophets) were from the Arabs: Hood, Saleh, Shu'aib and your Prophet." [5] Some of the *Salaf* referred to Shu'aib عليه السلام as the "Orator of the Prophets", due to his eloquence, grandeur of speech and powerful rhetoric, when calling upon his people to believe in his Message.

It is reported on the authority of 'Abdullah Ibn 'Abbas رضي الله عنه that he said: Whenever the Messenger of Allah ﷺ mentioned Shu'aib عليه السلام, he would say, "That was the Orator of the Prophets " [6]

The people of Madyan were disbelievers, who practiced highway robbery; they used to terrorize wayfarers and they worshipped *Al-Aikah*, which means a tree surrounded by tangled woods. They were the worst of people in their dealings with others, giving short weight and measure, while demanding more than their due from others. So Allah sent to them a man from among them and that was the Messenger of Allah, Shu'aib عليه السلام; he called on them to worship Allah, Alone, without ascribing partners to Him and he forbade them from engaging in the aforementioned sinful practices, such as cheating the people out of their rights and terrorizing them when they were on the road. Some of them believed, but most of them disbelieved and so Allah inflicted on them a severe punishment. And He is the *Wali* (Helper, Supporter, Protector, etc.), Worthy of all Praise. He, Most High, says, ﴿ And to (the people of) Madyan, (We sent) their brother Shu'aib. He said, "O, my people! Worship Allah! You have no other *ilah* (god) but Him. (*La ilaha ill-Allah* [none has the right to be worshipped but Allah]). Verily,

---

(5) This *hadeeth*, which was narrated in its entirety by Ibn Hibban in his Saheeh (2/77, No. 361) is extremely weak.

(6) This *hadeeth* was narrated by Al-Hakim in *Al-Hakim* (4071). Adh-Dhahabi did not comment on it in At-Talkhees, but in its chain of narrators is one Salamah Ibn Al-Fadhl, who has been declared weak by more than one scholar.

a clear sign from your Lord has come unto you." ❭ (*Soorah Al-A'raf* 7:85) That is, a proof, a clear argument and irrefutable evidence of the truth of what I have brought to you. ❮ "So give full measure and full weight and wrong not men in their things, and do not mischief on the earth after it has been set in order." ❭ (*Soorah Al-A'raf* 7:85) He commanded them to be fair and forbade them to commit injustice and he warned them against disobeying him in this, saying, ❮ "That will be better for you, if you are Believers. And sit not on every path." ❭ (*Soorah Al-A'raf* 7:85,86) That is, on every road "threatening…" . That is, threatening to take the people's money by exacting taxes and such like from the traders who entered the city and terrorizing the wayfarers.

As-Suddi said in his *Tafseer* on the authority of the Companions, ❮ "And sit not on every path, threatening" ❭ (*Soorah Al-A'raf* 7:86) means that they used to exact tithes from the money of the wayfarers.

It is reported on the authority of 'Abdullah Ibn 'Abbas ﷺ that he said, "They were a people who exceeded all limits and committed outrages; they would sit at the side of the road and exact tithes from the people's money – and they were the first people to practice that." ❮ "And hindering from the Path of Allah those who believe in Him and seeking to make it crooked." ❭ (*Soorah Al-A'raf* 7:86) So he forbade them to cut off the physical road in the life of this world and the spiritual, religious road: ❮ "And remember when you were but few, and He multiplied you. And see what was the end of the *mufsidoon*." ❭ (*Soorah Al-A'raf* 7:86) He reminded them of the blessings that Allah, Most High, had bestowed on them, by increasing their numbers, after they had formerly been only a few and he warned them of Allah's Vengeance being visited upon them, if they disobeyed the guidance that he brought to them, as Allah said to them in another account, ❲ "and give not short measure or weight, I see you in prosperity; and verily I fear for you the Punishment of a Day encompassing." ❳ (*Soorah Hood* 11:84), That is, do not (further) commit those sins that you are currently engaging in and do not continue to transgress in this way, for if you do, Allah will remove the blessing that is in your hands and He will cause you to become impoverished and remove the means by which you have become rich. This was in addition to the punishment of the Hereafter. A person upon whom both punishments are combined has acquired for himself the worst of bargains. So he forbade them from engaging in unacceptable practices, such as giving short measure to others, while taking more than one's due from them (*tatfeef*). He warned them that they would lose the benefits that Allah had bestowed on them in this earthly life and of the painful punishment that awaited them in the Hereafter, and he reprimanded them in the harshest manner. Then after rebuking them, he commanded them, saying, ❲ "And O, my people! Give full measure and weight in justice and reduce not the things that are due to the people, and do not commit mischief in the land, causing corruption. That which is left by Allah for you (after giving the rights of the people) is better for you, if you are Believers. And I am not set over you as a guardian." ❳ (*Soorah Hood* 11:85,86) 'Abdullah Ibn 'Abbas ﷺ and Al-Hasan Al-Basri said that ❲ "That which is left by Allah for you (after giving the rights of the people) is better for you" ❳ means that the sustenance which Allah bestows on you is better than the money that you take from the people by means of *tatfeet*. The Messenger of Allah ﷺ said, "Verily, *riba* (interest, usury, etc.), though it may multiply, the end result of it is less." [7] That is, little. The Messenger of Allah ﷺ also said,

---

(7) This is an authentic *hadeeth* narrated by Imam Ahmad, on the authority of

"The seller and the buyer have the right to keep or return goods as long as they have not parted or till they part; and if both the parties spoke the truth and described the defects and qualities (of the goods), then they would be blessed in their transaction, and if they told lies or hid something, then the blessings of their transaction would be lost." [8]

What is meant is that there is a blessing in lawful profit, even though it may be little, while the unlawful does not accrue any blessings, even though the profit from it may be great. This is why the Prophet of Allah, Shu'aib, said, ❨ "That which is left by Allah for you (after giving the rights of the people) is better for you, if you are Believers." ❩ (*Soorah Hood* 11:86) As for his saying: ❨ "And I am not set over you as a guardian." ❩ (*Soorah Hood* 11:86), it means: Do what I command you to do, seeking thereby Allah's Countenance and hoping for His Reward, not in order that I or any other may see you. ❨ They said, "O, Shu'aib! Does your *salah* (prayer) command that we leave off what our fathers used to worship, or that we leave off doing what we like with our property? Verily, you are the forbearing, right-minded!" ❩ They said these last words in order to mock him, belittle him and ridicule him. That is, do these prayers which you offer command you to forbid us to worship any deity except your God and order us to abandon that which our forefathers used to worship? Or do they command you to order us not to do business dealings except in the manner which pleases you and to abandon those dealings which you forbid, even though they please us? ❨ "Verily, you are the forbearing, right-minded!" ❩ (*Soorah Hood* 11:87)

'Abdullah Ibn Mas'ood ※ (3745).

(8) Narrated by Al-Bukhari (2079), Muslim (1532), Abu Dawood (3459), At-Tirmidhi (1246), An-Nasa'i (4457), Ahmad (14890) and Ad-Darimi (2548), on the authority of Hakeem Ibn Hizam ※.

'Abdullah Ibn 'Abbas ﷺ, Maimoon Ibn Mihran, Ibn Juraij, Zaid Ibn Aslam and Ibn Jareer said that they – the enemies of Allah – said these words in tones of mockery. ﴾ He said, "O, my people! Tell me, if I have a clear proof from my Lord, and He has given me a good sustenance from Himself (shall I corrupt it by mixing it with the unlawfully earned money). I wish not, in contradiction to you, to do that which I forbid you. I only desire reform so far as I am able, to the best of my power. And my guidance cannot come except from Allah, in Him I trust and unto Him I repent." ﴿ (*Soorah Hood* 11:88) He spoke to them using courteous and polite words and he called them to the truth with the clearest guidance. He said to them, "Do you consider, O deniers ﴾ "if I have a clear evidence from my Lord…" ﴿ (*Soorah Hood* 11:88). That is, if I am following a clear command from Allah, which is that He sent me to you ﴾ and He has given me a good sustenance from Himself ﴿ – meaning Prophethood and Messengership. That is to say, and knowledge of that was concealed from you, then what can I do with you?

Allah, Most High, says, ﴾ Enjoin you *al-birr* (piety and righteousness and each and every act of obedience to Allah) on the people and you forget (to practice it) yourselves, while you recite the Scripture (the Tawrah [Torah])? Have you then no sense? ﴿ (*Soorah Al-Baqarah* 2:44). In the *tafseer* of this Verse, it was authentically reported from the Messenger of Allah ﷺ that he said, "A man will be brought on the Day of Resurrection and thrown in the Fire, so that his intestines will come out and he will go around like a donkey goes around a millstone. The people of the Fire will gather around him and say, 'O, so-and-so! What is wrong with you? Did you not use to order us to do good deeds and forbid us to do bad deeds?' He will reply, 'Yes, I used to order you to do good deeds, but I did not do them myself, and I used to forbid you to do bad deeds, yet I used to do them myself.'" [9] This is the description of those adulterers and sinners and those who oppose the Prophets. While as for the superior and intelligent leaders from among the scholars who fear their Lord unseen, their situation is as described by the Prophet of Allah, Shu'aib: ❨ I wish not, in contradiction to you, to do that which I forbid you. I only desire reform so far as I am able, to the best of my power." ❩ (*Soorah Hood* 11:88) That is, in all of my commands, I desire naught but to exert my utmost efforts and abilities toward reforming your deeds and your words. ❨ And my guidance cannot come ❩. That is, in all of my affairs. ❨ Except from Allah, in Him I trust and unto Him I repent ❩ (*Soorah Hood* 11:88). That is, I place my trust in Him in all matters, to Him I will return and my destiny is in His Hands. This is a stance of (*targheeb*) [10] to do good.

Then he embarked on a form of *tarheeb*, [11] saying, ❨ "And my people! Let not my *shiqaq* cause you to suffer the fate similar to that of the people of Nooh or of Hood or of Salih, and the people of Loot are not far off from you!" ❩ (*Soorah Hood* 11:89) That is, do not let your opposition to me and your hatred of that which I have brought to you cause you to continue in your error and ignorance, for if you do, Allah will inflict upon you a similar punishment to that which He inflicted on those who were like you among the peoples of Nooh عليه السلام, Hood عليه السلام and Saleh عليه السلام, who belied and opposed their Prophets.

As for Shu'aib's saying: ❨ "and the people of Loot are not far off from you." ❩ (*Soorah Hood* 11:89), it is said that its meaning is that they were not far off from them in time; Qatadah

---

(9)   Narrated by Al-Bukhari (3267) and Muslim (2989).

(10) *Targheeb*: Incitement and encouragement.

(11) *Tarheeb*: To frighten, alarm or threaten.

said, "This means that they were only destroyed before you yesterday." It has also been said that it refers to place. But in actual fact, the Verse carries both meanings. It was also said that it means that they were similar to them in characteristics and repugnant deeds, such as highway robbery and taking money from the people both openly and in secret, through all kinds of tricks and sophisms. It is possible to reconcile to all of these opinions, because they were not far from them in time, distance or characteristics. Then he mixed *tarheeb* with *targheeb*, saying, ❴ "And ask forgiveness of your Lord and turn unto Him in repentance. Verily, my Lord is Most Merciful, Most Loving." ❵ (*Soorah Hood* 11:90) That is, abandon the sins you are engaged in and turn in repentance to your Lord, the Most Merciful, Most Loving, because if anyone turns in repentance to Him, He is Merciful toward His slaves – more merciful than a mother toward her child. ❴ "Most Loving" ❵ means, even if it is after He has accepted the repentance of his slave and even if the slave had repented of major sins. ❴ They said, "O, Shu'aib! We do not understand much of what you say, and we consider you a weak person (it is said that he was a blind man) among us." ❵ (*Soorah Hood* 11:91)

As for their saying: ❴ "Were it not for your family, we should certainly have stoned you; and you are not powerful against us" ❵ (*Soorah Hood* 11:91), this was due to their profound disbelief and their disgraceful obstinacy, as they said, ❴ They said, "O, Shu'aib! We do not understand much of what you say." ❵ (*Soorah Hood* 11:91) That is, we do not understand it, nor do we comprehend it, because we do not like it and we do not want it, so we have no eagerness for it and we will not follow it. And this is like the saying of the disbelievers of Quraish to the Messenger of Allah: ❴ And they say, "Our hearts are under coverings (screened) from that to which you invite us, and in our ears is deafness, and between us and you is a screen, so work you (on your way); verily, we are working (on our way)." 》 (*Soorah Fussilat* 41:5) As for their saying: 《 "and we consider you a weak person (it is said that he was a blind man) among us." 》 (*Soorah Hood* 11:91), it means despised and abandoned. 《 "Were it not for your family…" 》. means, your tribe and your kinsfolk among us. 《 "We should certainly have stoned you; and you are not powerful against us." He said, "O, my people! Is then my family of more weight with you than Allah?" 》 (*Soorah Hood* 11:91,92). That is, do you fear my tribe and my kinsfolk and hesitate to harm me because of them, yet you do not fear Allah's Anger or hesitate to harm me because I am a Messenger of Allah? That means that you consider my tribe more powerful than Allah! 《 And you have cast Him away behind your backs 》 (*Soorah Hood* 11:92). That is, you have placed fear of Allah behind your backs. 《 "Verily, my Lord is surrounding all that you do." 》 (*Soorah Hood* 11:92). That is, He is fully Aware of what you do and He encompasses all of that and He will recompense you for it on the Day when you are returned to Him. 《 And O, my people! Act according to your ability and way, and I am acting (on my way). You will come to know who it is on whom descends the punishment that will cover him with ignominy, and who is a liar! And watch you! Verily, I too am watching with you." 》 (*Soorah Hood* 11:93) This is a stern threat and a positive warning, that if they should continue on their path and in their (wicked) ways, they would come to know on whom Allah's Punishment would be inflicted and upon whom would destruction and annihilation be visited. In an earlier Verse in this *Soorah*, he said, 《 "and on whom will fall a lasting punishment." 》 (*Soorah Hood* 11:39) 《 "and who is a liar!" 》 (*Soorah Hood* 11:93) That is, which of us is the liar in the information, the glad tidings and the warnings he gave, you or I. ❨ "And watch you! Verily, I too am watching with you." ❩ (*Soorah Hood* 11:93). This is like the Words of Allah: ❨ "And if there is a party of you who believes in that with which I have been sent and a party who do not believe, so be patient until Allah judges between us, and He is the Best of judges." The chiefs of those who were arrogant among his people said, "We shall certainly drive you out, o, Shu'aib, and those who have believed with you from our town, or else you (all) shall return to our religion." He said, "Even though we hate it! We should have invented a lie against Allah if we returned to your religion, after Allah has rescued us from it. And it is not for us to return to it unless Allah, our Lord, should will. Our Lord comprehends all things in His Knowledge. In Allah (Alone) we put our trust. Our Lord! Judge between us and our people in truth, for You are the Best of the *fatiheen*." ❩ (*Soorah Al-A'raf* 7:87-89)

They demanded that those who had believed in Shu'aib's Message return to their religion and so Shu'aib ﷺ disputed with them on behalf of his people, saying, ❨ "Even though we hate it! ❩ (*Soorah Al-A'raf* 7:88) That is, these people (who have believed) will not return voluntarily to you; if they return, they will only do so under compulsion and that is because once the joy of faith has pervaded the heart, none will be discontented with it and none will reject it, and no one can avoid that. This is why he said, ❨ We should have invented a lie against Allah if we returned to your religion, after Allah has rescued us from it. And it is not for us to return to it unless Allah, our Lord, should will. Our Lord comprehends all things in His Knowledge. In Allah (Alone) we put our trust ❩ (*Soorah Al-A'raf* 7:89) That is, He is Sufficient for us, He is our Protector and we take refuge with Him in all of our affairs. Then he sought judgment from Allah against his people and asked his Lord to hasten the infliction of the punishment that they deserved upon them, saying, ❨ "Our Lord! Judge between us and our people in truth, for You are the Best of the *fatiheen*." ❩ (*Soorah Al-A'raf* 7:89) That is, of those who give judgment. So he invoked Allah against them – and Allah does not reject the invocations of His Messengers when they seek help from Him against those who reject Him, disbelieve in Him and His Messengers, and oppose them. But in spite of this, they remained determined to persist in what they were doing (i.e. disbelief, sins, etc.). ❨ The chiefs of those who disbelieved among his people said (to their people), "If you follow Shu'aib, be sure then you will be the losers!" ❩ (*Soorah Al-A'raf* 7:90) Allah, Most High, says, ❨ So the earthquake seized them, and they lay (dead), prostrate in their homes. ❩ (*Soorah Al-A'raf* 7:78) Allah mentioned (earlier) in *Soorah Al-A'raf* that the earthquake seized them (i.e. the people of Thamood); that is to say, the earth upon which they stood shook severely and caused their souls to be taken out from their bodies, while the animals in their land became like stone and their (i.e. the people's) bodies became corpses, without souls, unmoving and senseless. Allah had combined upon them a variety of punishments, lessons and afflictions and this was because of their wicked characteristics. Allah inflicted on them a severe earthquake, which stilled all movement and a great Shout extinguished their voices and He sent a shadow or cloud upon them which emitted fire and sparks from all sides and all directions. But He, Most High, informed us about them in every *Soorah* in which mention of them was appropriate. And in the course of the narrative in *Soorah Al-A'raf*, He mentioned that they spread false stories about the Prophet of Allah ﷺ and his companions and threatened them with expulsion from their town, if they did not return to their former religion. Allah says, ❨ So the earthquake seized them, and they lay (dead), prostrate in their homes. ⟩ (*Soorah Al-A'raf* 7:78) Allah responded to their spreading of falsehoods (*irjaf*) with the earthquake (*rajfah*) [12] and their intimidation (*ikhafah*) with terror (*kheefah*), [13] which was most appropriate in this context.

As for the narrative in *Soorah Hood*, He mentioned that the Shout seized them and they became lifeless in their homes. This was because they said to the Prophet of Allah in tones of derision, mockery and belittlement, ⟨ Does your *salah* (prayer) command that we leave off what our fathers used to worship, or that we leave off doing what we like with our property? Verily, you are the forbearing, right-minded!" ⟩ (*Soorah Hood* 11:87) So it was appropriate that He mentioned here the Shout, which was like a harsh rebuke for engaging in this wicked speech which they addressed to this noble, faithful and eloquent Messenger and so there came to them the Shout, which, along with the earthquake, silenced them.

As for Allah's Words in *Soorah Ash-Shu'ara'*, He mentioned that a punishment seized them on the Day of Shadow. And that was a response to their request and something approximating what they asked for, for they said, ⟨ "You are only one of those bewitched! You are but a human being like us and, verily, we think that you are one of the liars! So cause a piece of the heaven to fall on us, if you are of the truthful!" He said, "My Lord is the Best Knower of what you do." ⟩ (*Soorah Ash-Shu'ara'* 26:185-188)

Allah, Most High – Who is the All-Hearing, the All-Seeing – says, ⟨ But they belied him, so the torment of the Day of

_____

(12) *Irjaf* and *rajfah* are both from the same root verb *rajafa*.

(13) *Ikhafah* and *Kheefah* are both from the same root verb *khafa*.

Shadow (a gloomy cloud) seized them; indeed that was the punishment of a Great Day. ❳ (*Soorah Ash-Shu'ara'* 26:189)

Then Allah mentioned the same criticism regarding the Companions of the *Aykah* that He had made of the people of Madyan, which was that they used to cheat in their weights and measures and this proves that they were the one people, who were destroyed by a variety of punishments. Regarding Allah's Words: ❴ But they belied him, so the torment of the Day of Shadow (a gloomy cloud) seized them, indeed that was the punishment of a Great Day ❳ (*Soorah Ash-Shu'ara'* 26:189), scholars have said that they were afflicted by an intense heat and Allah sent against them a fierce wind, which blew for seven days and neither water nor shade, nor entering tunnels availed them against it. They fled from their homes into the countryside, where they were covered by a cloud. They gathered beneath it, in order to seek shade from it, but when they had all gathered under it, Allah caused it to cast sparks and flames of fire on them, while the earth shook beneath them and the Shout came to them from the heaven and their souls were extracted from them and destroyed. ❴ So the earthquake seized them and they lay (dead), prostrate in their homes. Those who belied Shu'aib became as if they had never dwelt there (in their homes). Those who belied Shu'aib, they were the losers. ❳ (*Soorah Al-A'raf* 7:91,92) So Allah saved Shu'aib ﷺ and the believers who were with him, as He, Most High, says, and He is the Most Truthful of Speakers, ❴ And when Our Commandment came, We saved Shu'aib and those who believed with him by a Mercy from Us. ❳ (*Soorah Hood* 11:94) He, Most High, says, ❴ So the earthquake seized them and they lay (dead), prostrate in their homes. Those who belied Shu'aib became as if they had never dwelt there (in their homes). Those who belied Shu'aib, they were the losers. ❳ (*Soorah Al-A'raf*

7:91,92) This was in response to their saying: ❨ "If you follow
Shu'aib, be sure then you will be the losers." ❩ (*Soorah Al-
A'raf* 7:90). Then Allah, Most High, mentioned regarding His
Prophet ﷺ that he reproached them and rebuked them, as
Allah, Most High, says, ❨ Then he (Shu'aib) turned from them
and said, "O, my people! I have indeed conveyed my Lord's
Messages unto you and I have given you good advice. Then
how can I sorrow for the disbelieving people's (destruction)."
❩ (*Soorah Al-A'raf* 7:93) That is, he turned away from their
place after they had been destroyed, saying, ❨ "I have indeed
conveyed to you the Message of my Lord, and have given you
good advice." ❩ (*Soorah Al-A'raf* 7:79). That is, I have fulfilled
what was incumbent upon me, by conveying to you the Message
in full and giving you the complete advice and I have striven
to guide you to the utmost of my ability and with all of the
means at my disposal. But that has not benefited you, because
Allah does not guide those who willfully go astray and they
have none to help them. So I do not regret what has befallen
you after all that, because you did not accept the advice and
you did not fear the humiliation. This is why he said, ❨ "Then
how can I sorrow...?" ❩ (*Soorah Al-A'raf* 7:93) That is, how
can I be sad for a disbelieving people, i.e. a people who do not
accept the truth and do not return to it or even look toward it.
So Allah inflicts His Punishment upon them – a punishment
which cannot be rescinded, nor can it be prevented or avoided
by anyone for whom it is intended?

Chapter: Mention of the Progeny of Ibraheem (عَلَيْهِ السَّلَام)

We shall embark at this point on a detailed discussion regarding the progeny of Ibraheem (عَلَيْهِ السَّلَام), because Allah placed Prophets among his offspring and revealed Scriptures to them; so every Prophet who came after him was from his progeny.

Mention of Isma'eel (عَلَيْهِ السَّلَام)

Allah, Most High, praises him and describes him as being gentle and patient, and the one who fulfilled his promises and offered his prayers regularly and ordered his family to do likewise, in order to protect them from Allah's Punishment, along with those other acts of worship of the Lord of lords to which he called, as He, Most High, says, ﴾ So We gave him the glad tidings of a forbearing boy. And, when he (his son) was old enough to walk with him, he said, "O, my son! I have seen in a dream that I am slaughtering you (offering you in sacrifice to Allah), so look what you think!" He said, "O, my father! Do that which you are commanded, *In sha' Allah* (if Allah wills), you shall find me of *As-Sabireen* (the patient ones, etc.)." 〗 (*Soorah As-Saffat* 37:101,102) So he obeyed his father in that matter and he promised him that he would be patient and he fulfilled that promise and was patient.

Allah, Most High, says, 〖 And mention in the Book (the Qur'an) Isma'eel (Ishmael). Verily! He was true to what he promised, and he was a Messenger, (and) a Prophet. And he used to enjoin on his family and his people *as-salah* (the prayers) and *zakah*, and his Lord was pleased with him 〗 (*Soorah Maryam* 19:54,55)

He, Most High, says, 〖 And remember Our slaves, Ibraheem, Ishaq, and Ya'qoob, (all) owners of strength (in worshipping Us) and (also) of religious understanding. Verily, We did choose them by granting them (a good thing, i.e.) the remembrance of the home (in the Hereafter and they used to make the people remember it, and also they used to invite the people to obey Allah and to do good deeds for the Hereafter). And they are with Us, verily, of the chosen and the best! And remember Isma'eel (Ishmael), Al-Yasa'a (Elisha), and Dhul-Kifl (Isaiah), all are among the best. 〗 (*Soorah Sad* 38:45-48)

He, Most High, says, 〖 And (remember) Isma'eel, and Idrees (Enoch) and Dhul-Kifl, all were from among *As-Sabireen*. And We admitted them to Our Mercy. Verily, they were of the righteous. 〗 (*Soorah Al-Anbiya'* 21:85,86)

He, Most High, says, 〖 Verily, We have inspired you (o, Muhammad) as We inspired Nooh and the Prophets after him; We (also) inspired Ibraheem, Isma'eel (Isma'eel), Ishaq, Ya'qoob, and *Al-Asbat* (the twelve sons of Ya'qoob). ﴾ (*Soorah An-Nisa'* 4:163)

He, Most High, says, ﴿ Say (Muslims), "We believe in Allah and that which has been sent down to us and that which has been sent down to Ibraheem, Isma'eel, Ishaq, Ya'qoob, and to *Al-Asbat* (the twelve sons of Ya'qoob).﴾ (*Soorah Al-Baqarah* 2:136) Something similar was related in another *Soorah.* [14]

He, Most High, says, ﴿ Or say you that Ibraheem, Isma'eel, Ishaq, Ya'qoob and *Al-Asbat* (the twelve sons of Ya'qoob) were Jews or Christians? Say, "Do you know better or does Allah (know better... that they all were Muslims)? ﴾ (*Soorah Al-Baqarah* 2:140). So Allah has described him as possessing a very fine quality and He made him a Prophet and a Messenger and declared him innocent of all that the ignorant people have attributed to him. He commanded His believing slaves to believe in what was revealed to him.

Al-'Umawi reported on the authority of 'Ali Ibn Al-Husain, who reported on the authority of his father (i.e. 'Ali Ibn Abi Talib صلى الله عليه وسلم), from the Prophet صلى الله عليه وسلم that he said, "The first person to speak clear Arabic was Isma'eel, when he was fourteen years old." [15] Yoonus said to him (i.e. the narrator), "You have spoken the truth, Abu Yasar! It was narrated to me in the same way by Abu Jurayy." He married an Amalekite woman when he was a young man, but his father ordered him to separate from her. Al-'Umawi said, "Her name was 'Umarah Bint Sa'd Ibn Usamah Ibn Akeel, the Amalekite. Then he married another

---

(14) See: *Soorah Ali 'Imran* 3:84.

(15) Al-Hafiz Ibn hajar attributed it in *Fath Al-Bari* (6/488, No. 3365) to Az-Zubair Ibn Bakkar in the book *An-Nasab*, on the authority of 'Ali صلى الله عليه وسلم and he declared its *isnad* to be *hasan*.

woman and his father ordered him to keep her with him and he did so. Her name was As-Sayyidah Bint Muduad Ibn 'Amr Al-Jurhumi. It was also said that she was his third wife and that she bore him twelve sons. And Muhammad Ibn Ishaq – may Allah have mercy on him – named them."

Isma'eel, the Prophet of Allah ﷺ, was buried with his mother in Al-Hijr and his age on the day of his death was one hundred and thirty-seven years.

Mention of Ishaq ﷺ, Son of Ibraheem ﷺ, the Noble, Son of a Noble

Allah, Most High, says, ﴾ And We gave him the glad tidings of Ishaq, a Prophet from the righteous. We blessed him and Ishaq, and of their progeny are (some) that do right, and some that plainly wrong themselves. ﴿ (*Soorah As-Saffat* 37:112,113) Allah praised him in a number of Verses in His Noble Book and we have previously mentioned in the *hadeeth* of Abu Hurairah ﷺ from the Messenger of Allah ﷺ that he said, "Verily, the noble, son of the noble, son of the noble, son of the noble is Yoosuf (Joseph), son of Ya'qoob, son of Ishaq, son of Ibraheem." [16]

The People of the Scripture said that when Ishaq ﷺ married Rifqa, daughter of Thabwa'eel, during the lifetime of his father (Ibraheem ﷺ), he was forty years of age and she was barren. So he invoked Allah on her behalf and she gave birth to twin boys. The elder of them they named 'Eesu and it is he who is known by the Arabs as Al-'Ees and he is held to be the father of Rome. The second came out holding onto the heel of his

_____

(16) The *takhreej* of this *hadeeth* has already been given.

brother and so they called him Ya'qoob. [17] He is also known as Isra'eel and the Children of Isra'eel claim descent from him. They (the People of the Scripture) said that Ishaq loved Eesu more than Ya'qoob, because he was his firstborn and that his wife, Rifqa loved Ya'qoob more, because he was the younger of the two.

Mention of the Amazing Events That Took Place During the Life of Isra'eel, Including the Story of Yoosuf, Son of Raheel

Allah revealed details of his life and his affairs in a *Soorah* of the Qur'an, in order that we might reflect on the wisdoms, warnings and manners therein. I seek refuge with Allah from the accursed Satan [18] ﴾ *Alif Lam Ra.* (These letters are one of the miracles of the Qur'an and none but Allah (Alone) knows their meanings). These are the Verses of the Clear Book (the Qur'an that makes clear the legal and illegal things, legal laws, a guidance and a blessing). Verily, We have sent it down as an Arabic Qur'an in order that you may understand. We relate unto you (Muhammad) the best of stories through Our Revelations unto you, of this Qur'an. And before this (i.e. before the coming of Divine Inspiration to you), you were among those who knew nothing about it (the Qur'an) ﴿ (*Soorah Yoosuf* 12:1-3)

In summary, we may say that He, Most High, praises His Noble Book, which He sent down to His slave and noble Messenger, in eloquent and clear Arabic language, which can

---

(17) The word for heel is *'aqib*, which is from the root verb *'aqaba*, meaning to follow; and it is from this that the name Ya'qoob is derived.

(18) This is recited before commencing the recitation of the Qur'an.

be understood by every rational and intelligent person and it is the most eminent Book sent down from the heaven to the most eminent of mankind in any time or place. Whether He is speaking of past events or contemporary ones, it mentions the best of them and the clearest of them and makes the truth apparent in matters in which people have differed, while refuting, invalidating and rejecting that which is false. When it deals with commands and prohibitions, it is the most just of legislations, the clearest of programs, filled with the most obvious wisdom and the fairest of judgments. As Allah, Most High, says, ﴾ And the Word of your Lord has been fulfilled in truth and in justice. ﴿ (*Soorah Al-An'am* 6:115) That is, truth in the information given and justice in the commands and prohibitions; and this is why Allah, Most High, says, ﴾ We relate unto you (Muhammad) the best of stories through Our Revelations unto you, of this Qur'an. And before this, you were among those who knew nothing about it. ﴿ (*Soorah Yoosuf* 12:3) That is, ignorant regarding what was revealed to you therein, as He, Most High, says, ﴾ And thus We have sent to you (O, Muhammad) *Roohan* (an Inspiration and a Mercy) of Our Command. You knew not what is the Book, nor what is Faith. But We have made it (this Qur'an) a light wherewith We guide whosoever of Our slaves We will. And verily, you (O, Muhammad) are indeed guiding (mankind) to the Straight Path (i.e. Allah's religion of Islamic Monotheism), the Path of Allah, to Whom belongs all that is in the heavens and all that is in the Earth. Verily, all the matters at the end go to Allah (for decision). ﴿ (*Soorah Ash-Shoora* 42:52,53)

And He, Most High, says, ﴾ Thus We relate to you (O, Muhammad) some information regarding what happened before. And indeed We have given you from Us a Reminder (this Qur'an). Whoever turns away from it (i.e. this Qur'an;

that is, does not believe in it or act on its orders), verily, they will bear a heavy burden (of sins) on the Day of Resurrection, They will abide in that (state in the Fire of Hell), and evil indeed will it be that load for them on the Day of Resurrection. ﴾ (*Soorah Ta Ha* 20:99-101) That is, whoever rejects this Qur'an and follows another book will have this threat fulfilled upon him, as reported in the *hadeeth* narrated in Imam Ahmad's *Musnad* and in the *Sunan* of At-Tirmidhi, on the authority of the Commander of the Faithful, 'Ali ﷺ, in a *marfoo'* form and also in a *mawqoof* form: "Whoever looks for guidance from some source other than it (i.e. the Qur'an), Allah will cause him to go (further) astray." [19]

Imam Ahmad narrated on the authority of Jabir Ibn 'Abdillah ﷺ that 'Umar Ibn Al-Khattab ﷺ came to the Prophet ﷺ with a book which he had obtained from one of the People of the Scripture and he read it to the Prophet ﷺ. The Prophet ﷺ became angry and said, "O, Ibn Al-Khattab, are we going to play in religion? By Allah, I have come to you with a pure Religion. Do not ask them about anything, for they may say something true and you do not believe what they say or they may say something false and you believe it. By Allah, If Moosa was alive he would not have done anything but follow me." Its chain of narrators is authentic. [20]

Allah, Most High, says, ﴿ (Remember) when Yoosuf said to

---

[19] Narrated by Imam Ahmad (706) and At-Tirmidhi (2906) and its chains of narrators is weak.

[20] Narrated by Imam Ahmad (14736) and declared authentic by the author (i.e. Ibn Katheer). But I say: In its chain of narrators is one Mujalid Ibn Sa'eed (who is weak, according to Al-Bukhari, who said in *At-Tareekh As-Sagheer*, "Ibn Al-Qattan said he is weak and Ibn Al-Mahdi would not narrate from him, while Yahya Ibn Ma'een, Ibn Hibban and Abu Hatim said that his *hadeeth* cannot be cited as evidence and he is weak.")

his father, "O, my father! Verily, I saw (in a dream) eleven stars and the sun and the moon; I saw them prostrating themselves to me." He (his father) said, "O, my son! Relate not your vision to your brothers, lest they arrange a plot against you. Verily! *Shaitan* is to man an open enemy! Thus will your Lord choose you and teach you the interpretation of dreams (and other things) and perfect His Favor on you and on the offspring of Ya'qoob, as He perfected it on your fathers, Ibraheem and Ishaq aforetime! Verily, your Lord is All-knowing, Most Wise." 》 (*Soorah Yoosuf* 12:4-6)

Ya'qoob عليه السلام had twelve sons and all of the twelve tribes of the Children of Isra'eel ascribe their ancestry to them. The noblest, the most revered and the greatest of them was Yoosuf عليه السلام. A group of scholars has stated the opinion that none was a Prophet except him and that his brothers did not receive any revelation. It is apparent from their actions and their words in this story that this view is correct. Those who claimed that they were Prophets cited as evidence the Words of Allah, Most High: ﴿ Say (Muslims), "We believe in Allah and that which has been sent down to us and that which has been sent down to Ibraheem, Isma'eel, Ishaq, Ya'qoob, and to *Al-Asbat*. 》 (*Soorah Al-Baqarah* 2:136) They claimed that these (the brothers of Ya'qoob عليه السلام) are *Al-Asbat*, but the evidence for this is not strong, because what is meant by *Al-Asbat* is the tribes of the Children of Isra'eel and none of them was Prophet to whom Revelation was sent down from the heaven. And Allah knows better.

What supports the claim that only Yoosuf عليه السلام was alone selected from among his brothers to be a Messenger and Prophet is the fact that his Prophethood and the receipt of Revelation are attested to in several Verses in the Qur'an and there is no evidence anywhere in the Qur'an that any of them except Yoosuf علیه السلام was a Prophet which proves what we said. But one must take into consideration the narration of Imam Ahmad, on the authority of 'Abdullah Ibn 'Umar رضی الله عنه, in which he reported that the Messenger of Allah ﷺ said, "Verily, the noble, son of the noble, son of the noble, son of the noble is Yoosuf, son of Ya'qoob, son of Ishaq, son of Ibraheem." [21]

The scholars of *tafseer* and others said that when Yoosuf علیه السلام was a boy – before he reached puberty – he saw in a dream as if ﴾ eleven stars ﴿ – this is a reference to his brothers – ﴾ and the sun and the moon ﴿ – and this is a reference to his parents – prostrating to him. His father understood that this meant that he would achieve a high rank and elevated status in the life of this world and in the Hereafter, since his parents and his brothers submitted to him in his dream. So he ordered him to keep it secret and not to relate it to his brothers, in case they became afflicted with envy and devise some plot to harm him. This proves what we have said (i.e. that they were not Prophets). This is why it has been reported in some traditions: "Seek help in attaining your needs by concealment of them, because every recipient of blessings is envied." [22]

﴾ Thus your Lord will choose you. ﴿ (*Soorah Yoosuf* 12:6) That is, as He showed you this great vision, if you keep it secret, ﴾ your Lord will choose you ﴿. That is, He will favor you with all manne of kindness and mercy ﴾ and teach you the interpretation of speech ﴿. That is, He will make you comprehend the meanings of speech and the interpretation of dreams, which none but you will understand ﴾ and perfect His

---

(21) The *takhreej* of this *hadeeth* has already been given.

(22) This is authentic, and it was also said that it is *hasan*, due to supporting narrations. It was narrated by At-Tabarani in *Al-Kabeer* (20/94, No. 183), on the authority of Mu'adh Ibn Jabal رضی الله عنه.

Favor on you ﴾. That is, with Revelation to you ﴿ and on the family of Ya'qoob ﴾. That is, because of you, and through you, they will attain the best of the life of this world and of the Hereafter ﴿ as He perfected it on your fathers, Ibraheem and Ishaq aforetime! ﴾ *(Soorah Yoosuf* 12:6). That is, He bestows His Blessings on you and favors you with Prophethood, just as He gave it to your father, Ya'qoob ﷺ, your grandfather, Ishaq ﷺ and your great-grandfather, Ibraheem, *Al-Khaleel.* ﴿ Verily, your Lord is All-Knowing, Most Wise ﴾ *(Soorah Yoosuf* 12:6), as He, Most High, says, ﴿ Allah Knows best with whom to place His Message ﴾ *(Soorah Al-An'am* 6:124).

This is why, when the Messenger of Allah ﷺ was asked which of the people was noblest, he said, "Yoosuf is the Prophet of Allah, son of the Prophet of Allah, the son of the Prophet of Allah, the son of Allah's *Khaleel.*" [23]

Allah, Most High, says, ﴿ Verily, in Yoosuf and his brethren, there were *Ayat* (proofs, evidences, Verses, lessons, signs, revelations, etc.) for those who ask. When they said: "Truly, Yoosuf and his brother Binyameen (Benjamin) are loved more by our father than we, but we are *'usbah* (a strong group). Really, our father is in plain error. Kill Yoosuf or cast him out to some (other) land, so that the favor of your father may be given to you alone, and after that you will be righteous folk (by intending repentance before committing the sin)." One from among them said, "Kill not Yoosuf, but if you must do it, throw him down to the bottom of a well, he will be picked up by some caravan of travelers." ﴾ *(Soorah Yoosuf* 12:7-10)

Allah, Most High, draws our attention to the signs, wisdoms, proofs, warnings and indisputable evidences contained in this

---

(23) Narrated by Al-Bukhari (3374), Muslim (3371) and Imam Ahmad (9284), on the authority of Abu Hurairah ﷺ.

story, Then He mentions the envy felt by Yoosuf's brothers towards him, because of the fact that his father loved him and his brother Binyameen more than them. (Yoosuf عليه السلام and his brother, Binyameen were both born to the same mother, while the others were born of another mother). They said, "We have more right to his love than these two." ﴾ "Really, our father is in plain error." ﴿ (*Soorah Yoosuf* 12:8) That is, by loving them more than us. Then they consulted one another regarding the idea of killing him or expelling him to a land from which he would not return, so that they would be left alone with their father, that his love would be devoted solely to them and would suffice them. They harbored within them the intention of repenting to Allah after that. So when they decided on their plan and agreed on it ﴾ One from among them said ﴿ (*Soorah Yoosuf* 12:10) – Mujahid said that the one referred to was Sham'oon. As-Suddi said that it was Yahooza. Qatadah and Muhammad Ibn Ishaq asserted that it was the oldest of them, Roobeel. ﴾ One from among them said, "Kill not Yoosuf (Joseph), but if you must do it, throw him down to the bottom of a well, he will be picked up by some caravan of travelers." ﴿ (*Soorah Yoosuf* 12:10) That is, some passing caravan of travelers. ﴾ "but if you must do it," ﴿. means, if you must do what you have mentioned, then do what I have suggested, rather than killing him or banishing him. So they agreed on their decision to do this, at which point they said, ﴾ They said, "O, our father! Why do you not trust us with Yoosuf, when we are indeed his well-wishers? Send him with us tomorrow to enjoy himself and play, and verily, we will take care of him." He (Ya'qoob) said, "Truly, it saddens me that you should take him away. I fear lest a wolf should devour him, while you are careless of him." They said, "If a wolf devours him, while we are *'usbah* (a strong group) (to guard him), then surely, we are the losers." ﴿ (*Soorah Yoosuf* 12:11-14)

They asked their father to send them with their brother, Yoosuf ﷺ, and they claim that they intended to take good care of him and to play with him and give him a good time, while in fact, they harbored feelings toward him of which Allah was fully Aware. The old man – may Allah's choicest prayers and blessings be upon him – answered them, saying, "O, my sons! It grieves me to be parted from him for even an hour of the day, and in addition to this, I fear that you will be busy with your games and you will not take care of him and that a wolf may come and devour him, and he will be unable to defend himself against it, due to his youthfulness and your neglect of him." ﴾ They said, "If a wolf devours him, while we are *'usbah* (to guard him), then surely, we are the losers." ﴿ (*Soorah Yoosuf* 12:14). That is, if a wolf attacks him and eats him while he is among us, or we are distracted from him and allow this to happen, then we must be a powerless group, and we will be destroyed (then surely, we are the losers).

Allah, Most High, says, ﴾ So, when they took him away, they all agreed to throw him down to the bottom of the well, and We inspired in him, "Indeed, you shall (one day) inform them of this affair of theirs, when they know (you) not." And they came to their father in the early part of the night weeping. They said, "O, our father! We went racing with one another, and left Yoosuf by our belongings and a wolf devoured him; but you will never believe us even when we speak the truth." And they brought his shirt stained with false blood. He said, "Nay, but you yonrselves have made up a tale. So (for me) patience is most fitting. And it is Allah (Alone) Whose help can be sought against that which you assert." ﴿ (*Soorah Yoosuf* 12:15-18)

They continued to press their father, until he sent Yoosuf ﷺ with them. But no sooner were they out of his sight than they began to revile him and insult him by words and deeds. They agreed to cast him into the depths of a well and they left him on the stone which projects from the middle of it, on which a person who descends into the well to fill his bucket would sit, when the water level is low. When they cast him into the well, Allah inspired him, by informing him that he would certainly be saved from this calamity into which he had fallen and that he would certainly inform his brothers of this deed of theirs, while he was in a position of power and they were in need of him and feared him ﴾ "when they know (you) not." ﴿ (*Soorah Yoosuf* 12:15)

Then, when they had placed him in the well and left him there, they took his shirt and stained it with blood and returned to their father at night and they were weeping, i.e. for their brother. This is why one of the *Salaf* said, "Be not deceived by the weeping of one who complains of having been wronged, because he may be a wrongdoer, though he weeps," and he mentioned the story of Yoosuf ﷺ and how they came to their father at night and they were weeping. They wept in the darkness of night, in order to hide their treachery (i.e. believing that their faces would not betray them in the poor light).

Allah, Most High, says, ﴾ They said, "O, our father! We went racing with one another, and left Yoosuf by our belongings." ﴿ (*Soorah Yoosuf* 12:17). That is, we left him by our clothes. ﴾ "and a wolf devoured him." ﴿ (*Soorah Yoosuf* 12:17). That is, while we were absent, racing with each other. They said, ﴾ "but you will never believe us even when we speak the truth." ﴿ (*Soorah Yoosuf* 12:17). That is, you will not believe what we are telling you regarding the wolf having devoured Yoosuf, even if you consider us truthful. So what about when you suspect that we are not truthful, especially since you feared that the wolf might devour Yoosuf and we guaranteed to you that he would be safe, due to our numbers around him and so we have come to be considered untrustworthy by you. So we do not blame you for not believing us in these circumstances. ❨ And they brought his shirt stained with false blood ❩. That is, with fabricated evidence; they had taken a baby goat and slaughtered it, then they took its blood and smeared it on his shirt, in order to lend credence to their claim that a wolf had eaten him. It was said that they forgot to tear the shirt and the ruin of lying is forgetfulness. When the signs of doubt became apparent in them, their deed did not surprise their father, because he knew of their enmity toward Yoosuf ﷺ and the envy they harbored toward him, because of the fact that he loved him more than them, due to the noble and venerable attributes he displayed in his childhood – attributes which Allah had bestowed on him, as He had destined Prophethood for him. Once they had persuaded him to let them take their brother, no sooner had they taken him, deprived him of him and removed him from his sight, than they returned, weeping over what they had done against him and claiming that they had been helpless to save him. This is why Ya'qoob ﷺ said, ❨ "Nay, but you yourselves have made up a tale. So (for me) patience is most fitting. And it is Allah (Alone) Whose help can be sought against that which you assert." ❩ (*Soorah Yoosuf* 12:18)

Allah, Most High, says, ❨ And there came a caravan; they sent their water-drawer, and he let down his bucket (into the well). He said, "What good news! Here is a boy." So they hid him as merchandise. And Allah was the All-Knowing regarding what they did. And they sold him for a low price - for a few *dirhams* (i.e. for a few silver coins). And they were of those who regarded him as insignificant. ❩ (*Soorah Yoosuf* 12:19,20)

Allah, Most High, informs that Yoosuf صلى الله عليه وسلم, when he was cast into the well, sat waiting for Allah to deliver him and bestow Kindness on him. ❨ And there came a caravan ❩. means, a party of travelers. ❨ He said, "What good news! ❩ That is, what good fortune for me! ❨ "Here is a boy." So they hid him as merchandise ❩. That is, they pretended that he was with them and that he was one of the slaves that made up their merchandise. ❨ And Allah was the All-Knowing regarding what they did ❩. That is, He was fully acquainted with the plot that his brothers had conspired against him and the way those who found him hid him amongst their merchandise. But He did not intervene due to His Great Wisdom, His All-Encompassing Omnipotence and the Mercy which would be bestowed on the people of Egypt at the hands of this young boy, who entered the land in the form of a captive slave, and after that, he came to hold the reins of power in his hands and Allah benefited them through him, in the life of this world and the Hereafter in ways too numerous to mention or describe. When Yoosuf's brothers realized that the caravan had taken him, they overtook them and said, "This is our slave who has run away from us," and they (the people of the caravan) purchased him from them for a low price. ❨ a few *dirhams* (i.e. for a few silver coins). And they were of those who regarded him as insignificant ❩ (*Soorah Yoosuf* 12:19)

Allah, Most High, says, ❨ And he (the man) from Egypt who bought him, said to his wife, "Make his stay comfortable." ❩. That is, be kind to him ❨ "may be he will profit us or we shall adopt him as a son." ❩ (*Soorah Yoosuf* 12:21) This was from Allah's Kindness, Mercy and Beneficence toward him, as it was His Will that He should make him feel at home and give him the goodness of this life and the goodness of the Hereafter. Scholars said that the person who bought him was an Egyptian and his title was *Al-'Azeez*; he was the minister in charge of the

treasury. Ibn Ishaq said, "His name was 'Atfeer, son of Ruhaib."
He said, "The Fir'awn of Egypt at that time was Ar-Rayyan,
son of Al-Waleed and the name of the wife of *Al-'Azeez* was
Ra'eel, daughter of Ru'aeel." Others said that her name was
Zulaikha; but it would appear that that was her nickname.

Ibn Ishaq said, "It was reported on the authority of 'Abdullah
Ibn Mas'ood ﷺ that he said, 'The noblest of people are three:
The 'Azeez of Egypt, when he said to his wife, ❴ "Make his stay
comfortable." ❵, the woman who said to her father, regarding
Moosa, ❴ "O, my father! Hire him! Verily, the best of men for
you to hire is the strong, the trustworthy." ❵ (*Soorah Al-Qasas*
28:26). and Abu Bakr *As-Siddeeq* ﷺ, when he appointed 'Umar
Ibn Al-Khattab ﷺ as his successor." [24]

Allah, Most High, says, ❴ Thus did We establish Yoosuf in
the land ❵ (*Soorah Yoosuf* 12:21) That is, just as We ordained
that *Al-'Azeez* and his wife should treat Yoosuf ﷺ kindly and
take care of him, so did We establish him in the land of Egypt
❴ that We might teach him the interpretation of events. ❵ That
is, the understanding of them; and the interpretation of dreams
is a part of that. ❴ And Allah has full power and control over
His Affairs ❵. That is, when Allah wills a thing, He ordains the
causes of it. This is why He, Most High, says, ❴ And he (the
man) from Egypt who bought him, said to his wife, "Make
his stay comfortable, that maybe he will profit us or we shall
adopt him as a son." Thus did We establish Yoosuf in the land,
that We might teach him the interpretation of events. And Allah
has full power and control over His Affairs, but most of men
know not. And when he (Yoosuf) attained his full manhood,
We gave him wisdom and knowledge (the Prophethood), thus

---

[24] Narrated by Al-Hakim (2/345) and it is authentic, due to supporting narrations, or it is *hasan*, due to supporting narrations. And Allah knows better. See: *Al-Majma'* (10/368).

We reward the *Muhsinoon* (doers of good deeds) ﴾ (*Soorah Yoosuf* 12:21,22)

He, Most High, says, ﴾ And she, in whose house he was, sought to seduce him (to do an evil act), she closed the doors and said, "Come on, you." He said, "I seek refuge in Allah (or Allah forbid)! Truly, he (your husband) is my master! He made my stay agreeable! (So I will never betray him). Verily, the *zalimoon* (wrongdoers and evil-doers) will never be successful." And indeed she did desire him and he would have inclined to her desire, had he not seen the evidence of his Lord. Thus it was, that We might turn away from him evil and illegal sexual intercourse. Surely, he was one of Our chosen, guided slaves. So they raced with one another to the door, and she tore his shirt from the back. They both found her lord (i.e. her husband) at the door. She said, "What is the recompense (punishment) for him who intended an evil design against your wife, except that he be put in prison or a painful torment?" He (Yoosuf) said, "It was she that sought to seduce me," - and a witness of her household bore witness (saying), "If it be that his shirt is torn from the front, then her tale is true and he is a liar! But if it be that his shirt is torn from the back, then she has told a lie and he is speaking the truth!" So when he (her husband) saw his (Yoosuf's) shirt torn at the back, he (her husband) said, "Surely, it is a plot of you women! Certainly mighty is your plot! O, Yoosuf! Turn away from this! (O, woman!) Ask forgiveness for your sin. Verily, you were of the sinful." ﴿ (*Soorah Yoosuf* 12:23-29)

Allah, Most High, informs us about *Al-'Azeez*'s wife's attempt to seduce Yoosuf ﷺ and her demand for him to do that which was inappropriate to his situation and station; she was a woman of great beauty, possessing wealth, high rank and youthfulness. He describes how she locked the doors on him and herself, then prepared herself for him, how she made herself up and donned her finest and most splendid garments, in spite of the fact that she was the wife of *Al-'Azeez*. Ibn Ishaq said, "She was the niece of Ar-Rayyan Ibn Al-Waleed, the king and ruler of Egypt. In addition to all of this, Yoosuf was an extremely handsome, young man; however, he was a Prophet, descended from a line of Prophets and his Lord protected him from committing evil deeds and from the plots of women; he was the master of the seven noble and God-fearing masters, mentioned in the authentic *hadeeth*, on the authority of the Seal of the Prophets, who reported the Words of the Lord of the heavens and the Earth: "Allah will give shade, to seven, on the day when there will be no shade but His. (These seven persons are) a just ruler, a youth who has been brought up in the worship of Allah (i.e. worships Allah sincerely from childhood), a man whose heart is attached to the mosques (i.e. to praying the compulsory prayers in the mosque in congregation), two persons who love each other only for Allah's sake and they meet and part in Allah's cause only, a man who refuses the call of a charming woman of noble birth for illicit intercourse with her and says: 'I am afraid of Allah,' a man who gives charitable gifts so secretly that his left hand does not know what his right hand has given (i.e. nobody knows how much he has given in charity), and a person who remembers Allah in seclusion and his eyes are then flooded with tears." [25]

What is meant is that she called him to her (i.e. she tried to seduce him) and she coveted that greatly; but he said, ❰ "I seek refuge in Allah (or Allah forbid)! Truly, he is my master!" ❱ (*Soorah Yoosuf* 12:23) That is, her husband was the owner of the house and his master. ❰ "He made my stay agreeable!" ❱

---

(25) Narrated by Al-Bukhari (660) and Muslim (1031).

That is, he has been kind and hospitable to me. ❨ Verily, the *zalimoon* will never be successful. ❩ And we have discussed previously His Words: ❨ And indeed she did desire him and he would have inclined to her desire had he not seen the evidence of his Lord. ❩ (*Soorah Yoosuf* 12:24) – in a manner which is sufficient and convincing in the *Tafseer*.

Most of the sayings of the scholars here are taken from the books of the People of the Scripture, but is more appropriate for us to avoid them. What is incumbent upon us is to believe that Allah, Most High, protected him and declared him innocent of committing any wrongdoing and He guarded him and preserved him from it. This is why He, Most High, says, ❨ Thus it was, that We might turn away from him evil and illegal sexual intercourse. Surely, he was one of Our chosen, guided slaves. So they raced with one another to the door ❩ (*Soorah Yoosuf* 12:24,25) That is, he ran from her, seeking to open the door and flee from the room and she chased after him. ❨ They both found her lord. ❩ That is, her husband ❨ at the door ❩ and she hastened to speak to her husband before Yoosuf عليه السلام could do so, and incited him against him: ❨ She said, "What is the recompense (punishment) for him who intended an evil design against your wife, except that he be put in prison or a painful torment?" ❩ (*Soorah Yoosuf* 12:25). She accused him, while in fact, she was the guilty one and she protected her reputation and acquitted herself of any blame. This is why Yoosuf عليه السلام said, ❨ He (Yoosuf) said, "It was she that sought to seduce me." ❩. It was necessary for him to speak the truth and defend himself, due to the need to protect his own honor. ❨ And a witness of her household bore witness. ❩ It was said that he was a child in his crib; this was the opinion of 'Abdullah Ibn 'Abbas رضي الله عنهما. Ibn Jareer At-Tabari preferred this saying and he narrated an authentic *hadeeth* to that effect, on the authority of 'Abdullah

Ibn 'Abbas ﷺ. Others claimed that the narration could only be ascribed to 'Abdullah Ibn 'Abbas ﷺ (that is, they did not ascribe it to the Prophet ﷺ). [26] It was also said that he was a man of approximately the same age as 'Atfeer, her husband. And it was also said that his age was close to that of Zulaikha.

Among those who said that he was a man were 'Abdullah Ibn 'Abbas ﷺ, 'Ikrimah, Mujhaid, Al-Hasan Al-Basri, Qatadah, As-Suddi, Muhammad Ibn Ishaq and Zaid Ibn Aslam. The witness said, ﴿ "If it be that his shirt is torn from the front, then her tale is true and he is a liar! ﴾ (*Soorah Yoosuf* 12:26) That is, because it will mean that he tried to seduce her and she defended herself, tearing the front of his shirt. ﴿ "But if it be that his shirt is torn from the back, then she has told a lie and he is speaking the truth!" ﴾ (*Soorah Yoosuf* 12:27) That is because, if he had fled from her and she had chased after him and grabbed him from behind, his shirt would be torn from the back – and such proved to be the case, which is why Allah, Most High, says, ﴿ So when he (her husband) saw his (Yoosuf's) shirt torn at the back, he (her husband) said, "Surely, it is a plot of you women! Certainly mighty is your plot!" ﴾ (*Soorah Yoosuf* 12:28). That is, this is from you women's plotting: you seduced him against his will, and then you falsely accused him. Then her husband turned away and said, ﴿ O, Yoosuf! Turn away from this! ﴾ (*Soorah Yoosuf* 12:27). That is, do not mention it to anyone, because keeping such matters secret is more appropriate and superior. He ordered his wife to seek forgiveness for the sin that she had committed and turn in repentance to her Lord. This is because when a slave repents to Allah, Allah forgives him. And

---

(26) Ibn Jareer At-Tabari narrated it in a *mawqoof* form (i.e. as a narration of 'Abdullah Ibn 'Abbas ﷺ) in his *Tafseer* (12/193) and he also narrated it in a marfoo' form (i.e. as a narration from the Prophet ﷺ) in his *Tafseer* (12/194).

while the people of Egypt used to worship idols, they knew that the One Who forgives sins and punishes the perpetrator of them is Allah, Alone, and He has no partners in that. This is why her husband spoke to her thus and pardoned her in some respects, because she had seen something that it was difficult to remain patient over. However, he was a virtuous and honorable man and so he said, ❨ "Ask forgiveness for your sin. Verily, you were of the sinful." ❩ (*Soorah Yoosuf* 12:29)

He, Most High, says, ❨ And women in the city said, "The wife of *Al-'Azeez* is seeking to seduce her (slave) young man, indeed she loves him violently; verily we see her in plain error." So when she heard of their accusation, she sent for them and prepared a banquet for them; she gave each one of them a knife (to cut the foodstuff with), and she said (to Yoosuf), "Come out before them." Then, when they saw him, they exalted him (at his beauty) and (in their astonishment) cut their hands. They said, "How perfect is Allah (or Allah forbid)! No man is this! This is none other than a noble angel!" She said, "This is he (the young man) about whom you did blame me (for his love), and I did seek to seduce him, but he refused. And now if he refuses to obey my order, he shall certainly be cast into prison, and will be one of those who are disgraced." He said, "O, my Lord! Prison is more to my liking than that to which they invite me. Unless You turn away their plot from me, I will feel inclined toward them and be one (of those who commit sin and deserve blame or those who do deeds) of the ignorant folk." So his Lord answered his invocation and turned away from him their plot. Verily, He is the All-Hearing, the All-Knowing ❩ (*Soorah Yoosuf* 12:30-34)

Allah informs us about the actions of the women of the city, the wives of the princes and the daughters of the powerful and influential, how they criticized, denounced and reviled the wife of *Al-'Azeez* regarding her attempted seduction of her slave and her extreme love for him; meaning that he was not worthy of it, since he was a slave, and nor, they said, did any other like him deserve it. This is why they said, ❨ "verily we see her in plain error." ❩ (*Soorah Yoosuf* 12:30) That is, by placing a thing (i.e. her affection) in a place that was unbefitting. ❨ So when she heard of their accusation. ❩ That is, their denunciation and belittling of her, their pointing accusing fingers at her and their censure of her for loving her slave and having passionate feelings for him. They displayed their condemnation of her, but at the same time, there was some excuse for her. For this reason, she wanted to make plain to them that there was indeed, some excuse for her and to show them that this young man was not as they thought, nor was he like their slaves. So she sent them an invitation, gathered them in her house and treated them with due hospitality. Among the things that she presented them was something that needed to be cut with a knife, like citron and the like. ❨ She gave each one of them a knife (to cut the foodstuff with) ❩ (*Soorah Yoosuf* 12:31) She had prepared Yoosuf ﷺ, dressing him in the finest clothes – who was at the peak of his youth and beauty – and she ordered him to come out to them while dressed thus. So he came out to them and he was, without doubt, more beautiful than a full moon. ❨ Then, when they saw him, they exalted him (at his beauty) ❩ (*Soorah Yoosuf* 12:31) That is, they extolled him, revered him and they cut their hands with the knives due to their distraction, and they did not notice their wounds. ❨ They said, "How perfect is Allah (or Allah forbid)! No man is this! This is none other than a noble angel!" ❩ (*Soorah Yoosuf* 12:31) It was related in the *hadeeth* of *Al-Isra'* that the Messenger of Allah ﷺ said, "Then

I passed by Yoosuf and he had been given half of all beauty." (27)

Allah, Most High, says, ❨ She said, "This is he (the young man) about whom you did blame me (for his love)." ❩ (*Soorah Yoosuf* 12:32) Then she praised him for his perfect chastity, saying, ❨ and I did seek to seduce him, but he resisted the temptation ❩ (*Soorah Yoosuf* 12:32) That is, he refused. ❨ "And now, if he refuses to obey my order, he shall certainly be cast into prison and he will be one of those who are disgraced." ❩ (*Soorah Yoosuf* 12:32) The other women incited him to hear and obey his mistress, but he vehemently refused and remained aloof, because he was from the stock of Prophets; he invoked the Lord of the worlds, saying in his supplication, ❨ O, my Lord! Prison is more to my liking than that to which they invite me. Unless You turn away their plot from me, I will feel inclined toward them and be one (of those who commit sin and deserve blame or those who do deeds) of the ignorant." ❩ (*Soorah Yoosuf* 12:33) That is, if You leave me to depend on myself, I will be weak and unable to resist. I possess not the ability to benefit or harm, except as Allah wills, because I am weak, unless You strengthen me, protect me and preserve me with Your Power and Your Strength. This is why Allah, Most High, says, ❨ So his Lord answered his invocation and turned away from him their plot. Verily, He is the All-Hearing, the All-Knowing. ❩ (*Soorah Yoosuf* 12:34)

He, Most High, says, ❨ Then it appeared to them, after they had seen the proofs (of his innocence) to imprison him for a time. And there entered with him two young men in the prison. One of them said, "Verily, I saw myself (in a dream) pressing wine." The other said, "Verily, I saw myself (in a dream) carrying bread on my head and birds were eating thereof."

---

(27) Narrated by Muslim (162).

(They said), "Inform us of the interpretation of this. Verily, we think you are one of the *Muhsinoon* (doers of good)." He said, "No food will come to you (in wakefulness or in dream) as your provision, but I will inform (in wakefulness) of its interpretation before it (the food) comes. This is of that which my Lord has taught me. Verily, I have abandoned the religion of a people that believe not in Allah and are disbelievers in the Hereafter (i.e. the *Kan'aniyoon* of Egypt who were polytheists and used to worship the sun and other false deities) And I have followed the Religion of my fathers, – Ibraheem, Ishaq and Ya'qoob, and never could we attribute any partners whatsoever to Allah. This is from the Grace of Allah to us and to mankind, but most men thank not (i.e. they neither believe in Allah, nor worship Him). O, two companions of the prison! Are many different lords (gods) better, or Allah, the One, the Irresistible? You do not worship besides Him but only names which you have named (forged), you and your fathers, for which Allah has sent down no authority. The command (or the judgment) is for none but Allah. He has commanded that you worship none but Him (i.e. His Monotheism), that is the (true) straight Religion, but most men know not. O, two companions of the prison! As for one of you, he (as a servant) will pour out wine for his lord (king or master) to drink; and as for the other, he will be crucified and birds will eat from his head. Thus is the case judged concerning which you both did inquire." ⟩ (*Soorah Yoosuf* 12:35-41)

Allah, Most High, tells us that after it became obvious to them that Yoosuf ﷺ was innocent, *Al-'Azeez* and his wife decided to imprison him until such time as the gossip about him and *Al-'Azeez's* wife died away. *Al-'Azeez* suppressed the facts, in order to make it appear that it was Yoosuf ﷺ who had tried to seduce her against her will and so he was imprisoned because

of it. So he was wrongfully and unjustly imprisoned. This was
a part of what Allah had ordained for him and it was the means
by which He protected him, for He removed him from their
company and the need to associate with them. It was based on
this that some Sufis claimed, according to what Ash-Shafi'i has
reported from them, that a part of chastity is to remove oneself
from temptation.

Allah, Most High, says, ❨ And there entered with him two
young men in the prison. ❩ (*Soorah Yoosuf* 12:36) It was said
that one of them was the king's cup bearer, and it has been said
that his name was Banu. The other was the king's baker, i.e.
the one who prepared his food, and is known to the Turks as
Jashankir, and according to what has been said, his name was
Mujallath. Both of them had been accused of something by
the king, who had them thrown in jail. When they saw Yoosuf
ﷺ in jail, they were amazed by his character, his dignified
demeanor, his faith, his words and actions, his frequent acts of
worship and his good conduct toward his fellow-man. Each of
them had a dream appropriate to him.

The scholars of *tafseer* said that they both had their dreams
on the same night. As for the cup-bearer, he saw three branches
from a grape-vine, which had produced leaves and ripe grapes
and he took them and squeezed them into the king's cup and
then he gave it to him to drink. The baker saw three baskets of
bread on his head and three birds of prey eating from the top
basket. They both related their dreams to Yoosuf ﷺ and asked
him to interpret them for them, saying, ❨ "Verily, we think you
are one of the *Muhsinoon* (doers of good)." ❩ (*Soorah Yoosuf*
12:36) He informed them that he was knowledgeable regarding
the interpretation of their dreams and skilled in such matters.
He said, ❨ "No food will come to you (in wakefulness or in

dream) as your provision, but I will inform (in wakefulness) its interpretation before it (the food) comes to you." ❭ (*Soorah Yoosuf* 12:37) It was said that the meaning is: no matter what visions you see, I will interpret them for you before it happens; and it will be as I said. It was also said that it means: I will inform you of what food will come to you before it arrives, whether it be sweet or bitter, as 'Eesa ﷺ said, ❬ "And I inform you of what you eat, and what you store in your houses." ❭ (*Soorah Ali 'Imran* 3:49) He said to them, "This is from the things that Allah has taught to me, because I believe in Him, affirm His Oneness and adhere to the Religion of my noble fathers, Ibraheem, *Al-Khaleel* ﷺ, Ishaq ﷺ and Ya'qoob." ❬ "And never could we attribute any partners whatsoever to Allah. This is from the Grace of Allah to us." ❭ That is, that He has guided us to this. ❬ "And to mankind." ❭ That is, that He has commanded us to call them to Him, guide them and direct them to Him. He (i.e. belief in Him) is firmly embedded in their innate natures and implanted in their natural dispositions. ❬ "But most men thank not.(i.e. they neither believe in Allah, nor worship Him)." ❭ (*Soorah Yoosuf* 12:38)

Then he called upon them to believe in Allah's Oneness and he censured the worship of anyone other than Allah and belittled and expressed scorn for the worship of idols. He said, ❬ "O, you two companions of the prison! Are many different (gods) better, or Allah, the One, the Irresistible? You do not worship besides Him but only names which you have named (forged), you and your fathers, for which Allah has sent down no authority. The command (or the judgment) is for none but Allah." ❭ (*Soorah Yoosuf* 12:39,40). That is, He is the Disposer of (the affairs of) His creation and He is the Doer of what He wills, Who guides whom He wills and increases in error whom He wills. ❬ "He has commanded that you worship none but

Him (i.e. His Monotheism)." ❳ (*Soorah Yoosuf* 12:40). That is, Alone, without ascribing partners to Him. ❲ "That is the straight Religion." ❳ (*Soorah Yoosuf* 12:40). That is, the true Religion and the Straight Path. ❲ "But most men know not." ❳ (*Soorah Yoosuf* 12:40). That is, they will not be guided to it, in spite of its clarity and its obviousness. His preaching to them both in this situation was of the utmost perfection, because their hearts extolled him and were ready to accept what he said. Therefore it was appropriate to call them to that which was more beneficial to them than about that which they asked and requested from him. Then he undertook that which was incumbent upon him and guided to that to which he had been guided, saying, ❲ "O, you two companions of the prison! As for one of you, he (as a servant) will pour out wine for his lord (king or master) to drink." ❳ (*Soorah Yoosuf* 12:41). The scholars said that he was the cup-bearer. ❲ "And as for the other, he will be crucified and birds will eat from his head." ❳ (*Soorah Yoosuf* 12:41) The scholars said that he was the baker. ❲ "Thus is the case judged concerning which you both did inquire." ❳ (*Soorah Yoosuf* 12:41). That is, this will happen, and it is inevitable, no matter what. This is why it was said in a *hadeeth*, "A vision flutters over a man as long as it is not interpreted, but when it is interpreted, it happens." [28]

Allah, Most High, says, ❲ And he said to the one whom he knew to be saved, "Mention me to your lord (i.e. your king, so as to get me out of the prison)." But *Shaitan* made him forget to mention it to his lord. So he (Yoosuf) stayed in prison a few (more) years. ❳ (*Soorah Yoosuf* 12:42)

---

[28] This is an authentic *hadeeth* narrated by Abu Dawood (5020), At-Tirmidhi (2279), Ibn Majah (3914), Ahmad (15749) and Ad-Darimi (2148), on the authority of Laqeet Ibn Sabirah ﷺ.

Allah, Most High, informs us that Yoosuf ﷺ said to the one whom he knew would be saved, which was the cup-bearer, ❲ "Mention me to your lord." ❳. That is, mention my case and the situation that I am in to your king; I am imprisoned, without having committed any crime. This is evidence of the permissibility of taking the necessary steps to achieve one's objective and this is not inconsistent with trusting in the Lord of lords (*tawakkul*). As for the saying of Him, Most High: ❲ But *Shaitan* made him forget to mention it to his lord ❳ (*Soorah Yoosuf* 12:42). That is, Satan caused the man who was saved to forget to mention what Yoosuf ﷺ had entrusted to him.

He, Most High, says, ❲ And the king (of Egypt) said, "Verily, I saw (in a dream) seven fat cows, whom seven lean ones were devouring - and of seven green ears of corn, and (seven) others dry. O, notables! Explain to me my dream, if it be that you can interpret dreams." They said, "Mixed up false dreams and we are not skilled in the interpretation of dreams." Then the man who was released (one of the two who were in prison), now at length remembered and said, "I will tell you its interpretation, so send me forth." (He said), "O, Yoosuf, the man of truth! Explain to us (the dream) of seven fat cows whom seven lean ones were devouring, and of seven green ears of corn, and (seven) others dry, that I may return to the people, and that they may know." (Yoosuf) said, "For seven consecutive years, you shall sow as usual and that (the harvest) which you reap you shall leave in ears, (all) – except a little of it which you may eat. Then will come after that, seven hard (years), which will devour what you have laid by in advance for them, (all) except a little of that which you have guarded (stored). Then thereafter will come a year in which people will have abundant rain and in which they will press (wine and oil)." ❳ (*Soorah Yoosuf* 12:43-49)

This was one of the means by which Yoosuf ﷺ obtained his release from prison, with honor and respect. To wit, this vision was seen by the king of Egypt, who was Ar-Riyyan Ibn Al-Waleed Ibn Tharwan, Ibn Arashah Ibn Faran Ibn 'Amr Ibn 'Imlaq Ibn Lawuz Ibn Sam (Shem) Ibn Nooh ﷺ.

The People of the Scripture said that he saw in the dream that he was on the edge of a river and seven fat cows had emerged from it and they began to graze in a meadow there; then seven lean, weak cows emerged from that river and they began to graze along with the first seven. Then they turned upon them and devoured them. Then he awoke in a state of alarm. Then he slept again and saw seven green ears of wheat on a single stalk and suddenly, seven thin, withered ears ate them. Then the king awoke in a state of alarm. When he informed his council of elders and his people about what he had seen, there was no one among them who was skilled in the interpretation of dreams. Indeed, ﴾ "Mixed up false dreams." ﴿ (*Soorah Yoosuf* 12:44). That is, these are a mixture of the dreams that you had during the night and it may be that there is no meaning to them; in addition to this, we have no expertise in this field. This is why they said, ﴾ and we are not skilled in the interpretation of dreams ﴿ (*Soorah Yoosuf* 12:44). At this moment, the one who had been freed from jail remembered the trust with which he had been charged by Yoosuf ﷺ.

This is why Allah, Most High, says, ﴾ Then the man who was released (one of the two who were in prison), now at length remembered and said. ﴿ (*Soorah Yoosuf* 12:45) That is, he remembered the trust after a few years had passed. He said to his people and to the king, ﴾ "I will tell you its interpretation, so send me forth." ﴿ (*Soorah Yoosuf* 12:45) That is, send me to Yoosuf; and he went to him and said, ﴾ (He said), "O, Yoosuf, the man of truth! Explain to us (the dream) of seven fat cows whom seven lean ones were devouring, and of seven green ears of corn, and (seven) others dry, that I may return to the people, and that they may know." ❳ (*Soorah Yoosuf* 12:46) He interpreted for them from the dreams of the king that which showed that seven years of abundance would be followed by seven years of drought. ❲ "Then thereafter will come a year in which people will have abundant rain." ❳ (*Soorah Yoosuf* 12:49). That is, they will experience rain, abundance and comfort ❲ "and in which they will press." ❳ (*Soorah Yoosuf* 12:49). That is, they will press or juice the things that they commonly used to press, such as sugar cane, grapes, olives, sesame seeds and other things. He interpreted the dreams for them and guided them as to what they should do during the years of plenty and the years of famine and how they should store the grain they had harvested during the seven years of plenty, i.e. in its ears, except for what they set aside for their use (i.e. to be eaten). He also told them to keep only a minimum of seeds during the seven lean years, since it was most likely that the seeds would not produce any return. This proves how complete was Yoosuf's knowledge, perception and understanding.

He, Most High, says, ❲ And the king said, "Bring him to me." But when the messenger came to him, (Yoosuf) said, "Return to your lord and ask him, "What happened to the women who cut their hands? Surely, my Lord (Allah) is Well-Aware of their plot." (The king) said (to the women), "What was your affair when you did seek to seduce Yoosuf?" The women said, "Allah forbid! No evil know we against him!" The wife of *Al-'Azeez* said, "Now the truth is manifest (to all), it was I who sought to seduce him, and he is surely of the truthful." He said, "It was in order that he (*Al-'Azeez*) may know that I betrayed him not in secret. And, verily! Allah guides not the plot of the betrayers.

And I free not myself (from the blame). Verily, the (human) self is inclined to evil, except when my Lord bestows His Mercy (upon whom He wills). Verily, my Lord is Oft-Forgiving, Most Merciful." 》 (*Soorah Yoosuf* 12:50-53). When the king realised the completeness of Yoosuf's knowledge, the perfect nature of his intellect, his acute powers of perception and his understanding, he ordered that he be brought in his presence, so that he might become a member of his inner circle. When the king's messenger came to him with this information, he preferred not to leave until it had become clear to everyone that he had been wrongly and unjustly imprisoned and that he was totally innocent of the crime they had falsely ascribed to him. 《 [Yoosuf] said, Return to your lord 》, that is, the king. 《 "and ask him, "What happened to the women who cut their hands? Surely, my Lord (Allah) is Well-Aware of their plot." 》 (*Soorah Yoosuf* 12:50) It was said that it means: Verily, my master, *Al-'Azeez* knows that I am innocent of what was attributed to me; i.e. so tell the king to ask them how I strongly rejected their advances, when they attempted to seduce me and encourage them to tell the truth about this matter, which is neither honorable nor right. So when they were asked about it, they acknowledged what had actually happened and confirmed Yoosuf's praiseworthy conduct. 《 The women said, "Allah forbid! No evil know we against him!" 》 (*Soorah Yoosuf* 12:51). At this point, 《 the wife of *Al-'Azeez* said 》. That is, Zulaikha. 《 "Now the truth has *hashasa*." 》 (*Soorah Yoosuf* 12:51). That is, now the truth has become manifest to all; and the truth has a greater right to be heeded (than falsehood). 《 "It was I who sought to seduce him, and he is surely of the truthful." 》 (*Soorah Yoosuf* 12:51). That is regarding his claim that he is innocent, that he did not attempt to seduce me and that he was wrongfully and unjustly imprisoned, based on false testimony.

And He, Most High, says, ❨ He said, "It was in order that he (*Al-'Azeez*) may know that I betrayed him not in secret. And, verily! Allah guides not the plot of the betrayers." ❩ (*Soorah Yoosuf* 12:52). It was said that this was the saying of Yoosuf ﷺ; i.e. I only requested this investigation in order that Al-'Azeez should know that I did not betray him in his absence. It was also said that it was the conclusion of the speech of Zulaikha, i.e. I only acknowledged this (sin) in order that my husband, Al 'Azeez should know that I did not actually betray him in this matter (by committing adultery). It was only an attempted seduction, and it did not result in unlawful sexual intercourse. This interpretation was supported by a great number of the later scholars and others. But Ibn Jareer and Ibn Abi Hatim only related the first interpretation.

❨ "And I free not myself (from the blame). Verily, the (human) self is inclined to evil, except when my Lord bestows His Mercy (upon whom He wills). Verily, my Lord is Oft-Forgiving, Most Merciful." ❩ (*Soorah Yoosuf* 12:53) It was said that this was from the speech of Yoosuf ﷺ and it was also said that from the speech of Zulaikha; the view that it is a continuation of the speech of Zulaikha is more apparent, more appropriate and stronger. And Allah knows better.

And He, Most High, says, ❨ And the king said, "Bring him to me that I may attach him to my person." Then, when he spoke to him, he said, "Verily, this day, you are with us high in rank and fully trusted." (Yoosuf) said, "Set me over the storehouses of the land; I am indeed *hafeez* and *'aleem*." (as Minister of Finance in Egypt, in place of *Al-'Azeez* who was dead at that time). Thus did We give full authority to Yoosuf in the land, to take possession therein, as when or where he likes. We bestow of Our Mercy on whom We please, and We make not to be lost the reward of *Al-Muhsinoon.* ❩ (*Soorah Yoosuf* 12:54-57)

When Yoosuf's spotless character and his innocence of the accusation they had leveled against him became apparent to the king, he said, ❨ Bring him to me that I may attach him to my person." ❩ That is, I will make him one of my inner circle members, a prominent member of my government and an eminent personage in my entourage. When he had spoken to him and heard his words and his situation had become clear to him, ❨ He said, "Verily, this day, you are with us high in rank and fully trusted." ❩ (*Soorah Yoosuf* 12:54) That is a person occupying a position of authority and trustworthiness. ❨ [Yoosuf] said, "Set me over the storehouses of the land; I am indeed *hafeez* and *'aleem.*" ❩ (*Soorah Yoosuf* 12:55) He asked the king to appoint him to oversee the grain stores, because of the expected depletion in the amount of grain stored after seven years of plenty, as he would then be in a position to manage the situation in a manner that was pleasing to Allah, by making provisions for them and treating them with kindness. He informed the king that he was ❨ *"hafeez"* ❩. That is, strong in preserving what was in his hands and he could be trusted not to deal with it in any dishonest way. He also said that he was ❨ *"'aleem"* ❩. That is, possessing full knowledge of things and of the best way to deal with the grain stores. In this, there is evidence of the permissibility of seeking an appointment for the one who knows himself to be trustworthy and capable.

Allah, Most High, says, ❨ Thus did We give full authority to Yoosuf in the land, to take possession therein, as, when and where he liked. ❩ (*Soorah Yoosuf* 12:56) That is, after imprisonment, hardship and confinement came freedom to do as he pleased within the lands of Egypt, ❨ to take possession therein, as, when and where he liked. ❩ That is, whatsoever he wished was made lawful for him; thus did Allah honor him, bestow on him an enviable reward and exalt him. ❨ We bestow of Our Mercy on whom We please, and We make not to be lost the reward of *Al-Muhsinoon* (those who do good deeds) ❩ (*Soorah Yoosuf* 12:56) That is, all of this is a part of Allah's Recompense and Reward for the Believer, in addition to the abundance of goodness and handsome reward that have been stored for him in the Hereafter. This is why Allah, Most High, says, ❨ And verily, the reward of the Hereafter is better for those who believe and used to fear Allah and keep their duty to Him (by abstaining from all kinds of sins and evil deeds and by performing all kinds of righteous good deeds) ❩ (*Soorah Yoosuf* 12:57) It was said that 'Atfeer died and the king appointed Yoosuf in his place and married his widow, Zulaikha, to him, and he was an honest and trustworthy minister.

Allah, Most High, says, ❨ And Yoosuf's brethren came and they entered unto him, and he recognized them, but they recognized him not. And when he furnished them forth with provisions (according to their need), he said, "Bring me a brother of yours from your father; (he meant Binyameen). See you not that I give full measure, and that I am the best of the hosts? But if you bring him not to me, there shall be no measure for you with me, nor shall you come near me." They said, "We shall try to get permission (for him) from his father, and verily, we shall do it." And he (Yoosuf) told his servants to put their money (with which they had bought the corn) into their bags, so that they might know it when they go back to their people, in order that they might come back. ❩ (*Soorah Yoosuf* 12:58-62) Allah, Most High, informs us about the arrival of Yoosuf's brothers in the lands of Egypt, where they had come to purchase food (grain, etc.) after the years of drought had spread throughout the lands surrounding Egypt. At that time, Yoosuf ﷺ was in charge of both secular and religious affairs in Egypt and when they entered in his presence, he recognized them, but they did not recognize him, for they could not have dreamed of the rise to high status and greatness that had come to Yoosuf عليه السلام; this is why he recognized them, but they did not recognize him.

Allah, Most High, says, ﴿ And when he furnished them forth with provisions (according to their need) ﴾. That is, he had given them the foodstuffs (grain etc.) which were in accordance with his custom, of giving to every person a camel-load and not more, ﴿ he said "Bring me a brother of yours from your father." ﴾ This was after he had asked them about their situation and how many they were, and they had replied, "We were twelve men, but one of us died and his full brother remained with our father." He then said, "If you come back next year, bring him to me." ﴿ "See you not that I give full measure, and that I am the best of the hosts?" ﴾ That is, I have treated you hospitably and entertained you well. Thus did he encourage them to return to him with their half-brother (Binyameen). In case they entertained the idea of not returning to him, he said, ﴿ "But if you bring him not to me, there shall be no measure for you with me, nor shall you come near me." ﴾. That is, I will not give you any supplies and I will not allow you to come to me at all. This was in contrast to the kindness that he had extended to them on their arrival. So he strove to ensure that they would bring Binyameen with them, in order to satisfy his desire to see him, by employing a carrot-and-stick-approach. ﴿ They said, "We shall try to get permission (for him) from his father." ﴾ (*Soorah Yoosuf* 12:61). That is, we will try our utmost to arrange that he accompanies us and to bring him to you. ﴿ "And verily, we shall do it." ﴾ (*Soorah Yoosuf* 12:61). That is, and certainly, we are able to accomplish that. Then he ordered his servants to place the merchandise they had brought with them to exchange for food in their saddle-bags, without them realizing it. ❬ So when they returned to their father, they said, "O, our father! No more measure of grain shall we get. So send our brother with us, and we shall get our measure and truly we will guard him." He said, "Can I entrust him to you except as I entrusted his brother (Yoosuf) to you aforetime? But Allah is the Best to guard, and He is the Most Merciful of those who show mercy." And when they opened their bags, they found their merchandise had been returned to them. They said, "O, our father! What (more) can we desire? This, our merchandise has been returned to us, so we shall get food for our family, and we shall guard our brother and add one more measure of a camel's load. This quantity is easy." He (Ya'qoob) said, "I will not send him with you until you swear a solemn oath to me in Allah's Name, that you will bring him back to me unless you are yourselves surrounded (by enemies, etc.)." And when they had sworn their solemn oath, he said, "Allah is the Witness over what we have said." And he said, "O, my sons! Do not enter by one gate, but enter by different gates, and I cannot avail you against Allah at all. Verily! The decision rests only with Allah. In him, I put my trust and let all those that trust, put their trust in Him." And when they entered according to their father's advice, it did not avail them in the least against (the Will of) Allah, it was but a need of Ya'qoob's inner-self which he discharged. And verily, he was endowed with knowledge because We had taught him, but most men know not. ❭ (*Soorah Yoosuf* 12:63-68) Allah, Most High, relates what happened to them after they returned to their father and how they said to him, ❬ "No more measure of grain shall we get." ❭ That is, after this year, unless you send our brother (Binyameen) with us; if you send him with us, we will not be prevented from receiving grain. ❬ And when they opened their bags, they found their merchandise had been returned to them. They said, "O, our father! What (more) can we desire? This, our merchandise has been returned to us." ﴾. That is, what else can you wish for, now that our merchandise has been returned to us? ﴿ "so we shall get food for our family." ﴾. That is, we will be able to provide for them and bring them that which is beneficial to them this year and which will relive the drought they are facing. ﴿ "And we shall guard our brother and add." ﴾. That is, because of his presence, ﴿ "one more measure of a camel's load." ﴾. Allah, Most High, says, ﴿ "This quantity is easy." ﴾. That is, in return for his other son going with them. Ya'qoob عليه السلام was very close indeed to his son, Binyameen, because he could smell in him the scent of Yoosuf عليه السلام and he found consolation in him for the loss of Yoosuf عليه السلام. This is why he said, ﴿ "I will not send him with you until you swear a solemn oath to me in Allah's Name, that you will bring him back to me unless you are yourselves surrounded (by enemies, etc.)." ﴾. That is, unless you are all prevented from bringing him back. ﴿ And when they had sworn their solemn oath, he said, "Allah is the Witness over what we have said." ﴾. He confirmed their oaths and validated their covenants and took precautions to ensure the safety of his son (Binyameen); but caution cannot avail against that which has been Divinely ordained. Had it not been for his need and the need of his people for supplies, he would not have sent his beloved son. But Allah's Divine Ordainment has its own rules; and the Lord, Most High, ordains what He Wills, chooses what He Wants and decides what He wills. And He is the Most Wise, the All-Knowing. Then he ordered them not to enter the city through one gate; but to enter it through different gates. It was said that he desired that none should afflict them with the evil eye of jealousy; this was due to the fact that they were all handsome

men of strong form. This was said by 'Abdullah Ibn 'Abbas
, Mujahid, Muhammad Ibn Ka'b , Qatadah, As-Suddi and
Ad-Dahhak. It was also said that he wanted them to separate,
that haply, they might find some trace of Yoosuf ﷺ. This was
said by Ibraheem An-Nakha'i. But the first opinion appears
more correct, which is why he said, ﴾ "and I cannot avail you
against Allah at all." ﴿. Allah, Most High, says, ﴾ And when
they entered according to their father's advice, it did not avail
them in the least against (the Will of) Allah, it was but a need
of Ya'qoob's inner-self which he discharged. And, verily, he
was endowed with knowledge because We had taught him, but
most men know not. ﴿ (*Soorah Yoosuf* 12:68)

He, Most High, says, ﴾ And when they went in before
Yoosuf, he betook his brother (Binyameen) to himself and
said, "Verily! I am your brother, so grieve not for what they
used to do." So when he had furnished them forth with their
provisions, he put the bowl into his brother's bag, then a crier
called out, "O, you (in) the caravan! Surely, you are thieves!"
They, turning toward them, said, "What is it that you have
missed?" They said, "We have missed the bowl of the king
and for him who produces it is (the reward of) a camel load; I
will be bound by it." They said, "By Allah! Indeed you know
that we came not to make mischief in the land, and we are no
thieves!" They (Yoosuf's men) said, "What then shall be the
penalty of him, if you are (proved to be) liars?" They (Yoosuf's
brothers) said, "The penalty should be that he in whose bag it
is found should be held for the punishment (of the crime). Thus
we punish the *zalimoon* (wrongdoers etc.)!" So he (Yoosuf)
began (the search) in their bags before the bag of his brother.
Then he brought it out of his brother's bag. Thus did We plan
for Yoosuf. He could not take his brother by the law of the king
(as a slave), except that Allah willed it. (So Allah caused the

brothers to bind themselves with their way of "punishment, i.e. the enslavement of a thief.") We raise to degrees whom We please, but over all those endowed with knowledge is the All-Knowing (Allah). They (Yoosuf's brothers) said, "If he steals, there was a brother of his (Yoosuf) who did steal before (him)." But these things did Yoosuf keep in himself, revealing not the secrets to them. He said (within himself), "You are in the worst case, and Allah knows best the truth of what you assert!" They said, "O, ruler of the land! Verily, he has an old father (who will grieve for him); so take one of us in his place. Indeed we think that you are one of the _Muhsinoon_ (those who do good)." He said, "Allah forbid that we should take anyone but him with whom we found our property. Indeed (if we did so), we should be _zalimoon_ (wrongdoers)." ﴾ (_Soorah Yoosuf_ 12:69-79)

Allah relates what happened to them when they entered with their brother, Binyameen, the presence of his full brother, Yoosuf عليه السلام, and how he received him and informed him in secret that he was his brother, ordering him to keep this knowledge to himself and not to share it with them. Then he ordered his servants to place the bowl from which he drank and which he used as a measure for the people during those times of drought among Binyameen's belongings. Then he told them that they (his brothers) had stolen the king's measuring bowl. And he promised them (the servants) that if it was returned to him, he would reward the finder with a camel-load of food. The caller guaranteed this to them. They (the brothers) approached the one who had accused them and they rebuked him and strongly censured him for what he had said to them. ﴿ They said, "By Allah! Indeed you know that we came not to make mischief in the land, and we are no thieves!" ﴾. That is, you know of us what contradicts the accusation of theft that you have made against us. ﴿ They (Yoosuf's men) said, "What then shall be the penalty of him, if you are (proved to be) liars?" They (Yoosuf's brothers) said, "The penalty should be that he in whose bag it is found should be held for the punishment (of the crime). Thus we punish the *zalimoon* (wrongdoers etc.)!" ⟩. This was their law, that the thief should be given up to the victim of the theft, which is why they said, ⟨ "Thus we punish the *zalimoon* (wrongdoers, etc.)!" ⟩

He, Most High, says, ⟨ So he (Yoosuf) began (the search) in their bags before the bag of his brother. Then he brought it out of his brother's bag ⟩ (*Soorah Yoosuf* 12:76) This was in order to avoid suspicion and to perfect the plot. Then He, Most High, says, ⟨ Thus did We plan for Yoosuf (Joseph). He could not take his brother by the law of the king (as a slave), ⟩ (*Soorah Yoosuf* 12:76) That is, had they not acknowledged that the punishment for one in whose luggage the bowl was found was that he be handed over to the victim of the theft, Yousuf ﷺ would not have been able to take him, according to Egyptian law. ⟨ Except that Allah willed it. (So Allah caused the brothers to bind themselves with their way of "punishment, i.e. the enslavement of a thief.") We raise to degrees whom We please ⟩, that is, in knowledge, ⟨ but over all those endowed with knowledge is the All-Knowing (Allah). ⟩ This is because Yoosuf ﷺ was more knowledgeable and more perceptive than his brothers and he possessed a stronger will and firmer resolution than they did. He only did what he did in accordance with Allah's Command to do so. This was because of the great benefit that resulted from it – and that was the coming of his father and his people to him and their approaching him in a delegation. When they saw the bowl being brought out from the baggage of Binyameen, ⟨ They (Yoosuf's brothers) said, "If he steals, there was a brother of his who did steal before (him)." ⟩ (*Soorah Yoosuf* 12:77). They were referring to Yoosuf ﷺ. It was said that he had stolen the idol of his maternal grandfather and destroyed it. It was also said that his paternal aunt had tied a belt belonging to Ishaq عليه السلام around him, under his clothing, when he was an infant; then they discovered it under his clothing and he (being a small child) was unaware of what she had done. And she had only done this because she wanted him to be in her care, because she loved him.

He, Most High, says, ❨ "You are in the worst case, and Allah knows best the truth of what you assert!" ❩. He answered them silently, in low voice – and his words were words of clemency and kindness, forgiveness, and pardon; they also spoke with kindness and gentleness, (though aloud) saying, ❨ "O, ruler of the land! Verily, he has an old father (who will grieve for him); so take one of us in his place. Indeed we think that you are one of the *Muhsinoon* (those who do good)." He said, "Allah forbid that we should take anyone but him with whom we found our property. Indeed (if we did so), we should be *zalimoon* (wrongdoers)." ❩ (*Soorah Yoosuf* 12:78). That is, if we let the accused go free and took an innocent person. This is something that we would not do and we would not permit it to be done. We will only take the person in whose possession we found our property.

He, Most High, says, ❨ So, when they despaired of him, they held a conference in private. The eldest among them said, "Know you not that your father did take an oath from you in Allah's Name, and before this you did fail in your duty with Yoosuf? Therefore I will not leave this land until my father permits me, or Allah decides my case and He is the Best of the judges. Return to your father and say, "O, our father! Verily, your son (Binyameen) has stolen, and we testify not except according to what we know, and we could not know the unseen! And ask (the people of) the town where we have been, and the caravan in which we returned, and indeed we are telling the truth." He (Ya'qoob) said, "Nay, but your ownselves have beguiled you into something. So patience is most fitting (for me). May be Allah will bring them all (back) to me. Truly, He, only He is All-Knowing, Most Wise." And he turned away from them and said, "Alas, my grief for Yoosuf]!" And he lost his sight because of the sorrow he was suppressing. They said, "By Allah! You will never cease remembering Yoosuf until you become weak with old age, or until you be of the dead." He said, "I only complain of my grief and sorrow to Allah, and I know from Allah that which you know not. "O, my sons! Go you and inquire about Yoosuf and his brother, and never give up hope of Allah's Mercy. Certainly no one despairs of Allah's Mercy, except the people who disbelieve." ❩ (*Soorah Yoosuf* 12:80-87)

Allah, Most High, informs us about them, saying that when they despaired of taking Binyameen from Yoosuf ﷺ, they began to whisper to one another in private. ❨ The eldest among them said, ❩ – that was Roobeel ❨ "Know you not that your father did take an oath from you in Allah's Name…" ❩. That is, you have broken your oath to him and you have been negligent with him (i.e. Binyameen) as you were formerly negligent with his brother, Yoosuf. Now I cannot face him. ❨ "Therefore I will not leave this land…" ❩. That is, I will continue to stay here ❨ "until my father permits me…" ❩. That is, to come to him ❨ "or Allah decides my case…" ❩. That is, He enables me to secure my brother's return to my father. ❨ And He is the Best of the judges. Return to your father and say, "O, our father! Verily, your son (Benjamin) has stolen…" ❩. That is, inform him of what you have seen of the matter with your own eyes. ❨ "And we testify not except according to what we know, and we could not know the unseen! And ask (the people of) the town where we have been, and the caravan in which we returned " ❳. That is, what we have told you about them seizing our brother because he had committed an act of theft is a matter which has become widely known in Egypt and the people of the caravan in which we returned know about it, because they were there. ❲ "And indeed we are telling the truth." He (Ya'qoob) said, "Nay, but your ownselves have beguiled you into something. So patience is most fitting." ❳. That is, the matter is not as you have described; he did not steal, because it is not in his nature to do so. It is only your own selves that have seduced you into believing something (that is not true), so patience is the most fitting thing for me.

Then he said, ❲ "May be Allah will bring them all (back) to me." ❳. That is, Yoosuf (عليه السلام), Binyameen and Roobeel. ❲ "Truly, He, only He is All-knowing." ❳. That is, regarding my situation and the separation that I am enduring from my loved ones. ❲ "Most Wise." ❳. That is, in all that He ordains and all that He does; and His is the most far-reaching Wisdom and the irrefutable evidence. ❲ And he turned away from them ❳. That is, Ya'qoob (عليه السلام) turned away from his sons. ❲ And said, "Alas, my grief for Yoosuf!" ❳ This new grief reminded him of his former grief and resurfaced that which had been latent, as someone said,

Let your heart roam wherever you wish for the sake of love,
But (true) love is only for the first love.

And someone else said,

My companion censured me for weeping at the graves,
For the tears that welled up and spilt forth,

And he said, "Do you weep for every grave that you see?
For a grave which consists of layers of sand?"
I said to him, "Verily, grief evokes grief, so leave me,
For all of this is the grave of Malik."

He, Most High, says, ❨ And his eyes became white because of the sorrow. ❩ That is, he became blind due to excessive weeping ❨ that he was suppressing. ❩ That is, the extreme grief, sorrow and longing that he was feeling for Yoosuf ﷺ. When his sons observed the emotional upset and the pain of being parted (from Yoosuf and Binyameen) that he was suffering, ❨ they said ❩ to him in tones of compassion, pity and concern for him, ❨ "By Allah! You will never cease remembering Yoosuf until you become weak with old age, or until you be of the dead." ❩ That is, you will continue to remember him until your body becomes weak and your strength departs, so if you take care of yourself, it will be better for you. ❨ He said, "I only complain of my grief and sorrow to Allah, and I know from Allah that which you know not." ❩ (*Soorah Yoosuf* 12:86). That is, I do not complain to you or to anyone among the people about my situation; I only complain to Allah, the Almighty, the All-Powerful, and I know that He will make a release and an escape for me from the situation that I am in. I also know that Yoosuf's vision must be fulfilled and that you and I will find no alternative to prostrating to him, as he saw. This is why he said, ❨ "and I know from Allah that which you know not." ❩ Then he said to them, in order to incite them to find Yoosuf ﷺ and his brother, that they should go and inquire about the matter: ❨ "O, my sons! Go you and inquire about Yoosuf and his brother, and never give up hope of Allah's Mercy. Certainly no one despairs of Allah's Mercy, except the people who disbelieve." ❩ (*Soorah Yoosuf* 12:87). That is, do not despair of attaining relief after hardship, because no one despairs of Allah's Mercy and Relief and the release from adversity that He can ordain, except the disbelieving people.

He, Most High, says, ❨ Then, when they entered unto him (Yoosuf), they said, "O, ruler of the land! A hard time has hit us and our family, and we have brought but poor capital, so pay us full measure and be charitable to us. Truly, Allah does reward the charitable." He said, "Do you know what you did with Yoosuf and his brother, when you were ignorant?" They said, "Are you indeed Yoosuf?" He said, "I am Yoosuf, and this is my brother (Binyameen). Allah has indeed been Gracious to us. Verily, he who fears Allah with obedience to Him (by abstaining from sins and evil deeds, and by performing righteous good deeds), and is patient, then surely, Allah makes not the reward of the *Muhsinoon* (those who do good) to be lost." They said, "By Allah! Indeed Allah has preferred you above us, and we certainly have been sinners." He said, "No reproach on you this day, may Allah forgive you, and He is the Most Merciful of those who show mercy! Go with this shirt of mine, and cast it over the face of my father, he will become clear-sighted, and bring to me all your family." ❩ (*Soorah Yoosuf* 12:88-93)

Allah, Most High, informs us about the return of Yoosuf's brothers to him, their visit to him and their desire for his grain and for him to show charity toward them by returning their brother, Binyameen to them. ❨ Then, when they entered unto him (Yoosuf), they said, "O, ruler of the land! A hard time has hit us and our family." ❩. That is, drought and straitened times, in addition to a large family ❨ "and we have brought but poor capital…" ❩. That is, we have brought money for the food we want to buy, but it is not substantial. It was said that they brought a mean sum of *dirhams*. It was also said that they were goods of little exchange value, except by the one who would be

kind enough to overlook this. It was also said that they brought
pine nuts, terebinth seeds [29] and such. It was reported on the
authority of 'Abdullah Ibn 'Abbas ﷺ that they were types of
straw sacks, ropes and the like. ❨ "So pay us full measure and
be charitable to us. Truly, Allah does reward the charitable."
❩. It was said by As-Suddi that it means by accepting what we
have brought. It was also said that it means by returning our
brother to us. This was the opinion of Ibn Juraij.

He saw the situation they were in and the pitiful payment
that they brought and he felt compassion for them and made
himself known to them, informing them about the Command
of his Lord and their Lord. When he had revealed his identity
to them, ❨ He said, "Do you know what you did with Yoosuf
(Joseph) and his brother, when you were ignorant? They said" ❩.
They were absolutely amazed to know his identity, for they had
visited him numerous times and they had not recognised him.
❨ "Are you indeed Yoosuf?" He said, "I am Yoosuf, and this is
my brother (Binyameen)" ❩. That is, I am Yoosuf with whom
you dealt as you did and whom you abandoned aforetimes. ❨
"And this is my brother (Binyameen)." ❩ He said this in order
to confirm the truth of what he had told them and to make clear
to them the envy that they had harbored toward them and the
deceitful stratagems they had employed against them, which
is why he said, ❨ "Allah has indeed been Gracious to us." ❩
That is, by the kindness and charity He has shown to us and
by gathering us together after having been separated. This was
the result of our obedience to Him and the patience we have
shown in the face of the trials that have beset us, in addition to
the obedience and filial piety we have shown toward our father
and his great love and affection for us. ❨ "Verily, he who fears

---

(29) Terebinth: Pistacia vera, a small tree which is grown for its edible seeds
     (akin to pistachio nuts).

Allah with obedience to Him (by abstaining from sins and evil
deeds, and by performing righteous good deeds), and is patient,
then surely, Allah makes not the reward of the *Muhsınoon*
(those who do good) to be lost." They said, "By Allah! Indeed
Allah has preferred you above us."〉 That is, He has favored
you over us and given you that which He has not given to us
(i.e. Prophethood). 〈 "And we certainly have been sinners."
〉. That is, in what we have done to you; and now here we are
before you. 〈 He said, "No reproach on you this day." 〉 That
is, I will not rebuke you for what you did to me after this day.
Then he went further, saying to them, 〈 "may Allah forgive
you, and He is the Most Merciful of those who show mercy!" 〉
Then he ordered them to go with his shirt, which he wore next
to his skin, and he told them to place it over their father's eyes
and he told them that his sight would be restored as a result, by
Allah's Permission, after he had lost it. This was an amazing
phenomenon, proof of his Prophethood and a major miracle.
Then he ordered them to bring all of their families to the lands
of Egypt, to enjoy goodness, abundant provision and unity,
after separation, in the most complete manner. 〈 And when the
caravan departed, their father said, "I do indeed feel the smell
of Yoosuf, if only you think me not a dotard (a person who has
weakness of mind because of old age)." They said, "By Allah!
Certainly, you are in your old error." Then, when the bearer
of the glad tidings arrived, he cast it (the shirt) over his face
and he became clear-sighted. He said, "Did I not say to you
that I know from Allah that which you know not?" They said,
"O, our father! Ask for forgiveness (from Allah) for our sins,
indeed we have been sinners." He said, "I will ask my Lord for
forgiveness for you, verily, He, only He is the Oft-Forgiving,
the Most Merciful." 〉 (*Soorah Yoosuf* 12:94-98)

'Abdur-Razzaq narrated on the authority of 'Abdullah Ibn

'Abbas ﷺ that he said regarding the Words of Allah, Most High: ❮ And when the caravan departed ❯, "When the caravan departed, a wind sprang up and it carried the smell of Yoosuf's shirt to Ya'qoob ﷺ and he said, ❮ I do indeed feel the smell of Yoosuf, if only you think me not a dotard (a person who has weakness of mind because of old age). ❯" Ibn 'Abbas ﷺ said, "He picked up his scent from a distance of eight days' (travel) away!" Ath-Thawri also narrated it thus, as did Shu'bah and others, on the authority of Abu Sinan. Al Hasan Al Basri and Ibn Juraij Al-Makki said that the distance between them was eighty *farsakhs* [(30)] and that he had been parted from him for eighty years. ❮ "If only you think me not a dotard (a person who has weakness of mind because of old age)." ❯ That is, you say that I have only said this because I have become old and senile. 'Abdullah Ibn 'Abbas ﷺ, 'Ata', Mujahid, Sa'eed Ibn Jubair and Qatadah said that it means: "you think me foolish." Mujahid also said – as did Al-Hasan Al-Basri – that it means "you think me senile and decrepit." ❮ They said, "By Allah! Certainly, you are in your old error." ❯ Qatadah and As-Suddi said that they spoke harsh words to him. Allah, Most High, says, ❮ "When the bearer of the glad tidings arrived, he cast it (the shirt) over his face and he became clear-sighted." ❯ That is, as soon as he arrived with the shirt, he put it over Ya'qoob's face and immediately, his sight returned, after having been blind. When this happened, he said to his sons, ❮ "Did I not say to you that I know from Allah that which you know not?" ❯ That is, I know that Allah will reunite me with Yoosuf ﷺ, that my eyes will be delighted by (seeing) him and that He will show me that which will please me regarding his situation. At this point, ❮ They said, "O, our father! Ask for forgiveness (from Allah) for our sins, indeed we have been sinners." ❯ They

---

(30) *Farsakh*: A parasang, which is an ancient Persian unit of distance.

requested from him that he ask Allah, the Almighty, the All-Powerful to forgive them for what they had done, what they had inflicted on him and his son and what they had resolved to do against him (i.e. Yoosuf عليه السلام). And because they had made the intention to repent before committing the deed, Allah caused them to seek forgiveness after they had committed it. Their father agreed to do what they asked. ❪ He said, "I will ask my Lord for forgiveness for you. Verily, He, only He is the Oft-Forgiving, the Most Merciful." ❫

Allah, Most High, says, ❪ Then, when they entered unto Yoosuf, he betook his parents to himself and said, "Enter Egypt, if Allah wills, in security." And he raised his parents to the throne and they fell down before him in prostration. And he said, "O, my father! This is the interpretation of my dream aforetime! My Lord has made it come true! He was indeed good to me, when He took me out of the prison and brought you (all here) out of the Bedouin life, after *Shaitan* had sown enmity between me and my brothers. Certainly, my Lord is the Most Courteous and Kind unto whom He Wills. Truly, He, Only He is the All-Knowing, the Most Wise. My Lord! You have indeed bestowed on me of the sovereignty, and taught me the interpretation of dreams; The (only) Creator of the heavens and the Earth! You are my *Wali* (Protector, Helper, Supporter, Guardian, etc.) in this world and in the Hereafter; cause me to die as a Muslim (the one submitting to Your Will), and join me with the righteous." ❫ (*Soorah Yoosuf* 12:99-101)

The People of the Scripture claim that Yoosuf عليه السلام was absent from his father for forty years; but the course of events related in the story is a fairly reliable guide to the length of his absence, because the woman attempted to seduce him when he was a young boy of seventeen, according to what has been related by a number of reporters, but he refused. Then he was in prison for a few years (seven, according to 'Ikrimah and others). Then he was released and the seven years of abundance occurred, then, when the people were suffering from the effects of the drought in the second year of the seven years, his brothers came, seeking food supplies in the first year. Then in the second year, they brought his brother, Binyameen with them. In the third year, he revealed himself to them and ordered them to bring all of their families with them and all of them came. ❨ Then, when they entered unto Yoosuf, he betook his parents to himself ❩. That is, he met with them alone, without his brothers ❨ "and said, "Enter Egypt, if Allah wills, in security." ❩ It was said that this means that he told them to enter and then he betook them to himself. This was described as weak by Ibn Jareer At-Tabari; but he is excused (for that). It was also said that he met them and betook them to himself in a tent (outside the city) and that when they approached the gate of Egypt, he said ❨ "Enter Egypt, if Allah wills, in security." ❩ This was said by As-Suddi. But if we said that the matter does not require this (explanation) and it is implicit in the word ❨ "Enter…" ❩ that means reside in Egypt ❨ "if Allah wills, in security." ❩ (*Soorah Yoosuf* 12:99) – it would be correct and also more appropriate.

Allah, Most High, says, ❨ and they fell down before him in prostration ❩. That is, his parents and his eleven brothers prostrated before him, in order to venerate and honor him and this was legislated for them (by Allah) and it continued to be acted upon in all of the Divine Legislations until it was made unlawful in the Revelation given to Muhammad. ❨ And he said, "O, my father! This is the interpretation of my dream aforetime!" ❩ That is, this is the interpretation of the dream that I related to you, in which eleven planets and the sun and moon, which prostrated before me when I saw them; and you told me to keep it secret and you promised me that which you promised me at that time. ❰ "My Lord has made it come true! He was indeed good to me, when He took me out of the prison." ❱ That is, after the affliction and hardship, He has made me a governor and a person whose words are heeded and implemented in the lands of Egypt, wherever I wish ❰ "and brought you (all here) out of the Bedouin life." ❱ That is, from the desert, for they lived in the region of the Arabs, in the lands of *Al-Khaleel.* ❰ "After *Shaitan* had sown enmity between me and my brothers." ❱ This refers to the envy and malice which Satan inspired in their hearts, which caused them to do what they did to Yoosuf عليه السلام, which we have already described. Then he said, ❰ "Certainly, my Lord is the Most Courteous and Kind unto whom He wills." ❱ That is, when Allah Wills something, He prepares the causes that will bring it about and makes them easy in ways of which the slaves are unaware. Indeed, He ordains them and facilitates them, as a Kindness from Him, by His Supreme Omnipotence. ❰ "Truly, He, Only He is the All-Knowing" ❱. That is, He possesses (complete and perfect) Knowledge of all affairs. ❰ "The Most Wise." ❱. That is, regarding His creation, His Legislation and His Divine Predestination.

Then, when Yoosuf عليه السلام saw that his blessing was complete and all of his family had been gathered, he realized this (earthly) abode will not remain and that everything in it and on it is transitory. He saw that there is nothing after completeness except deficiency. As he realized all this, he praised his Lord in a manner that befitted Him and he acknowledged His Great Kindness and Grace and asked Him – and He is the Best of those who are asked – to grant that when death came to him, he might die as a Muslim and be joined with His righteous slaves. Thus it is said in the words of the supplication: "O, Allah! Cause us to live as Muslims and to die as Muslims."

That is, when You bring death to us. It is possible that he asked this when death approached him, as the Prophet ﷺ asked, when death approached him, that Allah raise his soul to the heavenly host and the righteous companions from among the Prophets and the Messengers; he said three times, "O, Allah! Let me be with the highest companions," and then he died. [31]

As for our Islamic Law, it prohibits us from supplicating for death, except where we fear *fitnah*, [32] as in the *hadeeth* of Mu'az ﷺ, describing the supplication of death, which was narrated by Ahmad, "If You are going to send *fitnah* to a people, then cause us to die and come to You without being put to trial." [33] In another *hadeeth*, it is said: "Son of Adam! Death is better for you than *fitnah*." [34]

Maryam (peace be upon her) said, ﴾ "Would that I had died before this, and had been forgotten and out of sight!" ﴿ (*Soorah Maryam* 19:23). 'Ali Ibn Abi Talib ﷺ wished for death when the situation became grave, the discords and trials became oppressive, the fighting increased in intensity and rumor, gossip and hearsay became widespread. Abu 'Abdullah Al-Bukhari, the compiler of the famous *Saheeh* wished for it when circumstances became difficult for him and he encountered those who opposed him.

However, in circumstances of comfort and ease, it was narrated by Al-Bukhari and Muslim in their authentic compilations, on the authority of Anas Ibn Malik ﷺ that he said: "The Messenger

---

(31) Narrated by Al-Bukhari (4437), Muslim (2444), At-Tirmidhi (3496), Imam Ahmad (24253) and Imam Malik (562).

(32) *Fitnah*: Temptation, trial, discord, strife etc.

(33) This is an authentic *hadeeth* narrated by Imam Ahmad (15066); see the commentary of Al-Albani on *Al-Adab Al-Mufrad* (699).

(34) This is an authentic *hadeeth* narrated by Imam Ahmad (23113).

of Allah ﷺ said, "None of you should wish for death due to some harm that has befallen him, but if he has to wish for death, he should say, 'O, Allah! Keep me alive as long as life is better for me, and let me die if death is better for me.'" [35] What is intended by the word harm (*durr*) here is illness and the like, not harm in his religious affairs.

(35) Narrated by Al-Bukhari (5671) and Muslim (2680).

The Story of Ayyoob (Job) عليه السلام

Ibn Ishaq said, "He was a man from Rome and his name was Ayyoob, son of Moos, son of Razaah, son of Al-'Ees, son of Ishaq, son of Ibraheem, *Al-Khaleel*." Others said that he was Ayyoob (Job), son of Moos, son of Raghweel, son of Al-'Ees, son of Ishaq, son of Ya'qoob. And other genealogies have been given for him.

Allah, Most High, says, ❨ And (remember) Ayyoob (Job), when he cried to his Lord, "Verily, distress has seized me, and You are the Most Merciful of all those who show mercy." So We answered his call, and We removed the distress that was on him, and We restored his family to him (that he had lost), and the like thereof along with them, as a mercy from Ourselves and a Reminder for all who worship Us .❩ (*Soorah Al-Anbiya'* 21:83,84)

In *Soorah Sad*, He, Most High, says, ❨ And remember Our slave Ayyoob, when he invoked his Lord (saying), "Verily! *Shaitan* has touched me with distress (by losing my health) and torment (by losing my wealth)!" (Allah said to him), "Strike the ground with your foot: This is a spring of water to wash, cool and a (refreshing) drink." And We gave him (back) his family, and along with them the like thereof, as a Mercy from Us, and a Reminder for those who understand. "And take in your hand a bundle of thin grass and strike therewith (your wife), and break not your oath." Truly! We found him patient. How excellent (a) slave! Verily, he was ever oft-returning in repentance (to Us)! ﴾ (*Soorah Sad* 38:41-44)

Scholars of *tafseer* and history, and others have said that Ayyoob عليه السلام (Job) was a man of great wealth, consisting of grazing stock, slaves, cattle and vast lands in Batheniyyah, which is located in Hooran.

Ibn 'Asakir related that Ayyoob عليه السلام had all of this and he also had many children and a large family, but all of this was taken from him and he was afflicted in his body by a variety of illnesses; and it has been authentically reported that the Messenger of Allah ﷺ said, "The people who are tested the most severely are the Prophets, then the righteous, then the next best and the next best. A man is tried in accordance with his faith; if his faith is firm, then his affliction is hard and if his faith is weak, then his affliction is light." [36] But all of this only increased Ayyoob عليه السلام in patience, hope of Allah's Reward and praise and thanks for Him – to such an extent that his name has become a byword for patience; and it has also become a byword for tribulation, due to the many trials that he endured.

Ibn Abi Hatim and Ibn Jareer narrated on the authority of Anas Ibn Malik رضي الله عنه that the Prophet ﷺ said, "Allah's Prophet, Ayyoob, suffered for eighteen years from his affliction and was shunned by relatives and strangers alike, besides two men who were the closest of his brothers to him. They used to visit

---

(36) The meaning of this can be found in the *Saheehain* and it was narrated with an authentic chain of narrators by Imam Ahmad, on the authority of Sa'd Ibn Abi Waqqas رضي الله عنه (1484).

him every morning and every evening. One of them said to his companion, 'You know, by Allah, that Ayyoob committed a great sin which nobody in the world ever committed.' His companion said, 'Why are you saying that?' He said, 'For eighteen years he has been suffering and Allah has not had Mercy on him and relieve his suffering.' When he went to him the next morning, the (second) man could not wait to tell this to Ayyoob. Ayyoob said, 'I do not know what you are talking about, but Allah knows that if I passed by two men who were arguing and they mentioned the Name of Allah, I would go back home and offer expiation lest they had mentioned the Name of Allah in an improper manner.' Whenever he went out to answer the call of nature, when he finished, his wife would take his hand until he came back home. One day he took a long time, and Allah had revealed to Ayyoob, ﴾ Strike with your foot. This is (a spring of) water to wash, cool and a (refreshing) drink ﴿ (*Soorah Sad* 38:42) She thought that he had taken too long, so she turned to look at him, and saw that Allah had taken away the afflictions he had been suffering, and he looked better than he had ever looked. When she saw him, she said, "May Allah bless you! Have you seen Allah's Prophet, the one who is sorely tested By Allah? I have never seen a man who looks more like him than you, if he were healthy." He said, "I am he." He had two threshing floors, one for wheat and one for barley. Allah sent two clouds, and when one of them reached the threshing floor of the wheat, it rained gold until it was full. The other rained gold on the threshing floor of the barley until it was full." [37]

Ibn Abi Hatim narrated on the authority of Abu Hurairah 巡, from the Prophet 巡 that he said, "When Allah restored to health, Ayyoob 巡旅礼 He rained golden locusts down on him and

---

(37) Narrated by Ibn Jareer in his *Tafseer* (23/167).

he began to gather them up with his hands and place them in his garment. It was said to him, 'O, Ayyoob! Do you not have sufficient?' He said, 'O, my Lord! Who can ever have sufficient of Your Mercy?' [38] It was also narrated by Ibn Hibban in his *Saheeh,* [39] but none of the compilers of the (six authentic) books narrated it, though it conforms to the criteria required for a *hadeeth* to be accepted as authentic. And Allah knows better.

Imam Ahmad narrated on the authority of Abu Hurairah ﷺ that he said: The Messenger of Allah ﷺ said, "While Ayyoob ﷺ was bathing naked, locusts of gold fell upon him. Ayyoob, peace be upon him, began gathering them in his garment. Then his Lord called to him, 'O, Ayyoob, have I not made you so rich that you have no need of what you see?' He said, 'Yes, Lord! But I cannot do without Your Blessing'!" This was also narrated by Al-Bukhari, on the authority of 'Abdur-Razzaq ﷺ. [40]

Allah's Saying: ❨ Strike with your foot ❩ means: strike the ground with your foot; and he did as he was commanded to do, upon which, Allah caused a spring, whose water was cold, to gush forth for him. Then Allah commanded him to wash in it and to drink from it; he did so, and Allah removed thereby all of the pain, disfigurement and illness that had afflicted his body, both outside and inside. He replaced his former ill-health with good health, bestowing on him perfect beauty and great wealth, to such an extent that He rained down a shower of golden locusts upon him and He returned his family to him, as He, Most High, says, ❨ and We restored his family to him (that he had lost), and the like thereof along with them. ❩ (*Soorah*

---

(38) Narrated by Imam Ahmad (10260).

(39) This is an authentic *hadeeth* narrated by Ibn Hibban in his *Saheeh* (14/122, No. 6230).

(40) Narrated by Imam Ahmad (27376).

Al-Anbiya' 21:84) It was said that He restored the selfsame family to life. It was also said that He rewarded him for those he had lost and recompensed him in the life of this world with others, and that He reunited him with all of them in the life of the Hereafter.

He, Most High, says, ❨ as a Mercy from Ourselves. ❩ (*Soorah Al-Anbiya'* 21:84) That is, We relieved him of his hardship. ❨ and We removed the distress that was on him. ❩ (*Soorah Al-Anbiya'* 21:84) – as a Mercy from Us to him and a Kindness and Beneficence ❨ and a reminder for the worshippers. ❩ (*Soorah Al-Anbiya'* 21:84) That is, a reminder for those who are tested in their bodies, their wealth or their children, for they have an example in the Prophet of Allah, Ayyoob علیه السلام, who was tested by Allah with a test greater than that and he bore it patiently, hoping for Allah's Reward, until He relieved him of it.

He, Most High, says, ❨ And take in your hand a bundle of thin grass and strike therewith (your wife), and break not your oath. Truly! We found him patient. How excellent (a) slave! Verily, he was ever oft-returning in repentance (to Us)! ❩ (*Soorah Sad* 38:44) This is a license from Allah, Most High, to His slave and His Messenger, Ayyoob علیه السلام, because of the oath he had made to beat his wife with a hundred stripes. It was said that he made an oath to do this because she had sold her braids. It was also said that Satan appeared to her in a pleasant form and he described to her how to prepare a cure for Ayyoob علیه السلام and so she prepared it and informed Ayyoob علیه السلام of what had happened. He realized immediately that it was Satan and he swore an oath that he would beat her with a hundred stripes. When Allah, the Almighty, the All-Powerful cured him, He commanded him to take a hundred stems of thin grass and strike her with them once; and this would be equivalent to a hundred stripes. Thus he had fulfilled his oath and not broken it. This is a release and a way out for the one who fears Allah and obeys Him, especially with regard to the right of a patient wife, who hopes for Allah's Reward, who is long-suffering, honest, dutiful and rightly guided – may Allah be pleased with her. This is why Allah granted this license and explained it in His Words: ﴾ Truly! We found him patient. How excellent (a) slave! Verily, he was ever oft-returning in repentance (to Us)! ﴿ (*Soorah Sad* 38:44)

The Story of Dhul-Kifl ﷺ

Who, According to Some People, Was the Son of Ayyoob ﷺ

Allah, Most High, says, after relating the story of Ayyoob ﷺ in *Soorah Al-Anbiya'*, ❨ And (remember) Isma'eel, and Idris (Enoch) and *Dhul-Kifl* (Isaiah), all were from among *As-Sabireen* (the patient ones, etc.). And We admitted them to Our Mercy. Verily, they were of the righteous. ❩ (*Soorah Al-Anbiya'* 21:85,86)

Also after relating the story of Ayyoob ﷺ in *Soorah Sad*, He, Most High, says, ❨ And remember Our slaves, Ibraheem, Ishaq, and Ya'qoob, (all) owners of strength (in worshipping Us) and (also) of religious understanding. Verily, We did choose them by granting them (a good thing, i.e.) the remembrance of the home (in the Hereafter and they used to make the people remember it, and also they used to invite the people to obey Allah and to do good deeds for the Hereafter). And they are with Us, verily, of the chosen and the best! And remember Isma'eel (Isma'eel), Al-Yasa'a (Elisha), and *Dhul-Kifl* (Isaiah), all are among the best ❩ (*Soorah Sad* 38:45-48).

Ibn Jareer and Ibn Abi Najeeh narrated on the authority of Mujahid that he was not a Prophet, but that he was a righteous man, who was appointed to act on behalf of the Prophet sent to his people and to carry out his responsibilities towards them and to judge between them with fairness; as a result, he was known as Dhul-Kifl. [41]

And Ibn Abi Hatim said: It is reported on the authority of Kinanah Ibn Al-Akhnas that he said: I heard Al-Ash'ari (i.e. Abu Moosa) when he was at the pulpit, saying, "Dhul-Kifl was not a Prophet; but there was a righteous man among the Children of Isra'eel, who used to offer a hundred prayers every day. He died and *Dhul-Kifl* took his place, offering a hundred prayers every day. For this reason, he was called Dhul-Kifl." [42]

Mention of Communities That Were Completely Eradicated

This was before the revelation of the Torah, based on the evidence in the Words of Allah, Most High: ﴾ And indeed We gave Moosa (Moses), after We had destroyed the generations of old, the Scripture (the *Tawrah* [Torah]) ﴿ (*Soorah Al-Qasas* 28:43). Likewise, Ibn Jareer At-Tabari, Ibn Abi Hatim and Al-Bazzar narrated on the authority of Abu Sa'eed Al-Khudri رضي الله عنه that he said, "Allah did not destroy any people on the face of the Earth with a punishment from the heaven or from the Earth after the Tawrah had been revealed, except for the village

---

(41) This is because the word *kifl* is derived from the verb *kafala*, meaning to be responsible.

(42) See *Ad-Durr Al-Manthoor* (5/664). Al-Hafiz Ibn Katheer said in his '*Tafseer*' (3/192), "It is *munqati'* (broken) between Qatadah and Abu Moosa رضي الله عنه."

whose people were transformed into apes. Do you not see that Allah, Most High, says, ﴾ And indeed We gave Moosa, after We had destroyed the generations of old, the Scripture (the *Tawrah*) ﴿ (*Soorah Al-Qasas* 28:43) [43] In one version narrated by Al-Bazzar, he described it as *marfoo'*. But it appears most likely that it is *mawqoof* (i.e. that it may be attributed to Abu Sa'eed Al-Khudri, and not to the Messenger of Allah ﷺ). In any case, it proves that every nation that was completely destroyed was before Moosa ﷺ. Among them were the dwellers of Ar-Rass, of whom Allah, Most High, says, ﴾ And (also) 'Ad and Thamood, and the dwellers of Ar-Rass, and many generations in between. And for each of them We put forward examples (as proofs and lessons, etc.), and each (of them) We brought to utter ruin (because of their disbelief and evil deeds) ﴿ (*Soorah Al-Furqan* 25:38,39)

He, Most High, says in *Soorah Qaf,* ﴾ Denied before them (i.e. these pagans of Makkah who denied you, O, Muhammad) the people of Nooh, and the dwellers of Ar-Rass, and Thamood. And 'Ad, and Fir'awn (Pharaoh), and the brethren of Loot. And the dwellers of that wood, and the people of Tubba' Everyone of them denied (their) Messengers, so My Threat took effect. ﴿ (*Soorah Qaf* 50:12-14). The context of these *Soorahs* proves that they were destroyed, eradicated and annihilated. And this refutes the preferred opinion of Ibn Jareer At-Tabari, which was that they were the People of the Ditch, who were mentioned in *Soorah Al-Burooj*, because these people came after the Maseeh ﷺ, according to Ibn Ishaq and a number of others. And this

---

(43) Narrated by Ibn Jareer At-Tabari in his *Tafseer* (20/80). In *Al-Majma'*, Al-Haithami attributed it to Al-Bazzar in both *mawqoof* and *marfoo'* forms, while in *Ad-Durr Al-Manthoor* (5/129), As-Suyooti ascribed it to Ibn Abi Hatim. And Al-Haithami said, "…and its *rijal* (men) are all narrators of authentic *ahadeeth*."

claim also requires careful investigation.

Ibn Jareer At-Tabari narrated on the authority of 'Abdullah Ibn 'Abbas ﷺ that he said: "The dwellers of Ar-Rass were the inhabitants of one of the villages of Thamood." And at the start of his *Tareekh*, when describing the building of Damascus, Al-Hafiz Abul-Qasim Ibn 'Asakir related from the *Tareekh* of Abul-Qasim 'Ubaidullah Ibn 'Abdullah Ibn Khurdazbah and from other sources that the dwellers of Ar-Rass were in Hadoor [44] and Allah sent a Prophet to them whose name was Hanzalah Ibn Safwan, but they rejected him and killed him. So 'Ad, son of 'Aws, son of Iram, son of Sam, son of Nooh عليه السلام led his children from Ar-Rass and settled in Al-Ahqaf and they spread out through the land of Yemen and throughout all the lands, until Jairoon, son of Sa'd, son of 'Ad, son of 'Aws, son of Iram, son of Sam, son of Nooh settled in Damascus and built the city, calling it Jairoon and that is Iram of the Pillars. [45] And there is no place with more stone pillars than Damascus. Allah sent Hood, son of 'Abdullah Ibn Rabah, son of Khalid, son of Al-Khulood, son of 'Ad to the descendants of 'Ad at Al-Ahqaf, but they rejected him and so Allah, the Almighty, the All-Powerful destroyed them. This means that the dwellers of Ar-Rass lived a very long time before 'Ad. And Allah knows better.

Ibn Abi Hatim narrated on the authority of 'Abdullah Ibn 'Abbas ﷺ that he said, "Ar-Rass is a well in Azerbaijan." Ath-Thawri narrated on the authority of Abu Bukair, who reported on the authority of 'Ikrimah that he said, "Ar-Rass is a well in which they buried their Prophet." [46] Ibn Juraij said, "Ikrimah

---

(44) Hadoor: A town in Yemen.

(45) See: *Soorah Al-Fajr* 89:7.

(46) This is said to be derived from the Arabic verb *rassa*, which means to bury.

said that the dwellers of Ar-Rass were the dwellers of the town mentioned in *Soorah Ya Seen*, according to what 'Ikrimah has claimed, who were completely annihilated. Allah, Most high, says regarding them, ❴ It was but one *Saihah* (shout, etc.) and lo! They (all) were silent (dead – destroyed). ❵ (*Soorah Ya Seen* 36:29) And we shall relate their story after these people's story, though it would appear that they were another people (i.e. not the people referred to in *Soorah Ya Seen*); and they were also destroyed and eradicated. At all events, it contradicts what Ibn Jareer said.

The Story of the People of YaSeen

Who Were the Dwellers of the Town

Allah, Most High, says, ❨And put forward to them a similitude; the (story of the) dwellers of the town, when there came Messengers to them. When We sent to them two Messengers, they belied them both, so We reinforced them with a third, and they said, "Verily! We have been sent to you as Messengers." They (people of the town) said, "You are only human beings like ourselves, and the Most Beneficent (Allah) has revealed nothing, you are only telling lies." They said, "Our Lord knows that we have been sent as Messengers to you. And our duty is only to convey plainly." They (the people) said, "For us, we see an evil omen from you, if you cease not, we will surely stone you, and a painful torment will touch you from us." They (the Messengers) said, "Your evil omens be with you! (Do you call it an evil omen) because you are admonished? Nay, but you are a people *musrifoon* (transgressing all bounds by committing all kinds of great sins, and by disobeying Allah). And there came running from the farthest part of the town, a man, saying, "O, my people! Obey the Messengers; obey those who ask no wages of you (for themselves), and who are rightly guided. And why should I not worship Him (Allah, Alone) Who has created me and to Whom you shall be returned. Shall I take besides Him *alihah* (gods), (when) if the Most Beneficent (Allah) intends me any harm, their intercession will be of no use for me whatsoever – and nor can they save me? Then verily, I should be in plain error. Verily! I have believed in your Lord, so listen to me!" It was said (to him when the disbelievers killed him), "Enter Paradise." He said, "Would that my people knew! That my Lord (Allah) has forgiven me, and made me of the honored ones!" And We sent not against his people after him a host from heaven, nor do We send (such a thing). It was but one *Saihah* (shout, etc.) and lo! They (all) were silent (dead – destroyed). 〉 (*Soorah Ya Seen* 36:13-29)

It has been widely reported from many of the *Salaf* and the later scholars that this town was Antioch (Antakiyah). This was narrated by Ibn Ishaq, who reported it on the authority of 'Abdullah Ibn 'Abbas ﷺ, Ka'b Al-Ahbar and Wahb Ibn Munabbih. It was likewise narrated on the authority of Buraidah Ibn Al-Husaib, 'Ikrimah, Qatadah, Az-Zuhri and others.

But this saying is very weak, because when the Maseeh عليه السلام sent three of the Disciples to the people of Antioch (Antakiyah), they were the first city to believe in the Maseeh عليه السلام at that time. For this reason, it was one of the four cities in which there were Christian Patriarchs; and they were Antioch, Jerusalem, Alexandria and Rome. After them, Constantinople became a Patriarchal city, but none of them was destroyed, while the inhabitants of this village mentioned in the Qur'an were destroyed, as Allah says at the end of their story, after they had killed the one who believed in the Messengers. 〈 And put forward to them a similitude; the (story of the) dwellers of the town, when there came Messengers to them ❭ (*Soorah Ya Seen* 36:13) But if (it was said that) the three Messengers mentioned in the Qur'an were sent to the people of Antioch in the distant past and they rejected them and Allah destroyed them. The city was then rebuilt after that and then when it was the time of the Maseeh ﷺ, they believed in the messengers he sent to them, this cannot be ruled out. And Allah knows better.

He, Most High, says, ❬ And put forward to them a similitude. ❭ That is for your people, Muhammad . ❬ the (story of the) dwellers of the town ❭. That is, the city. ❬ when there came Messengers to them. When We sent to them two Messengers, they belied them both, so We reinforced them with a third. ❭ (*Soorah Ya Seen* 36:13,14) That is, We supported them by sending a third person to deliver the Message. ❬ They said, "Our Lord knows that we have been sent as Messengers to you." ❭ (*Soorah Ya Seen* 36:16). But they answered them by saying that they were only human beings, like them, as (all) the disbelieving nations said to their Messengers, deeming the idea that Allah would send a human Messenger to be farfetched. The Messengers replied that Allah knew that they were Messengers sent to them and that if they were lying about Him, He would have punished them and exacted condign Retribution on them. ❬ "And our duty is only to convey plainly." ❭ (*Soorah Ya Seen* 36:17) That is, the only obligation upon us is to convey to you the Message with which Allah has sent us to you; it is Allah Who guides whom He wills and increases in misguidance whomsoever He wills. ❬ They (the people) said, "For us, we see an evil omen from you." ❭ That is, we see an evil omen in that which you have brought. ❬ "...if you cease not, we will surely stone you." ❭. That is, we will revile you verbally. It was also said that it means we will physically stone you. But the first explanation is supported by His Words: ❬ "and a painful torment will touch you from us." ❩. So they threatened them with death and verbal abuse. ❨ They (the Messengers) said, "Your evil omens be with you!" ❩ That is, they are thrown back upon you. ❨ "(Do you call it " an evil omen") because you are admonished?" ❩ That is, because of the guidance to which we have called you, would you threaten us with death and verbal abuse? ❨ "Nay, but you are a people *musrifoon* (transgressing all bounds by committing all kinds of great sins, and by disobeying Allah)." ❩ That is, you do not accept the truth, nor do you desire it. And He, Most High, ❨ And there came running from the farthest part of the town, a man. ❩ That is, to support the two Messengers and to openly declare his belief in them ❨ saying, "O, my people! Obey the Messengers; those who ask no wages of you (for themselves), and who are rightly guided." ❩ (*Soorah Ya Seen* 36:20,21). That is, they call you to the pure truth, without receiving or expecting any payment or any recompense. Then he called upon them to worship Allah, Alone, without ascribing partners to him and he forbade them to worship any other deity besides Him, which can offer them no benefit in this world or in the Hereafter. ❨ "Then verily, I should be in plain error." ❩ (*Soorah Ya Seen* 36:24). That is, if I abandoned the worship of Allah and worshipped others besides Him. Then he said, addressing the Messengers, ❨ "Verily! I have believed in your Lord, so listen to me!" ❩ (*Soorah Ya Seen* 36:25). It was said that it means: Listen to my words and bear witness for me to them before your Lord. It was also said that it means: Hear, O, my people, my open testimony of belief in the Messengers of Allah. Upon hearing this, they killed him; it was said that they stoned him. It was also said that they tortured him to death. And it was also said that they leapt upon him as one man and killed him. Ibn Ishaq related from one of his companions, who reported on the authority of 'Abdullah Ibn

Mas'ood ﷺ that he said, "They stamped on him until they had spilled his cntrails."

'Abdullah Ibn 'Abbas ﷺ said, "He advised his people while he lived: ❴ "O, my people! Obey the Messengers." ❵ (*Soorah Ya Seen* 36:20) – and after his death: ❴ He said, "Would that my people knew! That my Lord (Allah) has forgiven me, and made me of the honored ones!" ❵ (*Soorah Ya Seen* 36:26,27) This was narrated by Ibn Abi Hatim. Qatadah said: "You will never find a believer but he is sincere and is never insincere. When he saw with his own eyes how Allah had honored him. He said, ❴ 'Would that my people knew! That my Lord (Allah) has forgiven me, and made me of the honored ones!' ❵ (*Soorah Ya Seen* 36:26,27). He wished that his people could know about what he was seeing with his own eyes of the honor of Allah." Qatadah added, "And no, by Allah! Allah did not censure his people after they had killed him." ❴ It was but one *Saihah* and lo! They (all) were silent (dead – destroyed). ❵ (*Soorah Ya Seen* 36:29)

And He, Most High, says, ❴ And We sent not against his people after him a host from heaven, nor do We send (such a thing). ❵ (*Soorah Ya Seen* 36:28) That is, We did not need to send down an army from the heaven in order to exact retribution upon them. This was the meaning narrated by Ibn Ishaq, who reported on the authority of one of his companions, who in turn reported on the authority of 'Abdullah Ibn Mas'ood ﷺ. Mujahid and Qatadah said, that His not sending upon them a host means: He did not send down to them another Message. But Ibn Jareer At-Tabari said, "But the first explanation is more appropriate."

I say that it is also stronger, which is why Allah says, ❴ nor do We send (such a thing). ❵ (*Soorah Ya Seen* 36:28) That is,

We did not need to do this in order to exact retribution, when they belied Our Messengers and killed Our *Wali*. ❨ It was but one *Saihah* and lo! They (all) were silent (dead – destroyed). ❩ (*Soorah Ya Seen* 36:29)

The scholars of *tafseer* said that Allah sent Jibraeel ﷺ to them and he seized the posts of the gates to their city, then he unleashed a single shout upon them ❨ and lo! They (all) were silent (dead – destroyed) ❩ (*Soorah Ya Seen* 36:29). That is, their voices were silenced and their movements were stilled, so that not even an eye movement remained among them. All of this proves that this village was not Antakiyak (Antioch), because these people were destroyed because of their rejection of the Messengers whom Allah sent to them, while the inhabitants of Antioch believed and obeyed the messengers of the Maseeh ﷺ from among the disciples whom he sent to them. For this reason it was said that Antioch was the first city to believe in the Maseeh ﷺ.

The Story of Yoonus (Jonah) ﷺ

Allah, Most High, says in *Soorah Yoonus*, ❨ Was there any town (community) that believed (after seeing the punishment), and its faith (at that moment) saved it (from the punishment)? (The answer is none,) – except the people of Yoonus (Jonah); when they believed, We removed from them the torment of disgrace in the life of the (present) world, and permitted them to enjoy for a while. ❩ (*Soorah Yoonus* 10:98)

He, Most High, says in *Soorah Al-Anbiya'*, ❨ And (remember) *Dhun-Noon* (Jonah), when he went off in anger, and imagined that We shall not punish him (i.e. the calamities which had befallen him)! But he cried through the darkness (saying), "*La ilaha illa Anta* (none has the right to be worshipped but You [O, Allah]), Glorified (and Exalted) are You (above all that [evil] they associate with You). Truly, I have been of the wrong-doers." So We answered his call, and delivered him from the distress. And thus We do deliver the Believers (who believe in the Oneness of Allah, abstain from evil and work righteousness). 》 *(Soorah Al-Anbiya'* 21:87,88)

He, Most High, says in *Soorah As-Saffat,* ﴿ And, verily, Yoonus was one of the Messengers. When he ran to the laden ship, He (agreed to) cast lots, and he was among the losers. Then a (big) fish swallowed him and he had done an act worthy of blame. Had he not been of them who glorify Allah, he would have indeed remained inside its (the fish) belly till the Day of Resurrection. But We cast him forth on the naked shore while he was sick. And We caused a plant of gourd to grow over him. And We sent him to a hundred thousand (people) or even more. And they believed; so We gave them enjoyment for a while. 》 *(Soorah As-Saffat* 37:139-148)

He, Most High, says in *Soorah Noon* (i.e. *Soorah Al-Qalam*), ﴿ So wait with patience for the Decision of your Lord, and be not like the Companion of the Fish, when he cried out (to Us) while he was in deep sorrow. (See the Qur'an, Verse 21:87). Had not a Grace from his Lord reached him, he would indeed have been (left in the stomach of the fish, but We forgave him), so he was cast off on the naked shore, while he was to be blamed. But his Lord chose him and made him of the righteous. 》 *(Soorah Al-Qalam* 68:48-50)

The scholars of *tafseer* said that Allah sent Yoonus ﷺ to the people of Neenawa, in the land of Al-Mawsil (Mosul); he called them to Allah, the Almighty, the All-Powerful, but they rejected him and arrogantly persisted in their disbelief and willful rejection of the truth. When this state of affairs had gone on for a long time, he departed from them and threatened them with the descent of Allah's Punishment upon them after three days.

'Abdullah Ibn Mas'ood رضي الله عنه, Mujahid, Sa'eed Ibn Jubair, Qatadah and more than one of the earlier and the later generations said that when he departed from among them and they became convinced of the imminent descent of Allah's Punishment upon them, Allah cast repentance and remorse into their hearts and they felt a sense of regret for the way they had treated their Prophet.

This is why Allah, Most High, says, ﴿ Was there any town (community) that believed (after seeing the punishment), and its faith (at that moment) saved it (from the punishment)? ﴾ That is, was there any town in past times whose whole population believed? This (rhetorical question) indicates that this did not happen. Indeed, as Allah, Most High, says, ﴿ And We did not send a warner to a township, but those who were given the worldly wealth and luxuries among them said, "We believe not in the (Message) with which you have been sent." ﴾ (*Soorah Saba'* 34:34). Then He, Most High, says, ﴿ except the people of Yoonus; when they believed, We removed from them the torment of disgrace in the life of the (present) world, and permitted them to enjoy for a while. ﴾ (*Soorah Yoonus* 10:98) That is, all of them believed. Scholars of *tafseer* have disagreed as to whether or not their belief would benefit them in the Afterlife and save them from the Punishment of the Hereafter, as it saved them from Punishment in the life of this world. The most apparent answer, according to the context, is yes. And Allah knows better. As He, Most High, says, ﴿ when they believed. ﴾ (*Soorah Yoonus* 10:98) And He, Most High, says, ﴿ And We sent him to a hundred thousand (people) or even more. And they believed; so We gave them enjoyment for a while. ﴾ (*Soorah As-Saffat* 37:147,148) This enjoyment for a while does not negate the possibility that there is another reward with it, that being the lifting of the Punishment of the Hereafter. And Allah knows better.

He, Most High, says, ﴾ And verily, Yoonus was one of the Messengers. When he ran to the laden ship, he (agreed to) cast lots, and he was among the losers. Then a (big) fish swallowed him as he had done an act worthy of blame. ﴾ (*Soorah As-Saffat* 37:139-141). That is to say, when he was the loser when they drew lots, he was cast overboard into the sea and Allah, the Almighty, the All-Powerful sent a great fish from the Mediterranean Sea and it devoured him; Allah, Most High, commanded it not to eat his flesh or break his bones, because he was not food for it. So it took him and swam through all of the seas. It was said that this fish was swallowed by another, even larger fish. They said that when he had stayed for some time in the fish belly, he thought that he had died; then he moved his limbs and saw that he was alive. He fell down in prostration before Allah in the belly of the fish, and he said, "O, Lord! I have taken as a place of worship to You a place which no other person has reached." They differed as to how long he spent in the belly of the fish. Some said three days; this was the view of Qatadah. Some said seven days; this was the view of Ja'far As-Sadiq, may Allah be pleased with him. Some said forty days; this was the view of Abu Malik. Mujahid said, narrating from Ash-Sha'bi, "It swallowed him in the morning and cast him forth in the evening." This is supported by the poetry of Umayyah Ibn Abi As-Salt

And You, by a Grace from You, saved Yoonus,
And He remained in the belly of the fish for a night.

What is meant is that when the fish began to swim with him

in the deep seas, and hurtled with him through the salty waves, he heard the sound of the fish praising the Most Beneficent and he even heard the praises of the pebbles for the Splitter of seeds and (fruit) stones ⁽⁴⁷⁾ and the Lord of the seven heavens and the seven earths and all that lies between them and that which is beneath the soil. On hearing these praises, he began to beseech Allah, silently and in words, as Allah has informed us, the Owner of Might and Majesty, Who knows the secrets and confidential talks and Who alleviates harm and affliction, Who hears all voices, even though they may be weak, Who knows the unseen things, even though they may be minute and Who answers the supplications of those who are in great distress, as He says in His Book, which was revealed to His trustworthy Messenger – and He is the Most Truthful of Speakers, the Lord of the Worlds and the God of the Messengers – ﴿ And (remember) *Dhan-Noon* (Jonah), when he went off in anger, and imagined that We shall not punish him (i.e. the calamites which had befallen him)! But he cried through the darkness (saying), "*La ilaha illa Anta* (none has the right to be worshipped but You [O, Allah]), Glorified (and Exalted) are You (above all that [evil] they associate with You). Truly, I have been of the wrong-doers." So We answered his call, and delivered him from the distress. And thus We do deliver the believers (who believe in the Oneness of Allah, abstain from evil and work righteousness). ﴾ (*Soorah Al-Anbiya'* 21:87,88)

As for His Saying: ﴿ and (he) imagined that We shall not punish him (i.e. the calamites which had befallen him)! ﴾ (*Soorah Al-Anbiya'* 21:87), it means: We would not constrain him. It was also said that it means: We would not ordain for him; and this is linguistically well-known, as the poet says (in '*Al-Bahr At-Taweel*),

---

(47) See *Soorah Al-An'am* 6:95.

There is no return for that time which has gone,

Blessed are You – that which You ordain will be,

And the matter is all in Your Hands.

As for His Saying: ❨ But he cried through the darkness ❩ (*Soorah Al-Anbiya'* 21:87), 'Abdullah Ibn Mas'ood الغيلا, 'Abdullah Ibn 'Abbas ﷺ, 'Amr Ibn Maimoon, Sa'eed Ibn Jubair, Muhammad Ibn Ka'b , Al-Hasan Al-Basri, Qatadah and Ad-Dahhak said that it means the darkness of the fish, the darkness of the sea and the darkness of the night. As for His saying: ❨ Had he not been of those who glorify Allah, He would have indeed remained inside its belly (the fish) till the Day of Resurrection ❩ (*Soorah As-Saffat* 37:143,144), it was said that it means: Were it not for the fact that he had praised Allah when he was in that situation, and spoken those words affirming Allah's sole right to be worshipped, glorifying Him, acknowledging Him with humility and repentance to Him and resorting to Him (in his hour of need), he would have remained there until the establishment of the Day of Resurrection – and he would have been sent forth from the belly of that fish.

This is supported by the narration of Imam Ahmad and some of the compilers of the *Sunan*, on the authority of 'Abdullah Ibn 'Abbas ﷺ, who said: The Messenger of Allah ﷺ said to me, "O, boy! I will teach you some words: Remember Allah and He will remember you. Remember Allah and you will find Him before you. Remember Allah in times of ease and He will remember you in times of hardship." [48]

He, Most High, says, ❨ But We threw him ❩ (*Soorah As-Saffat* 37:145). That is, We cast him forth ❨ on al-'ara' ❩ (*Soorah*

---

[48] This is an authentic *hadeeth* narrated by Imam Ahmad (2800) and At-Tirmidhi (2516).

As-Saffat 37:145). That is, in a deserted place, in which there
are no trees; rather, it is bare of them. ❨ While he was sick ❩
(*Soorah As-Saffat* 37:145). That is, physically weak. 'Abdullah
Ibn Mas'ood ﷺ said, "Like the body of a chicken without
feathers on it." [(49)] 'Abdullah Ibn 'Abbas ﷺ, As-Suddi and Ibn
Zaid said that his body was like the body of a child when it is
born, swollen and without anything on it. ❨ And We caused a
gourd plant to grow over him ❩ (*Soorah As-Saffat* 37:146).

Imam Ahmad narrated on the authority of Sa'd Ibn Abi
Waqqas ﷺ that he said: I passed by 'Uthman Ibn 'Affan ﷺ in the
mosque and I greeted him with salutations of peace; he looked
at me, but he did not return my salutations of peace. So I went
to 'Umar Ibn Al-Khattab ﷺ and said, "O, Commander of the
Faithful! Has anything happened in Islam?" Twice I repeated
this, but he replied, "No. Why do you ask?" I said, "Only
because I passed by 'Uthman Ibn 'Affan a short while ago in
the mosque and I greeted him with salutations of peace and
he saw me clearly. But he did not answer my salutations." He
said: So 'Umar ﷺ sent for 'Uthman ﷺ and said to him, "What
prevented you from replying to your brother's salutation?" He
said, "I did not (ignore his salutations)." Sa'd ﷺ said, "Yes
(you did)." They continued to contradict each other until they
both swore that they were telling the truth. He said: Then
'Uthman ﷺ remembered and he said, "Yes (I remember now).
I ask Allah's Forgiveness and I turn to Him in repentance. You
passed by me a while ago and I was preoccupied with thoughts
of a saying which I heard from the Messenger of Allah ﷺ which
I never think of except that a veil comes down over my eyes
and my heart." Sa'd said: And I will tell you what it was. The
Messenger of Allah told us the first part of the supplication

---

(49) Narrated by Ibn Abi Shaibah in *Al-Musannaf* (6/338, No. 31866) as part
of a lengthy narration.

then a Bedouin came and kept him busy, then the Messenger of Allah ﷺ got up and I followed him. When I felt worried that he would enter his house, I stamped my feet on the ground and the Messenger of Allah ﷺ turned toward me and said, "Who is this, Abu Ishaq?" he said, "I replied, "(What is the matter) I said, yes, O Messenger of Allah. he said: "keep silent" "Nothing, by Allah, except that you told us the first part of the supplication, then this Bedouin came and kept you busy." He said, "Yes, the supplication of *Dhun-Noon* when he was in the belly of the fish: ﴾ "None has the right to be worshipped but You. Glorified be You! Truly, I have been of the wrongdoers." ﴿ (*Soorah Al-Anbiya'* 21:87). No Muslim ever supplicates to his Lord with these words for anything, but He will answer his prayer. [50]

---

(50) This is an authentic *hadeeth* narrated by Imam Ahmad (1465), At-Tirmi-dhi (3505) and An-Nasa'i in 'Al-Kubra' (6/168, No. 10492)

Mention of the Virtue of Yoonus علیه السلام

Allah, Most High, says, ❨ And, verily, Yoonus was one of the Messengers ❩ (*Soorah As-Saffat* 37:139). Allah, Most High, mentioned him as being among the Noble Prophets in *Soorah An-Nisa'* and *Soorah Al-Anbiya'* – may the choicest prayers and blessings from Allah be upon them all.

Imam Ahmad narrated on the authority of 'Abdullah ﷺ that he said: The Messenger of Allah ﷺ said, "No slave should say that I am better than Yoonus, son of Matta." [51]

Al-Bukhari narrated on the authority of Abu Hurairah ﷺ that he reported from the Prophet ﷺ that he said, "No slave should say that I am better than Yoonus, son of Matta." [52]

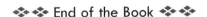 ❖❖ End of the Book ❖❖

---

[51] Narrated by Imam Ahmad (3695) and Al-Bukhari (4603).
[52] Narrated by Al-Bukhari (3416).